ID0626890

Springer Series on

ADULTHOOD and AGING

Series Editors:
Lissy F. Jarvik, M.D., Ph.D., and Bernard D. Starr, Ph.D.

Advisory Board:
Paul D. Baltes, Ph.D., Jack Botwinick, Ph.D., Carl Eisdorfer, M.D., Ph.D.,
Robert Kastenbaum, Ph.D., Neil G. McCluskey, Ph.D., K. Warner Schaie,
Ph.D., and Nathan W. Shock, Ph.D.

646.78
E84g

ETHNICITY AND AGING
Theory, Research, and Policy

Donald E. Gelfand
Alfred J. Kutzik,
Editors

with 25 contributors

TABOR COLLEGE LIBRARY
HILLSBORO, KANSAS 67063

SPRINGER PUBLISHING COMPANY
New York

810722

Copyright © 1979 by Springer Publishing Company, Inc.

All rights reserved

No part of this publication may be reproduced, stored in a
retrieval system, or transmitted in any form or by any means,
electronic, mechanical, photocopying, recording, or otherwise,
without the prior permission of Springer Publishing Company, Inc.

Springer Publishing Company, Inc.
200 Park Avenue South
New York, N.Y. 10003

79 80 81 82 83 / 10 9 8 7 6 5 4 3 2 1

Library of Congress Cataloging in Publication Data
Main entry under title:

Ethnicity and aging.

    (Springer series on adulthood and aging ; v. 5)
    "Most of the chapters . . . originally prepared for
the National Conference on Ethnicity and Aging held at
the University of Maryland in May 1978."
    Includes bibliographies and index.
    1. Aged—United States—Congresses. 2. Ethnicity—
Congresses. 3. Aged—Family relationships—Congresses.
4. Aged—Services for—United States—Congresses.
I. Gelfand, Donald E. II. Kutzik, Alfred J.
III. National Conference on Ethnicity and Aging, Univer-
sity of Maryland, 1978. IV. Series.
HQ1064.U5E8   301.43'5'0973   79-14046
ISBN 0-8261-2770-3
ISBN 0-8261-2771-1 pbk.

Printed in the United States of America

Contents

Contributors

William Bechill, M.S.W., is a member of the social policy and social administration faculty of the University of Maryland School of Social Work and Community Planning. He served as the first U.S. commissioner on aging in the Johnson administration. He is the author of several articles and monographs dealing with public policy issues in the field of aging. He is a fellow of the Gerontological Society and recently served as the chairman of the Social Policy Committee on Aging of the American Public Welfare Association.

Vern L. Bengtson, Ph.D., is professor of sociology at the University of Southern California. His publications reflect research in social stratification and aging, adult socialization, intergenerational relations, and social change. His interest in ethnicity and aging developed as he observed contrasts among members of his own family growing old in Sweden and in the United States. He is a graduate of the University of Chicago.

David E. Biegel, L.C.S.W., is director of the Neighborhood and Family Services Project and coordinator of professional development activities for the University of Southern California's Washington Public Affairs Center. A doctoral student at the University of Maryland School of Social Work and Community Planning, he has previously served as director of the Office of Planning and Program Development with Associated Catholic Charities, Inc. in Baltimore, Maryland.

Marilyn R. Block is faculty research associate, Center on Aging, University of Maryland, College Park; a visiting lecturer, Department of Psychology, Hood College, Frederick, Maryland; and director, Lifespan Research Associates, Silver Spring, Maryland. Her research interests are women and aging, retirement, and the aging family.

Marjorie H. Cantor is Brookdale Professor of Gerontology, Fordham University in New York, and research director, All-University Center on Gerontology. One of the founders of the New York City Department for the Aging and its director of research from its inception in 1969 until 1978, she is at present consultant to the department. She has lectured extensively and has authored over 25 publications and papers in the field of aging. She is a fellow of the Gerontological Society and a member of the Society for the Psychological Study of Social Issues.

Bertram J. Cohler is William Rainey Harper Associate Professor of Social Sciences in the College at the University of Chicago, and the Departments of Behavioral Sciences (Committee on Human Development) and Education. His research interests include the study of personality and mental health from a life-cycle perspective.

Donald E. Gelfand, Ph.D., is associate professor at the School of Social Work and Community Planning of the University of Maryland at Baltimore. A sociologist, he has been extensively involved in many applied areas of sociology including mental health, urban sociology, and aging. Formerly co-director of the Community Sociology Training Program at Boston University, his current research focuses on changes in the family related to aging and the role of ethnicity in the aging process.

David Guttmann, D.S.W., is director of the Catholic University of America's Center for the Study of Pre-Retirement and Aging in Washington, D.C., and was formerly assistant dean for academic affairs at the National Catholic School of Social Service. He is also the principal investigator of several large-scale research grants for the Administration on Aging and author of numerous articles on aging in the *Gerontologist* and other publications.

Robert Kastenbaum, Ph.D., is currently superintendent at Cushing Hospital in Framingham, Massachusetts. A psychologist, he was formerly on the faculties of the University of Massachusetts, Boston University, and Wayne State University, Detroit. A major contributor to the field of gerontology, his work on death and dying has been of importance to the growth of interest in "thanatology."

Alfred J. Kutzik, Ph.D., is on the faculty of the University of Maryland's School of Social Work and Community Planning. He is the author of several books and articles dealing with the relation of ethnicity and class to social welfare from a historical–sociological perspective.

Morton A. Lieberman, Ph.D., is professor in the Committee on Human Development at the University of Chicago. He is currently involved in two major areas of research: "people-changing groups" and the psychology of adulthood. He is the co-author of four books: *Crisis and Survival in Old Age* (1978); *Last Home for the Aged: Institutionalization Effects and Their Cause* (1976); *Psychotherapy Through the Group Process* (1974); and *Encounter Groups: First Facts* (1973).

David Maldonado, Jr., D.S.W., is associate professor at the Graduate School of Social Work at the University of Texas at Arlington, Texas. Besides his normal duties as a faculty member, Dr. Maldonado also serves as program director of the Chicano Aging Administration Program funded by the Administration on Aging.

Elizabeth W. Markson, Ph.D., is on the faculty of the Department of Sociology at Wellesley College, Wellesley, Mass. She has conducted extensive research in the areas of aging and mental health. She was formerly head of Research and Evaluation at the Department of Mental Health of Massachusetts and previously held a similar position at the Department of Mental Hygiene in New York State.

John Lewis McAdoo, Ph.D., is associate professor at the University of Maryland School of Social Work. He received his Ph.D. in 1970 from the University of Michigan in educational psychology. He received an M.S.W. from that institution in 1965. During the past year he was a gerontological fellow placed at the National Center on the Black Aged and also a postdoctoral fellow in mental health epidemiology at Johns Hopkins University in Baltimore.

Fred Medinger, M.S.W., is a doctoral student at the University of Maryland School of Social Work and Community Planning. He is also an instructor in psychology at Essex Community College and has served as a clinical social worker at the Walter P. Carter Mental Health Center in Baltimore.

Rolando Merino, M.D., is visiting assistant professor at the Mount Sinai School of Medicine of the City University of New York, Department of Community Medicine. He is a physician planner and biostatistician. He was a regional director in the Chilean health system, where he worked until 1973, the same year his involvement with Puerto Rican community groups concerned with health issues began.

Darrel Montero, Ph.D., is assistant professor, Department of Urban Studies, University of Maryland. A graduate of UCLA, he has done extensive analysis of that university's major study of Japanese Americans. His current activities involve a number of sociological areas including the problems of research among minorities and the adaptation of Vietnamese immigrants to American life.

Danuta Mostwin, D.S.W., is professor of social work and family mental health at the Catholic University in Washington, D.C. She has contributed to the field of ethnicity and family mental health and she has also published six novels and numerous articles in her native Polish.

Jody K. Olsen, Ph.D., is director of the Center on Aging at the University of Maryland. Her activities involve training as well as research programs at all campuses of the university. Formerly director of an area agency on aging, she is still extensively involved in short-term training for practitioners in gerontology.

Sarah Santana is health educator-administrator at the East Harlem Council for Human Services–Neighborhood Health Center. One of her duties is to coordinate a program for the elderly sponsored by this Puerto Rican community group. Her previous experience includes planning and grant proposal writing focusing on the health needs of the Hispanic community for the Erickson Educational Foundation, where she was assistant director.

Wendy R. Sherman, M.S.W., currently special projects director for the University of Southern California's Washington Public Affairs Center, formerly served as field coordinator and policy coordinator for the Neighborhood and Family Services Project. Her areas of concern include local, state, and national policy initiatives in neighborhood capacity building for human services.

Donald C. Snyder, Ph.D., economist at Goucher College, Towson, Maryland, is currently teaching courses in the area of poverty and discrimination, labor, and macro- and urban economics. His research centers around pensions, future income of the elderly, and work attachment of retirees; he has had grants from the Department of Labor, the Administration on Aging, and the National Science Foundation.

Jay H. Sokolovsky, Ph.D., is cultural anthropologist and assistant professor, Department of Sociology, University of Maryland, Baltimore County. He received his Ph.D. from Pennsylvania State University and has special interests in peasant societies, urbanization, and the anthropology of aging. He has recently been using social network analysis to research the adaptation of indigent elderly and ex-psychiatric hospital patients living in slum hotels in New York City.

James E. Trela, Ph.D., is associate professor of sociology at the University of Maryland, Baltimore County. His work in gerontology has centered around the political interest and participation of the elderly. He is also active in the Department of Sociology M.A. program in applied sociology, which emphasizes aging and medical sociology.

Raju Varghese, Ed.D., is assistant professor at the School of Social Work and Community Planning of the University of Maryland at Baltimore. He is also a consultant to the College Park Youth Services of Maryland. Before coming to Maryland, he taught at Kerala University in India and Temple University in Philadelphia. He has worked as a clinical social worker and served as consultant to several social welfare organizations.

Ruth E. Zambrana, M.D., is research associate and postdoctoral fellow at the Mount Sinai School of Medicine of the City University of New York, Department of Community Medicine. She has been working with the East Harlem community for the last few years in the areas of program development and planning.

Irving Kenneth Zola, Ph.D., is professor of sociology, Brandeis University, Waltham, Mass., and a counselor and board member of the Boston Self-Help Center—an organization devoted to advocacy and counseling for and by those with chronic diseases and physical handicaps. His research interests include the medicalization of society, patient interaction, patient health and illness behavior, and the consciousness of those with a disability.

Introduction:
Focuses and Issues

Donald E. Gelfand and Alfred J. Kutzik

Most of the chapters in this book were originally prepared for the National Conference on Ethnicity and Aging held at the University of Maryland in May 1978 under the co-sponsorship of the University's Center on Aging, the Interdisciplinary Coordinating Committee of the University's Baltimore campus, and the Institute on Pluralism and Group Identity of the American Jewish Committee. The purpose of the conference and this volume is to collate and make available the growing body of scientific knowledge and professional experience relating to ethnicity and aging.

Drawing on research in a variety of disciplines and practice in a variety of fields, the material collected here constitutes the most comprehensive consideration of the subject to date. A crucial dimension of this comprehensiveness is that, departing from the heretofore exclusive concern with "minority" ethnic aged of African, Asian, native American, and Hispanic origin, major attention is given to white ethnic aged of European descent.

This broad scope raises definitional issues concerning the term *ethnicity*. The different approaches of the contributors reflect the diversity that exists among scholars at this point. In line with prevailing general usage, some restrict the category of ethnicity to "minority groups." Following social scientific usage, others include white groups but tend to limit these to groups of immigrants and individuals who participate in social institutions that are clearly linked to their original nationalities. Only a few contributors consider WASPs or Mormons to be ethnics. All of the foregoing are included in our definition, which follows that of Milton Gordon (1964), who views an ethnic group as one set off from the rest of American society by race, religion, or national origin.

From this definition it can be inferred that every American is an ethnic, to some extent sharing the values of his or her ethnic group. In the study of ethnicity since the 1930s, scholarship has been virtually fixated on nonwhite racial groups, out of concern for combating and redressing discrimination. Despite the important differences in life chances, it is not clear that the situation and characteristics of the "minority" aged are essentially dissimilar from "white ethnic" aged. As spokesmen for minority groups caution, it is politically important, because of past and present discrimination, to recognize the differences among ethnic groups. The identification of similarities as well as dissimilarities by the contributors to this book is also essential to scientific understanding of sound professional practice.

The present heightened interest in ethnicity and aging can be ascribed to (1) the growing interest in ethnicity of the last two decades, (2) the increased numbers of aged during this same period, and (3) theoretical developments in gerontology.

It is hardly necessary to discuss in detail the ethnic situation that characterized the 1960s. Suffice it to say that it was a decade of racial turmoil. One crucial outcome was the movement away from integration to Black Power. This movement helped to strengthen and sanction the existence of ethnic identity among groups ranging from Chicanos to Poles. Whatever the social forces and political motivations underlying this development, ethnicity has since increased in importance in American life.

In the 1970s what has been termed the "ethnic revival" has been evidenced most strongly in urban neighborhoods, affecting the nature of services and the methods of community development. As ethnicity in all of its aspects has begun to be explored, it was only natural that an interest in older populations, who tend to be most oriented toward their ethnic groups, would emerge.

Even without these developments relating to ethnicity, the 1960s and 1970s would have promoted an interest in aging because of the unprecedented increase of the elderly proportional to the total population. As services have grown to meet their needs, those providing services have found that the backgrounds of the aged are extremely varied. The response of many service providers has been bewilderment at the different cultural norms, ranging from dietary requirements to family relationships, to which their programs had to attend. The ethnicity of the elderly person has become an important issue for program development at the state as well as local level, especially in central cities with large numbers of aged.

The understanding that service providers have gained of the diversity of the elderly in the United States has begun to be shared by researchers involved in developing knowledge of basic aging processes. Attention to ethnicity as a major variable in the aging process could probably not have occurred during the early development of the relatively new field of gerontology. The thrust of most researchers until recently was providing global explanations applicable to all the aged. The view of the aged as a monolithic social group with norms and values of their own denied their sociocultural diversity. Disengagement and activity theory disregarded and diverted attention from sociocultural differences. As the field of gerontology has grown, both internal criticism and knowledge from a variety of disciplines has begun to influence theoretical formulations. The field has shifted away from the dominant disengagement perspective, which in effect posited a "melting pot" for all the aged, toward a pluralistic approach recognizing the variety of sociocultural factors operating among the elderly no less than among other age groups. These factors include social stratification and ethnicity.

Adoption of a developmental approach has been a major step in bringing cultural variables into the study of the aging process. The developmental argument considers aging as one part of the individual's growth process. As many of the chapters indicate, the developmental approach has major strengths in exploring the role of ethnicity in aging.

Contributors to this volume are currently engaged in exploring issues of basic knowledge or in professional practice relating to the impact of ethnicity on the aging process. They were asked: "In addition to reporting your own activites, what is known about the area you are investigating?" Besides providing state-of-the-discipline assessments, this approach led to identifying gaps in our knowledge and provides direction for future research. For some readers the most important function of this book may be the delineation of the lack of knowledge in various unprobed areas of the subject.

Contributions to this volume have been divided into three sections: Part I deals with theory and policy issues in the area of ethnicity and aging; Part II focuses on ethnic factors shaping the family's relationship to its aged members; and the chapters in Part III focus on research in a variety of important areas relating to ethnicity and aging. The analyses of the issues highlighted in each of these sections should permit the development of general hypotheses about the relationship of ethnicity to aging and help set an agenda for further study in this area.

Reference

Gordon, M. M. *Assimilation in American Life*. New York: Oxford University Press, 1964.

Part I
Theory and Policy Perspectives

The first part of this volume provides an overview of important issues related to ethnicity and aging. The contributors provide a diversity of perspectives from which to view the relationship of ethnicity to aging. These include general approaches utilizing sociological and anthropological frameworks as well as historical discussions of policies toward ethnic groups that have been implemented by a variety of governmental and voluntary agencies. Because of our scanty knowledge about ethnicity and aging, there is a host of basic issues that need to be explored. Part I does not touch on all of them, but the individual chapters focus on topics that have long been deserving of intensive attention.

For students, researchers, and practitioners, an understanding of the current status of ethnicity and aging is an important starting point. An overview of the area is provided by Bengtson, whose research has focused on differences among whites, Blacks, and Spanish-speaking aged. He outlines the major problems that have made research in this area difficult, including the interpenetration of class and ethnicity. Bengtson's efforts to view the relationship of ethnicity to aging from the perspective of social stratification is a contribution to the growth of theoretical sophistication in gerontology. Exploring alternative explanations for some of his research findings, Bengtson notes the continued importance of ethnic differences among the aged. These differences might be even more evident if his sample differentiated groups commonly lumped under the term *white ethnics*.

Kutzik's analysis of the history of American social provision for the aged shows that this has always taken place under ethnic group auspices, including English-white-Protestant (EWP)-dominated public welfare. He finds the major means of assisting the needy aged from the early 1800s until the 1930s to have been not public welfare but organized mutual aid. These mutual aid groups were developed primarily by non-EWP ethnic groups who thereby avoided the degradation of being recipients of EWP public welfare. The generally good treatment of the aged in programs and institutions of their own ethnic group is contrasted with the generally poor treatment they received in those of another ethnic group.

Zola's discussion of the role of ethnicity in medical practice is based on a review of the literature, including his own studies. He notes that late 19th- and early 20th-century medicine had a negative view of ethnic factors as promoting illness (e.g., crowded living conditions and unhealthy foods), so that the "Americanization" of immigrants was considered medically as well as "socially" desirable. He ascribes the continuing resistance of medicine to recognizing the full significance of ethnicity for improved health care to its dominant view of health and illness as the individual's responsibility. Zola argues for sensitization of medical practitioners not only to their patients' but to their own ethnicity.

Kastenbaum's chapter reflects his recent experience as superintendant of a geriatric hospital. From this experience and his past work, he provides some insightful reflections on ethnicity and aging. His discussion ranges over the changing importance ethnicity might have for individuals at different times in their life and the relationship of ethnicity to status differentials. Most important, perhaps, is Kastenbaum's attempt to provide some clarity to the unending discussion of the systems used to classify people by ethnicity and the importance of ethnicity as a "dynamic" variable in the individual's life. Kastenbaum's work represents a psychologist's view and parallels to a large degree the sociological approach of Bengtson and the more anthropological approach utilized by Trela and Sokolovsky in their chapter.

Varghese and Medinger concentrate on an area of psychological inquiry that has not been sufficiently studied in gerontology. Their exploration of the effect of stress and fatalism on minority aged has important implications for the planners and implementers of programs for the aged.

Trela and Sokolovsky outline the basic stances toward ethnicity that have been dominant in the United States. From this perspective, the authors explore the "salience" of ethnicity for a wide variety of ethnic groups, and the possibilities for an "ethnically conscious" federal policy. Their discussion outlines the factors that both aid and hamper advocates of social policies based on ethnicity.

The final chapter, by Bechill, is clearly related to Trela and Sokolovsky's work. Analyzing the policy of the Administration on Aging toward ethnicity, Bechill shows that AOA originally disregarded ethnic differences among the aged. Since the strong thrust in this direction at the 1971 White House Conference on Aging, AOA has begun to place priority on projects developing services for minority groups. Bechill contends that in fulfilling its responsibility to foster programs to meet the needs of older Americans, AOA should expand its concern for the minority elderly to include white ethnic elderly. In addition, he advocates "retention of cultural and ethnic identities" of urban neighborhoods—by implication strengthening ethnic organizations and informal helping networks—as another essential means of meeting the needs of older people.

1

Ethnicity and Aging: Problems and Issues in Current Social Science Inquiry

Vern L. Bengtson

The analysis of social organization begins, as Durkheim long ago observed, with examining distinctions in social life which give rise to the formation of groups. How groups composing the society are defined and the ways in which those groups relate to each other are questions of social differentiation. This chapter explores two dimensions of social differentiation, ethnicity and age, in terms of some emerging problems and topics reflected in current social science literature.

It is obvious that contemporary American society is composed of many identifiable subgroups. What is less apparent is the way they occupy various positions relative to each other in the "division of labor," as suggested by Marx and by Durkheim; and in the possession of "honor" (status) as well as "power" (influence), as noted by Weber. Identifying such dimensions of social organization, and of subgroups that share common characteristics in terms of stratification, is important to enhanced understanding of social behavior both at the collective and at the individual level of analysis.

Preparation of this paper was supported in part by grant 90-A-10108 from the Administration on Aging to the University of Southern California (Fernando Torres-Gil and Stephen McConnell, Principal Investigators). Much of the data reviewed were collected under a grant from the National Science Foundation (#APR-75–21178). Conclusions and interpretations are those of the author and do not necessarily reflect views of the funding agencies or the University.

Ethnicity is increasingly recognized as an important dimension of social differentiation in modern pluralistic societies. The term *ethnic subcultures* is often used to describe groups distinctive from the majority population not only in racial or national background but also in terms of a shared history and cultural values. The question addressed in this chapter concerns to what extent there are ethnic or subcultural variations in patterns of aging.

It may appear obvious that groups differentiated by ethnicity or subcultural heritage have contrasting orientations toward age and aging. Certainly cross-societal research has demonstrated that definitions of old age, its rights and obligations, problems and opportunities, vary across cultures (Cowgill and Holmes, 1972; Simmons, 1945). But it may be equally argued that old age, a universal human challenge, brings with it similar problems and perceptions regardless of variations in social context (Bengtson, Dowd, Smith, and Inkeles, 1977). As Streib (1976) points out, little attention has been given by social scientists to stratification and aging within a particular social system; but, as he also observes, the heterogeneity of today's aged population means that there is marked differentiation among those now aged in terms of various criteria of stratification. Can such differentiation be seen with particular clarity as one examines ethnic groups growing old within the same broader cultural setting? Or are problems of aging generally common across groups to the point that social policy, programs, and theory may adopt a more universalistic perspective?

Ethnic and subcultural variations within the population of aged Americans have become increasingly discussed within the past decade, particularly as advocates for minorities point to the plight of elderly members of their communities. Yet researchers have only begun to accumulate a body of scientific generalizations concerning ethnicity as a mediator in problems of aging. Practitioners and policymakers have only recently begun to formulate programs reflecting the service implications of ethnic contrasts among elderly Americans. Criticisms are raised frequently to the effect that both research and policy are insensitive, and therefore ultimately irrelevant, to current realities of ethnic differentiation among the aged.

The purpose of this chapter is to examine some recurrent problems and some emerging potentials in the conduct of research on ethnicity and aging. Directly or by implication we will be exploring four questions of central relevance both to those social scientists involved in the conduct of research and to those professionals who make or influence policy affecting the pluralistic population of aged Americans. First, what is ethnicity? Second, does it matter as a dimension of social organization and behavior within contemporary American society? Third, what difference—if any—does ethnicity make in mitigating patterns or problems of growing old? Fourth, what are the possible implementations that can be made in policy, practice, and research, given answers to the first three issues? If professionals in gerontology succeed in answering these questions, criticism of irrelevance and insensitivity voiced by advocates of ethnic elderly can be addressed.

Problems in Research on Ethnicity and Aging

There are several problems recurrently faced by social scientists, policy-makers, and practioners as they attempt to consider more adequately the complex interplay between ethnicity and aging. These may be summarized as: (1) the lack of systematic information which spans both research and policy; (2) problems in concepts, vocabulary, and theory; (3) problems in the conduct of research among ethnic populations.

Lack of articulation between theory and policy. We must begin by acknowledging that until quite recently the state of scientific and policy-relevant knowledge concerning ethnicity and aging has been very much underdeveloped. There are few replicated generalizations concerning either differences or similarities among the large and identifiable population of aged ethnics within our society. We know relatively little concerning the varied needs and adaptations associated with aging, as these are differentially manifested in groups that vary by culture, ethnicity, or even by socioeconomic status.

Social scientists might be forgiven in some respects for this lack of knowledge. The study of aging and the characteristics of aged individuals has been pursued systematically for only two or three decades. It takes much longer than that for a science to develop a body of verified knowledge. Moreover, most of the research in social gerontology, at least until 1972, has been undertaken on respondents who are middle-class, white, predominantly native-born Americans, resulting in inadequate information concerning the wide diversity among the over-65 population. The lack of systematic knowledge concerning aging as mediated by ethnicity has unfortunate consequences for both theory and policy.

It should be obvious that any attempt to develop social policy for the aged which ignores the great range of cultural and social variation in the human experience runs the risk of mistakenly inferring universal and causal connections between the biological events of aging and the consequences of growing older in a pluralistic society such as America. Certainly there are biological imperatives in growing older. But what is truly remarkable is that these imperatives are handled in quite different ways by various cultural, socioeconomic, and ethnic groups. There appear to be wide variations in attitudes, values, and practices concerning aging which are social—not biological—in nature. Informed policy for the increasing numbers of older persons in American society must take such variations into account (Fandetti and Gelfand, 1976).

Relatively little is known, however, concerning the composition, needs, and potential resources of ethnic elderly. There is even a basic lack of accurate data on the numbers of elderly persons in the various minority groups in this country. Census data (U.S. Bureau of the Census, 1976) shows that of approximately 20.5 million elderly in the United States, about 18.3 million are white and the remainder Black, Spanish-heritage, Asian nationalities, and Native American (Indian). When broken down by individual minority groups, the census data on the 65-and-over population indicate approximately 1.5 million Blacks, 382,-000 Spanish heritage (Mexican, Puerto Rican, Cuban), 95,000 Asians (Japanese, Chinese, Filipinos), and 44,000 Native Americans. These figures would seem to represent few minority elderly, other than Blacks, in this country.

These figures, however, must be considered with a great deal of caution. Many minorities allege that the Census Bureau has undercounted the number of minority individuals, since many minority persons, especially the elderly, are fearful or suspicious of authority figures (they fear deportation or loss of benefits), and thus do not make themselves available; that inaccurate categories have been used in determining ethnicity; and that minority groups are "older" (i.e., higher mortality rates, lower life expectancy) at an age younger than 65, thus making the number of minority elderly larger than shown by census data. Finally, no census data are available on the numbers of so-called white ethnics over age 65.

Since 1940 some 9 million European immigrants have migrated to the United States (Fandetti and Gelfand, 1976). Greeley (1974) suggests that half of the population of American Catholic adults are either immigrants or the children of immigrants. Various estimates compiled by Woehrer (1978) indicate that in the 1970s there were 20 million Italian Americans, 6 million Mexican Americans, 5.5 million Eastern European Jewish Americans, 5 million Polish Americans, 1.5 million Puerto Ricans on the mainland, and over 0.5 million Japanese Americans. As Woehrer points out, older persons in all these groups are first- or second-generation Americans. Older individuals from other national or ethnic groups which emigrated to America earlier—Germans, Irish, Swedes, Greeks

—have spent much of their lives in culturally distinctive ethnic enclaves.

In the last several years various minority advocacy groups have attempted to focus attention on the unique cultures, lifestyles, languages, and problems of minority elderly. For example, in 1971, prior to the White House Conference on Aging, the National Caucus on Black Aged was formed to focus attention at the Conference on the needs and problems of Black elderly and to organize professionals, politicians, academicians, and service providers around the issues affecting the Black elderly. An outgrowth of this organization has been the National Center on the Black Aged (NCBA), devoted to research, education, and training in Black aging. In 1975 the first National Conference on the Hispanic Elderly was held, which brought together Puerto Ricans, Chicanos, Cubans, and Latin American seniors, professionals, and young people to discuss needs of Hispanic elderly and propose action to address many of their problems. An outgrowth of this conference was the formation of the Asociacion Nacional Pro Personas Mayores (National Association for Spanish-Speaking Elderly), which has become a prime force in representing Hispanic elderly in the public arena. Currently, there also exists a National Indian Council on Aging, and there is also discussion about the formation of a national group representing the Asian elderly. The conference on which the chapters in this volume are based suggests the emergence of advocates concerned about the special situation of white ethnics as well.

Efforts by, for, and within advocate groups have been hampered by a critical lack of information by which planners, decision-makers, politicians, and others can accurately assess the extent and parameters of specific problems—and therefore realistically plan and implement resolutions to these problems. Social policy for the elderly in the United States has generally considered the elderly to be white, English-speaking, and relatively well educated. Thus, most efforts by researchers and planners toward obtaining information in social gerontology has centered on the white elderly. In turn, the developments of policy and programs, to a large extent, have been geared exclusively to white elderly with the assumption being that any diverse groups would also be served by these programs. Yet the minority group advocates have repeatedly claimed that minority elderly have been denied many existing services and have been faced with culturally insensitive programs. Many feel that the ethnic and minority elderly are different by virtue of their language, lifestyle, socioeconomic status, and historical experiences in this country; thus, they require either a different array of social services, or at least modified and flexible regulations and requirements which permit greater accessibility.

The current situation is one where minority groups are advocating for the needs of minority elderly and sensitizing some decision-makers and government agencies to meet these needs. At the same time, some decision-makers are trying to incorporate the special needs of minority elderly in policy. Yet the data and information needed accurately to diagnose the extent of a given problem or situation is lacking. This suggests that either decision-makers will not redress some of these problems because they are not convinced of severity or importance; or that whatever changes do occur to benefit the minority elderly will be inaccurate, based on stereotypes or rhetoric, or be simply a politically expedient measure to placate groups advocating for the rights of the ethnic elderly. At this state in the development of ethnic gerontology, one of the greatest problems remains the lack of research in the field and the lack of policy-oriented data on needs, problems, and lifestyles of the ethnic elderly.

In short, information needed to understand ethnic or minority elderly and to develop programs geared for their particular needs is still quite limited. This is not to imply that there is no knowledge concerning ethnic aged. But it is as yet unsystematic, frequently reflecting a lack of articulation between social theory and policy; thus, available knowledge has had relatively little impact on day-to-day policy. This volume represents a beginning in redressing that lack.

Problems in concepts and theoretical relevance. A second problem we face in consideration of ethnicity and aging relates to general issues of theoretical relevance. Why is there, in 1978, relatively little policy-relevant knowledge concerning ethnicity and aging? I suggest the major reason is that we as professionals and advocates have not adequately articulated answers to the four questions posed at the beginning of this chapter: What is ethnicity? Does it matter in contemporary American social organization? What difference does it make in patterns of aging? What implications do the answers to the first three questions have, for policy, practice, and the conduct of research?

These issues, addressed explicitly or implicitly in this volume, reflect questions of conceptual and theoretical relevance, whether viewed from the perspective of social theory, of policy theory, of social work practice theory, or of service delivery models. For the basic issue concerns the degree to which *social stratification is important:* whether ethnic differentiation, a theoretical abstraction, has significant *demonstrable consequences* in the empirical world of data, policy, and practice.

Although we may be convinced—indeed, take it as a basic premise —that ethnicity is an important dimension in aging, my point is that we who are converted have not been particularly convincing to our colleagues, or to policy-makers, in answering these four questions. But we must, I think, develop systematic theory in answering these four questions. And we must disseminate our answers to academics, to practioners, and to policy-makers.

Why are our answers unconvincing? Possibly it is because they too frequently focus on ethnicity *per se,* rather than ethnic strata within the context of other social stratification dimensions. In short, our answers tend to be *descriptive* and atheoretical, and thus naive.

Any examination of ethnicity as a factor in social behavior must begin from the premise of social stratification: that in any society or group there is patterned social inequality. One universal dimension of social organization is the hierarchical arrangement of individuals or aggregates, reflected in divisions between those who have more power than others or who are more honored than others or who have more possessions than others. In short, social stratification reflects *inequality in the distribution of power, privilege, and prestige.*

The earliest modern sociologists—Marx, Weber, and Durkheim—developed typologies to describe such stratification and theories to account for inequality. Five points summarize the perspectives of these early theorists, as interpreted by C. Wright Mills and Sorokin:

1. The *economic order* is of primary importance in social position and inequality, both the structure and the mechanisms of stratification.

2. *Group consciousness* can and does emerge among persons in a similar stratum. This may then become an important dynamic in social change.

3. *Conflict and competition* are inevitable between strata as the ruling stratum attempts to increase its rewards at the expense of those subordinate.

4. *Ideologies and beliefs* of individuals are a reflection of the individual's position in the stratification system.

5. *Life histories and life chances*—an individual's biography from birth to death—are shaped by position in the class structure (Mills, 1963, pp. 81–95).

A vast body of research over the past 80 years has demonstrated the behavioral consequences of economic class stratification. The early preoccupation with class defined solely in economic or occupational terms has been revised. The traditional class perspective is considered by contemporary sociologists to be much too circumscribed or limited to reflect the complex social inequalities that are seen in modern societies. Instead, emphasis is placed on multiple hierarchies of inequality. Class defined in economic terms is one element in such hierarchies, but sex, age, and ethnicity have especially in the past decade been added. Current theory tends to focus on a multiple hierarchy model of stratification in which class, ethnicity, sex, and age are considered separate but inter-related aspects of social inequality. Each reflects social strata. Each can and must be examined separately and jointly, in terms of power, privilege, and prestige.

What, then, is ethnicity, and to what extent is it a dimension of social inequality in the context of aging? It is perhaps easiest to begin with a definition of "ethnic group." There are three distinctions that appear relevant in defining ethnic groups: (1) peoples distinguished primarily by visible physical criteria (for example, racial groups such as Blacks or Orientals); (2) peoples distinguished by cultural heritage or language (American Poles, Irish, or Italians); (3) peoples distinguished by conquest (Blacks, Mexican Americans, Indians, Hawaiians). It is obvious that often these physical, cultural, or political conditions are combined in the history of a particular group. And almost always, any of these criteria define "minority" group status, relative to the broader population.

Does ethnicity *per se* make a difference in terms of social inequality? Many commentators on American society have documented that it does. Indeed in the 1930s Gunnar Myrdal described the social organization of the American South as a "caste system." *Caste* connotes a rigid ascriptive form of stratification based on skin color, purity of blood, or other genetic or physical characteristics. One is born into, lives his life, and dies within a caste group with no chance of mobility. Consider the following description of caste etiquette in the deep South in the 1930s as described by Myrdal:

> Negroes and whites must not shake hands when they meet; the white man must start the conversation (although the Negro can hint that he wants to talk); the Negro must address the white person as Mr., Mrs., or Miss, but he must never be addressed by these titles himself (Negroes are addressed by their first name or called uncle, aunty, darky, nigger, or in some cases —for politeness sake—may be called by their last name or by such titles as doctor, professor, or teacher). The topic of conservation must be limited to specific job matters or to personal niceties (e.g., inquiries after one's health); it must never stray over to bigger matters of politics or economics or to personal matters such as white husband-wife relationships. Negroes should never look into the eyes of white people when they talk to them but generally keep their eyes on the ground or shifting, and their physical posture in front of white people when they talk to them should be humble and self-demeaning [trans. Rose, 1948, p. 358].

Such caste etiquette represents an extreme example of what we are calling *unequal privilege* in the social sense of norms and conventions. That is, Blacks were locked into highly circumscribed roles under a caste system.

It may appear quaint, if not irrelevant, to review Myrdal's depiction of Black–white relations in caste-stratified Southern society five decades ago. But it is relevant to our discussion to be reminded that many of today's aged Blacks were born into and grew up within such rigid social differentiation. Many other aged ethnics—born in Mexico, Ireland, Eastern Europe, Italy, Puerto Rico—have lived their adult lives within a social context where they experienced continual reminders of inequality. They were disadvantaged from the beginning in terms of the *economic order*. Undoubtedly they held some degree of *group consciousness*, a sense of differentness which either motivated attempts at assimilation or the elaboration of distinctive cultural symbols to provide meaning. They felt *competition* and perhaps *conflict* with the dominant majority, and certainly their *life chances* were shaped by their position of structured inequality—a condition many sought to redress by providing their children with an education to gain upward mobility. Growing old today, their biographies and circumstances reflect a lifetime of inequality within a political ideology that states "all men are created equal."

But again this is a unidimensional and perhaps stereotypic view. Many elderly ethnics reflect upward mobility within their own lifetimes. Patterns are different for those who held higher positions in the economic order, and for males as compared with females. Just as we are uninformed if we ignore the classical sociological concepts concerning class stratification and inequality, so are we naive if we do not examine current theory concerning multiple dimensions of stratification.

Does ethnicity make a difference? Yes: but an adequate answer cannot be given convincingly to our colleagues unless appropriate concepts such as those reflected in the multiple hierarchy stratification model are articulated. Data are needed that allow for analysis of ethnicity *and* economic class, as well as age and sex. Research is needed that focuses on individual variations as well as model types of aging within ethnic subgroups (such an approach is illustrated below).

Problems in the conduct of ethnic research. This leads to a consideration of a third major challenge: issues of conducting research in ethnic communities. Research on ethnic and subcultural aging is fraught with problems requiring special considerations, issues not usually treated in textbooks or courses in research methodology. Four are as follows:

1. Identification of problems, questions, and issues: The perspective of the middle-class, white, nonimmigrant researcher or practitioner may be quite irrelevant to the life circumstances of ethnic aged, particularly those from racial minority backgrounds.

2. Goals of the research: Well-intentioned efforts to gain information may be viewed as another example of Establishment rip-off using ethnic aged as "subjects" with no payoff to the populations from which data are gathered.

3. Methods of the research: Sampling and questionnaire construction may be quite irrelevant to the populations from which information is elicited. Or so they may appear to advocates representing groups under study, as well as to professionals having an "insider" perspective of the ethnic groups.

4. Politics and accountability in research: The conduct of scientific inquiry always involves adjudicating among special interest groups (researchers; funding agencies; academic institutions; professional peers). Thus negotiation ("politics") is an inevitable, if not openly acknowledged, aspect of research. Ethnic studies encounter another interest group, advocates of the collectivity from which data are sought. Too frequently researchers are quite unprepared to negotiate for the right to carry out their studies, or to consider accountability beyond their own academic reference group.

Experiences with a cross-ethnic research program at the University of Southern California will be drawn from, in discussing these problems. This project has had a highly unusual history according to standards of current research methodology textbooks, but its biography may be fairly typical of future cross-ethnic research projects. It has not followed the usual course of social science research, in which academics define the plan of study, gather data, analyze and report findings, all within the confines of a scholarly community. Rather, from the beginning the researchers became directly involved in the politics of community research with subsequent alterations in both the organization and the spirit of the program. The researchers came to accept a new definition of accountability in the conduct of ethnic studies.

In fact, the program was suspended prior to its anticipated starting date because of community protest about the research. The protest was caused by failure of the investigators to involve and gain support of important community constituencies when the research plans were first formulated. Representatives of the Los Angeles Mexican American and Black communities formally protested to the funding foundation, requesting a role in setting policy for the studies so as to avoid the implicit racism and elitism which, they noted, had characterized other cross-ethnic research.

The history of the project has been described in several publications (Bengtson, Cuellar and Ragan 1977) and will be summarized only briefly here. The major vehicle for gaining community involvement and trust was the establishment of the Community Research Planning Committee, comprised of concerned members of the Black and Mexican American constituencies. Over the past five years the Committee has been the decision-making body at each stage of the program and at each level of project organization.

Regularly quarterly meetings have been held, reviewing each segment of the program and ratifying or modifying staff decisions concerning procedures. It is important to note that the major substantive goals of the program remained unchanged, while alterations were made in the means of data-gathering and the targets of dissemination. The result has not only been community support for the program, but also an unusual degree of confidence in its products: confidence that the inferences drawn from the data are valid and that the dissemination products are relevant beyond the usual academic audiences.

The costs of such unusual collaboration between academics and community representatives have been high in terms of time and energy for the various interest groups involved. It is estimated that perhaps one year was added to the original time frame in order to build mutual understanding and trust, as well as to make necessary modifications in organization. But the rewards have also been high. The original concerns of the community advocates—for greater minority involvement, for greater relevance to the needs of their aged, and for greater effectiveness in dissemination of results—have been achieved.

In short, as one publication from the project concludes, the recurrent conflicts with community groups which have confronted many social scientists in recent years are often the consequence of naiveté and unwarranted inflexibility on the part of academic researchers. Thus, the process of this research may be of as much interest to future investigators as are the eventual substantive scientific products.

Potentials for Developing Policy-Relevant Knowledge in Ethnicity and Aging

Substantial problems confront those who take seriously the challenge of relating ethnic or subcultural variations in aging to social policy or practice in gerontology. But there are significant potentials as well, both for development of social science theory and for relevant policy. Two examples from recent research explore the question of whether ethnicity makes a difference in patterns of growing old within a pluralistic society such as the United States. In addition they employ a multiple-hierarchy model of stratification in addressing the following issues: the "multiple jeopardy" of ethnic minority aged versus the idea that aging is a "leveler" of prior social and economic distinctions; perceptions of aging as reflecting common problems versus perceptions particular to specific groups such as of ethnic and minority aged.

The question of multiple jeopardy among ethnic elderly. The situation of elderly individuals who are members of identifiable ethnic or minority populations has been characterized by minority group advocates as that of "double jeopardy" or "multiple hazards" (Jackson, 1970, 1971; National Council on Aging, 1972; National Urban League, 1964). These descriptions refer to the additive negative effects of being old *and* in a racial/ethnic minority (the focus of these publications was on Black elderly) on frequently cited indicators of quality of life such as income, health, housing, or life satisfaction.

Like other older people in industrial societies, ethnic aged experience the devaluation of old age found in most modern societies (Cowgill and Holmes, 1972). Unlike other older people, however, these aged must bear the additional economic, social, and psychological burdens of living in a society in which racial equality remains more myth than social policy. It has been noted that, compared to the white aged, most of the minority aged "are less well educated, have less income, suffer more illnesses and earlier death, have poorer quality housing and less choice as to where they live and where they work, and in general have a less satisfying quality of life" (U.S. Senate Special Committee on Aging, 1971).

But another perspective suggests that problems of ethnic elderly may not be all that unique. While differences among ethnic groups are frequently observed and incontestable, it also is true that the aging individual, regardless of ethnic background, is subject to a variety of influences which cut across racial lines and may mediate or level differences in patterns of aging (Kent and Hirsch, 1969). True, the relative numbers of ethnic minority *aged* having good health and adequate income, may be less than those of aged whites. If, however, the percentage differences between middle-aged Blacks or Mexican Americans and their white counterparts are greater yet, a characterization of the minority aged as being in double jeopardy would be an incomplete description. It may be that age exerts a *leveling* influence on the ethnic differences found among the younger cohorts.

In short there are two apparently contradictory perspectives on ethnicity and aging. The first perspective suggests that the minority aged suffer from a situation of double jeopardy, the second perspective views advancing age as a leveler of racial inequalities that existed in mid-life.

The empirical question of whether either of these perspectives characterizes the situation of ethnic-minority aged has been examined by Dowd and Bengtson (1978). Data from the University of Southern California's community survey of aging and social policy, involving 1,269 individuals from Black, Mexican American, and white communities, were analyzed on four dimensions reflecting quality of life: income, health, social interaction, and life satisfaction. Comparisions were made so as to contrast three ethnic strata and three age strata (age 45–54, 55–64, 65–74 years) to determine the extent of ethnic variation within each stratum. Statistical controls were introduced to examine contrasts attributable to the additional stratum dimensions of socioeconomic status and sex.

One important limitation in this community survey is the lack of further ethnic differentiation within the "white" or "Anglo" subsample of 418 individuals. In Los Angeles, as in most major American cities, there are geographic and subcultural enclaves of Eastern European Jews, Greeks, Armenians, Poles, and so forth. Undoubtedly these groups carry with them distinctive patterns and needs associated with growing old. But to attempt representative sampling of such white ethnics would have reduced sample cells to numbers inadequate for comparative analysis (to say nothing of the practical problems of linguistic equivalence for the survey questionnaire). Moreover, the qualitative analyses carried out by anthropologists within the same project (Myerhoff and Simic, 1978) was expected to provide a more focused and informative portrait of at least two white ethnic groups.

Results from the USC survey suggest that in terms of relative *income* the minority elderly may indeed be characterized as experiencing double jeopardy. While income of both white and minority respondents declined by age stratum, the mean income reported by older Mexican American and Black respondents is considerably lower than any other age-ethnic subgroup in the sample (3.36 and 3.49, respectively, compared to 6.89 for whites age 65–74 and 10.94 among whites 45–54). Further, the relative *decline* in income within the 30-year age span represented in the sample studied here is much greater for minority respondents than it is for whites. The mean income reported by Blacks declined 55% across the three age strata. Mexican Americans showed an even larger drop in mean income, 62%. The income of older white respondents, by contrast, declined only 36%. Thus, the rather large income "gap" that exists between middle-aged minority and white respondents becomes an even larger one among the respondents aged 65 or older. These differences in income cannot be explained by the Socioeconomic Status (SES), sex, or health differences that exist between whites and either Mexican Americans or Blacks. Even with these variables held constant, the net incomes of the respondents over 65 are significantly different.

Similar results can be seen with respect to self-rated *health*. Older minority respondents were significantly more likely to report poorer health than white respondents even with the effects of SES, sex and income held constant. The differences in health among the three ethnic groups were less apparent among younger respondents, particularly those aged 55 to 64. While the mean health scores of Blacks and Mexican Americans across the three age strata dropped, respectively, 13% and 19%, the mean score of white respondents declined less than 9%. As was the case with income, the self-assessed health of whites is greater than that of minority respondents at each age stratum with the greatest disparity occurring among those aged 65 and older. Consequently the label "double jeopardy" appears appropriate when describing the health categorizations of older Blacks or Mexican Americans; the same may be true for other older minority ethnics.

A third dimension explored in Dowd and Bengtson's (1978) analysis concerned subjective dimensions of *life satisfaction*. Here there is less support for the double jeopardy hypothesis. On the first factor dimension, labeled "Tranquility," there was little indication of stable age-stratum differences within or across ethnic strata. Although the mean scores for 65- to 74-year-old Mexican Americans are somewhat lower than for the 45- to 54-year-olds, the contrast is not statistically significant, and the scores of Blacks are virtually the same (interestingly, there is a slight *increase* in tranquility scores by age within the white sample).

On the second dimension, called "Optimism," the responses of the Mexican American minority group do appear supportive of the double jeopardy hypothesis. Among the 449 respondents in this group there was a significant decline in optimism scores with age; optimism scores among aged respondents (age 65–74 years) were significantly lower than scores for whites in the same age stratum; and the contrast is greater in the older, as contrasted with the middle-aged group. However, no such indication of double jeopardy characterizes the Black respondents—where on both tranquility and optimism, differences in comparision to the white sample of respondents in each age group become *smaller* with increasing age. On the tranquility dimension there is substantively no difference between 65- to 74-year-old Black and white respondents, though in the 45- to 54-year-old age stratum Blacks score slightly higher than whites. In this ethnic contrast controlling for income, SES, health, and sex, the hypothesis of age as a leveler receives some support while the double jeopardy hypothesis is *not* suggested by the data. What this indicates, in passing, is the multiple complexity of assessing ethnic contrasts in varying aspects of aging.

Indicators of *social interaction* were used to explore a fourth dimension of quality-of-life as varying by ethnicity, indicative of either the double jeopardy or age-as-leveler hypotheses. Primary group interaction indicates a source of reward available to individuals in the course of daily living: directly in terms of potential assistance when in need, indirectly as a form of insulation from the breakdown in self-esteem and diminution of coping skills often associated with the transition to old age. Both are important elements in alleviating the "social breakdown syndrome" which jeopardizes competence in old age (Kuypers and Bengtson, 1971).

On two measures of primary group interaction, frequency of contact with children and grandchildren, the data showed the white respondents reporting the lowest frequency of contact. Mexican Americans at each age stratum reported the most frequent interaction. Even with controls for income, occupational prestige (SES), sex, and health of respondent, the differences between Mexican Americans and whites remain striking. Blacks showed slightly higher rates of contact than whites, but not in the oldest age category.

On a third measure, frequency of contact with other kin, whites again have lower rates of interaction in the two middle-age categories (age 45–64 years), but the difference becomes smaller with increasing age: the pattern of contact with relatives among minority respondents declines while that reported by whites remains relatively stable. The result suggests a leveling of ethnic differences with advancing age.

On the fourth dimension, frequency of contact with friends, neighbors, and acquaintances, whites reported higher levels of interaction at all age levels. Contact increases for whites with each age stratum, but there are are no such increases for the Black and Mexican American respondents. Thus, the ethnic differences in 65- to 74-year olds are greater than in any other age category. These findings are not supportive of the double jeopardy hypothesis, however, because for the minority respondents the lower interaction scores are not explained to any degree by *age:* younger Blacks, for example, are not substantially higher than aged Blacks in contact scores.

Thus, the greater frequency of *familial* interaction among the ethnic minority respondents, particularly Mexican Americans, suggests that primary group needs of minority aged are being met within the extended family. But the fact that Mexican Americans also report the *least* amount of interaction with nonrelated individuals suggests a certain amount of social isolation.

In summary, the southern California community survey data on various dimensions of quality-of-life suggests that differences among the three ethnic groups do exist, but there is also support for the hypothesis that age exerts a leveling influence on some aspects of ethnic variation with advancing age. While longitudinal research across ethnic groups would be necessary in order to definitively explore the age-as-a-leveler hypothesis, the data reviewed offers some support for Kent's (1971a) suggestion that the problems older people face are substantially similar regardless of their ethnic background: "This is not to say that the same proportion of each group faces these problems; obviously they do not. The point, however, is that if we concentrate on the group rather than the problem, we shall be treating symptoms rather than causes."

Put differently, to presume that ethnic differences are alone sufficient to understand the personal and social situation of the aged ignores tremendous variation both across ethnic boundaries and within ethnic categories (as has been underscored, for example, by Jackson, 1970; 1971). The existence of double jeopardy, therefore, is an empirical, not a logical, question. To assume otherwise would be to ignore the warning of Kent (1971a) that "age may be a great leveller with regard to both racial and social influences. . . ."

Perceptions of aging. Perhaps the most basic philosophical assumption common to those who consider ethnicity crucial to understanding contemporary aging relates to the importance of *social definitions of age and aging,* in contrast to chronological or biological parameters. Consistent with the "sociology of knowledge" perspective articulated by Thomas (1931), Mannheim (1953), and more recently Berger and Luckman (1966), the assumption here is that reality is socially constructed: humans think, feel, and act in the context of shared expectations. The experience of aging depends to a large extent on socially defined patterns deriving from learned and shared "definitions of situations" which influence action and behavior. Such definitions vary according to location in the social system, especially in terms of broader systems of meaning provided by cultural interpretations of normative events such as growing old. Thus, analysis of *perceptions* of aging and the ways such perceptions vary across social strata such as ethnic subcultures is of considerable importance in understanding the phenomenology of aging.

Analysis of perceptions of age, pursued within the context of a "social construction of reality" theoretical perspective, has several important implications for researchers and policy-makers in aging (Bengtson, Kasschau, and Ragan, 1977). First, the social categorization of individuals by age (as young, middle-aged, elderly, and frail or "dependent") may vary among subgroups, reflecting differential placement in terms of social stratification. Moreover, the basic notion of time, while usually defined in terms of chronological events such as birthday to birthday, can more meaningfully be defined in terms of developmental or historical events which have influenced an individual's life. The *occurrence* of such events, as well as their *meaning* for the person, varies among groups and between individuals. Therefore the basic constructs of interest to gerontologists (time and aging) may have quite different meaning for one group of humans in contrast to another.

A second implication concerns the definition of "social problems." What is or is not seen as a difficulty associated with aging reflects what is collectively defined as normal or deviant, and these definitions may vary across societies, across locations within a given society, across historical periods. So also do the solutions proposed to deal with problematic aspects of aging—how much it is the responsibility of public collectivities (such as governmental agencies) to provide needed assistance to older individuals, and how much it is the responsibility of the older person himself or his family (Ragan and Grigsby, 1976)? Thus, the public recognition of problems and their appropriate amelioration is a complex social and political process based on the emergence of collective definitions of the situation, definitions which may vary considerably from one ethnic or cultural group to another in a pluralistic society.

In short, aging represents one of many aspects of reality that are socially defined; and old age is a social category whose properties and problems are constructed within the context of shared expectations particular to specific groups. It is useful to examine evidence concerning perceptions of aging among contrasting groups to explore patterns of reality construction. Many ethnic elderly were born into and grew up within one culture, learning one set of expectations regarding what old age is marked by and how it should be negotiated, only to migrate and grow old themselves in a quite different cultural context in which aging is viewed very differently. To what extent are there marked ethnic differences in perceptions of aging? To what extent are there commonalities, despite ethnic or subcultural variations?

In the southern California studies several indicators were used to examine ethnic contrasts in perceptions of aging. The first concerned *subjective assessments of age,* self-categorizations by respondents of whether they define themselves as "young," "middle-aged," or "elderly." Self-categorizations varied considerably by ethnic group membership. Over 30% of the Mexican Americans identified themselves as "old" at age 57, while the same percentage of Black respondents was not reached until age 63 and among whites until nearly age 70 (Bengtson, Kasschau, and Ragan, 1977). In discussing contrasts between Black and white elderly, Jackson (1970) suggests that in the United States minority group members perceive themselves as "old" at a considerably earlier chronological age than whites because of the repeated hardships they have faced through a lifetime of economic and social disadvantage.

A different method of assessing subjective age is to ask respondents to estimate the amount of time left to them to live. This has been termed *"awareness of finitude"* by Munnichs (1968). These estimates may be expected to vary by social location, since mortality rates indicate significant contrasts between males and females, between racial groups, and among economic status levels.

Results from the southern California survey again indicate significant ethnic differences in this perception of aging (Bengtson, Cuellar and Ragan, 1977). The Black subsample as a group expressed the greatest longevity expectancy, with a mean of 26 years, and the Mexican Americans the least with a mean of 19 years (it will be recalled that these respondents range in age from 45 to 74 years old). The ethnic contrasts were maintained after controlling for potentially confounding effects of SES differentials.

These results may be somewhat surprising. The patterns of Black responses are in marked contrast to age-specific mortality data showing differences between minorities and whites. According to current United States Census figures, additional life expectancy at age 50 for nonwhites is about 24 years, while for whites it is 26 years. At age 70 it is slightly under 12 years for nonwhites, slightly over 12 years for whites (Vital Statistics, USDHEW, 1972). Comparable census life expectancy data are not available for Mexican Americans, but it is estimated that these will be even lower than for Blacks (Moore, 1971).

Thus, the Blacks in this particular sample subjectively considered themselves to have more years to live than the other two ethnic groups. Perhaps this is an indication of the "pride of survivorship" described by Jackson (1970) in the face of lifetime adversity as a minority group member. Perhaps it is indicative of a lessened sense of futurity in some social groups than others.

A third indicator of perceptions regarding age and aging is obtained from asking older individuals to indicate the *best* (and the worst) *things about being their age.* In the USC survey we asked respondents for such evaluations and coded up to three responses. The results suggest cross-ethnic similarities as well as contrasts.

Perhaps the most frequent response concerned relaxation, not having to work so hard, having more leisure time. This was mentioned more by the Blacks and Mexican Americans than by the whites; a 66-year-old Black man said, "I got the time now to think and appreciate life, and do all the little things I can do to help my fellow man less fortunate than I am." A second theme concerned health: an unexpected, but welcomed, aspect of old age. A 74-year-old Black woman said, "I feel pretty good health-wise, which is a blessing." Another said, "I'm surprised that I'm as healthy as I am, because I expected old age to be a lot worse, and it hasn't turned out that way." A third common response was pleasure from children and other family members; one Mexican American woman noted that "when my children return and come to see me" is the best thing about being 73 years old, while another 70-year-old mentioned the other side of the coin: "Children are grown so they're not a problem as far as raising them." Yet a fourth theme is independence and freedom, mentioned about equally by the three ethnic groups.

But there are distinctive ethnic patterns in these responses to what is best liked about being the age they are. A common response among Blacks—mentioned by 22% of the men, 32% of the women—concerned the theme of just being alive, having reached this age. In the words of one respondent, "God let me stay here as old as I am, strong, being as well as I am. It's a beautiful age and I'm proud of it." Typical Mexican American responses focused on characteristics of home and family. A 72-year-old woman responded, "More time for myself. I don't have to rush like I did before . . . ," while a 65-year-old woman said, "That I have my husband; that's another thing that I should be proud of." Older whites tended to mention independence and being glad to be retired. Travel was mentioned by 22% of the men and 22% of the women. In addition, a higher percentage of whites said "nothing" in response to the question. "I can't think of anything. I just accept it," said a 74-year-old woman. A man the same age voiced a more negative view: "I wish I was younger; I don't like being my age."

A fourth aspect concerns *major problems encountered* in old age. In the USC survey we asked members of each ethnic group what were the three greatest problems they currently faced (Ragan and Simonin, 1977). Again there were cross-ethnic similarities as well as differences.

All three ethnic groups reported finances as the number one problem (mentioned by 76% of the Blacks and Mexican Americans, 67% of the whites). Health was the second greatest problem volunteered (48% of the Mexican Americans, 35% of the whites, 31% of the Blacks).

Cross-ethnic contrasts were evident in additional responses. Over one-quarter of the Black elderly, for example, mentioned crime as a problem; about the same percentage of the Mexican Americans volunteered the cost of food specifically as a difficulty. Slightly more whites (12%) than Blacks (5%) mentioned medical costs. More whites (13%) indicated problems of morale—loneliness, isolation, or feeling "blue."

The fifth and perhaps most general assessment of perceptions of age involved analysis of responses to *opinion items regarding characteristics of old age,* both positive and negative. The USC survey respondents were asked to agree or disagree to such statements as, "Most older people are set in their ways and unable to change," and "older people can learn new things just as well as younger people can." A battery of items taken from previous studies was constructed to measure both positive and negative attributes of aging. Items were then factor-analyzed and two scales constructed which demonstrated cross-stratum equivalency of response dimensions (Morgan and Bengtson, 1976).[1] These were then tested for significant differences, by ethnicity, age, and sex.

Results were somewhat surprising. First, there was substantial similarity among the various social categories represented in the survey on the scale measuring Negative Attributes of the Aged. Evaluations tended overall to be highly negative (indicating, for example, that many respondents agreed that "Most older people spend too much time prying into the affairs of others"). Although overall differences by ethnicity did not attain significance, whites were less negative than were Blacks or Mexican Americans. There were no statistically significant differences by age (though older respondents were slightly more negative than 45- to 54-year-olds) or by sex.

Second, there were group differences on the scale measuring Positive Potential of the Aged (questions such as, "Older people can learn new things just as well as younger people can"). Ethnic differences were highly significant, with Blacks the most positive, Mexican Americans the least positive. Age differences also emerged, with the oldest respondents the least positive.

In these data one sees perhaps the clearest example of the complex interplay between broadly shared cultural perceptions regarding old age and subgroup or ethnic variations. There is general agreement that old age has pervasive negative attributes; there are insignificant ethnic variations on this theme. But there are wide group contrasts on assessments of positive aspects of aging. Responses from a sample of diverse white ethnic elderly would probably reflect an even wider spectrum of culturally influenced orientations on this issue, as is suggested in the analyses of Greeley (1974), Woehrer (1978), Fandetti and Gelfand (1976), as well as the chapter by Cohler and Lieberman in this volume.

Anthropological data from the USC project provides a sixth source of information concerning ethnicity and perceptions of aging. Here the

1. It should be mentioned that this analysis focused on a frequently overlooked methodological problem in comparing attitudes of respondents from different social categories, that of cross-stratum equivalence of meaning in research instruments. It was found that the scales originally constructed using 14 items contained serious problems of cross-group equivalency in terms of reliability and validity—the same questions appeared to have different meanings for Black, Mexican American, and white respondents. A second stage of analysis involving reduction of items revealed two orthogonal dimensions that could be justified as operating similarly across ethnic, sex, and age groups (see Morgan and Bengtson, 1976). These are the dimensions reported in the present discussion.

information focuses on life histories of individuals, allowing construction of biographies concerning those who have grown up in one cultural setting and grown old in another, maintaining their ascribed membership as "ethnics" with the minority status which the term connotes (Myerhoff and Simic, 1978).

The elderly Jews studied by Barbara Myerhoff and the Mexican Americans of East Los Angeles researched by Jose Cuellar reflect in their old age dramatic discontinuities not experienced by many of their "Anglo" counterparts. Both have been essentially cut off from the sources of their childhood experience in another country. Both are separated by a cultural gap from their more Americanized children. Thus, these aging people within a large urban center are the product of a number of ruptures to biographical continuity: migration from their place of birth; survival of severe persecution (in the case of the Jews); separation from the culture that socialized and nurtured them into adulthood; partial alienation within their present cultural environment; language barriers; and often severance of expected intergenerational ties (Myerhoff, 1976).

But the ethnographic analysis of these ethnic migrants points to an important generalization: their ethnicity represents a significant resource in dealing with problems of aging. Perhaps this is best illustrated by Barbara Myerhoff's study. She describes the community created by her group of increasingly frail elderly Jews, built around a Community Center, in which symbols and ritual shared with other individuals from a common background provide meaning and support in old age. These provide the affirmation continuities in the lives of these dislocated Jews who regard themselves as survivors in a hostile environment, collectively and individually. In a sense, autonomous existence has become their very "career" in old age, and their peers provide continued validation of their being "a good Jew" to the end. Other studies of ethnic Americans support this point—for example, Helena Lopata's research on Polish Americans (1976).

Three summary statements can be drawn from this survey of evidence regarding ethnicity and perceptions of age. The most obvious is that ethnic group membership *does* appear to reflect an important dimension of social stratification among the aged. In pluralistic populations, which increasingly characterizes most contemporary nation-states, gerontologists would do well to acknowledge the importance of ethnic group membership as reflecting important collective characteristics that are manifest in patterns of behavior in old age.

Second, in the complex configuration of differences and similarities among ethnic groups, norms and values of the predominant culture are an important consideration. Whether these represent positive or negative forces, the data point to many cross-group similarities as well as differences, some of which are quite subtle, many problems and potentials reflecting slight variations on common themes.

Third, it is important to emphasize that although minority status brings problems, membership in an ethnic group, with its shared culture, symbols, rituals, and meanings, is an important resource in dealing with the problems of aging. These must be recognized and indeed exploited by the elderly themselves and by their advocates.

References

Bengtson, V. L., Cuellar, J. B., and Ragan, P. K. Stratum contrasts and similarities in attitudes toward death. *Journal of Gerontology,* 1977, *32*(1), 76–88.

Bengtson, V. L., Kasschau, P. O., and Ragan, P. K. The impact of social structure on the aging individual. In J. Birren and K. W. Schaie (Eds.) *Handbook of the Psychology of Aging.* New York: Van Nostrand Reinhold, 1977.

Bengtson, V. L., Dowd, J. J., Smith, D. H., and Inkeles, A. Modernization, modernity and perceptions of aging: A cross-cultural study. *Journal of Gerontology,* 1977, *30*(6), 688–695.

Berger, P. L., and Luckman, T. *The Social Construction of Reality.* New York: Doubleday, 1966.

Cowgill, D. O., and Holmes, L. D. *Aging and Modernization.* New York: Merideth, 1972.

Dowd, J. J., and Bengtson, V. L. Aging in Minority Populations: An examination of the double jeopardy hypothesis. *Journal of Gerontology,* 1978, *33*(3), 427–436.

Fandetti, D. V., and Gelfand, D. E. Care of the aged: Attitudes of white ethnic families. *Gerontologist,* 1976, *16,* 544–549.

Greeley, A. M. *Ethnicity in the United States.* New York: Wiley, 1974.

Jackson, J. J. Aged Negroes: Their cultural departures from statistical stereotypes and rural-urban differences. *Gerontologist,* 1970, *10,* 140–145.

Jackson, J. J. Compensatory care for the Black aged. In occasional paper #10 Institute of Gerontology, (Ed.), *Minority aged in America.* University of Michigan, 1971.

Kent, D. P. The Negro Aged. *Gerontologist,* 1971a, *11,* 48–50.

Kent, D. P. The elderly in minority groups: Variant patterns of aging. *Gerontologist,* 1971b, *11,* 26–29.

Kent, D.P., and Hirsch, C. Differentials in need and problem solving techniques among low income Negro and White elderly. Paper presented at the 8th International Congress of Gerontology, Washington, D.C., 1969.

Kuypers, A., and Bengtson, V. L. Generational difference and the "developmental" stake." *Aging and Human Development,* 1971, *2*(1), 249–60.

Lopata, Helena. *The Polish Americans.* Englewood Cliffs, N.J.: Prentice-Hall, 1966.

Manheim, K. The problem of generations. In. D. Kecskemeti (Ed. and Trans.), *Essays in Sociology of Knowledge*. London: Routledge and Kegan Paul, 1953.

Mills, C. W. *Power Politics and People*. New York: Ballantine Books, 1963.

Moore, J. Mexican Americans. *Gerontologist*, 1971, *11*, 30–35.

Morgan, L. A., and Bengtson, V. L. Measuring perceptions of aging across social strata. Paper presented at the annual meeting of the Gerontological Society, New York, October 15, 1976.

Munnichs, J. M. *Old Age and Finitude: A Contribution to Psycho-gerontology*. New York and Basel: S. Karger, 1968.

Myerhoff, B. *Number Our Days*. Film produced for Public Broadcasting Corporation, 1976.

Myerhoff, B. G., and Simic, A. (Eds.). *Life's Career—Aging: Cultural Variations in Growing Old*. Beverly Hills: Sage Publications, 1978.

Myrdal, G. *An American Dilemma*. Boston: Beacon, 1956.

National Council of Aging. *Triple Jeopardy: Myth or Reality*. Washington, National Council on Aging, 1972.

National Urban League. *Double Jeopardy: The Older Negro in America Today*. New York: National Urban League, 1964.

Ragan, P. K., and Grigsby, J. E. Responsibility for meeting the needs of the elderly for health care, housing, and transportation: Opinions reported in a survey of Blacks, Mexican Americans and Whites. Western Gerontological Society, San Diego, 1976.

Ragan, P. K., and Simonin, M. Community Survey Report. A brief report reproduced for dissemination, March, 1977.

Rose, A., (Trans.) G. Myrdal's *The Negro in America*. Boston: Beacon, 1948.

Simmons, L. W. *The Role of the Aged in Primitive Society*. New Haven: Yale University Press, 1945.

Streib, Gordon. Social stratification and aging. In Robert H. Binstock and Ethel Shanas (Eds.), *Handbook of Aging and the Social Sciences*. New York: Van Nostrand Reinhold Company, 1976, pp. 160–85.

Thomas, W. I. *The Unadjusted Girl*. Boston: Little, Brown, 1931.

U.S. Bureau of Census. *Current Population Reports*. Series P-23, No. 59. Demographic aspects of aging and the older population in the U.S. Washington, D.C.: U.S. Government Printing Office, 1976.

U.S. Senate Special Committee on Aging. *The Multiple Hazards of Age and Race: The Situation of Aged Blacks in the U.S.* Washington, D.C.: U.S. Government Printing Office, 1971.

Vital Statistics of the United States. *Vol. II, Sec. 5, Life Tables: 1972*. Rockville, Maryland: U.S. Department of Health, Education and Welfare, 1972.

Woehrer, C. E. Cultural pluralism in American families: The influence of ethnicity on special aspects of aging. *Family Coordinator*, 1978, *27*(4).

2

American Social Provision
for the Aged:
An Historical Perspective

Alfred J. Kutzik

This book represents long overdue recognition by those studying and serving the aged that ethnicity is important for correctly understanding and adequately providing for the aged in the present period. This chapter discusses the importance of ethnicity throughout American history in social provision for the aged on the assumption that knowledge of past experience can clarify current research and policy (Watson and Maxwell, 1977, p.100).

The Colonial Period

In the Colonial period the needy aged were cared for no differently than the needy non-aged. It has long been understood that by the late 1600s, following English Poor Law precedent, public assistance was being provided by every politically organized American community to those of its members in need of it. However, this has also long been misunderstood to have been punitive, inadequate care largely in almshouses, with even harsher extra-institutional treatment for the considerable number of poor and dependent annually auctioned off by public officials to the lowest bidders willing to care for them in order to cut down on almshouse expenditures. This erroneous view has recently been corrected by scholars who have studied the heretofore neglected historical data. As Rothman generalizes:

> The colonial community typically cared for its dependents without disrupting their lives. Whenever possible it supported members in their own families; in extenuating circumstances of old age, widowhood or debility, it boarded them in a neighboring household. Only a handful of towns maintained an almshouse, and they used it as a last resort for very special cases; ... The colonists normally supported the poor in community households, not in separate institutions. ... Communities dispensed relief straightforwardly, without long investigation or elaborate procedures, without discomfort or dislocation [Rothman, 1971, pp. 30–31].

The facts that by the late 1700s a few small communities in New England and New York were auctioning off their public charges and some in Pennsylvania even forcing "paupers" to wear a "P" does not call this overall characterization into question. However, the fact that poor "strangers," i.e., nonmembers of the community, were denied public assistance throughout Colonial times seems to raise questions with it. In explaining this policy inherited from England, Trattner notes: "most localities had so many of their own poor to maintain, and thus were forced to spend so much money for their aid, that it is understandable that they pursued a vigorous policy of attempting to exclude poor strangers." But he stresses "the apparent readiness with which the colonists accepted responsibility for the indigent" members of their communities and that "by and large, the poor were dealt with humanely and wisely" (Trattner, 1974, pp. 19, 26–27). What is pertinent here is that the aged were rarely if ever among these "strangers." A small number of aged were among the few residents of the few Colonial almshouses, nearly always being "not only very old but infirm, sickly and weak." Despite the accepted Dickensian stereotype, the data show that these almshouses were homelike facilities whose mode of operation was "patterned after the family." In fact, the Colonial almshouse, unlike the oppressive late 19th-century institution of the same name with which it is confused, was a "substitute household for those who lacked their own and could not easily fit in with a neighbor" (Rothman, 1971, pp. 38–43). Some disabled or senile elderly were cared for in the almshouses that existed in Boston (1680), New York (1736), Charleston (1738), Philadelphia (1742), and Baltimore (1773), but most of the needy aged in these cities and elsewhere were assisted in their own homes or those of their neighbors. While the benign nature of assistance in the recipient's own home is self-evident, it might be mistakenly assumed that being cared for in a neighbor's home at taxpayers' expense was a problematical, far from benign expedient. The historical evidence, however, shows that this was the normal, respectable means of providing for the familyless non-poor as well as the poor of all ages (Modell and Hareven, 1973). Finally, it must be borne in mind that the great majority of the aged, i.e., those over 60, who constituted about 10% of the population by the late 1600s, did not require public assistance (Demos, 1978).

The foregoing presents an overview of early American public provision for the aged. But what does this have to do with ethnicity? I contend that the characteristically sympathetic, generous treatment of the needy aged (and non-aged) by Colonial public welfare was largely due to the fact that it was an ethnic social institution in which both those receiving and those providing assistance, from overseers of the poor to almshouse staff, were nearly always of the same English (-white-Protestant) background. The English ethnicity of most of those involved in Colonial public welfare can be surmised from the predominance of the English among settlers and immigrants prior to the 19th century. It can be documented by the almost invariably English names in the public assistance records of the period (e.g., see those of Boston, New Haven, and Fairfield, Conn., in Pumphrey and Pumphrey, 1961). The following typical records of public assistance to the aged bring this out as well as support the general position presented above.

In 1670 Watertown, Mass,. recorded these expenditures to maintain Goodman (i.e., citizen) Henry Bright in his own home:

	£	s	d
To widow Bartlett, for dieting old Bright	10	00	00
To John Bisko, for a bushel of meal to old Bright, and 7 loads of wood	01	11	06
To William Perry, for work for old Bright	00	03	03
To Michael Barstow ... for cloth for a coat for old Bright	01	18	06

[in Demos, 1978, p. 240]

A decade later, Fairfield, Conn., town records note:

Nov. 30, 1682. The towne are willing to give Thomas Bennet Thirteen pounds provided he mayntayn old patchin with meat drink clothing washing and Lodging for the Term of a Twelve month: & render him in clothing at the years end as he is at this present [in Pumphrey and Pumphrey, 1961, p. 22].

In addition to relief in kind, i.e., food, clothing, and services, poor old people capable of caring for themselves were granted cash relief, as when in about 1650 New Haven authorities provided "old Bunnill," among other assistance, two shillings a week for self-maintenance (Demos, 1978).

The sympathy as well as humanity that characterized the treatment of aged welfare recipients in Colonial times is epitomized by the way they are referred to in these official records from three different communities: "old Bright," "old Bunnill," "old Patchin." Such familiarity and quasi-familial treatment can be ascribed to the *Gemeinschaft* character of these small preindustrial communities. I contend, however, that both the treatment and *Gemeinschaft* relationships themselves are largely attributable to the ethnic homogeneity of those involved. This is brought out by evidence that the few non-English as far as possible avoided public welfare to which they were legally entitled and developed an institutional alternative under their own control in which those receiving assistance were of the same ethnicity as those providing it: mutual aid.

It is generally understood that informal mutual aid among neighbors preceded and accompanied public assistance in Colonial time, although the shared ethnic identity of these neighbors has been disregarded. The far more significant formal mutual aid of organizations established for this purpose chiefly by non-English groups has been recognized by some but their significance underestimated. As many have noted, the earliest of these, the Scots Charitable Society, was founded by some two dozen Scottish citizens of Boston in 1657. (To understand the leading role of Scots in the development of Colonial mutual aid, it must be remembered that Scotland was independent until annexed by England in 1707 after centuries of subjugation and conflict.) Despite its name, this "charitable" organization primarily provided mutual aid benefits to its dues-paying members with minimal emergency charity for Scottish nonmembers. In these respects it was typical of later mutual aid societies. However, it was atypical in its initial reliance on public assistance with the society's benefits being considered no more than a supplement to the latter. This 1657 policy was necessitated by the group's limited resources. For in 1684 when the society had some 180 members, including several wealthy ones, it revised the original policy so as to operate in complete independence from Boston's public welfare system with the objective that not only members and their families but "the poor strangers and families and children of our natione . . . may be more ordourly and better relieved" (in Pumphrey and Pumphrey, 1961, p. 31). This change in the manner of relief of Scottish Bostonians three years after Boston established its almshouse is evidently due to the problems posed for poor Scots by being placed in an English institution and those posed for non-poor Scots by having poor Scots readily identifiable recipients of English assistance. Other ethnic mutual aid societies were organized along similar lines in Boston during the next century. These included an Irish one, which clearly supports this analysis, as well as an English one, which appears to contradict it. But this Episcopal Charitable Society (1754) was founded by Anglicans, who were a nondominant ethnic subgroup among the dissenting Protestant English of Boston.

Scots pioneered the development of ethnic mutual aid organizations in other cities where they lived in substantial numbers. For example, in Charleston they founded such a society in 1730. What would now be considered community relations caused them to proclaim that it was not just for Scots but "to assist all people in distress, of whatsoever Nation or Profession [i.e., religion]." But they ensured it would primarily assist Scots by naming it the St. Andrew's Society after Scotland's patron saint. In 1737 Charleston's Protestant (Huguenot) French established the South Carolina Society, which like the Scots' organization had a few members of different ethnic background. That an English mutual aid Ubiquarian Society had been organized in 1736 again does not contradict our position on mutual aid organizations. A clue to the different, subdominant English ethnicity of members of the Ubiquarian Society is that one of its officers was a Jew named Moses Solomon. In the absence of a Jewish mutual aid society, two Jews were members of the St. Andrew's Society in its early days. However, once a Jewish congregation was established in Charleston in the 1730s, it functioned as a mutual aid institution for its congregants, who included all the city's Jewish residents (Kutzik, 1967). By 1750 a congregational mutual aid society, the *Hebra Gemilut Hassadim* ("good deeds" or "charity" society) was organized specifically to care for the sick and bury the dead. In 1784, as the Hebrew Benevolent Society, it became independent of the congregation. However, throughout the Colonial period the congregation itself provided assistance to poor and dependent members, as evidenced by its 1791 request for incorporation on grounds of "the wish [of the Jews of Charleston] to exercise their religion publicly: the desire to provide for their poor; and, finally, the need to support and educate their orphans" (in Marcus, 1959, p. 182). A development similar to Charleston's occurred in other large cities like Philadelphia and New York where, by the time of the Revolution, English, French, German, Irish, and Scottish societies and Jewish congregations provided mutual aid to their members along with some charity to the destitute of their respective ethnic groups.

Reversing the earlier question, what does the foregoing discussion of the ethnic mutual aid characteristic of Colonial, particularly, 18th-century, America have to do with social provision for the aged? As with the treatment of public welfare recipients of all ages, it can be assumed that the aged members of mutual aid societies received benefits that were no different from, i.e., as adequate and acceptable as, those received by non-aged members. However, to answer this specifically, let us turn to the records of the Scots' Charitable Society of Boston and New York City's equally prototypical Shearith Israel Congregation, which also dates from the late 1660s. As with the mutual aid organizations that followed it, the Scots' Charitable Society at first concentrated on assisting orphans and widows, nursing the sick, and burying the dead. These functions, of course, involved the aged to some extent. However, as time went on a great deal of assistance was specifically provided to the increasing number of aged members unable to support themselves. This is reflected in the following items from the records of the Scots' Charitable Society:

> *Nov. 1718.* On reading a petition from James Maxwell praying for relief in his old age—alledging yt he was a Contributor [i.e., dues-paying member] while he was in a capacity—The Society voted that he, sd James Maxwell, be allowed out of the box [i.e., treasury] Twenty Shillings, and time to come during life Ten shillings each quarter after this & the Treasurer is ordered to pay the same. . . .

> Memo. *Feby. 11, 1756* Died Eliza. Wdo Wilson one of the oldest pensioners who was relieved by the Charity of this Society quarterly for these twenty-three years past . . . [in Pumphrey and Pumphrey, 1961, pp. 32, 33].

A similar development occurred at Shearith Israel. While its records at first do not differentiate among "the poor" assisted by the congregation, the detailed accounts of Shearith Israel's "charity" during the second half of the century show minor expenditures for nonmember transients and major ones for widows and orphans, the sick, and the aged. As with the Scots' Charitable Society, by the 1760s Shearith Israel's support of the aged had become so institutionalized that they were being given "pensions" (Grinstein, 1947).

Granting that, whether provided through societies or congregations, mutual aid rather than public welfare supported most of the non-English needy aged, what was the quality of this support? One can infer its material adequacy and psychological acceptability from the fact that both the Scots' Charitable Society and Shearith Israel Congregation not only survived but increased in size and status throughout the Colonial period after having assisted several generations of aged members. The adequacy and sympathy with which these organizations provided for the dependent aged is evident in their records, as epitomized by the following two items. One is that the same Elizabeth Wilson, "one of the oldest pensioners," whom the Scots' Charitable Society had supported for 23 years, upon her death in 1756 "left what Estate she died possessed of to the Society" (in Pumphrey and Pumphrey, 1961, p. 33); the other is that the "pension" that had been granted by Shearith Israel to "D. H. Sr." in 1773 was increased in 1774 ("Minute Book of Congregation Shearith Israel," 1913, pp. 115, 121). Evidently, needy non-English aged received as much if not more support and consideration from their groups' mutual aid as the English did from their public welfare.

The Early Republic (1780–1830)

Traditional Colonial norms of humanity and ethnicity in providing for the needy prevailed during the first five decades of the United States. Again, literary fictions and ideological suppositions notwithstanding, the historical evidence leads to the following conclusions concerning public welfare during this period:

> Few people questioned the community's responsibility to satisfy the pressing needs of dependents as directly and simply as possible or pondered alternatives to their methods of relief. . . . [T]hroughout these decades, household relief seemed an equitable and reasonable way to carry out a traditional function. The poor were usually spared the animosity and suspicion as well as the ameliorative efforts of their neighbors [Rothman, 1971, p. 156].

Even when taking into account the increasing deterioration of almshouses after 1830, the historical data of the antebellum period have been generalized as follows:

> Given the circumstances of the people the almshouses served and the fact that urban almshouses were largely free hospitals extending good medical care, these 19th century communities *were* making admirable provision for their "worthy" and even "unworthy" poor [Coll, 1969, p. 27].

Relating the last point to this discussion, it will be shown below that the "unworthy" poor were treated well because most of those being assisted in and out of the almshouses were considered "worthy" due to both their circumstances and their ethnicity. As regards circumstances, recipients were nearly all the traditional "worthy poor": widows and orphans, the physically and mentally ill, and the aged. Ethnically, they were predominantly of English provenance until about 1820 and substantially so for some time thereafter.

The English "American" identity of most public assistance recipients theretofore is apparent from the novel, widespread criticism around 1820 of "foreign paupers," when for the first time significant numbers of non-English received public assistance during America's first depression of 1817–1821. Coinciding with the unprecedentedly high level of immigration after 1815, this long, deep depression forced not only recent immigrants but native-born non-English to turn to public assistance as individual resources and even mutual aid societies' benefits became exhausted. Reflecting this, the 1820 annual report of New York's newly organized Society for the Prevention of Pauperism identified "emigrants from foreign countries" as making up most of the city's "paupers." Here as elsewhere the "paupers" were found to be chiefly Irish and, to a lesser extent, German, the two groups furnishing America's typical relief recipients during the remainder of the century.

That this was an issue of ethnicity rather than immigration is brought out by the fact that in Philadelphia, where among a large community of free Blacks some required public assistance, Blacks were also identified as a group prone to pauperism. This formerly stigmaless status of the English poor now became a vilifying charge against those of other ethnic groups—and against the groups themselves which, in permitting members to become public charges, were viewed as failing to conform to the American norm of "taking care of one's own." As early as 1817, an official Philadelphia committee, formed to investigate the mysterious sudden increase in the number of "paupers" in that city, found that they were mainly Irish and Blacks "as well as the intemperate and day laborers" and proposed as a remedy teaching those groups "to cherish a regard for religious and moral obligation" (Wolf and Whiteman, 1957, p. 275). A Pennsylvania Society for the Promotion of Public Economy was actually established for this purpose. New York's Society for the Prevention of Pauperism charged in its 1821 annual report that the city's paupers, which it had already identified as predominantly "foreigners," were "for the most part ... depraved and vicious and require support because they are so" (in Rothman, 1971, p. 162), a position soon widely held among the Anglo-American establishment.

This ethnicity-laden welfare crisis, which recurred during the depressions of 1827–1829 and 1837–1843 when immigration was at even higher levels, led to two ethnicity-related welfare developments, one among the English and the other among the non-English. As Rothman notes: "In the 1820s and 1830s ... Americans began to reverse" their traditional "premises" as to the worthiness of the poor and the community's responsibility to adequately and nonpunitively meet their needs (Rothman, 1971, p. 156). More precisely, this reaction among English Americans of the governing and taxpaying upper strata was one of the major factors resulting in the rapid proliferation of almshouses from which it was believed the "vices" causing pauperism could be excluded and in which "vicious" paupers could be reformed. On the other hand, among the non-English this led to an equally great expansion of mutual aid so as to avoid the double stigma of degeneracy on the part of public assistance recipients and irresponsibility on the part of fellow-ethnics who failed to "care for their own."

Even before the economic depressions and their social and ideological concomitants, mutual aid societies had substantially increased in number and resources. While underestimating their expansion, Trattner observes of the post-Revolutionary period that "just as in prior years . . . numerous ethnic and nationality groups, no less than religious organizations aided their compatriots in need" (Trattner, 1974, p. 40). The need for such private alternatives to the public welfare system was understood by all concerned. The social requirement for non-English or nondominant English groups to care for themselves explains why a contemporary observer could report that in 1810 in Philadelphia there were not only a French and an Irish, but two German and two Scottish as well as numerous "American" benefit societies (Mease, 1811). Modern historians have found that Philadelphia then had more than 20 major mutual aid societies (Wolf and Whitemen, 1957). Generally overlooked then and now is the fact that the city's two Jewish congregations functioned as mutual aid organizations for their congregants.

Until 1815 assistance was provided needy Philadelphia Jews from the congregations' general treasury which, as elsewhere, was called the *sedaca,* i.e., "charity fund." That year a mutual aid society for the Visitation of the Sick and Mutual Assistance was formed at the long-established Mikveh Israel Congregation, which in 1820 permitted non-congregants to join this group. Earlier, a few Jews participated in various non-Jewish mutual aid organizations, at least ten being members of the English St. George Society. After several years of economic depression and unusually high immigration of Jews, many of whom joined neither the congregations nor Mutual Assistance Society, an additional institutional mechanism became necessary. Following the example of Philadelphia's English establishment, the more well-to-do Jews provided help to the Jewish poor through two charity organizations: the Female Hebrew Benevolent Socity (1819) and the United Hebrew Beneficent Society (1822). However, as soon as possible, most of the actual and potential recipients of this charity provided for themselves through the mutual aid of their own small congregations. These developments within the Philadelphia Jewish community were more or less paralleled in New York and other cities, as was the expansion of mutual aid among different ethnic groups of European origin. But the most extraordinary development of mutual aid during this period, that of Philadelphia's Blacks, was matched only in Baltimore, which also had a large free-Black community.

The country's first Black mutual aid organization, the Philadelphia Free African Society was founded in 1787, serving as a model for similar organizations in Boston, Newport, and New York within the next decade. By 1813 in Philadelphia there were ten additional Black mutual aid societies (Du Bois, 1967 [1899]), by 1831 a total of more than 40 (see the incomplete listing in Aptheker, 1951, pp. 113–114), and by 1838 exactly 100 (Du Bois, 1967 [1899]). While to some extent reflecting the steady growth of the free Black population of Philadelphia during these decades from about 2,500 in 1795 to about 18,000 in 1840, this development was more related to the economic and social pressures of the period. Keeping the dates of depressions in mind, the impact of economic conditions is apparent from the facts that only a half-dozen societies were founded before 1817, but about 16 between 1817 and 1826, about 20 between 1827 and 1831, and about 50 between 1831 and 1838. The extremely large number of such societies established from the late 1820s is related to an additional factor—the marked deterioration in race relations resulting from 1829 on in "a series of riots directed chiefly against Negroes which recurred frequently until about 1840 and did not wholly cease until after the war" (Dubois, 1967 [1899], pp. 26–27). The consequent inaccessibility of "white" English public assistance—and "white" English organized charity (discussed below)—strengthened the already strong motivations for Blacks to care for themselves. By 1838, the city's 100 mutual aid societies had 7,448 members, who must have included practically every adult and every family of Philadelphia's Black community of about 17,500. A similar development appears to have taken place in Baltimore even earlier, where 35 to 40 Black mutual aid societies were in existence by 1821 (Fishel and Quarles, 1970). Like their conterparts in other ethnic groups, these Black organizations originally were formed, as was the Philadelphia Free African Society, "in order to support one another in sickness, and for the benefit of . . . widows and fatherless children" (in Aptheker, 1951, p. 18). However, they too inevitably had to provide benefits to aged members. In addition to direct assistance to the latter, mutual aid benefits to non-aged members of a family, of course, better enabled it to care for its aged members. [It appears that, rather than racial discrimination, it is the extent and effectiveness of Black mutual aid that primarily accounts for the relatively small number of Black public assistance recipients in Philadelphia (and Baltimore) during this and the following period.]

A major factor in the extraordinary development of mutual aid among antebellum free Blacks is that, like white public welfare, the white charities established about this time were considered to be unavailable to them. These were also considered unavailable by other non-English groups. Except for the very few Jewish ones, these charities were nearly all English-Protestant. There had been practically no organized charity during the Colonial period and relatively little during the post-Revolutionary decades. But the unprecedented poverty due to the depression of 1817–1821 in combination with the equally unprecedented wealth accumulated during the wartime and postwar boom of 1812–1816—and the absence of other socially acceptable means of using wealth to attain or maintain high status—resulted in a proliferation of charity societies. At first mainly congregational, many of these societies soon became or were founded as independent "nonsectarian" organizations in order to make themselves available to the poor of different Protestant congregations and denominations ("sects"). The need for nondenominationalism became particularly clear when a federal census in 1807 found that the great majority of citizens—who were mainly Protestants—were unaffiliated with any congregation. Increasingly after 1815, such "nonsectarianism" had to be broadened and strengthened in order for these Protestant-led and -supported charities to assist impoverished Catholic immigrants. These religious differences were compounded by the fact that most affiliated Protestants were of English ethnicity, whereas many of the unaffiliated ones were German and most Catholics were Irish or German. While "as early as 1820 the larger cities had an embarrassment of benevolent [charity] organizations" (Bremner, 1960, p. 47), nearly all these societies, whether church-sponsored or "nonsectarian," were led and supported by the English-Protestant rich and primarily used by the English-Protestant poor. It was the more or less manifest English-Protestant identity of these organizations that forced the Irish Catholic poor, who had few mutual aid resources, to turn to the manifestly nonreligious and more latently English public welfare, just as it was the Christian and white identities of both "nonsectarian" charity and public welfare that made them unavailable to Jews and Blacks, forcing these groups to rely on their own mutual aid and, to a lesser extent, charity.

The welfare patterns of Blacks, Irish, Jews, etc.—and English— established during the second and third decades of the century persisted in the following ones.

The Middle Decades (1830–1860)

Although the traditional humanitarian attitudes toward public welfare of the English-American establishment had begun to change earlier, it was not until mid-century, when escalating immigration and recurrent depressions led to "foreigners" comprising the majority of the country's "paupers," that this was generally expressed in policies and programs. With depressions in each decade, the number of immigrants, mainly from Ireland and Germany, rose from 129,000 in the 1820s to 540,000 in the 1830s, 1.5 million in the 1840s and 1.75 million in the 1850s. It was during this period that the previously dominant methods of "outdoor relief" were eclipsed by "indoor relief" and the creditable care provided in the almshouse became increasingly inadequate and repressive. From the late 1830s on, government reports and other well-publicized evidence of terrible conditions in many almshouses formed the stereotype that has been misapplied to the almshouse of the Colonial and early Republican periods. While largely reflecting mid-19th-century reality, this totally negative stereotype has obscured the good care that inmates of a significant number of almshouses continued to receive through the 1850s (Coll, 1969; Rothman, 1971). It has been recognized that the immigrant, i.e., non-English, identity of most of their inmates was the key factor in the deterioration of almshouses during this period, when they were increasingly "filled with first- and second-generation immigrants" (Rothman, 1971, p. 200). Evidence of the poor conditions in the immigrant-dominated almshouses of states like New York and Massachusetts also supports this interpretation, which is clinched by the fact that those almshouses that maintained traditional high standards tended to have predominantly English American populations.

The very different effects of English as opposed to other ethnic identities of inmates on the quality of almshouse care can be inferred from the findings that major seaports and other large cities where immigrants congregated tended to have deplorable almshouses, while cities and towns where there were few if any recent immigrants, like those in Kentucky and New Jersey, tended to have adequate and even comfortable ones. The most striking evidence of this is provided by the Baltimore almshouse. For unlike those of other major seaports like Boston, Philadelphia, and New York, during the decades under discussion Baltimore's almshouse continued to provide what has been accurately characterized by Coll as "outstanding care." I contend this is primarily attributable to the fact that, while first- and second-generation immigrants of non-English background then constituted a majority of the almshouse population of other port cities, in Baltimore they were a minority. As late as 1844, an English visitor to the Baltimore almshouse, who was critical of its overly comfortable conditions "in contrast to similar institutions in some of the other large towns," observed that "about two thirds of the paupers are native Americans [i.e., of English extraction], the rest almost entirely Irish and Germans" (in Carroll, 1966, pp. 13–14).

Another factor that mitigated the treatment of almshouse inmates is that many—and very many of the English Americans among them— were old and therefore "worthy" poor. Records of this period show that the aged were typically the second largest category of the almshouse population after the medically indigent. For example, in 1848 the Philadelphia almshouse's "old men's infirmary and incurable" and "old women's asylum and incurable" sections contained 444 of its 1,509 white inmates and, evidently, most of its 78 unclassified Black inmates were aged and/or disabled. Since immigration was with few exceptions undertaken by the non-aged, it seems warranted to assume that in these early decades of mass immigration most of the white aged in the Philadelphia and other almshouses of the time were American-born of English ancestry.

It is generally believed that the poor and dependent, including the aged, were exclusively provided for in almshouses during this period. However, it has now been shown that while indoor relief prevailed, substantial amounts of outdoor relief continued to be provided (Coll, 1969). Much if not most of this went to the aged. In New York City, for example, outdoor relief was specifically provided by statute to widows with young children, sick or otherwise disabled breadwinners and their families, and "aged and infirm persons whose relatives were able to provide shelter but no other subsistence." That the aged constituted the largest part of those receiving such favored treatment is suggested by a contemporary analysis of Philadelphia's outdoor relief recipients in the early 1830s, which found that of the total of 549 such recipients 390 were over 60 with six of these over 100 (in Coll, 1969). How this humanitarian approach to providing for the largely English American aged poor was undermined by the period's increasingly repressive, cost-conscious approach to "foreign paupers" is dramatized by developments in this city.

In 1835, upon completion of a new larger almshouse, Philadelphia's Board of Guardians of the Poor decided that it would therafter grant only emergency outdoor relief and no more "pensions," i.e., long-term income maintenance of the aged (and disabled). While this decision was revoked in 1839 and by 1857 the Board of Guardians indicated a preference for outdoor relief as more humane and less expensive than indoor relief, the inadvisability of relying on public assistance, even for the "worthy" aged, had come to be understood by all Philadelphians. This was most clearly understood and consistently acted upon by the most insecure of the city's ethnic groups, Blacks and Jews.

The cessation of outdoor relief in the late 1830s resulted in an unusually large number of Blacks being admitted to the Philadelphia almshouse. In 1837, for example, there were 235 Blacks among its 1,673 inmates, constituting 14% of the almshouse population, although the Black community then formed only 7% of Philadelphia's total population. Yet, as noted above, in 1848 there were only 78 Blacks among the Philadelphia almshouse 1,588 inmates. What accounts for this reduction is not just the resumption of outdoor relief but the continuing development of Black mutual aid societies within a context of intensifying racism. By 1848 the number of such organizations had only increased to 106 from the 100 in existence a decade before, but their membership had considerably expanded with commensurate expansion in resources and expenditures. Since the Black population of Philadelphia had hardly risen during this decade, it can be concluded that nearly all of the city's approximately 30,000 Blacks—including the aged—were covered by their mutual aid welfare system.

The only ethnic group which surpassed free Blacks of the antebellum period in "caring for their own" were the Jews. As noted above, the comprehensive mutual aid and minor charity by which the latter had met their welfare needs prior to the 1820s had been structured into congregations. In the following decades, the American Jewish welfare system consisted mainly of non-congregational mutual aid and charity societies, with the latter playing an increasingly important but still minor role. The principal factor underlying the development of Jewish welfare organizations independent of the congregation, also noted above, is that after 1815 the immigration of large numbers of poor Jews who were not members of established congregations or mutual aid societies, or were members of newly organized ones whose limited resources were depleted during depressions, could be helped only by noncongregational organizations. This trend became more marked in the 1840s and 1850s, when immigration multiplied the Jewish population of cities like New York, Philadelphia, and Chicago within a context of rampant anti-alien sentiment and burgeoning anti-Semitism. Another less evident but equally important factor in this development brings out a dimension of ethnicity not discussed to this point, i.e., the existence within ethnic groups of ethnic subgroups motivated to "take care of their own" rather than rely on the charity of the more well-established of their fellow-ethnics. In fact, many of the new mutual aid and charity societies were organized and used by recently arrived immigrants to obviate their having to turn for help to those of an earlier generation of immigrants or native-born with the social status as well as cultural differentials this involved. Such subgroup differentiation among other ethnic groups is suggested in the above-mentioned datum that in 1810 there were two German, two Scottish, and several English benevolent societies in Philadelphia. It is explicit, moreover, in the abundant data available concerning the development of Jewish charities in Philadelphia and other cities (Kutzik, 1967). For example, it was the recently arrived immigrant Jews of Philadelphia who founded the German Hebrew Benevolent Society in 1842 and the German Hebrew Ladies Benevolent Society in 1845 "duplicating" the established Jews' longstanding Hebrew Beneficent and Female Hebrew Benevolent societies. By the mid-1840s the newcomers were meeting most of their emergency needs through their own charity societies and most of their long-term needs through their own congregational mutual aid, including care of the dependent aged. The necessity for these newly arrived Jewish immigrants to care for and be cared for by "their own" within the Jewish welfare system even though the established Jews were themselves largely second- and third-generation immigrants from Germany underscores the subtlety as well as salience of ethnic factors in welfare organization.

A similar development took place in New York City, where the three Jewish charity societies dating from the 1820s were augmented by six others between 1839 and 1843, including a German Hebrew Benevolent and (German) Hebrew Ladies Benevolent societies "duplicating" the established Hebrew and Ladies Benevolent societies. But, while New York's Jewish population increased from about 11,000 in 1844 to 40,000 in 1859, no additional charity societies were organized. Yet this large community was able to meet the welfare needs of its members in such a way that the records prior to 1860 show that only two Jews had ever been inmates of the city's almshouses (Grinstein, 1947). This was achieved by New York Jewry's mutual aid system whose extensive development during these decades is obscured by the more visible, socially influential charity societies.

By 1860 the city's 27 congregations performed only certain minor mutual aid functions for their needy members, such as providing the special foods required for Passover. For, anticipating later developments in Philadelphia and elsewhere, in New York by this time the major functions of caring for widows, orphans, sick, disabled, and dependent aged were carried out by 34 mutual aid societies, most independent of and others loosely affiliated with these congregations.

There had been only one Jewish mutual aid society in New York from 1795 to 1825, when the Jewish population was gradually increasing from about 350 to 500 and the congregations provided needy members a full range of mutual aid benefits. But five more were organized by 1836, when immigration had expanded the Jewish population to 2,000. By 1842 there were ten mutual aid groups for a Jewish population of 10,000; 15 by 1846 for 12,000; 25 by 1850 for 16,000; 30 by 1855 for 30,000; and 34 by 1860 for 40,000. This proliferation of immigrant mutual aid societies cannot be accounted for by population increase alone, since the existing societies and congregations welcomed new members. As with charity organizations, ethnicity was obviously a key factor in the development of immigrant German mutual aid societies "duplicating" established "American" ones. But the multiplicity of German Jewish organizations further "duplicating" one another was also due to essentially the same ethnic factor. For immigrant mutual aid societies and congregations typically involved members of the same subgroup who had emigrated from a given part of Germany (e.g., Bavaria, Posen). This *landsmanshaft* ("association of fellow countrymen") principle has long been recognized as the basis of mutual aid and congregational organization among East European Jewish immigrants in the late 19th and 20th centuries. It was already typical of Jewish immigrants from central Europe in the antebellum period, just as to some extent it characterized the welfare organization of other ethnic groups.

A mutual aid organization of a non-*landsmanshaft* type was founded by immigrant German Jews in New York City in 1843. After some had been refused membership in that city's non-Jewish German Order of Odd Fellows, they organized the Independent Order B'nai B'rith. Like most other mutual aid organizations, the original objectives of B'nai B'rith were "alleviating the wants of the poor and needy; visiting and attending the sick; . . . providing for, protecting and assisting the widow and orphan" (in Schappes, 1950, p. 217). However, since lodges of this national organization quickly sprang up in city after city collectively accumulating substantial financial resources, only five years after its founding B'nai B'rith was able to provide institutional care for the dependent aged of its members' families. In 1848 it established the country's first Jewish home for the aged in New York City. This institution was patterned less after the American almshouse than German Jewish homes for the aged in Hamburg (1796), Berlin (1839), and Frankfurt (1844).

In 1849 the Independent Order Free Sons of Israel was founded, but such fraternal organizations were first widespread among Jews later in the century. On the other hand, fraternal orders like the Odd Fellows were already well-established among German Americans by the 1840s. This affords a clue as to why immigrants from Germany entering the United States in numbers matching those from Ireland—approximately two million came from each country between 1830 and 1860—formed a much smaller proportion of those receiving public assistance. In addition to the better financial and physical condition of most German immigrants, the combination of these national fraternal organizations with their local mutual aid and charity societies provided the German communities of New York, Philadelphia, Chicago, Cleveland, Cincinnati, etc., fairly substantial welfare resources. The Irish, who generally arrived in a far more impoverished and debilitated condition (Woodham-Smith, 1963) had far fewer such resources. The relatively few Irish "emigrant aid societies" of the well-to-do and more numerous but financially limited immigrant Irish mutual aid organizations of various types (discussed below) could not cope with the deluge of penniless Irish entering the country after 1845. In conjunction with general recognition of the English-Protestant nature of "nonsectarian" charities, this made public welfare the major means of survival for the large number of these newcomers who were jobless or too sick, too young, or too old to work. Indicating the extent of this situation, in 1852 70,000 of the 131,000 recipients of public assistance in New York State were Irish. That there were so many Irish recipients does not seem so strange when placed within the context of the 159,548 Irish who entered the U.S. that year, mainly at the port of New York, and the 221,253 the year before on top of the nearly 600,000 in the five previous years. However, it may seem problematical that the Irish turned to public welfare in such numbers in face of the disapproval of doing so by dominant public opinion with the then-on-the-rise Know-Nothing party singling out the Irish for attack as much for being "paupers" as "papists." Central to understanding why 19th-century Irish immigrants who required it applied for public assistance with few if any qualms is the fact that there was no public assistance in Ireland until 1837 when the English Poor Law was first put into effect there and its use became socially sanctioned in the following decades of starvation during which most Irish immigrants came to this country. So, unlike the other American ethnic groups, the Irish had no sociocultural bias against, but actually one for those in need receiving public assistance. Further, living in insulated Irish neighborhoods, they were initially unaware of and later unconcerned with the anti-welfare norms of the American establishment. However, they did become concerned with the increasingly demeaning and inadequate nature of the public assistance the Irish poor and dependent received, primarily in the form of indoor relief.

An ironic consolation is that few elderly Irish were subjected to the rigors of almshouses since few Irish immigrants were aged and few lived long enough to be aged. This was most evident in Boston, where an 1843 municipal census found the average longevity of the Irish to be 13 years (Woodham-Smith, 1963), and a reliable observer in 1846 noted that he rarely saw a "gray-haired Irishman" (in Shannon, 1963, p. 29). It is still probable that a high proportion of the few Irish aged were provided for in almshouses since the Irish as a group were so greatly overrepresented in them.

Although public welfare was the major means by which most newly arrived and sick or disabled Irish met their survival needs for income maintenance and health care, the abuse and obloquy this entailed encouraged the development of organized charity among the established Irish and mutual aid among the immigrant Irish.

By the 1850s, charity societies patterned after Philadelphia's Friendly Sons of St. Patrick for the Relief of Emigrants from Ireland (1771) had been created by the well-to-do in Brooklyn, Charleston, Chicago, New York, Rochester, St. Louis, Toledo, and other cities. The earliest of these had been at least as much mutual aid as charity societies, but as their members prospered, the mutual aid benefits became unnecessary. Until the late 1840s, they functioned more as social than charitable organizations, some meeting only once a year to celebrate St. Patrick's day. But they then resumed their welfare function with a vengeance under the double burden of collecting charity for famine-stricken Ireland and providing assistance to the multitude of refugees fleeing from that calamity. Reflecting the increased number and activity of Irish charity societies, an Irish Emigrant Aid Convention was held in Buffalo in 1856.

While Irish charity helped some poor immigrants avoid or extricate themselves from public welfare, far more were helped to do so by their own mutual aid efforts. Much of this was informal, with neighbors in the typical all-Irish neighborhood helping one another in emergencies and fellow-workers of dead breadwinners collecting house-to-house donations for widows and orphans (Shannon, 1966). Some of this mutual aid, however, was organized in a characteristically Irish-American way: trade unions. The earliest Irish "trades associations" in the 1820s and 1830s were, in fact, not unions but mutual aid societies for those in a given occupation. From the 1830s on, most of these became actual unions concentrating on improving wages and working conditions, but they continued to provide mutual aid benefits to members and their families. For example, in 1843 Irish tailors in Boston established a "cooperative" organization that a decade later was known as the Journeymen Tailors Trade and Benevolent Association. Soon Irish "benevolent societies" were being organized as such in city after city. Reflecting the extent of this development was the formation in 1869 of a national umbrella organization, the Irish Catholic Benevolent Union, which was the most important nonecclesiastical Irish organization of the time (O'-Grady, 1973).

Another Irish mutual aid development was the fraternal organization, the Ancient Order of Hibernians, founded in 1836 although first incorporated in 1853 and not to become a major organization for several decades.

Finally, by midcentury in cities like Boston and New York, where they were a large portion of the population, the Irish had begun to develop what amounted to their own public welfare system through the political machine they controlled. Little of the assistance provided by Irish politicians went directly to the aged. However, like other forms of Irish American welfare, it enabled Irish families to care for their aged members, constituting a humane and dignified outdoor relief alternative to the increasingly inhumane and anti-Irish indoor relief.

The Late 19th Century: 1860–1900

Despite almost exclusive scholarly attention to the public welfare and organized charity of the time, mutual aid continued to be the means by which most Americans met their welfare needs during the rest of the century. Still primarily in the form of local societies of particular ethnic groups or subgroups, mutual aid increasingly took place through local chapters of national ethnic, so-called fraternal, organizations. The cash benefits to widows, the sick and, in some instances, elderly long-time dues-payers which both types provided their members enabled most of the needy aged among them to manage or to be cared for at home. However, for some of the few who could not be maintained at home the larger fraternal organizations established congregate "homes" for the aged. Many more such institutions were founded under charitable ethnic auspices. This first American welfare program specifically for the elderly developed as an alternative to the almshouse, which had now become the abomination from which asylums were rescuing children and the mentally ill. Except for the relatively few private homes for the aged, the almshouse was the only life-sustaining resource of the severely incapacitated aged of limited means and often of the physically and mentally competent aged with no problem other than poverty. For outdoor relief—which, it should be remembered, went largely to the elderly—was now greatly reduced and in some places abolished. By 1880, for example, only indoor relief was provided by cities like New York and Philadelphia. Since most communities did not have separate workhouses for what the authorities now considered the "unworthy" able-bodied unemployed adult, all the inmates of the almshouse were subjected to the same harsh conditions and iron discipline designed to drive the former back to work. After 1880 the situation was not much better in those cities whose almshouses contained only the "worthy" aged, sick, etc., as the Charity Organization Society movement's campaign against all public welfare for fostering pauperism gained adherents among most of those in control. The operation of the late

19th-century almshouse with particular reference to the elderly is all-
too-aptly characterized by Coll as follows: "Physical care was minimal,
recreation unheard of, and emotional needs ignored, as old couples
were separated—the husband sent to the men's, the wife to the wom-
en's wing of the almshouse" (Coll, 1969, pp. 81–2).

One if not the major factor in such treatment of almshouse inmates
irrespective of age was that they were preponderantly "foreigners." As
already noted, by the 1850s a majority of the nation's almshouse population was foreign-born. By the 1860s this reached as high as 75% in the
Atlantic port cities. In 1871, only 8% of Chicago's and half of the rest
of Illinois' almshouse population had been born in this country. A reliable national survey reported in 1880 that "almost forty percent of all
almshouse inmates were immigrants" (in Rothman, 1969, p. 291).

None of the investigations which produced the foregoing information paid attention to the large number of inmates who were American-
born of immigrant ancestry. Statistically, they were categorized as
"Americans" along with tenth-generation English. But they were generally viewed as part of the immigrant population and treated accordingly. That the foreign-born and their American-born offspring were
considered members of the same ethnic group is evident in the following excerpt from a federal government report on immigrants: "The
census of 1890 shows that the Irish still lead the list of paupers, as they
did 50 years ago, the proportion of paupers to the thousand of population of the same race element for the whole country being 7½ for the
Irish, 2½ for the Germans, a little over 2 for the English, 1½ for the
Bohemians, eight-tenths for the Italians, and six-tenths for the Russians
(Hebrews)" (United States Industrial Commission, 1901, pp. 171–2).

That these "Bohemians" must have included other Slavs and these
Russian-Jewish "paupers" were not on public assistance but receiving
what was then conceived of as private outdoor relief from Jewish
charity societies and indoor relief from Jewish charitable institutions is
beside the point—which is that the multigenerational ethnic groups
that furnished most of the nation's public charges were the target of
investigations of the "welfare mess" of the time. However, when one
transforms the 7½ per thousand Irish to ¾ per hundred, 2½ per thousand Germans to ¼ per hundred, etc., the question of 19th-century
authorities, "Why the high proportions of various ethnic groups among
the dependent poor?" is changed to the present one of, "Why more
than 99% of the millions of Irish, German, and English poor, of the
hundreds of thousands of Jewish, Italian, and Polish poor, etc., were able
to subsist without public assistance during this period of unprecedented
economic hardship?" The general answer has already been indicated:

through their own mutual aid and, to a certain extent, their own ethnic group's charity.

Despite the omission of Blacks from this discussion of immigrants, as in the past, they were confronted with essentially the same kinds of problems and developed the same kinds of coping mechanisms as other ethnic groups. The evidence suggests that at this time a somewhat larger proportion of Blacks than other groups may have been receiving public assistance. Specifically, in the early 1890s an average of 600 Blacks were in the Philadelphia almshouse of a Black population of about 40,000, i.e., 15 per 1,000. Blacks constituted about 10% of the almshouse's inmates, although they were less than 4% of the city's total population. In recognizing this overrepresentation, Du Bois (1967 [1899]) attributes the increase from the far lower Black welfare rates of the antebellum period to the migration of large numbers of unskilled southern Blacks to Philadelphia and increased job competition with white immigrants in an atmosphere of racism. However, another trustworthy contemporary student of the subject reports that in several cities, including Baltimore and Washington, which had the largest Black communities of the day, Blacks were less prone than others to apply for public assistance, doing so mainly when forced to by illness since they "have a dread of taking relief, especially when they think an institution will be recommended. . . ." (in Pumphrey and Pumphrey, 1961, p. 250). While the national rate of Blacks receiving public assistance was evidently considerably lower, the way in which Philadelphia's Black community kept all but 1.5% of its many poor off the welfare rolls exemplifies the operation of white as well as Black ethnic welfare systems of this period.

At the end of the century, according to Du Bois (1967 [1899]), the approximately 40,000 Blacks of Philadelphia had "several hundred" mutual aid societies of the traditional kind and several dozen lodges of various national and regional fraternal orders. The latter had some 4,000 members, mainly affiliated with the Odd Fellows and the Masons, each of which had no less than 19 lodges in the city. In addition, there were a considerable number of local "insurance societies" and branches of regional ones, which resembled the mutual aid societies and fraternal orders but operated along the lines of commercial insurance. The largest of these, the United Order of True Reformers, had "several" Philadelphia branches. Other organizations with mutual aid characteristics included building and loan associations and trade unions.

The indirect impact on the aged of mutual aid coverage for their children's families was crucial. For those without families, moreover, direct coverage was so important that some of Philadelphia's elderly Blacks who had either not taken out membership in their younger days

'or had allowed it to lapse, being too old to meet the entrance requirements of other mutual aid societies, formed their own Old Men's Association. Others were cared for at the Home for Aged and Infirm Colored
Persons, founded by a Black philanthropist in 1864, or the Home for the
Homeless, affiliated with the Black community's leading church. The
former was a typical home for the aged, the latter primarily for "temporary lodgers" and "transients." (It should be noted that these were only
two of a variety of Black charitable institutions established during this
period ranging from a hospital to a Y.M.C.A.).

The existence in Baltimore of a similar, even more extensive network of Black mutual aid organizations complemented by charitable
institutions is documented by Brackett (1890). While most developed in
these largest Black communities, that this pattern was not restricted to
them is indicated by the facts that the ("Colored") Odd Fellows, which
had 2,300 Baltimore members in the late 1880s and 1,188 Philadelphia
members in the late 1890s, then had about 200,000 members nationally. Odd Fellows lodges had been organized by Baltimore and Philadelphia Blacks as early as the 1840s, but the True Reformers, which had
branches in these and other cities, had been founded in Richmond in
1881 and, by the turn of the century, had established homes for the
aged at Westham and Tampico, Virginia. More typically, homes for the
aged were located in big cities with sizable Black populations, like
Philadelphia and Chicago, as part of a small but growing number of
Black charitable institutions and organizations (Drake and Cayton,
1945; Osofsky, 1963).

A similar pattern was characteristic of other ethnic groups. All
tended to be comprehensively covered by mutual aid organizations
and all but some of the more recently arrived supplemented these
with charity societies, orphan asylums, hospitals, and homes for
the aged.

Among the old (mainly pre-1880) immigrant groups, local mutual
benefit societies tended to be replaced by or become branches of national fraternal orders. It was in these decades, for example, that the
Ancient Order of Hibernians and the Independent Order B'nai B'rith
along with newer rivals like the Knights of Columbus and Independent
Order Brith Abraham came to the fore. The earlier prevalence of fraternal orders among Germans has been mentioned. The widespread
existence of such organizations among WASPs (a newly developed
grouping dominated by the English but now including Scottish, Scotch-
Irish, and Welsh and assimilated Dutch, Swedes, etc.) has been little
noted. However, most of the ubiquitous white Odd Fellows and Masons
lodges were WASP organizations (Anderson, 1970). Working-class
WASPs participated in their own Order of United American Mechanics

and Junior Order of American Mechanics which in 1903 together had nearly 160,000 members in over 2,000 chapters in 33 states and disbursed $527,431 in benefits.

Local mutual benefit societies abounded among the new immigrant groups from Eastern and Southern Europe. Although members of these groups first arrived in substantial numbers in the 1880s, by the turn of the century they had developed local mutual aid organizations as extensively as the old immigrant groups. This is evidenced by a 1914 Massachusetts report that found that the state's Greeks, Italians, Lithuanians, Poles, and Eastern European Jews (mainly from Poland and Russia) had large numbers of mutual benefit societies. While fraternal orders were not as prevalent as among the long-settled groups, the report noted the presence of branches of the Pan-Hellenic Union, the National Polish Alliance, and unnamed regional Jewish "mutual aid associations." Both old and new immigrant Jewish charity societies were singled out for attention but the existence in Boston of an Italian Immigrant Aid Society and a Polish "temporary lodging house" was also reported (in Handlin, 1959). The only two of these groups whose welfare patterns have been studied nationally, Poles and Jews, have been found to have similar ones wherever they lived (Thomas and Znaniecki, 1958 [1918–1920]; Lopata, 1976; Schappes, 1958; Kutzik, 1967), so it can be assumed that the Massachusetts situation was typical.

While charity was a very small component of the welfare system of new immigrants, the old immigrant groups had by this time developed numerous charitable organizations and institutions.

With the exception of WASP "nonsectarian" ones, charity societies of a particular ethnic group provided its needy members minimal outdoor relief of short duration, going principally to newly arrived immigrants before the breadwinners among them had found jobs and to nonimmigrants temporarily jobless due to layoffs, illness, or injury. Comparatively little went directly to the aged, but many were supported as part of the multigenerational families being assisted. Together with some direct assistance to the familyless aged, especially in cities with no public outdoor relief, this added up to a substantial amount of support for the elderly. Although secondary to mutual aid, the significant role of ethnic charity societies in assisting the needy aged and non-aged in the late 19th century has been overlooked largely as a result of scholarly fixation on large charity societies that provided much less relief (e.g., the Associations for the Improvement of the Poor) or next to none (e.g., the Charity Organization Societies). In fact,the very existence of most ethnic charity societies has generally been overlooked. This is partly because they do not appear to be ethnic. While the comparatively few Jewish and even fewer German charity societies are readily identifiable as such, many of the far more numerous WASP ones are not, due to their "nonsectarian" form. On the other hand, the "sectarian," Catholic form of most of the great many Irish charity societies has obscured their ethnic identity. For during this period, the patently Irish self-designated Irish Emigrant Aid Societies were increasingly supplemented and finally supplanted by units of the Catholic Church's Society of St. Vincent de Paul. By the turn of the century "conferences" of this official church organization, supported and administered by laymen along the lines of other charity societies of the day, existed in hundreds of city parishes, which were predominantly Irish. In fact, the American Catholic Church at this time was so predominantly Irish in membership and totally Irish in leadership that it was justifiably considered an Irish institution (Handlin, 1959). More specifically, the Irishness of the Society of St. Vincent de Paul is evident from the name of the organization's publication during this period: *The Irish Bulletin.*

The quality of assistance provided by ethnic charity societies has not been studied. However, it is significant that, throughout the second half of the century, they were criticized by the spokesmen of WASP "scientific philanthropy" based in the Association for the Advancement of the Condition of the Poor and the Charity Organization Society (Kutzik, 1972) for overly generous and insufficiently discriminating relief-giving. This suggests that ethnic charity societies were more humane and sympathetic to "their own" poor than "nonsectarian" ones to those they assisted "without regard to race, creed, or color." However, the extent to which the many charity societies of the Irish, WASPs, and Jews met the welfare needs of these groups should not be exaggerated. Jewish charity societies, which provided at least as much assistance as any, are reliably reported to have covered a small fraction of the needs of a small fraction of the Jewish poor between 1880 and 1910 (Price, 1958 [1894]; Waldman, 1949). An authoritative participant-observer primarily attributes this to the fact that the Eastern European Jewish immigrant was "resourceful in creating mutual benefit societies of various types to which he could repair in case of emergencies due to unemployment or illness" (Waldman, 1949, p. 27). The same can be said of the Irish and WASPs and even more so of other old immigrant groups like the Germans and Norwegians, who relied less on charity societies.

Whatever the combined strength of their mutual aid organizations and charity societies in providing outdoor relief, ethnic groups had to develop residential institutions to provide indoor relief to those of their members who could not be maintained in their homes and whose only alternative was the now-unacceptable almshouse.

Institutions for children were establshed first not so much to provide them better care as to remove the many Irish-Catholic and
German-Catholic as well as German-Protestant children from
English-Protestant almshouses, orphan asylums, or foster homes, in all
of which they were being raised as English-Protestant "Americans." On
the other hand, given the unshakable ethnic identity of the aged and
their generally good treatment in the early 19th-century almshouse, it
was not until the deterioration of this treatment largely because of their
non-WASP ethnicity that an institutional alternative to the almshouse
was required. Consequently, homes for the aged date from the middle
decades of the century. (The special case of the Jews, who had never
used the almshouse, makes the development of their own homes for the
aged at about the same time even more clearly ethnicity-related.)

Among the Irish, who needed them most and founded the most,
homes (henceforth used for "homes for the aged") were under Catholic
auspices. These official church institutions were doubly Catholic in appearance since they were staffed by nuns and overseen by priests. But
the nuns and priests were as Irish as the residents! The Irish identity of
the scores of such institutions established throughout the country during these decades is generally obscured by their religious names—e.g.,
St. Ann's Home or Sacred Heart Home—but occasionally it is evident,
as in Louisville's O'Leary Home for Catholic Men or Denver's J. K.
Mullen Home, both official church institutions staffed by members of
religious orders.

WASP homes were generally differentiated by denomination even
when not officially under denominational auspices. But most German
ones were not church-related and their names typically proclaimed that
they were German Old Folks Homes. In line with Jewish tradition, none
of the 18 Jewish homes founded by 1906 was under religious auspices.

Until the 1890s the dozen or so Jewish homes then in existence
(with the exception of Cleveland's, discussed below) had been organized and supported by the then predominantly German Jewish communities of the same number of cities. However, at the turn of the
century, the large subcommunities of Eastern European newcomers
began to "duplicate" these institutions with Eastern European-style
ones of their own (Szold, 1901). This is what accounts for 18 Jewish
homes for the aged in only 12 cities, again demonstrating the necessity
for different welfare programs for ethnic subgroups, particularly in the
provision of care for the aged. Dramatizing this, the Montefiore Home
for the Aged established in Cleveland in 1881 by the Eastern European
fraternal order Kesher Shel Barzel (1860) was later "duplicated" by
new, more traditionalistic Eastern European Clevelanders who
founded the Jewish Orthodox Home for the Aged in 1906.

What was the quality of care provided in these ethnic homes for the aged? In the absence of studies of this issue, one basis for assuming it was good—certainly better than that of the "nonethnic" almshouse— is the proliferation of such institutions among long-settled groups and their development among immigrant groups during the ensuing decades.

The Early 20th Century: 1900–1940

According to the U.S. Bureau of Labor Statistics in 1929, there were 1,268 homes for the aged. With few exceptions, these were under eth- nic group auspices. This was clearly so for the 444 under "religious" aegis, most of the 102 run by "fraternal orders," and the 32 run by "nationality groups." Another 360 under "private philanthropic aus- pices" were mainly "nonsectarian" WASP ones. Most of the remainder were "non-," that is, multi-ethnic: 55 were clearly so, being government institutions for veterans; another 5 were for "union members" and 38 were unclassified. Great ethnic diversity existed among the some 250 church-related Protestant homes, particularly evident as regards the many Lutheran ones identified with one or another Northern European group. The category of Protestant homes also included some of the dozen or so Black ones. Most of the 156 Catholic homes were Irish, but an increasing number were supported, staffed, and used by other groups ranging from Poles to French Canadians. Maintaining the tradi- tional independence from the synagogue of all their communal institu- tions, the great majority of the 63 Jewish homes were now Eastern European with frequently two or more organized in the larger commu- nities by subgroups from different countries. Most of the homes spon- sored by "nationality groups" were German. The intense anti-German prejudice engendered by World War I discouraged the founding of new ones, but pre-existing German homes were expanded, sometimes un- der protective fraternal or religious auspices.

Among the factors underlying the development of this large num- ber of ethnic homes is one particularly relevant to this discussion. It is that these (and other) ethnic welfare institutions received not only strong social sanction but substantial financial support by government. Public subsidy of private welfare institutions irrespective of the nature of their (almost invariably ethnic and generally "sectarian") auspices had increased steadily since this policy was adopted early in the 19th century to help support institutions for children. It was extended to other institutions, primarily hospitals and homes for the aged, as they developed during the second half of the century. By 1900 half the states, including most of the long-established ones with heavy immigrant populations, provided and encouraged localities to provide such subsidies. Despite increasing WASP political and professional opposition, the subsidization of ethnic welfare institutions with tax funds greatly increased during the early decades of the 20th century. Most spectacular in this regard was Pennsylvania, whose allocations rose from $348,000 for 22 institutions in 1885 to about $2,500,000 for 176 in 1901 and nearly $8,000,000 for 273 in 1908 (Warner, 1908). From the 1920s on, nativist political and "nonsectarian" professional pressure succeeded in reducing and later eliminating direct support of "private," ethnic welfare institutions by "public" tax funds. But this continued in the more acceptable forms of government payment-for-service to private institutions caring for those eligible for care by the government and the tax exemption of charitable and religious institutions.

Of the 1,268 homes in existence in 1928, 1,022 reported a daily average of 68,661 residents. Since the country's 2,046 almshouses had only 41,980 inmates over 65 about this time (1923), one must question the conclusion that "the almshouse remained the last refuge for most aged persons well into the 20th century" (Coll. 1969, p. 81). In fact, despite the massive immigration and natural population increase in the first three decades of the century, the combination of ethnic homes, ethnic mutual aid, and ethnic charity societies steadily reduced the number of aged in almshouses. In 1904 the latter amounted to 52,795, in 1910 to 46,032 and, as already noted, in 1923 to 41,980. Nevertheless, the presence in almshouses of this many "worthy" aged in this period of reform now became a matter of broad social concern. For they were more visible than ever: with dependent children in special institutions and the mentally and physically ill removed to hospitals, almshouses had, in effect, become institutions for the aged (Coll, 1969).

Given the well-known conditions within them, which had not improved much since the late 19th century, this concern led to social and political action. Particularly after 1911, when laws establishing "mothers' pensions" began to be passed for the express purpose of keeping the children of young husbandless but worthy mothers out of public institutions, agitation for state "old-age pensions" developed. The first such law was passed in 1915 and was operative in seven states by 1929. In the next five depression years 19 more states legislated old-age pensions. Unlike the earlier permissive statutes which allowed localities to provide pensions from local tax funds—thereby reestablishing outdoor relief—most post-1929 legislation required that pensions be granted to all eligible aged throughout the state with state supplementation of local funds. Consequently, from a 1929 national total of some 1,000 aged individuals receiving $222,000 "by 1932 more than 100,000 persons were receiving old-age assistance, at a total cost of $22 million a year" (Coll, 1969, p. 81).

One can agree with Coll that these meager relief grants averaging $220 per person per year and equally inadequate financial assistance of charity societies is what was responsible for the presence of so many aged in the almshouse. Yet one can maintain that, however limited, these minimal supports helped keep many more out of the almshouse. This was particularly true of the assistance provided by ethnic charity societies during the first three decades of the century when public outdoor relief was negligible where it existed at all.

Keeping in mind that ethnic mutual aid organizations met the greatest part of welfare needs (e.g., Balch, 1969 [1910]), the large number of ethnic charity societies still played a significant role in this. One reason this has not been noted is that the thousands of small WASP charity societies, "sectarian" and "nonsectarian," have been overshadowed by the much-discussed single large WASP C.O.S. or family welfare society in each city, much as the hundreds of small Eastern European Jewish charity societies have been obscured by the few large German-Jewish ones which were constituents of the influential German-Jewish welfare federations that developed during this period. However, the cumulative amount of assistance provided by these many small organizations by far surpassed that of the few large ones. This is particularly evident with respect to Catholic charities since in 1928 there were only 41 city-wide diocesan agencies but units of the Society of St. Vincent de Paul existed in 1,400 parishes.

Admitting its great aggregate quantity, what was the quality of the assistance provided by such small ethnic charity societies, particularly to the aged? The following excerpt from the summary of an actual case reflects the way in which one Catholic—typically, Irish—charity society assisted the needy aged of its parish and suggests how diocesan Irish-Catholic hospitals and homes served them in the early 1920s:

> Family of an elderly couple with no children. . . . The old couple had no relatives who could be counted on for assistance and as they were unwilling to enter a home for the aged the Conference [parish unit of the St. Vincent de Paul Society] gave them a weekly allowance. The man was referred to a Catholic hospital. . . . The woman was finally taken ill and removed to a hospital, where she died. . . . After his wife's death the man deprived of the [sic] comfort and companionship was then willing to enter an institution. A vacancy was obtained for him in a home conducted by the Sisters (Galbally, 1923, p. 81).

The understanding, respect, and helpfulness evident in this case appears to have characterized the treatment of the dependent aged by ethnic charity societies. Such considerate treatment would have been improbable in the contemporary C.O.S.-dominated "nonsectarian" family welfare societies and impossible in the cost-conscious, regulation-ridden public welfare system.

All three sectors of U.S. welfare—private ethnic, private "nonsectarian" and public—were transformed by the Great Depression and the Social Security Act. Already by 1930 most charity societies had exhausted their funds and their major function of providing cash relief was assumed by government. It was not much longer before mutual aid societies, until this point the mainstay of American social welfare, had to curtail and, in many instances, cease functioning as benefits were paid out and dues not paid in. The *coup de grâce* to charity societies and a devastating blow to mutual aid societies was the passage of the Social Security Act in 1935. Its public assistance provisions for the poor aged and blind and dependent children permanently removed much of the charity societies' relief caseload, while its unemployment and retirement insurance programs and burial grants duplicated most of the benefits of mutual aid societies and fraternal orders. With the addition of life ("survivors") insurance in the 1939 amendment to the Act and the spread of private health insurance from the early 1940s on as a "fringe benefit" in union contracts, mutual aid and fraternal organizations lost their historic near-monopoly in these areas for the majority of Americans.

Now that charity societies were no longer giving relief, the largely professionally staffed "nonsectarian" agencies focused on their former minor function of giving advice which, as "counseling" or "therapy," became their new *raison d'être*. With few exceptions, the largely volunteer ethnic charity societies could not make this change, particularly since they had not considered those they helped as needing much advice or any rehabilitation. Consequently, most ethnic charity societies went out of existence. Only the largest were able to survive by emulating the "nonsectarian" family service societies. (Ironically, the most successful of these, the city-wide Jewish and Catholic family agencies, also emulated "nonsectarian" agencies in disregarding ethnic differences among their clientele who were generally viewed as just Jews or Catholics.)

The secondary function of sociability could not maintain mutual aid organizations once the welfare benefits they had provided were given to most people by other programs in which they were compulsorily enrolled. The equity that long-time members had in mutual benefit societies kept these going for another decade or two, but few new members joined. As a result they became organizations of the aged, largely of the immigrant generation, performing important social as well as welfare functions for them, but dying when they did. On the other hand, most fraternal orders survived and generally expanded their membership by adding to actuarially sound life insurance benefits and social activities various cultural and service programs generally related to the members' ethnic group. These still play an important role in the lives of several million Americans, particularly first- and second-generation immigrants, a large proportion of whom are aged.

While ethnic mutual aid and charity were undermined by Social Security programs, these same programs supported and strengthened ethnic welfare institutions. For the very public assistance that eliminated private outdoor relief promoted private indoor relief by permitting grants to residents of private institutions while denying them to those in public ones—thereby simultaneously hastening the demise of the moribund almshouse. In this way, the federal government now adopted the longstanding policy of states and localities paying private charitable institutions for services rendered to those who would otherwise have to receive public services. This is evidently why in 1937, after nearly a decade of depression, the number of homes for the aged had increased 20% since 1928 to about 1,500 with more than 80,000 residents.

In addition to enabling many incapacitated aged to be cared for in ethnic institutions, that year old-age assistance supported many of the approximately 150,000 able-bodied people over 65 living in boarding houses, most of which can be assumed to have been located in ethnic neighborhoods. A number of these boarding houses later developed into proprietary nursing homes which tended to isolate residents from their neighborhoods and other ethnic institutions—but that is one of the post-1940 developments which this chapter can not discuss. (For such discussion see Kamerman and Kahn, 1976; and Manard and Kart, 1976.)

To sum up, during the first three decades of the 20th century, alongside the more evident "nonsectarian" private and public welfare sectors, private ethnic welfare outstripped both in meeting the needs of the country's dependent population, particularly the aged. But in the 1930s, as an unintended consequence of fundamental changes in public welfare policy, the major organizational means through which this had been achieved, ethnic mutual aid and charity societies, were virtually destroyed. While ethnic welfare institutions not only survived but thrived, these served a very small percentage of the needy. Even the fraternal orders with their greatly expanded memberships met only a small part of the welfare needs of a small part of the needy population. This is underscored by the fact that, despite the large number of well-supported Black fraternal orders (Frazier, 1957), from the 1930s on Blacks were unprecedentedly overrepresented on public assistance.

By the mid-20th century—with the principal exception of the stronger-than-ever Jewish welfare system on which the survival of the Jews as a group depends (Kutzik, 1967)—welfare organizations, agencies, etc., supported by and serving members of the same ethnic group no longer played the leading role they had since Colonial days in meeting the welfare needs of Americans, including the aged.

Conclusions and Implications

This analysis revises or at least raises question with many accepted views of the history of American social welfare ranging from the ethnic neutrality of the auspices and policies of public welfare to the absence of a tradition of mutual aid among Blacks (e.g., Glazer and Moynihan, 1958). More specific to the focus of the present discussion, this analysis challenges the popular if not scholarly views that until the 20th century the aged who could not be cared for by their families were mainly cared for in public institutions where they were uniformly maltreated and that their only other resource was almost as inhumane and equally "nonsectarian" charity.

Our general finding is that extrafamilial assistance for the aged throughout American history was primarily provided them in their own homes by public or private organizations under ethnic auspices and that, even for the relatively small number in public or private institutions, such provision tended to be humane when those helped were of the same ethnicity as their helpers. Incorporated in the above is the finding that extrafamilial provision for the aged was—with the negligible exception of short-term neighborliness—always organized. While first organized by the English settlers in the form of public assistance, the preferred form of organization for non-English groups and non-dominant English ones was mutual aid, with its structured self-determination and self-respect. But even public welfare and charity, with their built-in tendencies toward authoritarianism of administrators and status-degradation of recipients, was less dysfunctional in these regards when administrators and recipients shared the same ethnic identity.

One of the major implications of these findings is that the disregard of ethnicity that has characterized both private and public provision for the aged in recent decades is a departure from three-and-a-half centuries of American experience. Another implication is that the current disesteem of formal organizations in favor of informal natural helping networks as the mainstay of service provision for the aged (e.g., Borman, 1976) also flies in the face of American historical experience.

In light of this analysis, it can be concluded that a major objective of planners and providers of services to the aged should be to bring ethnicity and organization together to recreate at a higher level the natural ethnic organizational network that helped most of the aged throughout most of American history. A corollary objective should be to bring a sophisticated understanding of ethnicity into the policies of the "nonethnic" organizational network of "nonsectarian" and "integrated" agencies so they can more adequately serve their ethnically diverse clientele.

References

Anderson, C. H. *White Protestant Americans*. Englewood Cliffs, N.J.: Prentice-Hall, 1970.

Aptheker, H. (Ed.). *A documentary history of the Negro people in the United States*. New York: Citadel Press, 1951.

Balch, E. G. *Our Slavic fellow citizens*. New York: Arno Press, 1969 [1910].

Borman, L. D. Barn-raising re-visited: The upsurge in self-help groups. *Center Report*, June 1976, 16–17.

Brackett, J. *Notes on the progress of the colored people of Maryland since the war*. Baltimore: Johns Hopkins University Press, 1890.

Bremner, R. H. *American philanthropy*. Chicago: University of Chicago Press, 1960.

Carroll, D. History of the Baltimore city hospitals. *Maryland State Medical Journal*, 1966, 15, 1–47.

Coll, B. D. *Perspectives in public welfare*. Washington, D.C.: United States Department of Health, Education and Welfare, United States Government Printing Office, 1969.

Demos, J. Old age in early New England. In Michael Gordon (Ed.), *The American family in social-historical perspective*. New York: St. Martin's Press, 1978 (2nd ed.), 220–256.

Drake, S., and Cayton, H. R. *Black metropolis*. New York: Harcourt, Brace and World, 1945.

Du Bois, W. E. B. *The Philadelphia Negro*. New York: Schocken Books, 1967 [1899].

Fishel, L., and Quarles, B. (Eds.). *The black American—A documentary history*. New York: William Morrow, 1970.

Frankel, L. K. Charity and charitable institutions—Modern times. *Jewish Encyclopedia*, 1906, 672–676.

Frazier, E. F. *The Negro in the United States*. New York: Macmillan, 1957 (revised).

Galbally, E. J. What can the parish do? In *Proceedings, Ninth Session of the National Conference of Catholic Charities*. Philadelphia, 1923.

Glazer, N., and Moynihan, D. P. *Beyond the melting pot*. Cambridge, Mass.: M.I.T. Press, 1958.

Grinstein, H. *The rise of the Jewish community of New York, 1654–1860.* Philadelphia: The Jewish Publication Society of America, 1947.

Handlin, O. *Immigration as a factor in American history.* Englewood Cliffs, N.J.: Prentice-Hall, 1959.

Kamerman, S. B., and Kahn, A. J. *Social services in the United States.* Philadelphia: Temple University Press, 1976.

Kart, C. S., and Manard, B. B. Social factors and institutionalization of the elderly. In C. S. Kart and B. B. Manard (Eds.), *Aging in America,* New York: Alfred Publishing Co., 1976, 401–420.

Kutzik, A. J. Class and ethnic factors. In F. W. Kaslow, et al. *Issues in human services.* San Francisco: Jossey-Bass, 1972, 85–114.

Kutzik, A. J. *The social basis of American Jewish philanthropy.* Unpublished doctoral dissertation, Brandeis University, 1967.

Lopata, H. Z. *Polish Americans.* Englewood Cliffs, N.J.: Prentice-Hall, 1976.

Marcus, J. R. *American Jewry: Documents eighteenth century.* Cincinnati: The Hebrew Union College Press, 1959.

Mease, J. *The picture of Philadelphia.* Philadelphia: B. & T. Kite, 1811.

Minute Book of Congregation Shearith Israel. *Publication of the American Jewish Historical Society,* 1913, *21,* 1–17.

Modell, J., and Hareven, T. K. Urbanization and the malleable household: An examination of boarding and lodging in American families. *Journal of Marriage and the Family.* August 1973, *35,* 467–479.

O'Grady, J. P. *How the Irish became Americans.* New York: Twayne Publishers, 1973.

Osofsky, G. *Harlem: The making of a ghetto.* New York: Harper and Row, 1963.

Price, G. N. The Russian Jews in America. *Publication of the American Jewish Historical Society,* September 1958 (1894), *XLVIII.*

Pumphrey, R. E., and Pumphrey, M. W. (Eds.). *The heritage of American social work.* New York: Columbia University Press, 1961.

Rothman, D. J. *The Discovery of the asylum.* Boston: Little, Brown, 1971.

Schappes, M. U. (Ed.). *A documentary history of the Jews in the United States, 1654–1875.* New York: Citadel Press, 1950.

Schappes, M. U. *The Jews in the United States.* New York: The Citadel Press, 1958.

Shannon, W. V. *The American Irish.* New York: Collier Macmillan Publishers, 1963.

Szold, H. "The Year." *American Jewish Yearbook, 1901.* Vol. II. Philadelphia: Jewish Publication Society of America, 1901.

Thomas, W. I., and Znaniecki, F. *The Polish Peasant in Europe and America.* New York: Dove, 1958 [1918–1920].

Trattner, W. I. *From poor law to welfare state.* New York: Free Press, 1974.

U.S. Industrial Commission. *Reports,* Vol. XV, "Immigration and Education," House Document no. 184, 57th Congress, First Session, Washington, D.C., 1901.

Waldman, M. J. A backward look. *Jewish Social Service Quarterly,* September 1949, *XXVI,* 23–28.

Warner, A. G. *American charities.* New York: Thomas Y. Crowell, 1908 (2nd ed.).

Watson, W. H., and Maxwell, R. J. *Human aging and dying: A study in sociocultural gerontology.* New York: St. Martin's Press, 1977.

Wolf, E., II, and Whiteman, M. *The history of the Jews in Philadelphia: From colonial times to the age of Jackson.* Philadelphia: The Jewish Publication Society of America, 1957.

Woodham-Smith, C. *The great hunger.* New York: Harper and Row, 1963.

3

"Oh Where, Oh Where Has Ethnicity Gone?"

Irving Kenneth Zola

"Oh Where, Oh Where Has Ethnicity Gone?" conveys in tone, if not in substance, the thrust of this chapter. In part, I am forced to take a reflective approach in regard to ethnicity and health care. For despite the dates of my publications, (Zola 1963, 1966, 1972b, 1973) I have not done an empirical study on the topic in nearly 20 years. I have, however, paid the price for my early research for I am continually asked to consult and speak on the topic. This is a speech or consultation which usually goes quite well until someone asks either, "What will you do next?" or "What have you done recently?" The answer to both questions is most often a slightly regretful, "Nothing." I state this not as a caution but a context. I am both an insider and an outsider on the topic of ethnicity and health care.

As an outsider it was clearly time to look again at the field. After reviewing the literature provided by a medline search, I was confronted with the problem of pulling it together. An encyclopedic article by Chrisman and Kleinman provided a provocative take-off point. In the early pages of their paper they asked themselves. "Why study ethnic health beliefs and practices?" Their answer was an interesting one.

> Because ideas about health, illness and healing are so closely tied to the values and behaviors of people's lives, knowledge about health ways affords significant insight into the nature of ethnicity in the United States. Folk illnesses and cures are frequently an element in an individual's maintenance of a particular ethnic identity [in press].

This link to identity recalled the cautions of Shibutani and Kwan (1965). They noted that "since ethnic identity lies at the core of the self-conception of so many people, it is not surprising that this subject matter is so explosive and . . . difficult to contemplate dispassionately." As a result they claimed that all too many of the scientific positions on the issue are little more than "political positions." This suggested that one way of understanding "ethnicity and its relation to health services" was *not* to review the literature itself but the ideas behind it—a sociopolitical history of ideas. And so that is what I am offering—a reflective and admittedly speculative interpretation of the development of ethnic and cultural research in the field of health care. My discussion will not focus specifically on the elderly. Since they are major consumers of health care, however, the issues raised herein are certainly applicable to the growing population of elderly from diverse ethnic backgrounds.

The Growth of Ethnic Research

To paraphrase The Virginia Slim cigarette ads, we the ethnic researchers have "come a long way." My surmise is, however, that in the health care area we have come slower, had less impact, and are in for more resistance than in almost any other area of applied research. Let me first document the progress.

1. Pick up any textbook on ethnic relations or monograph about an ethnic group written more than a decade ago and you will find barely any mention of health care or illness treatment except to document some exotic custom. Now every year there are dozens of books and hundreds of articles detailing ethnic and cultural factors in health practices and delivery.

2. Where once there was no academic forum for such topics, now there are many international journals, several devoting themselves specifically to cross-cultural and ethnic themes and a professional organization, The Society for Medical Anthropology, which devotes much of its newsletter to reports and conferences on cultural patterning of health practices.

3. In the all-important area of professional practice, references to ethnic and cultural factors have taken a positive turn. Where once such traits were only documented in order to stamp them out, now they are documented so that they can be used to heighten the sensitivity and available resources of health workers. The most common academic rubric is a course entitled medical anthropology. At very least we are likely to find attention to cultural factors part of any course or book on the psychosocial care of patients.

4. Finally, in the public arena, from a period of despairing of such differences to one of merely noting them, we are now in an era of almost celebrating them. From educational to popular television, from the *National Geographic* to *Psychology Today,* the health practices of different ethnic and cultural groups are no longer described for their exotic aspects but their therapeutic ones, not for their distancing functions but for their integrative ones.

Whether or not this is a "success" story can be put aside for a minute. What seems worth examination is the social, historical, and even political aspects of this progression.

Ethnic Research and Mental Health

As I said in the beginning, research in this area has in general been slow. But *within* the broad area of health care, there has been a discernible difference. For the greatest impact not only in the study but also the delivery of health care seems to be in regard to mental health. As Kleinman (1977) has noted it is a difference which persists even today:

> . . . clinically oriented anthropologists . . . have concentrated their investigations on psychiatric problems, while leaving general medical disorders virtually unexamined [1977, p. 12].

Tracing this development may well tell us something.

Early research efforts. Without calling it the first such study, I would venture a guess that the importance of social and cultural factors in mental health was crystallized in both the scholarly and popular world by the work of Margaret Mead (1928, 1930, 1935). Over 50 years ago she began the first of a long train of cross-cultural investigations. In studying Samoan girls, she claimed that adolescence need not everywhere be a time of turbulence and struggle but in certain cultural circumstances could be a time of calm transition. This questioning of universal myths she continued in the 1930s when she began her New Guinea studies of the Arapesh, the Mundugumor and the Tschambuli. Emphasizing the different value orientations and family structures in these different societies she noted that to the Arapesh an aggressive person was sick, while to the Mundugumor it was one who was peaceful and considerate and to the Tschambuli a dominant male or gentle female was likely to be thought of a neurotic. In short, with these early investigations there was a growing recognition that what was considered normal in one culture was not necessarily normal in another. But the literature more often referred to faraway places with strange sounding names (Opler, 1959). So while there was some recognition that categories of mental health and illness were not as universal as we might like to think, it seemed to have little empirical and theoretical relevance for work in the United States. I do not mean that Americans were unaware of any relationship between culture, ethnicity, and mental functioning but that it was essentially a negative one. On the crassest level, differences in rates of mental illness between different ethnic groups—differences documented since the mid-1800s—were used to demonstrate that "the more foreign" group, whoever they might be at the time—Irish in the mid-1800's, southern and eastern Europeans in the late 19th and early 20th century—were in some ways inferior to the dominant culture. Where the research was more sophisticated it did not focus on the ethnic groups *per se* but rather the issue of migration and immigration. In the retrospect of some 50 years these studies too had a built-in evaluative component. For while the investigators were often sympathetic to the plight of these immigrants, their explanations for this plight focused on some flaw in these ethnic groups, on variables which affected their ability to cope. Rarely was there any analytic attention, let alone blame, focused on the receptivity of the host environment. America was, even in the minds of these researchers, "the land of opportunity." That America might take advantage of, use, even destroy such people was left primarily to the writings of the muckrakers (Weinberg and Weinberg, 1961), not the ethnic researchers.

Postwar ethnic research. While World War I only reinforced this phenomenon, World War II had quite a different impact on scientific thinking about ethnicity, mental illness, and their relationship to one another. World War II shook to the core certain of America's notions of insularity, both politically and culturally. For much of the population it mitigated their isolation and complacency if only by forcing them to be aware of different ways of defining as well as handling problems. Though occasionally romanticized in novels about the era, much of the war effort *was* a forced intermixing and with it a reliance on people of varying backgrounds, religions, even races on one another. Geographically, much of this took place in areas known to the participants previously only through folk tales or movies. And all of these long-term events were symbolically capped by a real one—the possibility of our ultimate destruction through the A-bomb and its successor the H-bomb. With this a certain American rootlessness became evident. All these provoked a deep questioning of who we were and what life was all about. One outcome of this searing of our social conscience was a societal commitment to money in the solving life's problems. From a technology to kill, we sought a technology to save. And so in the immediate postwar era the National Institutes of Health began to flourish and the wars against killer diseases began. But this did not answer who we were. America suffered a kind of "existential schmerz"—what Allan Wheelis (1958) called "the quest for identity." And it was reflected in an upsurge of all sorts of group-related phenomena, from the human potential movement to religious revivals to ethnic consciousness. This social consciousness was accompanied by a rising political consciousness. One after another civil rights and liberation movements arose. Each demanded more positive attention to their specialness, their uniqueness, their previous exclusion, discrimination, and oppression. And the research of the '50s reflected it. Cultural variables become more prominent than ever but while the researchers (Hollingshead and Redlich, 1958; Srole et al., 1962; Leighton et al. 1963) again documented ethnic differences in mental health rates, they added something else: a documentation of a fairly systematic exclusion of ethnic groups from the services they needed. And sometimes the researchers began, albeit mildly, to criticize the therapeutic models of the providers of services.

   Changing conceptions of mental illiness. The very thinking about mental illness also changed. Theorists called neo-Freudians— Sullivan, Horney, Fromm, Kardiner—spoke of the social interactional, the social, and the environmental aspects of mental illness. Treatment followed suit and expanded from one-to-one to more social methods, from milieu, group, and family therapy to a consideration of cultural alternatives (Kiev, 1964, 1968). General research paid more attention to differing perceptions of mental illness by both status (Gurin, Veroff, and Feld, 1960; Starr 1955, 1957; Woodward 1951) and ethnicity (Opler and Singer 1956, Singer and Opler 1956). In this era Social Psychiatry as a theoretical discipline and Community Psychiatry as a practical application were born.

Ethnicity and Physical Illness

In the medical as opposed to the psychiatric world, however, no such dramatic change was evident. Kleinman again echoes this observation.

> It is curious that applied clinically-based anthropology, which has already contributed substantially to an understanding of the culture-specific categories of ethnic minorities and non-Western populations, had contributed so little an appreciation of the historicity and culture-specific nature of biomedical constructs, or to refurbishing the narrowly conceived and notoriously inadequate medical model [1977, p. 12].

This is no accidental phenomenon. Simply put, there was much greater resistance to admitting the importance of culture in regard to physical disease than mental disorder. There was much more politically at stake. And this showed itself in both macro-societal explanations and micro-professional concerns.

As with rates of mental disorder, there had long been a documenting of cultural and ethnic differences in regard to physical illness. The early data focused on acute infectious diseases and their concomitants: tuberculosis, pneumonia, influenza, scarlet fever, measles, diarrhea. It is again in the explanations that the unverbalized value positions of the investigators were revealed. While the words *working conditions, living arrangements,* and *poverty* dotted the findings, the major attention and ultimately the blame was directly placed on the individuals themselves:

their wish to live in crowded cramped quarters led to the spread of infections

their eating incorrect and often ethnic foods led to nutritional difficulties

their washing insufficiently and poor hygiene led to unsanitary conditions

their bizarre customs of dress got them caught in machines or made them either over- or underdressed in what were once called sweatshops.

While thus recognizing ethnic and cultural differences in rates of illness as well as in health care itself, America's ideological, political, and economic system blamed the ethnics and their culture for their own physical ills. In other words, the physical disorders which each person suffered were the result in some way of individual ills and faults not societal ones. And there was an ideological out—social mobility—the notion that anyone in America could get out of the mire of poverty and their cultural background by simply trying harder and assimilating.

Physical Illness in the 1970s

I must stress the political implications of this by jumping to the mid-1970s. Today we are confronted *not* by marked differences in the acute infectious diseases but in the chronic diseases. Pneumonia, influenza, tuberculosis are replaced by lung cancer, heart disease, obesity, and stroke. But the political consequences of our explanatory models are still the same. Today the newest "buzz word" is *lifestyle behavior,* a term which easily incorporates ethnic health practices. The elements to my hearing are the same as several generations ago. Again the lip

service exists. Most speakers and writers on the health care of Americans acknowledge that America is a very materialistic, achievement-
oriented, indeed stressful society. And yet beneath these apparent
negatives lurks the feeling that it can be overcome if we the public only
lived right. So now the people who are "sicker" are criticized:

for not knowing how to relax, thereby exacerbating their hyperten-
sion

for eating greasy and fast foods, which contribute to their obesity
and circulatory troubles

for smoking too much, which leads to lung cancer and heart attacks

for relying too heavily on alcohol and drugs, which leads to all
manner of addictions.

Once more it is the individual who is indicted. Once more it seems
easier to point a finger at the individual behavior and practices that
correlate with specific diseases rather than to ask what is it about American society economically, socially, or politically which makes us un-
relaxed, eat unnutritiously, smoke, drink, and use drugs prodigiously,
and what political and economic interests might be served by our so
doing (Navarro, 1976; Waitzkin and Waterman, 1974).

My point is a simple one. As long as we view disease as an individual
problem we will seek individual solutions. It is no wonder that we are
the last of the large industrial nations to provide any kind of national
health insurance or any kind of national health care. How could it be
otherwise? For if we conceive of getting ill as an individual problem and
responsibility, then preventing and treating the illness is similarly an
individual problem. Based on such assumptions, good health care is a
privilege of those who can pay for it, not a right of all. And providers
who give services to the poor do it out of sense of charity for some, not
of equality for all.

The Acceptance of Ethnic Research
in Mental and Physical Health

The playing out of this scenario is perhaps best seen in further contrasting the political threats of cultural research in the mental and physical
health areas. While incorporating social causes into thinking about the
etiology of mental illness did imply a criticism of the American way of
life, it was less threatening to its basic fabric. The societal forces that
affected our mental health often seemed more ephemeral and indirect.
To say that America was inhospitable, materialistic, achievement-oriented—in short stressful—for segments of our population seemed a long
way from saying it was inherently destructive. Societal forces in regard

to physical illness seemed to imply a more causal and direct relationship. A look at history may clarify this point. Mental illness is claimed (Rosen, 1968) to have always existed with its form changing from country to country, from era to era. Not so with many of the physical diseases that plague us today. While some forms of heart disease, stroke, and arthritis are found in many ancient civilizations, many others, like the varying cancers, lung and circulatory problems, and the vast number of occupational diseases are not. Our industrial society has created them. If the blame is to be placed anywhere it is as much to be placed at the heart of what we often call industrial progress than in the hearts and minds of our industrial workers. To look closely or to accept this relationship between society and disease might mean that we would have to do something about it—elimate the causes and provide for treatment.

In this light it is not surprising that the recognition of ethnic and cultural forces in relation to physical disease has a shorter and more tortured history than that of mental disorder. There are no comprehensive reviews of ethnicity and physical illness as there are of ethnicity and mental disease (Giordano, 1973; Giordano and Giordano, 1977), no famous impactful surveys (Gurin, Veroff, and Feld 1960; Leighton et al., 1963; Srole et al., 1962), no treatises integrating cultural factors into theoretical models (Kiev, 1972; Opler, 1967; Leighton, 1959; Spiegel and Papajohn, 1975), no centers of cross-cultural research (as McGill University and University of Washington are for mental illness). The same political drama that we noted at the societal level of explanation is thus played out when we look at the micro-professional level. This should, of course, be no surprise, since recent thinkers are finally beginning to debunk the myth that scientific and medical thinking is independent of social and political events (Kuhn, 1964; Foucault, 1965; Ackerknecht, 1967).

Again the contrast between mental and physical illness is helpful. The most well-known critic of psychiatry is Thomas Szasz. And yet his series of books, *The Myth of Mental Illness* (1964) or *The Manufacture of Madness* (1970), wherein he questions and chides his fellow workers, somehow do not threaten the basic enterprise of psychiatry or psychotherapy. Not so I would contend with the critics of physical medicine. Though occasionally divided into camps, the criticisms of both groups go deep to the basic service that medicine offers. One group—Navarro's *Medicine Under Capitalism* (1976) and Waitzkin and Waterman's *The Exploitation of Illness in a Capitalist Society* (1974)—criticize the basic priorities, organization, and delivery of health care. But the most well-known and caustic critic, Ivan Illich, writes books entitled *Medical Nemesis* (1975) and *Disabling Professions* (1977), in which he indicts medicine for its role in maintaining, if not causing, the very illnesses it is supposed to treat.

So too the data of ethnic medical research reflects a potentially more critical perspective. For it emphasizes not merely differing perceptions of physiological phenomena but different physiological states which the people consider worthy of attention, not merely complementary methods of dealing with disorder but often alternative or conflicting ones (Newell 1975). Kleinman, Eisenberg, and Good, reflecting on cultural research, stated it well when they noted:

> Modern physicians diagnose and treat diseases (abnormalities in the structure and function of body organs and systems) whereas patients suffer illnesses (experience of disvalued changes in states of being and in social function) [1978, p. 251].

In short, the true impact of ethnic research confronts the provider with changing not merely his language but his priorities. It calls into question the basis of medicine, the very boundaries of its territory.

This then is my rendering of the history of ethnic and cultural research into the delivery of health services. It is slow in coming because it has been and is threatening to established interests. If we somewhat arbitrarily divide the work into mental and physical aspects, there is a differential path, precisely along dimensions of threat.

Problems and Pitfalls of Ethnic Research

Although this trail of progress has been convoluted, one can argue that the implications of ethnic research are being gradually accepted. And so they are, but I would further contend that the success carries with it certain problems, and it is to these dangers I wish to devote my final paragraphs.

Conceptual problems. The first is the one-sided way we continue to use the concepts of culture and ethnicity. In light of the resistance to thinking of illness as anything but a biological entity, the need to emphasize that it is much more is understandable. But it is not merely the illness and hence its recipient which need to be regarded as multifaceted but also the service and its provider. The latter is simply no longer, if it ever truly was, a technical task, expertly and actively given to a passive and grateful taker.

Let me illustrate how logically absurd the one-sided approach is. In recent years, there has been some documentation that the attitudes and beliefs of an experimenter have an influence on the results of their animal experiments. Surely if the background and beliefs of an experimenter can effect the behavior of his rats, is it too much to expect that the backgrounds and beliefs of a practitioner will similarly affect not only how and what she/he transmits but how and what is received? Yet we never seem to tire of denying this. We see endless books and papers on the doctor–patient relationship, but they deal overwhelmingly with the patient, not the doctor, and little with the dyadic nature of the relationship. Being more specific, they deal with the patient's feelings about the doctor but rarely if ever vice versa. Analytically speaking, they deal with transference and not countertransference. (And the few that deal with both are interestingly enough in psychiatry and the most provocative of these deal with cultural contacts [Spiegel, 1959, 1976].) In the medical world this literature itself is virtually nonexistent.

Ethnicity and compliance. The medical area of compliance illustrates all the dilemmas of which I am writing (Zola, 1977a). The culture that *is* examined is still only the patients' and still the negative side— how the individual's culture gets in the way of his/her obeying or complying with the doctor's orders. It is claimed that patients will not take a drug or follow a regimen for a long period of time, and yet there is research that indicates that people are quite willing to self-medicate on a regular basis. In fact, from studies I've analyzed I would estimate that between 67% and 80% of adult Americans self-treat and medicate themselves in any given 36-hour-long period. It is claimed that many cultural forces weigh against the integration of health practices into one's daily life. In fact, the study of popular and folk medicine claims the opposite—it is this integration that lies at the heart of many ethnic health practices. Thus, perhaps the culture that is getting in the way of integrating certain medical recommednations is not that of the recipients of care but that of the providers. For the sake of argument I would say that for every study or technique we create to understand the culture and ethnicity of the recipient of help we must match it with one of the provider and to the interaction of the two worlds. In the sociomedical world, we too easily feel that someone else, the recipient of care, is the one with a culture, not the provider.

It is probably not an accident that I learned this insight from a person who made his early reputation in ethnic research—Everett C. Hughes (1943). Yet he was also the guiding spirit behind the now classic *Boys in White* (Becker et al., 1961), which documented the overwhelming socialization of students into the medical world, the development of a changing ideology where idealism gradually died in the service of other needs, the evolution and persistence of a medical culture, reflective of their gender, class, and ethnicity, which subsequently colored all

of their future service orientation. The lesson we need to remind ourselves of is an old and ancient truism: to know others we must first know
ourselves.

But the ignoring of culture of the provider on the micro-level is not
my only concern. Again we must return to the macro-level. For medicine itself is part and parcel of a cultural system and thereby embodies
albeit implicitly, unwittingly, and unconsciously certain social values
and political and economic beliefs (Kleinman, 1973; Navarro, 1976;
Waitzkin and Waterman, 1974) which, if not fully understood, may
undermine human dignity, reinforce certain negative social roles, and
become a major instrument of social control (Zola, 1972a). Let me dwell
a final moment on each of these three dangers.

Ethnic research and stereotypes. In the pressure to be practical
we may be seduced into stereotyping. From the very first time that my
research appeared I was asked to write manuals on the handling of
American ethnics groups. Although the overt intent was to help the
health providers in their work, I always feared my efforts would do just
the opposite. I felt I was being asked to construct a social reality that
paralleled the biological one. Today we realize that even biological
realities do not remain the same over time. Not only the general environment but the varying treatments we use alter that reality. Thus,
society is not only continually creating new diseases but constantly
altering the forms of the old ones (Dubos 1961). Thus too with social
reality (Berger and Luckman, 1966). Pure ethnics, in fact, rarely exist
in U.S. culture. Being an Italian, even a southern Italian, was not the
same at the turn of the century as it is now. And its subjective experience and persistence varied not only through time but also through
space—whether you lived in Palermo, Sicily, or the North End of Boston or in Mobile, Alabama. It depended on who you married and lived
near, what education you attained, your social mobility, and your degree of exposure to the "American way."

My original research point was (Zola 1963, 1966, 1973), and is, that
everyone has a cultural heritage which is part and parcel of an individual's health practices. The practical answer is not to learn in detail the
infinite varieties of culture but to be aware of these varieties and how
they *might* affect one's health practices (Kleinman, Eisenberg, and
Good, 1978, offer an exceptionally useful model in this regard). Thus,
I am totally opposed to training anyone in the details of a particular
ethnic group, for this will ultimately squeeze people into unreal categories, and reify their culture as we have rigidified diagnoses. What I
favor is making practitioners sensitive to the patient's heritage, their
own heritage, and to what happens when different heritages come
together.

Ethnicity and professional control. On the social role level I am wary of giving anyone the tools to make them even more powerful in interaction over someone else. The language of medical compliance is not a socially irrelevant one. It uses the words *comply, obey,* and *orders.* Thus, it reinforces in the society certain hierarchical relations to which I am politically opposed and blocks awareness to other therapeutic alternatives of which I am in favor. The women's movement has, for example, recently pointed out that the sick role and the labeling of many of their physical issues as sickness has to a very large extent been a way of keeping them in their place (Boston Women's Health Book Collective, 1976). This has given meaning to the battle cry that anatomy is *not* destiny. On the therapeutic level, I feel the patient should have much more say as well as a role in anything that has to do with his health and illness, his living and dying. I worry that success in dealing with or, more cynically put, manipulating the patient to do what the health provider feels is in the patient's best interest raises important moral questions.

Ethnicity and medicalizing. And finally I am concerned with an evergrowing "medicalizing of daily life," a medicalizing fostered by a certain kind of chemical and surgical success in which the real problems of survival in modern society are trivialized and reduced to treatable medical symptoms, with social problems too often reduced to individual pathologies, all treated symptomatically, with little regard for the larger moral and political consequences (Zola, 1977b). For example, despite the increasing recognition of the so-called stress-related diseases, all efforts to reduce this stress are not on the social level but the individual one. One is instructed on all sides how to deal with these socially induced tensions, from the soothing effects of chemical tranquilizers to the relaxing effects of meditation, from the techniques of mind control to the techniques of centering—each method in the end is an individual one. I do not question the success of these therapies. In a sense I fear them. For with each successful so-called coping method the original source problem, be it social, economic, political, becomes further removed from vision. They are not only ignored, they are perpetuated.

Conclusion

The specific rendering of this history may be a novel one but certainly my basic point—the need to continually reexamine the basic assumptions under which we do our research—is not. I can do little better than end where I began, with the cautionary words of Shibutani and Kwan:

... There is a moral responsibility of scientists for the use made of their work. The successful development of more adequate knowledge will not automatically solve social problems. Knowledge is a source of power for it facilitates control—a person who understands how something works can manipulate some of the conditions so that the course of events can be redirected to his benefit. But knowledge is ethically neutral. In itself it is neither good nor bad, and it can be used in many ways. Although it is generally used to implement the values accepted in a society, in our pluralistic world men are not always agreed on what ought to be done. Generalizations about inter-ethnic contacts might be used to facilitate exploitation as well as to further the welfare of mankind. Colonial governments may use the generalizations to devise more effective techniques of suppression, just as social reformers may use them to implement their values. Precisely because of the possibilities of exploitation the problems of the development of knowledge cannot be separated from the considerations of political power and moral standards [1965 p. 19].

References

Ackerknecht, E. H. *Medicine at the Paris Hospital: 1794–1848* Baltimore: The Johns Hopkins Press, 1967.

Becker, H. S., Geer, B., Hughes, E. C., and Strauss, A. *Boys in white: Student culture in medical school.* Chicago: University of Chicago Press, 1961.

Berger, P. L., and Luckman, T. *The social construction of reality.* Garden City, N.Y.: Doubleday, 1966.

Boston Women's Health Book Collective. *Our bodies, ourselves.* New York: Simon and Schuster, rev. ed., 1976.

Chrisman, N. J., and Kleinman, A. Health beliefs and practices among American ethnic groups. *Harvard Encyclopedia of American Ethnic Groups,* in press.

Dubos, R. *The mirage of health.* Garden City, N.J.: Anchor Books, 1961.

Foucault, M. *Madness and civilization: A history of insanity in the age of reason.* New York: Pantheon, 1965.

Giordano, J. *Ethnicity and mental health.* New York: Institute on Pluralism and Group Identity, 1973.

Giordano, J., and Giordano, G. P. *The ethno-cultural factor in mental health. A literature review and bibliography.* New York: Institute on Pluralism and Group Identity, 1977.

Gurin, G., Veroff, J., and Feld, S. *Americans view their mental health.* New York: Basic Books, 1960.

Hollingshead, A., and Redlich, F. *Social class and mental illness: A community study.* New York: Wiley, 1958.

Hughes, E. C. *French Canada in transition.* Chicago: University of Chicago Press, 1943.

Illich, I. *Medical nemesis: The expropriation of health.* London: Calder and Boyars, 1975.

Illich, I., Zola, I. K., McKnight, J., Caplan, J., and Shaiken, H. *Disabling professions.* London: Marion Boyars, 1977.

Kiev, A. (Ed.). *Magic, faith, and healing.* New York: Free Press of Glencoe, 1964.

Kiev, A. *Curanderismo: Mexican-American folk psychiatry.* New York: Free Press of Glencoe, 1968.

Kiev, A. *Transcultural psychiatry.* New York: Free Press, 1972.

Kleinman, A. Toward a comparative study of medical systems. *Science, Medicine, and Man,* 1973, *1,* 55–65.

Kleinman, A. Lessons from a clinical approach to medical anthropological research. *Medical Anthropology Newsletter,* 1977, *8,* 11–15.

Kleinman, A., Eisenberg, L., and Good, B. Culture, illness and care: Clinical lessons from anthropological and cross-cultural research. *Annals of Internal Medicine,* 1978, *88,* 251–258.

Kuhn, T. *The structure of scientific revolutions.* Chicago: University of Chicago Press, 1964.

Leighton, A. H. *My name is legion—Foundations for a theory of man in relation to culture.* New York: Basic Books, 1959.

Leighton, D. C., Harding, J. S., Macklin, D. B., Macmillan, A. M., and Leighton, A. H. *The character of danger—Psychiatric symptoms in selected communities.* New York: Basic Books, 1963.

Mead, M. *Coming of age in Samoa.* New York: Morrow, 1928.

Mead, M. *Growing up in New Guinea.* New York: Morrow, 1930.

Mead, M. *Sexual temperament in three societies.* New York: Morrow, 1935.

Navarro, V. *Medicine under capitalism.* New York: Prodist, 1976.

Newell, K. W. (Ed.). *Health by the people.* Geneva: World Health Organization, 1975.

Opler, M. K. (Ed.). *Culture and mental health.* New York: Macmillan, 1959.

Opler, M. K. *Culture and social psychiatry.* New York: Atherton Press, 1967.

Opler, M. K., and Singer, J. Ethnic differences in behavior and psychopathology: Italian and Irish. *International Journal of Social Psychiatry,* 1956, *2,* 11–22.

Rosen, G. *Madness in society.* Chicago: University of Chicago Press, 1968.

Shibutani, T., and Kwan, K. M., *Ethnic stratification.* New York: Macmillan, 1965.

Singer, J. L., and Opler, M. K. Contrasting patterns of fantasy and mobility in Irish and Italian schizophrenics. *Journal of Abnormal and Social Psychology* 1956, 53, 42–47.

Spiegel, J. P. Some cultural aspects of transference and countertransference. In J. Masserman (Ed.), *Science and psychoanalysis: Individual and family dynamics.* Vol. 2. New York: Grune and Stratton, 1959, 160–182.

Spiegel, J. P. Some cultural aspects of transference and countertransference revisited. *Journal of the American Academy of Psychoanalysis,* 1976, *4,* 447–467.

Spiegel, J. P., and Papajohn, J. *Transition in families: A modern approach for resolving cultural and generational conflicts.* San Francisco: Jossey-Bass, 1975.

Srole, L., Langner, J. S., Michael, S. T., Opler, M. K., and Rennie, T. A. C. *Mental health in the metropolis: The midtown Manhattan study.* New York: McGraw-Hill, 1962.

Star, S. The public's ideas about mental illness. Paper presented to the Annual Meeting of the National Association for Mental Health, Indianapolis, 1955.

Star, S. The place of psychiatry in popular thinking. Paper presented at the Annual Meeting of the American Association for Public Opinion Research, Washington, D.C., 1957.

Szasz, T. S. *The myth of mental illness.* New York: Harper and Row, 1964.

Szasz, T. S. *The manufacture of madness.* New York: Harper and Row, 1970.

Waitzkin, H., and Waterman, B. *The exploitation of illness in capitalist society.* Indianapolis: Bobbs-Merrill, 1974.

Weinberg, A., and Weinberg L. (Eds.). *The muckrakers.* New York: Simon and Schuster, 1961.

Wheelis, A. *The quest for identity.* New York: W.W. Norton, 1958.

Woodward, J. Changing ideas on mental illness and its treatment. *American Sociological Review,* 1951, *16,* 443–454.

Zola, I. K. Problems of communication, diagnosis and patient care: The interplay of patient, physician, and clinic organization. *Journal of Medical Education,* 1963, *38,* 829–838.

Zola, I. K. Culture and symptoms—An analysis of patients' presenting complaints. *American Sociological Review,* 1966, *31,* 615–630.

Zola, I. K. Medicine as an institution of social control. *Sociological Review,* 1972a, *20,* 487–504.

Zola, I. K. The concept of trouble and sources of medical assistance—To whom one can turn, with what and why. *Social Science and Medicine,* 1972b, *6,* 673–679.

Zola, I. K. Pathways to the doctor—From person to patient. *Social Science and Medicine,* 1973, *7,* 677–689.

Zola, I. K. Taking your medication—A problem for doctor or patient: In Ivan Barofsky (Ed.), *Medication compliance—A behavioral management approach.* Thorofare, N.J.: Charles B. Slack, 1977a, 3–9.

Zola, I. K. Healthism and disabling medicalization. In I. Illich, I. K. Zola, J. McKnight, J. Caplan, H. Shaiken, *Disabling professions.* London: Marion Boyars, 1977b, 41–69.

4

Reflections on Old Age, Ethnicity, and Death

Robert Kastenbaum

Consider a person in a life-threatening situation. The immediate threat is in the form of a diseased leg. A team of physicians advises that the leg be amputated and without delay. Consent to the amputation and one will still have a future—perhaps years, and perhaps reasonably good health. Refuse surgery? Death will be relatively swift and certain.

The person refuses. Neither the physicians's reasons nor the family's urgings persuade otherwise. Death is chosen over amputation.

This is the gist of a case reported in the Boston newspapers recently. What are we to make of it? Anyone seriously interested in trying to understand the dynamics involved would probably seek further information. Fair enough. Is the surgical procedure itself the critical factor? In other words, would the person have consented to life-saving interventions that did not involve surgery? Or that involved surgery, but not amputation? It could be that either surgery or the amputation of a limb had such powerful emotional connotations to this person that these took precedence over the desire to stay alive. But maybe that was not it at all. The patient was old. Did this "oldness" contribute to a reduced will to live? Did the life-threatening physical condition provide a convenient, even a welcome occasion to conclude an existence that was no longer valued? The self-destructive interpretation might be consistent with the high suicide rates for old men. Yet this person was an old *woman*. Do we now have to introduce a different set of considerations, or weigh them differently, because of gender-associated factors?

And which "source of variation" is the more critical in leading to the decision against amputation: the patient's "oldness" or "womanness?" Would she be making the same decision if she were 30 years younger? Or if she were a he? Still again, is the really important issue one that centers on idiosyncratic attitudes toward surgery and amputation rather than either age or sex? Is it not also possible that the fact of hospitalization itself—or, alternatively, the realization that one's body is vulnerable—established a sense of fatalism or despair?

It may seem pedantic and aloof to raise such questions when a person's life is at stake. In a sense, what does it matter *why* this old woman refused surgery; it is the decision itself and its likely outcome that is most important. And yet if knowledge and insight have any value at all, should not this value be even greater in life-and-death situations? Would it not be helpful to understand more clearly the various strands that go into life-and death decisions? Would not a better understanding at least occasionally provide the would-be helping person with a more effective, more appropriate guideline? Let us then persevere just a little longer with this one particular example of many that might be examined.

This old woman with a life-threatening condition had strong ethnic roots (or so it appears from the available information). Is it not possible that here ethnicity might have had a significant bearing on the way she confronted the decision? Turn the question around: would it not be difficult to believe that the ethnic tradition that has influenced her throughout a long life has abruptly *stopped* affecting thought, feeling, and behavior in a critical situation? It would appear more reasonable to assume that ethnicity has some influence on this decision. But how much influence? And what is the process through which the ethnic influences express themselves?

These questions generate others. For example:

1. Can ethnicity be regarded as "one more variable" whose influence is to be computed and weighed along with such other variables as age and sex? Or must we take a more complex view of ethnicity and the total person-in-the-situation?

2. Does ethnicity influence thoughts, feelings, and actions in the same way and to the same extent throughout the lifespan, or are the processes and dimensions different, say, in early development, adulthood, and old age?

3. Do powerful environmental systems (such as the health care establishment when one is hospitalized) overwhelm and reduce the influence of ethnicity, or, instead, arouse fierce ethnic responses?

4. How important is the *particular* ethnicity of an individual as compared with his/her embeddedness in *any* ethnic tradition?

5. To what extent are the interaction and discrepancies *between* different ethnic orientations and the gradients and shifts *within* a particular ethnic orientation critical in their implications for the individual?

6. And, while we are at it, would it not also be useful to know: What *is* ethnicity in the first place?

Ideally, we would have data-based answers to questions such as these, along with the perspective of an expert ethnologist. Instead, all this chapter can offer are the observations of a psychologist who has been around the aged and the dying and life-threatened for about two decades. The above questions come out of my experience; satisfactory answers I have not been able to find. This admission once made, it might be the decent thing to conclude right here and not waste the reader's time. But I will continue in the hope that there might be some value in setting forth problems and possibilities that could make it easier for other clinicians, researchers, administrators, and educators to fathom the interrelationships of death, aging, and ethnicity.

Let us first identify and sort out some of the problems that have been touched upon fleetingly above.

Who Is Ethnic and What Does It Matter?

We are concerned here with the possible significance of ethnicity in the total situation of the old person with particular reference to dying, death, suicidality, bereavement, and related problems. But this relatively specific focus assumes that we have our bearings straight on ethnicity in general. I have allowed myself the luxury of trying to think this through for myself without consulting the technical literature on this subject.

When ethnicity does not matter. Imagine a population of 9-year-olds or a population of 90-year-olds. Imagine an all-female or an all-male population. Would age be an important variable in the first example, or gender in the second? Similarly, if a population were comprised entirely of people with the same shared cultural tradition, what significance could be attributed to ethnicity? In a hypothetically air-tight situation (the population has internal interactions only), a characteristic common to all would essentially disappear. The actions of a particular individual could not be predicted or explained on the basis of age, gender, or ethnicity if either of these was the universally shared characteristic. Age, gender, and ethnicity become background factors, constants, rather than sources of variation. A transcendent observer might

be fascinated by differences between isolated and homogeneous populations. But ethnicity would not be an "interesting" variable if indeed
it was any variable at all within a particular population.

When we do concern ourselves with ethnicity, then, it is usually
because of differences, discrepancies, interactions rather than "pure"
ethnicity as such. At times we may not be as interested in ethnicity as
we think we are: what concerns us are the misunderstandings, the
differential response sets, the "over-" or "under-" reactions of people
whose interactions start from *un*shared ethnic orientations. Looked at
in this way, ethnicity certainly does seem to matter for many old people
in death-related situations. Hospitals, nursing homes, and other congregate settings are becoming increasingly the "final environment" of the
elderly in our society, whether for a few hours or days or for many
months and years. The ethnic mixture is often both broad and patterned, but with the specific mix variable from region to region and
time to time. The modal resident in a geriatric facility, for example, may
be an "Old Yankee" woman whose most frequent interactions are with
lower-echelon staff of Black and Spanish-speaking heritages, supervised
by registered nurses of Italian or Irish background, and diagnosed and
treated when necessary by physicians from India and the Phillipines. A
few miles away the ethnic mixture might be appreciably different.

It is also possible that ethnicity counts for little in some circumstances because it is overwhelmed by environmental pressure, physiological extremity, or some combination of these. We should be cautious
about accepting such conclusions at face value, however. The advanced
stages of senile dementia, for example, devastate thought and personality. To put it bluntly, the wreckage of the person is likely to appear
much more evident than what remains. And yet the individual's gestures, speech fragments, rudimentary ways of interacting—do these not
still convey something central to the kind of person he/she was in
better times? Does this old man's neat, precise (but environmentally
un-oriented) gestures tell us something about a style of life instilled
three-quarters of a century ago in an Asiatic or northern European
milieu? Does this other man's more expansive and expressive gestures
perpetuate the lifestyle acquired from his Mediterranean heritage?
Extreme sensory deprivation, nutritional deficit, and chemical strait-
jacketing of vulnerable old people can also inhibit the expression of any
clear individual characteristics, whether these represent mostly "ethnic" or "personality" attributes (a distinction that itself will have to be
examined).

Should we see a depressing commonality among a set of ill and
impaired old people, it may be hasty to conclude that ethnicity has
disappeared. Dream and imagery fragments, not available for the

casual observer to note, may be providing a pulse of inner continuity and be richly laden with ethnic connotations.

Furthermore, has ethnicity been nonoperative as a variable on the interpersonal scene? Or is it not a distinct possibility that some characteristics of the controllers-of-the-environment have served to reduce the apparent ethnic expression of the elders? Take one ugly kind of situation for example. It is not necessary to specify the precise ethnic groups involved; their relative positions in society are more to the point. Let us say the setting is a nursing home and that its people can be divided into members of an "upper" and a "lower" ethnic group. By these terms I mean the group's place in the informal status hierarchy of a multi-ethnic society. The important point here is not *which* group is upper and lower, although this is certainly relevant. Rather, it is the fact that most of the residents/patients are in one group, most of the staff/controllers in the other.

When the staff is comprised of "uppers" (ethnically speaking), there may be little consideration given to the lifestyle, the complaints, the specific needs of the residents. The uppers, virtually by definition, know better. They enjoy a double source of power: vested control of the environment, and the security of social superiority. When views of resident and staff differ, this can be accounted for readily by the former's crudeness and peculiarities as well as illness and age—in other words, "error variance." The situation is not necessarily improved when the leather boot is on the other foot. Debilitated and devalued (because old and sick), members of an "upper" group can become the role-reversal captives of "lowers" who have acquired contol of the institutional setting because nobody else has taken sufficient interest in it— an excellent opportunity for revenge, especially if working conditions generate frustration and low morale. In either situation, the *ethnic disparity* can work massively against the institutionalized elder. The patient/resident we see who appears virtually depleted of personality and its ethnic overtones may have reached that condition in part because of complex interactions and decision-making practices which have been subject to the influence of ethnic factors. I am not saying that this is a conscious, deliberate, bad-willed process, but just that such things do seem to happen. The apparent draining off of ethnic features in an old, enfeebled person, then, might itself be an outcome of ethnic interplay.

The increasing physical weakness and powerlessness that often accompanies the approach to death can further erode the expression of ethnic values and styles. Along with the reduced strength of the dying old person one must consider the possibly increased discomfort of the caretakers or environmental managers. The latter are likely to call ever more intently on their own sources of comfort, such as reliance on rationalizations and maneuvers that derive from *their* ethnic traditions as well as the pseudo-professional, technobureacratic "management" of the terminally ill person that has become commonplace. When the old person becomes institutionalized, then, there may be significant environmental forces that operate to reduce the expression and utilization of ethnically derived resources, and the subsequent dying process may be accompanied by even further reductions. I am not saying that this is the only pattern that can be observed; fortunately, it is only one of a number of patterns that would repay close examination. However, when this pattern does exist, we see an apparent fade-out of ethnicity just when the individual needs whatever strength he or she can muster from every personally relevant source.

Some ways of looking at ethnicity.   There is more than one way of looking at ethnicity. To some extent, we are free to select the approach that is most useful to our purpose. If it is a large epidemiological study we have in mind, then it makes sense to establish tight and specific criteria that can be determined easily and objectively. If, by contrast, we are working on a direct personal level with people experiencing life problems, then more subtle and shifting criteria might be appropriate within broad guidelines. There should be something in common, however, between relatively "tight" and relatively "loose" definitions of ethnicity if the term itself is to retain useful meaning.

In my own work it has sometimes seemed useful to classify old people by fairly clear-cut ethnic criteria. A person might be classified as "Old Yankee," for example, if born in New England of parents both of whom were also born in New England, and whose ocean-crossing ancestors came from England or Scotland. One could make this particular definition either tighter or looser, but it does seem to identify an ethnic tradition. Any fairly tight definition of ethnicity runs into many problems in the application, of course (e.g., mixed and at times indeterminate lineage).

There are times when more subjective definitions appear to be just as useful, or even preferable. Two old people appear equally Polish or Irish in their ethnic credentials. Yet one person shows little adherence to the customs and mannerisms associated with his tradition, while the other lives almost exclusively within that tradition. On paper, both are ethnic; in observable behavior, they have little in common. Furthermore, the subjective assessment of ethnicity can be made either by an observer or by the person him/herself. The purity of classification may be lost if we permit the person to speak for himself—but why shouldn't he? A person who is "half-Greek" might take much pride from this heritage and express it in every possible way, while one who is "all-Greek" in lineage might, for his own reasons, attempt to live as though of no particular ethnic lineage at all. The external observer might or might not agree with the individual's self-assessment. The more an individual attempts to deny his/her ethnic heritage, for example, the more it may seem to the observer that the heritage is asserting itself. Both perspectives (self and other) have their claim on reality.

It is reasonable to use either ancestry, self-assessment, or other-assessment as a basis for classifying people by ethnicity. The rationale for classification should be made clear, of course, and it might be helpful if we eventually came up with appropriate terminology to distinguish these differential bases. If our aim is to understand and perhaps help people, then it would also be reasonable to use these three general classification approaches together. A (too simple) illustration is given in Table 4–1. Suppose that we are chiefly interested in working with old people who may be of either Old Yankee, Irish, or Italian ethnic backgrounds (which happen to be the more populous groups among the aged whom I see regularly). Lineage often can be determined by available records and/or the individual's own statements. Self-definition of ethnicity can be assessed both by direct and indirect questioning. The behavioral observations can be sophisticated and matched to specific self-definition inquiries, or as broad-gauged as noting that the person will speak only Italian and eat only ethnic dishes unless pressed to do otherwise. Include the provision for recording whether the individual is a more or less totally "saturated" representative of his/her ethnic tradition (e.g., perhaps Irish only on the father's side of the family). This could be a continuous gradation, especially on the self and other definitional approaches, but the table has limited itself to "total" and "partial" positions.

We have classified three hypothetical old people in Table 4–1. A person who thinks of herself in OY terms and is a perfect model of "Old Yankee-ness" turns out to come from a mixed lineage that includes no OYishness per se. Yet she has developed a lifestyle around OY characteristics—an "adopted Old Yankee," one might say. Should we exclude her from consideration as an "ethnic" because she lacks the lineage pedigree, or include her because she has made the central characteristics of his orientation her own? Next, we have charted a person fully qualified for Irish ethnicity by virtue of lineage. However, this person steadfastly maintains that there is nothing especially "Irish" about himself. One has the impression that early in his life he encountered severe discrimination on the basis of ethnic identity and cultivated a self-image and behavioral style that was intended to elude the bias. An objective observer, however, sees a number of indices of "Irishness" in his

Table 4-1. Multiclassification of Ethnicity: Three Hypothetical Individuals

Type of Classification	Illustrative Ethnic Groupings and Degree of Saturation								
	Old Yankee			Irish			Italian		
	Total	Partial	None	Total	Partial	None	Total	Partial	None
By lineage			X	X			X		
By self-definition	X					X	X		
By observed behavior	X				X		X		

thought and behavior, although it is not in full bloom. The final example we have selected is of a person who is as Italian as she can possibly be, whether classified by lineage, self-definition, or behavioral observation. It is only this latter person who would be taken as a full exemplar of ethnicity. But each of the others has a particular constellation of ethnicity that deserves consideration on its own terms. And each could be compared with complete representatives of their own respective ethnic traditions. For some purpose we might want to compare only people who are fully ethnic in their own traditions on the basis of all three classificatory approaches. But more often we will probably want to consider all the patterns of partial ethnicity. Each pattern could well have distinct implications for interpretation of illness, orientation toward dying and death, and type of personal, social, and symbolic resources available to cope with the challenges.

We can return briefly now to two of the questions raised earlier. Does the individual's particular ethnicity matter the most, or is the degree of what might be called "ethnic saturation of personality" more important? In other words, is it possible that there is something about living within a firm ethnic tradition—almost *any* ethnic tradition—that must be considered in trying to understand the individual's orientation toward aging, dying, and other significant life events? I do not see how this question can be answered firmly at this time. But it does seem to me that we will make better observations if we distinguish between ethnic saturation and the particular type of ethnicity involved. As an old Russian Jew and an old Italian Catholic face death, each may have deeply carved pathways for the flow of thoughts and feelings, clear guidelines for what should and should not be done, clear standards for determining what has been laudable and what has been deficient in their lives. The details are likely to differ appreciably and should not be ignored. Yet both of these people may be more similar to each other than to an individual who is no longer attached significantly to any ethnic tradition. Thus, it is reasonable to distinguish people according to their personal configuration of ethnicity and their overall saturation as well as according to the specific ethnicity.

The related question centers on the consistency of ethnic influence and expression throughout the individual's lifespan. Take our semi-Irishman, for example. It is possible that as a preschooler he was as Irish as could be within the, say, second-generation immigrant subtradition. This means among other things that his sense of fantasy, of basic inter-personal affiliation, of language, etc., had their origins within this ethnic tradition. The *processes* by which this ethnic tradition became part of his life were those associated with early development. The *acquisition* of ethnicity must be understood in the context of infant and child development in general, including neurological maturation, stage of cognition, formation of attachment relationships, and all the rest. Later this person could exercise more choice, attempting to emphasize some aspects of personality and downplay others. He might have deliberately expunged ethnic characteristics from his thought and identity. Now, in old age, it is possible that ethnicity has become *resurgent.* This would be in keeping with the oft-noted resurgence of early life characteristics (including childhood memories) in general. It would also be consistent with a reduced need to deny one's ethnicity in order to be more em-ployable or for other advantages in society. Disengagement dynamics (Cumming and Henry, 1961) also might be relevant, including the theorized heightening of "interiority" as distinguished from affiliations with the external world (Henry, 1965).

Let us take just one more possible interpretation that points in the same direction. Studies of mental performance over the lifespan indi-cate that there are two broad types of cognitive operations that have different trajectories. (Both types have been named and pioneered in research by Cattell, 1968.) *Crystallized* intelligence refers to the build-up of knowledge, skills, information that enables the individual to func-tion successfully in society. Vocabulary and the use of cultural symbols in general are important components of crystallized intelligence. This form of mental functioning has a good chance of continuing to flourish, to reach even higher levels in late adulthood and old age (depending on the individual and his particular circumstances). But *fluid* intelli-gence, essentially the ability to cope with *new* situations and problems, tends to decline with age. This suggests that it might be to the individu-al's advantage to rely more heavily on his fund of previously acquired information and his most firmly established coping strategies. These, in turn, began during his early days of high ethnic embeddedness. The "Irishness" that was partially set aside in earlier adulthood may now return as part of his mustering of long-established knowledge and coping strategies.

Simple thinking about ethnicity is not encouraged by such considerations. We must take into account the possibility that an individual's "ethnic saturation" not only may differ from that of another person who ostensibly has the same lineage, but that it may change during the course of his lifespan. Furthermore, it might receive either greater or lesser expression as the person encounters critical situations. We have already discussed some of the circumstances in which the expression of ethnicity can be inhibited (e.g., the anxious and technological treatment at the hands of environmental managers when an old person is approaching death). But these can be the same circumstances in which the resurgence of ethnicity might be of special benefit to the individual. Here, surely, is a zone of conflict that could use careful examination.

At least one other source of complication should be noted: *generational shift in ethnic saturation.* the most obvious case is the one in which succeeding generations appear less and less ethnic than their predecessors. First-wave immigrants to the United States sometimes have pressured their children to grow up as "American" as possible. It was a matter of pride and vicarious satisfaction for the foreign-born parents to see their children win acceptance as Americans (i.e., nonethnics). In other family configurations, it has been the children who have taken the initiative in breaking away. The "old country" ways have embarrassed them. They may cringe to hear the accented speech, the grammatical errors of their parents. This process of shedding ethnicity and becoming "Americanized" has usually been ambivalent. It was not easy to achieve a balance between learning the new ways and holding on to the more important older values and practices.

Every cohort of old people today represents a different time-slice of ethnicity and acculturation. In general, we expect that the oldest of the old will also be the more ethnically saturated. Accordingly, their orientation toward dying, death, and bereavement must be understood with clear reference to the values they acquired under specific ethnic-influenced circumstances that are somewhat apart from the mainline of development today.

But we should be ready for some surprises. I think a careful look at ethnic saturation among generations of the same family will now reveal at times a partial return to tradition. The immigrant generation was heavily ethnic. The second and third generations labored to become more American than the Americans. This need is no longer dominant. Later generations (younger people today) have been seeking "roots" and rallying points for enduring values even before the popular book and television series struck its responsive chord. Certainly, one sees fewer people going out of their way to deny ethnicity than was true around the turn of the century (e.g., changing the family name from a long, hard-to-spell, or decidedly ethnic name to a short and innocuous WASPish name). Ethnic saturation can shift, then, between generations as well as within the individual's own lifespan. There is another reason why we may limit ourselves unnecessarily if we consider ethnicity as meaning lineage and nothing but.

Ethnicity: As variable and as mediating process. The person whose interest in ethnicity is highly research oriented and whose favored tool is the computer package of multivariate statistics can "plug" this variable in and out and perform numerous operations with it. The problem arises (in my mind, at least) when method is identified with substance. It becomes possible to say that ethnic membership adds this or that much to predicting a certain characteristic or outcome. Unfortunately, this kind of information, useful in itself, sometimes is applied simplistically. We may act as though ethnicity itself is "one more variable." In "real life," however, we do not encounter pure ethnicity—any more than we encounter pure age, pure gender, pure renal failure, pure fluid intelligence, or pure anything else. We are always dealing with a person in a situation—with neither person nor situation holding completely still.

Statistical techniques provide the opportunity to peel many aspects of the total person and situation apart from each other. (There are more integrative-type statistical techniques as well, but seldom utilized as yet and still difficult to manage.) In our own thinking there is no need to restrict ourselves to an essentially analytic and static view of ethnicity. Instead, we can explore ethnicity as a shaping process and mediator. We do not see old age and ethnicity as two separate features of the same person and wonder which is the more important. The age is steeped in ethnicity, and the ethnicity steeped in age. Ethnicity became a characteristic of the person from the first pattern of parent–child contact. No: make that from the selection of mates and the genetic pool available for the offspring, from the timing of conception, from the mother's nutritional status during pregnancy, from the family's expectations for the child even before it was born. It is useful but artificial to separate ethnicity from the total pattern of personality development. It is still rather simple to construe ethnicity as a mediator of thought, feeling, and action, simple because ethnicity itself is mediated by many influences that we have scarcely mentioned here. Nevertheless, it is more appropriate to look at ethnicity as a dynamic, active set of influences inseparable from the total individual than as a monolithic, static variable that can be plugged in and out.

Some Practical Considerations

Recall to mind the life-threatened person who was mentioned at the onset. How much of her attitude was influenced by ethnicity as compared with age, gender, and other factors cannot be determined. In fact, I have been suggesting that trying to separate ethnicity as though it were a static, isolatable variable does violence to the dynamic integrity of the individual. Yet this person did have a well saturated ethnic identity: Italian. Again, we cannot be sure whether it was mostly her "Italian-ness" or her rootedness in ethnic tradition in general that played the greater role in her resolve against a life-saving amputation. In my experience, old people with high ethnic saturation of almost any persuasion do not take as easily to hospitalization as those with less ethnic affiliation. The hospital is alien turf that does not look sound, or smell like home, nor take much account of the individual's in-family status.

   In the geriatric hospital best known to this writer, I learned that a person who was at the same time old, life-threatened, female, and strongly within the Italian tradition usually expressed a keen desire for interpersonal support. There should be people around, responsive people who would really pay attention. Family members were the most preferred, but staff who also came from Italian background and could still converse in that language were also welcome. There is nothing strange about a person seeking familiar interpersonal supports during such a crisis situation. But it should be added that this is not the only pattern one can observe in the same institution. The Old Yankee, life-threatened male often behaved differently. He was more likely to draw himself up and put on a display of independence. (Couldn't be feeling better. No, I can do that for myself, thank you!) After a while I learned that a sudden show of autonomy and inclination to be left to his own devices might be the sociobehavioral signal presaging rapid decline and death. Especially through the psychological autopsy procedure (Weisman and Kastenbaum, 1968) we developed the impression that a number of people with this configuration (Old Yankee male) had premonitions of death that led them to take one last walk in the sun. The decline and death, while not out of keeping with the individual's physical condition, would not have been clearly expected at the time. Some people, then, behaved in ways that seemed designed to bring family and staff to their side, while others seemed to prefer going it alone. We never were able satisfactorily to distinguish the ethnicity per se from gender, type, and degree of physical disorder, and the environmental and treatment situation.

The old woman who refused amputation was in a general hospital and not known to this writer personally. After reading the first account of her situation, a nurse (Beatrice Kastenbaum) well experienced with people of Boston-area ethnicities thought that she could sense what was happening. This woman expects an outpouring of concern from her family, she suggested, especially from the children. It is not enough that they show sympathy and interest. What she expects is an absolutely central place in their lives at this time, wave after wave of love, convincing proof that everybody is giving everything. But the family probably has many other concerns as well—their own children, their jobs and obligations. More "Americanized" (less ethnically saturated) than the old woman, the family expected a balance between skilled technical help (as represented by the physicians and the hospital) and themselves. This differential expectation might have contributed significantly to the problem. The old woman would feel rejected, brood, threaten to let herself die, and make good her threat unless the family gave her the unstinting time and attention she considered to be her just due.

The follow-up newspaper account did not give enough details to test the nurse's thesis conclusively, but the results were certainly consistent. The sons pledged their devotion; the old woman agreed to the surgery. Nothing is proven by this example, but it is of the type that we have seen over and again, and which will also be familiar to many others who have worked with people highly embedded in particular ethnic traditions.

The education of health care professionals is not complete if ethnicity is excluded. Effective education would include raising the individual's own ethnic predilections to his/her awareness and learning how to use these self-facets to the patient's advantage rather than as subtle distortions of the communication and decision-making processes. It is no secret that many stereotypes exist about the aged (e.g., Butler and Lewis, 1977) and the terminally ill (e.g., Kastenbaum, 1977). The person who is not aware of these stereotypes in general or of his/her own blindspots is that much less effective in the helping role. But when a patient is old *and* terminally ill *and* embedded in an ethnic tradition, there is an even greater challenge. Can the would-be helping person get out of his own skin, see the world as the other person sees it? Experiential exercises represent one educational approach that is worth exploring in all three related domains (age, terminal illness, ethnicity). The scholarly literature in these areas can also be consulted. Just as important is the availability of mature role-models, people who have already learned to respect both the individuality of a terminally ill or bereaved old person and also the common themes and styles that are associated with their ethnic traditions. This is also one more reason why it is worthwhile to encourage people of diverse cultural backgrounds to be active in geriatrics and in terminal care. We can then not only see diverse cultural traditions in action from both the care-giver's and the patient's standpoint, but also gain insights about aging and death in general from what other traditions have to offer.

The hopelessness-suicidality route to death is taken by some old people both in the community and in institutions. Awareness of what values are held especially dear by people of a particular ethnic tradition —and of what can sustain them in times of massive stress and loss—can make the difference between a premature and degraded form of death and the continued will to live (a concept as hard to define as it is to discard). If we are clumsy and inattentive, we may inadvertently deprive the individual of that small comfort or that vital symbol of pride and respect that might otherwise have kept him going. Years ago we learned that something as "ordinary" as a glass of wine in a mature and congenial atmosphere seemed to have a positive effect on depressed institutionalized elders, though more so for members of ethnic groups for whom wine drinking in the family setting had long-established meaning (Kastenbaum, 1972). The physiological effects of wine counted for something, but more important still were the sociosymbolic messages conveyed: you are still adult; you are still important; you can still give and receive pleasure. This is but one type of life-favoring symbol and support that can be offered. Some offerings may be valuable to a broad spectrum of aged and life-threatened people, while others may be specific to a certain ethnic cohort. Discovering what sustains or revivifies is not necessarily that difficult once we commit ourselves to the search.

In what ways can ethnic sensitivity enable us to do better justice by the old person whose death is imminent? The hospice movement offers some cues. In the medieval hospice, the dying person would be placed in a position to gaze upon religious icons and thus draw strength from a shared tradition (Stoddard, 1978). Modern hospices often maintain a religious-ethnic "presence" for those who are apt to take comfort, while not neglecting control of pain and other facets of physical care. Hospice care is not widely available, however, and often is restricted to people with cancer (for reasons that are more economic-bureaucratic than humanistic). Furthermore, the challenge of providing care to persons of many ethnic backgrounds within the same hospice system does not seem to have been fully addressed as yet.

The winding down of an old person's life in an institutional setting often does not call forth sensitive interpersonal response (e.g., Glaser and Strauss, 1968; Gubrium, 1975). As long as the person is not dying in a way that especially alarms the staff, the situation is something to be "managed," not a profoundly important rite of passage or leave-taking. The efficient (cost-effective) processing of an old person's final scene (including body disposal and minimal or nonexistent memorialization) is at odds with most ethnic traditions. Birth and death are major events for most peoples. Ethnic cohesion loses strength when these critical events pass into public settings. Both the dying old person and the ethnic tradition he/she represents are likely to suffer when the passage from life is allowed to be reduced in emotional significance.

Perhaps we see today a renewed interest in "possessing" birth and death rather than leaving it to specialists who are expected to check their ethnicities at the door. Various forms of "natural" childbirth are gaining popularity, as is the greater participation of the father-to-be. More people are also seeking to breathe humanity into the dying-and-death situation. The old person who represents a strong ethnic tradition could benefit from the emerging movement toward recapturing our own lives. But the old person also can contribute much both in health and in illness. As others have pointed out, every wave of old people represents a kind of person whose like will never be seen again. Our own heritage—no matter what our particular ethnicity—can only be enhanced by opening ourselves to their uniqueness.

References

Butler, R. N., and Lewis, M. I. *Aging and mental health* (2nd edition). St. Louis: C. V. Mosby, 1977.

Cattell, R. B. Fluid and crystallized intelligence. *Psychology Today*, 1968, *3*, 56–62.

Cumming, E., and Henry, W. E. *Growing old.* New York: Basic Books, 1961.

Glaser, B. G., and Strauss, A. L. *Time for dying.* Chicago: Aldine, 1968.

Gubrium, J. F. *Living and dying at Murray Manor.* New York: St. Martin's Press, 1975.

Henry, W. E. Engagement and disengagement: Toward a theory of adult development. In R. Kastenbaum (Ed.), *Contributions to the psychobiology of aging.* New York: Springer, 1965, 19–36.

Kastenbaum, R. Beer, wine, and mutual gratification in the gerontopolis. In D. P. Kent, R. Kastenbaum, and S.S. Sherwood (Eds.), *Research, planning, and action for the elderly.* New York: Behavior Publications, 1972, 365–394.

Kastenbaum, R. *Death, society, and human experience.* St. Louis: C. V. Mosby, 1977.

Stoddard, S. *The hospice movement.* Briarcliff Manor, N.Y.: Stein and Day, 1978.

Weisman, A. D., and Kastenbaum, R. *The psychological autopsy: A study of the terminal phase of life.* New York: Behavioral Publications, 1968.

5

Fatalism in Response to Stress among the Minority Aged

Raju Varghese and Fred Medinger

This chapter explores the impact of stress in the lives of aged people who are members of certain disadvantaged minorities and considers the role of perceived fatalism as an adaptive response to the severe stress these individuals commonly face. Fatalism—a disbelief in one's power to control his own destiny—is often assumed to preclude a higher level of functioning as measured by active attempts to master adverse circumstances and secure outcomes favorable to oneself. Thus, in some ways the fatalistic person is exposed to even more stress. Yet fatalism may protect an aging Black, Indian, or Spanish-speaking person from the severe depression and anxiety that would ensue were he or she to assume complete personal responsibility for the stressful, poverty-related circumstances present in his/her life. These circumstances are the product of a socially imposed gap between cultural goals, including the goal of financial self-sufficiency, and the institutionalized means for their attainment. For certain minority groups this gap exists today (Bultena, 1976).

The Stress of Poverty

Situational resources and the mediation of stressors. All of us at one time or another have experienced stress arising from the burden of major responsibilities, occasional reversals in fortune, emotional conflicts, physical disorders, or other events that strain our psychophysiological resources and pose a threat to something we value, such as our social status, health, or self-respect. The term *stress* refers to this cognitive appraisal of threat in the absence of a readily available coping response (Lazarus, 1966; Monat and Lazarus, 1977). A "stressor" is the particular event or circumstance that elicits this assessment of threat from the person exposed to that event.

Dispositional and situational factors can mediate the impact of a stressor upon the individual, either intensifying or diminishing the magnitude of that person's appraisal of threat (Dohrenwend and Dohrenwend, 1970; Figure 5-1). To illustrate, a worker with a large family living on a subsistence wage may feel more threatened by the possibility of his becoming ill than will the healthy individual who is well-covered by insurance. In the same manner, a "C" grade may prove more stressful to the student who aspires after admission to Harvard Medical School than to another student who has no plans for graduate study.

The impact of stress upon the aged is often greater than upon the young since the elderly as a group usually possess fewer personal resources for coping effectively with stressful circumstances. Old age is the first stage of life that brings systematic status-loss for an entire generation (Rosow, 1973). The loss of social roles in the family and at work excludes many elderly people from significant participation in the society and therefore restricts their access to and control over needed social and economic resources. In the give-and-take of social exchange, the aged usually find themselves at a disadvantage. They have fewer financial resources and fewer sanctioned opportunities to offer what resources they do have, such as their labor or their expertise in a given area, in exchange for something of value to themselves, including housing, food, medical care, respect, or social status. Problems of aging therefore are problems of decreasing power resources, rendering the aged more vulnerable to the impact of social and biological stressors, including illness, poor housing, and the death of loved ones (Blau, 1964, 1973; Dowd, 1975).

This deficit in personal resources is acute in the case of the minority aged, leaving them even more vulnerable to stress than the aged in general. Elderly Blacks, Indians, and Spanish-speaking Americans often face double jeopardy with respect to the impact of stress in their lives: not only are they exposed to greater numbers of stressors, they also have fewer coping resources after a lifetime of financial deprivation, subordination to other groups, and systematic exclusion from access to social and economic opportunity (Moore, 1976). Race and ethnic origin themselves account for little of this differential impact of stress in the lives of the minority aged; it is the presence, instead, of certain situational deficits and dispositional elements commonly associated with member-

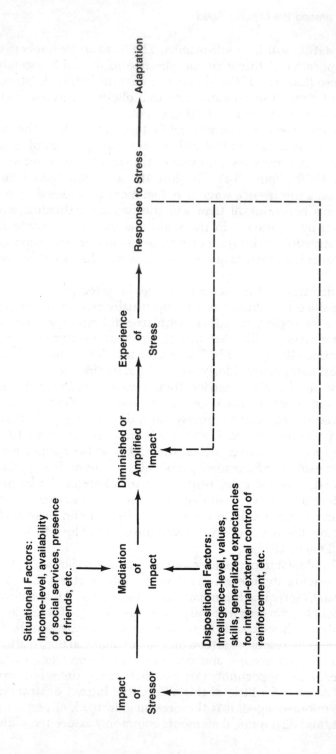

Figure 5–1 Environmental Mediation of Stress

ship in a particular racial or ethnic group which explains the nature and magnitude of the threats experienced, as well as the responses made to those threats by the group members (see Figure 5-1).[1]

For example, elderly whites and Blacks of the same income level show insignificant individual differences in life-satisfaction as measured by the Life-Satisfaction Index-A, a measure of subjective well-being (Clemente and Sauer, 1974; Larson, 1978; Neugarten, Havighurst and Tobin, 1961; Spreitzer and Snyder, 1974). Significant differences in life-satisfaction appear, however, when elderly whites are compared on the whole with elderly Blacks because of the lower economic status of aged Blacks as a group (Larson, 1978). It is the economic deprivation of the minority aged which is the single most important source of stress in their lives, and which most contributes to their dissatisfaction with their immediate situation.

Poverty among the minority aged. Poverty is the situational deficit most salient to the status of the minority aged. The lack of adequate financial resources limits the choices available to alleviate the impact of those stressors that could be handled by people with sufficient financial means (Kimmel, 1974). Over one-third of Black persons past the age of 65 fall below the poverty line, as compared with 14% of elderly whites (Schulz, 1976; U.S. Bureau of Census, 1974). The per capita income of all American Indians is one-third that of the total population; 55% of all Indians on reservations live below the poverty line (Kimmel, 1974; Levitan and Johnston, 1975). This poverty leads to a precarious existence for those few Indians who manage to live to age 65.

Financial circumstances are similar for aged Spanish-speaking Americans. For all Mexican Americans, the likelihood of being poor is nearly three times as great as for Anglos (U.S. Senate Special Subcommittee on Aging, 1971); significant numbers of Mexican Americans over age 65 have worked in occupations that were not covered by Social Security until recently and therefore receive minimal or no Social Security benefits. Overall, 38.8% of aged Black families and 25.4% of aged

1. An "ethnic group" is distinguished by a special history, a collective experience which has led to their present position in the American social system (Moore, 1976). In the case of oppressed ethnic groups, their collective experience has been shaped partly by discrimination and prejudice directed toward them from the more dominant and powerful groups in society. "Race" as a concept is subsumed under "ethnic group." Ethnic groups in America include members of different races, such as Blacks, Indians, and Chinese peoples. However, different ethnic groups can be found within the same race. Witness the "white ethnics," including the Poles, Lithuanians, the Irish, and so forth. This chapter focuses mainly upon the aged of those groups who have yet to attain socioeconomic parity with the remainder of society. This refers to aged Blacks, Indians, and Spanish-speaking peoples such as Chicanos and Puerto-Ricans.

Spanish-speaking families were living in poverty in 1970, as compared to 15.6% of aged white families (U.S. Bureau of Census, 1973).

The extreme impoverishment of the minority aged leads to undesirable living conditions, exposing them to stressors not commonly experienced by other segments of society. Housing is one example. Forty-one percent of elderly Blacks living in the South lack one or more basic plumbing facilities (Carp, 1976). Substandard conditions characterize 54% of all Black housing, and the situation is probably worse for elderly Blacks (Frieden, 1977). The conditions are no better for aged Indians; 63% live in homes with inadequate heating and 21% in homes with no electrical power (U.S. Senate Special Subcommittee on Aging, 1971). As is true of their Black and Indian counterparts, elderly Mexican Americans in the Southwest and inner-city Puerto Ricans in the Northeast also live in less adequate housing than do Anglo American elderly (Carp, 1976).

In addition to their substandard housing, the economic deprivation of the minority aged contributes to their lower standard of nutrition (Carp, 1976; Clark, 1971) and more limited access to adequate health care and residential services with adequate treatment resources (Brody, 1973; Carp, 1976; Jackson, 1971; Kart and Beckham, 1976; Kosberg and Tobin, 1972). These inequities lead to higher rates of illness and shorter life expectancies for aged minorities in relation to aged whites. To illustrate, 15% of whites over the age of 65 are unable to carry on daily activities because of a chronic medical condition; for aged Blacks and other minorities, that figure is 25%. Elderly whites on the average have 33 days per year in which their activity is restricted due to poor health; for the minority aged, that figure rises to 48 days per year (National Center for Health Statistics, 1971).

The impact of poverty-related stressors produces shorter life expectancies for minorities, insuring that very few of their numbers reach old age. In 1975 the average life expectancy for white males was 69.4 years, but only 63.6 years for nonwhite males living in America. The life expectancy for white females was 77.2 years, but only 72.3 years for nonwhite females (*Information Please Almanac,* 1978). Life expectancies for American Indians in particular are severely limited, being only about 46 years (Kimmel, 1974).

Poverty and the loss of control over stressors. The insidious concurrence of debilitating stress with the impoverishment of the minority aged has two dimensions: (1) impoverished, minority status is associated with exposure to greater numbers of stressors, including poor health, poor nutrition, and poor housing, coupled with social ostracism and discrimination; and (2) impoverishment magnified by social discrimination restricts access to institutionalized means for income gain, denying the minority aged the resources necessary to cope with and control the greater magnitude of stress in their lives. The second point in particular is significant. Subjective stress in part results from an inability to mobilize resources to cope directly with a potentially harmful stimulus (Lazarus, 1966). The less control over the malignant stimulus perceived, the greater the intensity of threat experienced. A sense of personal control over threatening circumstances is correlated with stress reduction.

By reason of their poverty and their exposure to systematic discrimination from more powerful elements of society, the minority aged are denied access to and control over financial resources and supportive services such as medical and transportation benefits and legal services. These services and resources are necessary for greater control over the timing and force of impact of situations that threaten the well-being of the minority elderly. It is this lack of available resources to counter the force of stressful circumstances, rather than simply the stressful circumstances themselves, which often creates the greater stress experienced by the minority aged (cf. McGarth, 1977; Mechanic, 1974; Watson and Kivett, 1976).

Numerous experimental studies point to the debilitating consequences of perceived helplessness in the face of stressful situations (Lazarus, 1966; Lefcourt, 1976; Seligman, 1975). Aversive events experienced by subjects who believe they cannot remove themselves from the source of duress have more destructive effects in terms of increased anxiety and decreased task performance than when these same events are thought to be controllable (Lefcourt, 1976). Subjective ratings of the stress produced by experimentally induced noxious stimuli such as electric shock and loud noise are lower when subjects believe their behavior can reduce the onset as well as the duration of the aversive stimulus (Averill, 1973; Craig and Best, 1977; Glass et al., 1973; Hokanson et al., 1971; Lefcourt, 1976). In the same manner, subjects who have control over the aversive situation experience less disorganization of their problem-solving behavior, as measured by their performance in tasks immediately following the presentation of the aversive event (Golin, 1974; Lefcourt, 1976).

Lowenthal, Thurnher, and Chiriboga (1975) have reported that the most highly stressed elderly people, as measured by anxiety level and preoccupation with past misfortune, are not necessarily those who have encountered the greatest number of stressors in their lives. Those who have retained some sense of control over their destiny experience less stress, even in the presence of many stressors. Control over the source and duration of threats is precisely what the minority aged lack as a result of their limited financial resources and systematic exclusion from access to supportive services.

An example may help illustrate the magnification of stress by situational deficits. Arthritis is likely to be stressful for any aged person, rich or poor, Black or white. For the aged Black person living in the inner city, however, impoverishment amplifies the stress. For keeping clinic appointments the nearest busline may be too long a walk and a taxi unaffordable. Perhaps there are no organized programs in the community offering free transportation services to the elderly (Carp, 1971; Cutler, 1972). Assuming the individual finally gains access to a medical unit, his/her economic and social status as an aged member of a minority may result in treatment by a succession of physicians or even medical students at a hospital emergency room or public health clinic. Medicaid and Medicare may not provide complete financial coverage for whatever medicines, special diets, or medical appliances are required for treatment. In short, the minority elderly person's latitude of choice for coping with this stressor, arthritis, may be curtailed due to the unavailability of those situational resources that could modify and ease the impact of this stressor upon the individual's life. Instead the impact of this stressor triggers off a series of secondary concerns involving money, transportation, and the quality of medical care.

Threatened Values and Objectives

Life-threatening stress.   The psychoanalytic, humanistic, and existential perspectives on human behavior all concur that the maintenance of life itself is of highest priority to each individual. Most human behavior reflects what psychoanalysis labels the *life instinct,* the person's innate tendency to act in such a manner as to preserve life (Freud, 1949). Similarly, humanists posit the "maintenance and enhancement of the organism" as the fundamental basis for most human behavior (Rogers, 1973). All other values and goals must be given lesser priority to the preservation of life itself. Events or circumstances that threaten this one objective will prove especially stressful. As the existentialists remind us, the greatest threat possible is the threat of nonbeing.

This principle explains the magnitude of stress experienced by the minority elderly, who often must cope with life-threatening stressors. The shorter life expectations of Blacks, Mexican Americans, and Indians attest to the life-endangering circumstances faced by these groups. Impoverishment and the inaccesibility of needed resources heighten one's vulnerability to premature death from disease, including the complications arising from malnutrition, and those from social causes, including the destructive consequences of urban crime. Old age itself brings a more immediate threat of nonbeing. The most basic threat faced by the minority aged, then, is the threat to life itself, as produced by extreme poverty, systematic exclusion from social opportunity and resources, and finally old age itself, with its expectancy for fewer years left to live.

Threats to self-esteem. Besides the will to live, other needs and aspirations of the minority aged are routinely frustrated or threatened as a consequence of their social status. This systematic disjuncture between ends and means frustrates a motive significant to people of all ages, namely the need for a sense of personal competence and mastery over the environment in service of immediate and long-range objectives. The sense of helplessness produced by this discrimination-based cleavage between objectives and the means for their attainment further exacerbates the impact of the numerous stressors encountered by the minority aged.

This inability to develop a sense of personal effectiveness in achievement of desired outcomes, and the lessening of opportunity to accomplish earlier objectives because of the loss of social roles associated with entry into old age, both undermine the self-confidence of the aged Black or Indian, rendering them even more susceptible to the injurious influence of negative labeling by others (cf. Aaronson, 1966; Bell and Stanfield, 1973; Kuypers and Bengtson, 1973; Slater, 1963). Unconditional positive regard from others, along with positive self-regard, are essential ingredients for a sense of well-being (Rogers, 1973). For the minority aged, these two important values—positive self-regard and unconditional regard from others—are seriously threatened by the negative stereotypes commonly attached to the minority aged, as well as by their sense of helplessness resulting from exposure to systematic discrimination (Bell and Stanfield, 1973; Kuypers and Bengtson, 1973).

The threat from dependency conflicts. Dependency conflicts create a cruel dilemma for the minority aged. On the one hand, many of their needs are either frustrated altogether or granted only precarious fulfillment by the prevailing system of resource distribution, and the lack of an adequate response to cope with this perceived injustice produces rage. On the other hand, the minority elderly remain largely dependent upon this same system of distribution for many of the resources they do receive. So the minority aged, as a group and individually, cannot act upon their anger with impunity, for fear of further jeopardizing their position with respect to the agencies of resource distribution (e.g., hospitals, housing authorities, social-service agencies, governmental agencies). The lack of alternatives available to poor

Blacks living in a nursing home with numerous deficiencies, for example, may effectively preclude their acting vigorously upon their grievances. This and similar conflicts between frustration-produced anger and continuing dependence upon the source of frustration form the basis for a type of stress commonly resulting in chronic anxiety and depression (Horney, 1950; Sullivan, 1953).

Stress and age-related tasks. These stressful conflicts and frustrations present obstacles to the completion of certain psychosocial tasks essential for a sense of well-being in old age; including: (1) adjusting to waning physical strength and declining health, (2) adjusting to retirement, (3) coping with the death of spouse, (4) establishing relations with members of one's age group, (5) establishing satisfactory living arrangements, and (6) affirming the value and dignity of one's past life (Erikson, 1968; Havighurst, 1972). The completion of these tasks is difficult for the minority aged, due to the situational deficits associated with minority status. The failure to come to terms with these objectives itself creates further stress. Unsatisfactory living arrangements, for example, can impede adjustment to retirement.

Origins and Incidence of Minority Fatalism

Disjunction of behavior and reward. A lifetime of exposure to socially sanctioned discrimination and systematic exclusion from those opportunities for economic, educational, and social betterment available to nonminority people can leave the aged minority person with little sense of personal control over his own destiny. Personal efforts on behalf of greater social status and economic security are likely to have met with failure, given the institutionalized exclusion of Blacks, Indians, and certain other minority groups from the middle and upper strata of society until only recently. Aged Blacks and members of other minorities have lived most of their lives in the pre-Civil Rights era and therefore have not enjoyed the full benefit of the widening social and economic opportunities that have resulted from recent Civil Rights legislation.

Repeated failures in the pursuit of desired objectives can prove discouraging for anyone, not just members of a minority group. This discouragement may lead in turn to a generalized expectancy that such instrumental efforts are doomed to failure and that securing desired objectives is not contingent upon anything the person does. Similarly, someone may be exposed to an environment where rewards and punishments are distributed haphazardly and do not seem to follow upon any one particular behavior. This person also will conclude that personal behavior makes little difference in terms of receiving reward or punishment.

Blacks and other minorities have been exposed to circumstances wherein reinforcement has been dissociated from antecedent behavior. The now-retired Black office worker, for example, probably could not have been promoted into the ranks of middle management with a white firm back in the 1940s and 1950s in his prime, regardless of the excellence of his work. This same person may also have discovered that his salary and employment security were subject to factors outside his control rather than to his job performance. He may have been suddenly laid off during the Depression, rehired again in the late 1930s as business improved, only to be laid off again (assuming he was not already drafted) after the war, when a great swell of white veterans returned home looking for work.

Experiences such as this build the foundation for fatalism. Any individual who does not experience a consistent association between his/her own behavior and subsequent reward (or punishment) will develop a general belief that reinforcing events (rewards) are subject to outside forces, including pure chance, fate, the wishes of powerful others, or the invisible forces of the larger socioeconomic system (Rotter, 1966, 1975). Fatalism is thus a generalized expectancy for *external control* of reinforcement in the form of fate, chance, or other forces outside the individual's control. This belief is described as an *external locus of control* (Rotter, 1966).[2] Someone with an *internal locus of control,* on the other hand, believes reinforcement to be contingent upon his own behavior or personal attributes.

Comparative prevalence of fatalism. Significant differences in locus of control between ethnic groups and social classes have been reported in several studies (e.g., Joe, 1971). Nearly all studies using scalar measures of locus of control[3] indicate that Blacks and lower-class people are more fatalistic in their outlook than are whites and middle-class people (Lefcourt, 1976; Lefcourt and Ladwig, 1966; Lessing, 1969; Scott and Phelan, 1969; Strickland, 1972). Significant levels of fatalism are found among American Indians (Coleman et al., 1966; Lefcourt, 1966), as might be expected from their deeply rooted cultural reverence for the powerful forces of nature. An external locus of control is also more prevalent among Spanish Americans as compared to Anglo Americans (Clark and Anderson, 1967; Justin, 1970; Lefcourt, 1966; Saunders, 1954; Scott and Phelan, 1969), as well as being more common

2. For the purpose of presentation, those with an external locus of control are referred to alternately as "externals," "fatalists," or "externally oriented persons."
3. The most widely used scale is Rotter's Internal-External Locus of Control Scale (Rotter, 1966).

among other ethnic minorities, including certain groups of Italian Americans and Chinese Americans (Hsieh, Shybut, and Lotsof, 1969; Jessor et al., 1968; Kiefer, 1974).

While the fatalism of American Indians may be due primarily to their culture, several recent studies indicate the fatalism of Blacks and Spanish-speaking Americans may be due more to economic factors than to religious beliefs or other cultural considerations. When personal income is controlled for, Blacks and Spanish-speaking Americans do not appear to be significantly more fatalistic than whites of the equivalent economic status (Cassavantes, 1970; Garza and Ames, 1974; Lefcourt, 1976; Reitz and Groff, 1974).

Fatalism and Stress Management

Maladaptive consequences of fatalism. What are the consequences of the disposition to fatalism for aged members of these populations who must cope with the stressors produced by poverty and discrimination? The consequences are mixed and can be fully interpreted only in light of the situational constraints under which the aged minority person operates.

At first glance, the fatalism of aged minority groups would seem to be maladaptive. Fatalism, or a generalized expectancy for external control of reinforcement, is associated with a poor self-concept (Duke and Nowicki, 1973; Fish and Karabenick, 1971; Ryckman and Sherman 1973; Wall, 1970), as well as mood disorders such as chronic anxiety and depression (Burnes, Browne, and Keating, 1971; Feather, 1967; Hountras and Scharf, 1970; Joe, 1971; Patton and Freitag, 1977; Powell and Vega, 1972; Strassberg, 1973; Watson, 1967). Externally oriented people tend to be less sociable and tolerant of others (using scale-assessments of these variables; Hersch and Scheibe, 1967; Williams and Vantress, 1969), as well as less trusting of others (Hamsher, Geller, and Rotter, 1968).

As might be expected, fatalists generally exhibit less initiative in their efforts to attain goals and control their environments than do internally oriented people (Phares, 1965). They exhibit lower levels of achievement-motivation (Duke and Nowicki, 1973; Hersch and Scheibe, 1967), and are less likely to persist longer at skill-governed activities that are instrumental to the achievement of valued goals (Mischel, Zeiss, and Zeiss, 1974).

Believing reinforcement generally is not related to their behavior, fatalists generally seem less willing to intervene actively in the environment on behalf of definite objectives. This has implications for their management of stressful situations. Fatalists have been reported to feel more subjective stress and to make less use of task-oriented coping strategies in the face of natural disasters (Anderson, Hellriegel, and Slocum, 1977). Those with generalized expectancies for external control of reinforcement experience greater anxiety and depression during hospitalization for chronic or acute illness and do not as actively seek out information pertinent to their recovery as do those with an internal locus of control (Goldstein, 1976; Phillips, 1975). This information-seeking behavior extends to other problems as well; in general fatalists make less use of information relevant to the solution of a particular problem (Phares, 1968; Prociuk and Breen, 1977). This in part may be due to the relative inflexibility of the fatalist's beliefs and problem-solving strategies, as well as the presence of ideas with little factual basis more commonly found among fatalists (Martin, McDonald, and Shepel, 1976; Sherman, Pelletier, and Ryckman, 1973).

Many of the investigations reporting a strong correlation between fatalism and various indices of maladjustment and vulnerability to stress have been conducted with college-aged adults; their generalizability to aged adults might be called into question. Several recent studies involving the aged, however, point to the deleterious effects of fatalism on the self-concept, social involvement, and mood level of the aged person as well (Hamrick, 1977; Kivett, Watson, and Busch, 1977; Kuypers, 1971; Palmore and Luikhart, 1972; Wolk and Kurtz, 1975).

Conditional effects of fatalism. All of this would seem to lead to the conclusion that fatalism among the minority aged is detrimental to their management of stress, due to the poor self-concept, mood disorders, lack of initiative, and lack of achievement-motivation commonly associated with an external locus of control. This conclusion may be unwarranted. Fatalism may be an adaptive response to stress for those faced with circumstances that reduce their capacity to cope directly with the stressor. It is this particular factor of *situational constraint* which is overlooked in most of these studies linking fatalism to poor adjustment and which is so important to the *Weltanschauung* of the minority aged.

The well-replicated association of fatalism with maladjustive behaviors is valid for situations of *low constraint,* that is, circumstances that do not arbitrarily limit the person's capacity to intervene actively in the environment on his own behalf. In *high constraint* situations, however, where forces outside the individual severely limit the capacity to deal with stressors and pursue objectives, the association disappears between locus of control and psychosocial adjustment (Wolk, 1976). In his study of the predominantly white, elderly people in a retirement home with significant situational constraints, Wolk (1976) found that the presence of an external locus of control among many of the residents did *not* predict a lower level of psychosocial adjustment for these residents, as measured by their mood, self-concept, and certain other indices of adjustment.

Adaptive consequences for minority aged. In certain respects aged minority people living in the community face a situation analogous to that confronting the residents of the retirement home: their latitude of choice in daily activity and coping style is restricted, but it is poverty and ethnic discrimination that are the limiting factors, rather than the rules and regulations of the institution. One reason that fatalism is no longer closely associated with poor adjustment in situations of high constraint is that it is realistic to develop a generalized expectancy for external control of reinforcement in environments that severely restrict the instrumental behavior of those living within. In such circumstances fatalism represents accurate reality-testing, one of the most reliable indicators of mental health.

Fatalism has other adaptive consequences for people living under restraining conditions. Recent attention has been directed to the defensive value of an external locus of control (Rotter, 1975). By shifting blame for failure and low status onto forces outside of themselves, stigmatized people, including the minority aged, can relieve themselves of some of the self-recrimination that would otherwise follow their unsuccessful attempts to improve their position. In the case of the minority aged, blaming the system is often justified, instead of being simply a "cop-out." Rather than leading to behavioral inertia, system-blaming may sometimes motivate the minority person, permitting him/her to focus on systemic discrimination and the many ways social forces structure one's fate. This realization can lead to greater involvement in social action (Gurin et al., 1969).

It has been reported that internally oriented people prefer activities whose outcome depends upon skill and place greater value on objects that can be obtained through skill and effort (Cherulnick and Citrin, 1974; Schneider, 1968). Fatalists, on the other hand, disavow significant interest in skill-based activities, preferring instead projects whose outcome is chance-determined. Similarly, objectives that can be secured through skill and effort often have less appeal to the fatalist than objectives that are reached on the basis of chance alone. Congruent with these reports, Srull and Karabenick (1975), in a study of cheating behavior among internally and externally oriented individuals, concluded that success may be more important to the internally oriented in situations whose outcome has been defined as skill-determined. For the fatalist, however, success in these conditions is not as highly valued as success in those situations whose outcome is considered chance-determined.

These reports have an important bearing on the adaptive consequences of fatalism in response to stress among the minority aged. Many of the culturally sanctioned goals and social positions in American society (attainments such as educational degrees, business success, possession of a fine home) allegedly are acquired through skill and effort. These are precisely the attainments that have been denied the aged minority person, regardless of how much effort has been expended for their sake. We have seen that many of the minority aged are fatalistic. Since fatalists devalue skill-based activities and objectives, as reported above, the minority aged as a group probably now are interested less in those skill-determined activities and goals that have been denied them for so long. They may feel less stress than if they continued to pursue these objectives and met with failure time after time. Thus, the fatalistic stance of the minority aged may have spared them from the fruitless pursuit of and competition for those skill-based objectives, such as educational and economic advancement, which have been outside their reach because of systematic discrimination. They may thus have been spared a great deal of stress and frustration.

Korman (1971) has reported that people with an internal locus of control experience greater subjective well-being in situations that allow them freedom to exercise personal control over reinforcement as compared to conditions that limit their capacity to control the outcomes of their instrumental behaviors. From this comes the conclusion that were the minority aged less fatalistic and more internally oriented with respect to perceived control of reinforcement, they might experience even less life satisfaction than is now the case. This would be understandable, since maintaining an expectancy for internal control of reinforcement would produce cognitive dissonance every time they acted on this expectation and found it untrue. Fatalism circumvents the cognitive dissonance that would be generated by the aged minority person's having to experience disconfirmation of a generalized expectancy for internal control of reinforcement.

As Weiss (1971) has demonstrated in his stress research with monkeys, stress is a function, not only of feedback regarding the success or failure of coping responses, but also of the number of coping responses made. When feedback is held constant, the animal who responds more to a given stressor without success generally experiences more stress than the animal who gives up early and makes fewer responses (cf. Averill, 1973). Extrapolating to the minority aged, the elderly Black or

Indian who becomes fatalistic and makes little attempt to cope with the adverse conditions in his repressive environment may experience less stress than the person who keeps trying and fails to do much about the stressors he encounters, due to lack of situational supports such as a decent income.

Conclusion

The adaptive consequences of the fatalism prevalent among the minority aged cannot be considered apart from the environmental context in which it occurs. The impact of stressors is mediated by situational factors and internal, dispositional factors (see Figure 1). We have seen that situational deficits amplify the magnitude of stress in the lives of the minority elderly, who must face life-threatening stressors without many of the environmental resources enjoyed by other groups. Fatalism is a dispositional element that may counteract some of the injurious effects of stressors confronting the minority elderly and diminish their impact.

In situations of low constraint, which allow for significant personal control of desired objectives, fatalism is associated with maladaptive responses to stress. In the presence of the circumscribed choices and resources deficits faced by the minority elderly, however, a different picture emerges. The low-status individual who assumes complete personal responsibility for his social status becomes vulnerable to depression. A belief in the power of chance factors and other forces outside one's control provides a defensive rationale for past failures and present status. Fatalism may also lead to a devaluation of skill-based objectives that have been denied the minority elderly by reason of social discrimination. A disbelief in one's personal competence leads to lowered expectations, which in turn offers some protection from the stress of broken dreams. Fatalism may represent a realistic response to the situational deficits faced by the minority elderly; even today, much of their destiny has been controlled by forces outside their control.

Therefore, mental health, defined by the presence of certain beliefs and tendencies, may have to be interpreted flexibly in the case of the aged minority person. In some contexts fatalism could conceivably be an adaptive response to a difficult and unjust environment. This may be the case with the minority elderly.

We have learned, however, that in low-constraint environments personal costs are incurred from fatalism, in the form of diminished self-esteem, depression, and chronic anxiety born out of a sense of helplessness. In situations permitting the successful completion of most goal-oriented behaviors, fatalism is maladaptive and stress-inducing. As more and more opportunities for personal control of reinforcement become available to ethnic minorities and the aged in coming years, fatalism will become less useful and appropriate as a response to stress in old age. It is reasonable to predict that fatalism will be less prevalent with each succeeding generation of minority aged in the future decades.

Expectancies regarding the locus of control of reinforcement respond to individual or group therapy in certain cases (Brannigan, Rosenberg, and Loprete, 1977; deCharms, 1972; Diamond and Shapiro, 1973; Foulds, 1971; Lefcourt, 1976; Nowicki and Barnes, 1973; Smith, 1970). Former fatalists sometimes gain a greater sense of personal control over their own destiny while in therapy. For the present, however, clinical intervention on behalf of developing within the aged minority person a greater sense of his having internal control of reinforcement may be insufficient and even counterproductive for helping that person cope with stress, without some form of concomitant social action designed to create environments that provide aged minorities with resources sufficient to provide effective means of coping with stress. Effective stress management is a function of person–situation congruence, wherein the aged person is provided access to those situational resources that will enable him/her to cope with the source of stress.

References

Aaronson, B. Personality stereotypes of aging. *Journal of Gerontology,* 1966, *21,* 458–462.

Anderson, C., Hellriegel, D., and Slocum, J. Managerial response to environmentally-induced stress. *Academy of Management Journal,* 1977, *20*(2), 260–272.

Averill, J. Personal control over aversive stimuli and its relationship to stress. *Psychological Bulletin,* 1973, *80,* 286–303.

Bell, B., and Stanfield, G. The aging stereotype in experimental perspective. *Gerontologist,* 1973, *13,* 341–344.

Blau, P. *Exchange and power in social life.* New York: Wiley, 1964.

Blau, Z. *Old age in a changing society.* New York: New Viewpoints, 1973.

Brannigan, G., Rosenberg, L., and Loprete, L. Internal-external expectancy, maladjustment and psychotherapeutic intervention. *Journal of Personality Assessment,* 1977, *41,*(1), 71–78.

Brody, S. Comprehensive health care for the elderly: An analysis. *Gerontologist,* 1973, *13,* 412–418.

Bultena, G. Life continuity and morale in old age. In B. Bell (Ed.), *Contemporary social gerontology.* Springfield, Ill.: Charles C Thomas, 1976.

Burnes, K., Brown, W., and Keating, G. Dimensions of control: Correlations between MMPI and I-E scores. *Journal of Consulting and Clinical Psychology,* 1971, *36,* 301.

Carp, F. The mobility of retired people. In E. Cantilli and J. Shmelzer (Eds.), *Transportation and aging: Selected issues.* Washington, D.C.: U.S. Government Printing Office, 1971.

Carp, F. Some components of disengagement. In B. Bell (Ed.), *Contemporary social gerontology.* Springfield, Ill.: Charles C Thomas, 1976.

Cassavantes, E. Pride and Prejudice: A Mexican-American dilemma. *Civil Rights Digest,* 1970, *3,* 22–27.

Cherulnick, P., and Citrin, M. Individual difference in psychological reactance: The interaction between locus of control and mode of elimination of freedom. *Journal of Personality and Social Psychology,* 1974, *29,* 398–404.

Clark, M. Patterns of aging among the elderly poor of the inner city. *Gerontologist,* 1971, *11,* 58–66.

Clark, M., and Anderson, B. *Culture and aging: An anthropological study of older Americans.* Springfield, Ill.: Charles C Thomas, 1967.

Clemente, F., and Sauer, W. Race and morale of the urban aged. *Gerontologist,* 1974, *14,* 342–344.

Coleman, J., Campbell, A., Hobson, B., McParland, C., Mood, D., Weinfield, E., and York, E. *Equality of Educational Opportunity.* Report of the Office of Education. Washington, D.C.: U.S. Government Printing Office, 1966.

Craig, K., and Best, J. Perceived control over pain: Individual differences and situational determinants. *Pain,* 1977, *3*(2), 227–235.

Cutler, S. The availability of personal transportation, residential location, and life satisfaction among the aged. *Journal of Gerontology,* 1972, *27,* 383–389.

deCharms, R. Personal causation training in the schools. *Journal of Applied Social Psychology,* 1972, *2,* 95–113.

Diamond, M., and Shapiro, J. Changes in locus of control as a function of encounter group experiences. *Journal of Abnormal Psychology,* 1973, *82,* 514–518.

Dohrenwend, B. S., and Dohrenwend, B. P. Class and race as status related sources of stress. In S. Levine and N. Scotch (Eds.), *Social stress.* Chicago: Aldine, 1970.

Dowd, J. Aging as exchange: A preface to theory. *Journal of Gerontology,* 1975, *30,* 584–594.

Duke, M., and Nowicki, S. Personality correlates of the Nowicki-Strickland Locus of Control Scale for Adults. *Psychological Reports,* 1973, *33,* 267–270.

Erikson, E. *Identity: Youth and crisis.* New York: W. W. Norton, 1968.

Feather, N. Some personality correlates of external control. *Australian Journal of Psychology,* 1967, *19,* 253–260.

Fish, B., and Karabenick, S. Relationship between self-esteem and locus of control. *Psychological Reports,* 1971, *29,* 784.

Foulds, M. Changes in locus of internal-external control. *Comparative Group Studies,* 1971, *2,* 293–300.

Freud, S. *An outline of psychoanalysis.* New York: W. W. Norton, 1949.

Frieden, B. Housing. In *Encyclopedia of social work.* Washington, D.C.: National Association of Social Workers, 1977.

Garza, R., and Ames, R. A comparison of Anglo and Mexican-American college students on locus of control. *Journal of Consulting and Clinical Psychology,* 1974, *42*(6), 919.

Glass, D., Singer, J., Leonard, H., Krantz, D., Cohen, S., and Cummings, H. Perceived control of aversive stimulation and the reduction of stress responses. *Journal of Personality,* 1973, *41,* 577–595.

Goldstein, A. Denial and external locus of control as mechanisms of adjustment in chronic medical illness. *Essence,* 1976, *1*(1), 5–22.

Golin, S. The effects of stress on the performance of normal and high anxious subjects under chance and skill conditions. *Journal of Abnormal Psychology,* 1974, *83,* 466–472.

Gurin, P., Gurin, G., Lao, R., and Beattie, M. Internal-external control in the motivational dynamics of Negro youth. *Journal of Social Issues,* 1969, *25,* 29–53.

Hamrick, N. Learned helplessness and internal-external locus of control in the elderly. *Dissertation Abstracts International,* 1977, *37*(11-B), 5812.

Hamsher, J., Geller, J., and Rotter, J. Interpersonal trust, internal-external control, and the Warren Commission Report. *Journal of Personality and Social Psychology,* 1968, *9,* 210–215.

Havighurst, R. *Developmental tasks and education.* New York: David McKay, 1972.

Hersch, P., and Scheibe, K. On the reliability and validity of internal-external control as a personality dimension. *Journal of Consulting Psychology,* 1967, *31,* 609–614.

Hokanson, J., DeGood, D., Forrest, M., and Brittain, T. Availability of avoidance behaviors in modulating vascular stress responses. *Journal of Personality and Social Psychology,* 1971, *19,* 60–68.

Horney, K. *Neurosis and human growth.* New York: W. W. Norton, 1950.

Hountras, P., and Scharf, M. Manifest anxiety and locus of control in low-achieving males. *Journal of Psychology,* 1970, *74,* 95–100.

Hsieh, T., Shybut, J., and Lotsof, E. Internal versus external control and ethnic group membership. *Journal of Consulting and Clinical Psychology,* 1969, *33,* 122–124.

Information please almanac, 1978 (32nd edition). New York: Information Please Publishing, 1978.

Jackson, J. Negro aged: toward needed research in social gerontology. *Gerontologist,* 1971, *11,* 52–57.

Jessor, R., Graves, T., Hanson, R., and Jessor, S. *Society, personality and deviant behavior.* New York: Holt, Rinehart and Winston, 1968.

Joe, V. Review of the internal-external construct as a personality variable. *Psychological Reports,* 1971, *28,* 619–640.

Justin, M. Culture, conflict and Mexican-American achievement. *School and Society,* 1970, *98,* 27–28.

Kart, C., and Beckham, B. Black-white differentials in the institutionalization of the elderly: A temporal analysis. *Social Forces,* 1976, *54*(4), 901–910.

Kiefer, C. *Changing cultures, changing lives: An ethnographic study of three generations of Japanese Americans.* San Francisco: Jossey-Bass, 1974.

Kimmel, D. *Adulthood and aging.* New York: Wiley, 1974.

Kivett, V., Watson, J., and Busch, J. The relative importance of physical, psychological and social variables to locus of control orientation to middle age. *Journal of Gerontology,* 1977, *32*(2), 203–210.

Korman, A. Environmental ambiguity and locus of control as interactive influences in satisfaction. *Journal of Applied Psychology,* 1971, *55,* 399–402.

Kosberg, J., and Tobin, S. Variability among nursing homes. *Gerontologist,* 1972, *12*(3), 214–219.

Kuypers, J. Internal-external locus of control and ego-functioning correlates in the elderly. *Gerontologist,* 1971, *11,* 39 (abstract).

Kuypers, J., and Bengtson, V. Social breakdown and competence: A model of normal aging. *Human Development,* 1973, *16,* 181–201.

Larson, R. Thirty years of research on the subjective well-being of older Americans. *Journal of Gerontology,* 1978, *33,* 109–125.

Lazarus, R. *Psychological stress and the coping process.* New York: McGraw-Hill, 1966.

Lefcourt, H. Internal-external control of reinforcement: A review. *Psychological Bulletin,* 1966, *65,* 206–220.

Lefcourt, H. *Locus of control: Current trends in theory and research.* New York: Wiley, 1976.

Lefcourt, H., and Ladwig, G. Alienation in Negro and white reformatory inmates. *Journal of Social Psychology,* 1966, *68,* 152–157.

Lessing, E. Racial differences in indices of ego functioning relevant to academic achievement. *Journal of Genetic Psychology,* 1969, *115,* 153–167.

Levitan, S., and Johnston, W. Indian giving: Federal programs for native Americans. *Policy studies in employment and welfare,* No. 20. Baltimore: Johns Hopkins University Press, 1975.

Lowenthal, M., Thurnher, M., and Chiriboga, D. *Four stages of life.* San Francisco: Jossey-Bass, 1975.

Martin, R., McDonald, C., and Shepel, L. Locus of control and two measures of irrational beliefs. *Psychological Reports,* 1976, *39*(1), 307–310.

McGrath, J. Settings, measures and themes: An integrative review of some research on social-psychological factors in stress. In A. Monat and R. Lazarus (Eds.), *Stress and coping: An anthology.* New York: Columbia University Press, 1977.

Mechanic, D. Social structure and personal adaptation: Some neglected dimensions. In G. Coelho, D. Hamburg, and J. Adams (Eds.), *Coping and adaptation.* New York: Basic Books, 1974.

Mischel, W., Zeiss, R., and Zeiss, A. Internal-external control and persistence: Validation and implications of the Stanford Preschool Internal-External Scale. *Journal of Personality and Social Psychology,* 1974, *29,* 265–278.

Monat, A., and Lazarus, R. (Eds.). *Stress and coping.* New York: Columbia University Press, 1977.

Moore, J. Situational factors affecting minority aging. In B. Bell (Ed.), *Contemporary social gerontology.* Springfield, Ill.: Charles C Thomas, 1976.

National Center for Health Statistics. *Health in the late years of life: Data from the National Center for Health Statistics.* Washington, D.C.: U.S. Government Printing Office, 1971.

Neugarten, B., Havighurst, R., and Tobin, S. The measurement of life satisfaction. *Journal of Gerontology,* 1961, *16,* 134–143.

Nowicki, S., and Barnes, J. Effects of a structured camp experience on locus of control orientation. *Journal of Genetic Psychology,* 1973, *122,* 247–252.

Palmore, E., and Luikhart, C. Health and social factors related to life satisfaction. *Journal of Health and Social Behavior,* 1972, *13,* 68–79.

Patton, J., and Freitag, C. Correlational study of death anxiety, general anxiety and locus of control. *Psychological Reports,* 1977, *40*(1), 51–54.

Phares, E. Internal-external control as a determinant of amount of social influence exerted. *Journal of Personality and Social Psychology,* 1965, *2,* 642–647.

Phares, E. Differential utilization of information as a function of internal-external control. *Journal of Personality,* 1968, *36,* 649–662.

Phillips, B. Internal-external locus of control and recovery from orthopedic surgery. *Dissertation Abstracts International,* 1975, *35*(9-B), 4632.

Powell, A., and Vega, M. Correlates of adult locus of control. *Psychological Reports,* 1972, *30,* 455–460.

Prociuk, T., and Breen, L. Internal-external control and information-seeking in a college academic situation. *Journal of Social Psychology,* 1977, *101*(2), 209–310.

Reitz, H., and Groff, G. Economic development and belief in locus of control among factory workers in four countries. *Journal of Cross-Cultural Psychology,* 1974, *5*(3), 344–355.

Rogers, C. A theory of personality. In T. Millon (Ed.), *Theories of psychopathology and personality.* Philadelphia: W. B. Saunders, 1973.

Rosow, I. The social context of the aging self. *Gerontologist,* 1973, Vol. 13, 82–87.

Rotter, J. Generalized expectancies for internal versus external control of reinforcement. *Psychological Monographs,* 1966, *80*(1).

Rotter, J. Some problems and misconceptions related to the construct of internal versus external control of reinforcement. *Journal of Consulting and Clinical Psychology,* 1975, *43,* 56–67.

Ryckman, R., and Sherman, M. Relationship between self-esteem and internal-external control for men and women. *Psychological Reports,* 1973, *32,* 1106.

Saunders, L. *Cultural difference and medical care: The case of the Spanish-speaking people of the Southwest.* New York: Russel Sage Foundation, 1954.

Schneider, J. Skill versus chance activity preference and locus of control. *Journal of Consulting and Clinical Psychology,* 1968, *32,* 333–337.

Schulz, J. Income distribution and the aging. In R. Binstock and E. Shanas (Eds.), *Handbook of aging and the social sciences.* New York: Van Nostrand Reinhold, 1976.

Scott, J., and Phelan, J. Expectancies of unemployable males regarding source of control of reinforcement. *Psychological Reports,* 1969, *25,* 911–912.

Seligman, M. *Helplessness.* San Francisco: W. H. Freeman, 1975.

Sherman, M., Pelletier, R., and Ryckman, R. Replication of the relationship between dogmatism and locus of control. *Psychological Reports,* 1973, *33,* 749–750.

Slater, P. Cultural attitudes toward the aged. *Geriatrics,* 1963, *18,* 308–314.

Smith, R. Changes in locus of control as a function of life-crisis resolution. *Journal of Abnormal Psychology,* 1970, *75,* 328–332.

Spreitzer, E., and Snyder, E. Correlates of life satisfaction among the aged. *Journal of Gerontology,* 1974, *29,* 454–458.

Srull, T., and Karabenick, S. Effects of personality-situation locus of control congruence. *Journal of Personality and Social Psychology,* 1975, *32*(4), 617–628.

Strassberg, D. Relationship among locus of control, anxiety, and valued goals and expectations. *Journal of Clinical and Consulting Psychology,* 1973, *41,* 319.

Strickland, B. Delay of gratification as a function of race of the experimenter. *Journal of Personality and Social Psychology,* 1972, *22,* 108–112.

Sullivan, H. *The interpersonal theory of psychiatry.* New York: W. W. Norton, 1953.

U.S. Bureau of the Census. *1970 census of population.* United States summary. Detailed characteristics. Washington, D.C.: U.S. Government Printing Office, 1973.

U.S. Bureau of the Census. Characteristics of the low-income population: 1973. *Current Population Reports,* Series P-60, No. 94, Washington, D.C.: U.S. Government Printing Office, 1974.

U.S. Senate Special Subcommittee on Aging. *A pre-White House conference on aging: Summary of development and data.* Washington, D.C.: U.S. Government Printing Office, 1971.

Wall, J. Relationship of locus of control to self-actualization. *Psychological Reports,* 1970, *27,* 282.

Watson, D. Relationship between locus of control and anxiety. *Journal of Personality and Social Psychology,* 1967, *6,* 91–92.

Watson, A., and Kivett, V. Influences on the life-satisfaction of older fathers. *Family Coordinator,* 1976, *25*(4), 482–488.

Weiss, J. Effects of coping behavior with and without a feedback signal on stress pathology in rats. *Journal of Comparative and Physiological Psychology,* 1971, *77,* 22–30.

Williams, C., and Vantress, P. Relation between internal-external control and aggression. *Journal of Psychology,* 1969, *71,* 59–61.

Wolk, S. Situational constraint as a moderator of the locus of control-adjustment relationship. *Journal of Consulting and Clinical Psychology,* 1976, *44*(3), 420–427.

Wolk, S., and Kurtz, J. Positive adjustment and involvement during aging and expectancy for internal control. *Journal of Consulting and Clinical Psychology,* 1975, *43,* 173–178.

6

Culture, Ethnicity, and Policy for the Aged

James E. Trela and Jay H. Sokolovsky

The appropriateness of ethnicity as a focal point of social policy largely hinges on whether ethnic differences are objectively and subjectively important for those who are identified as ethnic. The salience of ethnicity can be judged in terms of at least three separate dimensions. The first is *cultural distinctiveness.* An ethnic group may be minimally or maximally distinct in terms of its cultural values and norms and related social patterns. More subjectively, ethnic groups may display higher or lower attachment to their ancestral culture, independent of the degree to which they are culturally distinct. *Ethnic identity,* then, is an important dimension of ethnicity insofar as it is a function of feelings of solidarity with fellow ethnics and is reflective of the personal subjective salience of ethnicity. Finally, quite apart from the above, ethnicity is part of the system of stratification, a dimension of intergroup relations and related to *life chance,* including education, life expectancy, income, and other social desirables.

There are several models of ethnicity in American society which attempt to account for the salience of ethnic status and which bear upon the question of ethnicity in old age. These models present different conceptions of the nature and importance of cultural differences, ethnic identity, and life chances.

The melting pot. The melting pot model of ethnicity is perhaps the best known and most closely associated with our national ideals and conventional wisdom. This model suggests that with time the cultural distinctiveness of all groups is reduced and there emerges a unique

American nationality which is a distillation of the plural cultural patterns which currently exist. In short, people cease being ethnic and are "melted" into a dominant culture that is an amalgam of its various contributors. Implicit in this model is the value of assimilation: the notion that little value is attached to distinctive cultural patterns and that individuals are eager to embrace the dominant culture.

Support for the melting pot model is not difficult to find. English, for example, has become the dominant language for all ethnic groups — even though some members of these groups may remain bilingual. The model becomes problematic, however, when the relationship between ethnicity and life chances is examined. These life chances, including life expectancy and income, vary significantly by ethnicity in spite of the distillation that has occurred.

To the degree that the melting pot model is viable, certain implications for aging inevitably follow. As individuals grow older, as a result of their exposure to the dominant culture, the degree to which they embody an ethnic tradition should be reduced and their sense of subjective identification with a distinct cultural heritage should decline. Similarly, there should be important cohort differences with regard to cultural distinctiveness, ethnic identification, and attendant life chances. Within a family, for example, younger generations may be expected to replace traditional values and social patterns with more modern ones and many ethnic rituals might be expected to be discarded. The relationship between ethnic status and life chances would similarly be expected to decline with each successive cohort. To the extent that an ethnically conscious social policy would be appropriate, it would necessarily be ephemeral in nature.

Integrated pluralism. This model recognizes that persistence of ethnic and racial diversity and contains the argument that America is not a melting pot but a society made up of numerous ethnic and racial groups and hence a plurality of subcultures. Pluralists hold that ethnic and racial groups maintain distinctive cultures, forms of organization, and identities while participating in the larger American society. Members of ethnic groups share a sense of community and interact intimately among themselves, whether or not they live in more-or-less well-defined communities. This interaction sustains and promotes their cultural distinctiveness and identity.

Pluralism as generally conceived not only implies that subcultural groups are distinct but that they are equal in the sense that patterns of subordination and superordination are absent from intergroup relations. In this model the distribution of power and life chances would not be a function of ethnic group membership. Nor is support for this model difficult to find. Attempts to explain local and national politics as well as our national economy and cultural life rely heavily on ethnic factors (Glazer and Moynihan, 1963).

There are several implications of this model for aging. We are led to focus on the distinctiveness of various cultures, particularly with regard to the relative social status of various age groups, the values and norms governing the treatment of the aged, and the roles these cultures provide for older people. Of particular importance would be the role of older people in the transmission of subcultural patterns. Indeed, of the several models possible, the pluralistic model most clearly mandates an ethnically conscious social policy.

Invidious pluralism.   Because the above model implies harmonious intergroup relations, another pluralist model is possible. Pluralism is invidious to the degree that ethnic status is important in patterns of subordination and is closely related to how a group shares in desired things produced by a society. This is generally conceived in terms of the distribution of wealth, power, and prestige. The invidious pluralism model applies where some groups are included in and others are excluded from full participation in society on the basis of racial and ethnic ancestry. Here particularly, social class emerges as an important concept insofar as class-related factors are functions of and sustain apparent forms of cultural distinctiveness.

With regard to aging, the distinction between integrated pluralism and invidious pluralism is critical. The former implies a resistance to assimilation, while the latter implies that society has failed to permit assimilation. Here we are led to inquire into the relationship between distinct cultural patterns and their implications for aging (Fandetti and Gelfand, 1976). When the invidious pluralism model applies we must focus on life chances for the aged of various ethnic groups. The "double jeopardy" hypothesis referring to the additive negative effects of being old and of minority status on various life chances is an example of research stemming from this model (Dowd and Bengtson, 1978).

The ethnic revival.   Somewhat distinct from pluralism is the thesis that there is a revival of ethnicity taking place (Friedman, 1971). Certainly the 1960s saw a rise in the social consciousness and political activity of Blacks and other groups, largely as a result of longstanding patterns of prejudice and discrimination. Similarly, and in part as a result of this, white ethnics showed an increase in ethnic consciousness. Italian Americans, for example, began to protest stereotyping of people of Italian extraction as gangsters, and ethnic groups in cities became aware of the need to work politically in local and state politics on behalf of ethnic neighborhoods.

To the extent that this model reflects social reality, not only is an ethnically conscious social policy supported, but a certain beneficial impact on old people may be hypothesized. Particularly in families where the generations are sharply differentiated by their ethnic behavior and identity, older people may find new roles. Not only may the ethnic characteristics of old people be a source of pride for adult children (whereas they may be a source of embarrassment where assimilation is valued), but the aged, as repositories of knowledge about ethnic rituals and customs, may be a vital link to an ancestral past.

Each of the above models takes ethnicity in general as its focal point and examines ethnicity in an historical context. In each we are drawn to the cohort as a way of examining changes in ethnic salience. Several other models can be identified which focus on aging. These may be identified as the age-as-leveler and the ethnic compensation models.

Age-as-leveler. This model posits that aging exerts a leveling influence on ethnic differences. The process of aging is seen to be sufficiently potent to cut across ethnic lines and mediate or level differences in patterns of aging which are reflective of distinct cultural norms and values (Kent and Hirsch, 1969). At least limited support for this model is available. Dowd and Bengtson (1978), for example, found that frequency of interaction with relatives and the life satisfaction factors of tranquility and optimism showed a decline in ethnic variation across age strata.

Ethnic compensation. While direct empirical support is lacking, it can be argued theoretically that ethnic identity and attendant cultural patterns may be seized upon in old age as a way of compensating for other losses. This model posits that losses related to occupational and other roles require individuals to develop compensatory roles. The endorsement of one's ethnic status and assumption of ethnic roles here is a form of adaptation to aging contributing to the social integration of old people. While this hypothesis has not been tested, research has demonstrated that older people tend to increase commitments to some roles as a way of compensating for losses (Glenn and Grimes, 1968) and that association with similar others increases the significance of commonly held statuses (Trela, 1972).

The above models of ethnic salience, none of which is either without some support or adequate by itself, suggest different policy stances. The melting pot model argues that the importance of ethnicity is ephemeral. The invidious pluralism model points to socioeconomic factors and suggests that inequality needs to be addressed. Concern for cultural distinctiveness and ethnic identification in this context becomes a "false consciousness" obscuring the "real" source of disadvantage. The integrated pluralism and ethnic revival models, however, suggest that cultural distinctiveness and ethnic identify of various groups is enduring and critical in the lives of members of these groups.

But while there is little doubt that ethnicity is an important source of variation in the attitudes and behaviors of people in general and the aged in particular, whether this single status should generate an ethnically conscious social policy is problematic, particularly because little is known about the most important policy-related dimensions of cultural variation.

Ethnicity, Culture, and Aging

The relationship of ethnicity and aging must be placed within the context of cultural variation of whole societies. Anthropological data leave little doubt as to the impact varying cultural contexts have on roles, prestige, interaction, and the physical and mental well-being of the aged (see especially Shelton, 1965). Individual ethnographics of non-state or minimally incorporated societies have shown that elders among, for example, the Samoans (Maxwell, 1970; Holmes, 1974); Samburu of East Africa (Spencer, 1965); Igbo of Nigeria (Shelton, 1965); Abkhasian people of the Caucasus (Benet, 1974); and Middle Eastern highland Druze (Guttman, 1964) maintain important functions and prestige in many crucial areas such as family activities, socialization, political groupings, and religious behavior. In these cases status seems to increase as persons make the transition into some culturally defined period of old age (see especially Guttman, 1964; Benet, 1974).

However, these works should not lead one to suspect that all pre-state societies ordain beneficent treatment of the elderly in contrast to universal degradation of this age group in the industrialized world. On the one hand, studies of the Siriono (Holmberg, 1969), the Kapauku Papuans (Pospisil, 1971), and the Jivaro (Harner, 1972), each a band or tribal society, demonstrate the perils of aging even in small face-to-face autonomous cultures. On the other hand, certain state organized societies, particularly China (Chin, 1944) and Japan (Palmore, 1975), have been noted for developing cultural norms which maintain and sanctify the importance of elders even in the context of industrialization. A lesson emerging from such considerations is that one must not assume an invariate link of folk-primitive cultures to high status of the aged nor expect the reverse always to exist in modern industrialized contexts.

Our task then is to identify those factors in both traditional and modern societies which affect the aging experience. To the degree that such factors are more or less present or absent in various contemporary ethnic groups, the viability of an ethnically conscious social policy may be examined.

Cultural variation and the position of the aged. Researchers have for some time been interested in the culture–aging relationship and are now able to identify those aspects of culture that most strongly impact on the life of the elderly (Simmons, 1945; Clark and Anderson, 1967; Maxwell and Silverman, 1970; Press and McKool, 1972; Cowgill, 1972, 1974; Sheehan, 1976). Most useful for our purposes are the work of Cowgill (1972, 1974), Press and McKool (1972) and Maxwell and Silverman (1970), which employ qualitatively a limited number of ethnographies and build upon the early statistical work of Simmons to elucidate universal factors linked to the well-being of the elderly. The first two works arrive independently at almost an identical set of factors, which they predict will positively correlate with high status of the aged. The status of aged will be maximized:

1. when knowledge they possess is important.

2. when the control of important family/community resources is in the hands of the old.

3. when useful and valued functions are continued as long as possible.

4. when there are fewer role shifts and a greater role continuity through the life cycle.

5. when these roles sequentially involve higher responsibility, authority or advisory capacity.

6. when the extended family is a viable residential or economic unit into which the elderly are integrated.

7. when there is less emphasis upon individual ego development.

In one of the few recent cross-cultural statistical studies relating culture and treatment of the elderly, Maxwell and Silverman (1970) hypothesize that "the esteem in which the aged are held in a given society varies directly with the degree of control they maintain over the society's information resources." The criteria for "informational resources" are quite broad, including participating in ritual, consulting, decision-making, entertaining, arbitrating, and teaching. In actuality these factors not only encompass informational flow but also specify types of activity and power within important societal groups. Based on a worldwide sample of 27 cultures, the authors find confirmation for their hypothesis, and it is noted that the relationships hold regardless of whether the information being processed is instrumental or expressive.

In summary, research suggests that three interrelated sets of culturally bound phenomena should impact most on the well-being of the aged. These are: (1) An available role-set emphasizing continuity and important decisional and activity-dependent responsibilities, and involving links to an extended family unit and/or community organization; (2) Control of some important material and information resources; (3) A value system deemphasizing a concept of self-esteem dominated by self-reliant individualism.

It has been suggested that the modernizing influences of our industrial society have provided a national cultural model antithetical to the traits proposed as most benefiting the aged (Cowgill, 1972; Rosow, 1974). Most often noted are conspicious alienation from the family, loss of work roles, devaluation of traditional knowledge, a series of institutionalized social losses, and a stress on self-reliance as a core value. This is summed up by Rosow (1974) in stating that our current institutions do not offer a choice between marginality and integration of the aged, but simply between alternative forms of alienation. However, empirical research is beginning to indicate that the prevalence of some of these negative traits, especially the isolation from family and nonkin social networks, is not as severe as once thought. Even among what are theorized to be the most isolated aged, the SRO (single room occupancy) Euro-American poor, the works of Sokolovsky and Cohen (in press) and Erickson and Eckert (1977) indicate that this population has an important informal social support system. Nevertheless, such studies give little indication as to what part, if any, ethnic variation plays in the patterns found.

When we turn our concern directly to ethnicity and the aged, the crucial question becomes to what extent do the traits identified above as benefiting the aged differentiate American ethnic groups? Unfortunately, little qualitatively oriented research has been done on the culturally distinct lifestyles of America's ethnic aged. Rather, to date most studies on the subject have focused on quantitative surveys hoping to delineate demographic and socioeconomic differences (see especially the special issue of the *Gerontologist*, 1971). Yet a small literature is emerging which can give us a broad perspective on the sociocultural distinctiveness that exists and how this relates to the problems of aging. For purposes here it is suggested that we can roughly differentiate ethnic groups into high, moderate, and low levels of distinctiveness from American cultural norms. However, one must caution that culturally specific homogeneity cannot be expected within the levels distinguished and even culturally similar ethnic features may have varied impact on the life of the aged depending on many situational factors such as differential migration patterns, age structure, or degree of ethnic stigmatization.

High levels of ethnic distinctiveness. There are a small number of groups in our society that have maintained sociocultural systems that are not only distinct from American cultural norms but also stress factors that foster high status for the aged. Among the most distinct are people such as the Amish, Hasidic Jews, and certain American Indian groups such as the Navaho and Zuni. The long-term positive maintenance of their ethnic divergence has been possible so far as they have remained economically independent of outside groups. There is only limited research, especially on the latter two groups, detailing the meaning of old age in the contemporary context. Rather, many of the assumptions about the aged Indian stem from the anthropologist's "ethnographic present" prior to the reservation system, when traits such as communal sharing, mandated family and community care of the frail aged, and the control by the aged of important ceremonial positions and important esoteric knowledge where observed. Among these most poverty-stricken of all ethnic groups it is not known to what extent such traits remain as a buffer to their forms of triple jeopardy. However, the work of Marjorie Schweitzer (1978) in two Oklahoma Indian communities shows that the prestige of the elderly is based on their role as storyteller and the demand the seniors are in for sharing their knowledge of ritual and religious matters. Nevertheless, judging by the health statistics and life expectancy figures for the American Indian, the biggest problem an old Indian may have is the government's perception that a viable traditional support system still exists and can adequately deal with the needs of the aged.

The clearest data on the importance of sociocultural distinctiveness comes from the studies of old order Amish who have largely rejected the "worldly" nature of our industrial society (Hostetler and Huntington, 1971). In their tight-knit agrarian communities old age is defined functionally, with a varied timing of a retirement process which is voluntary and gradual. Movement into the "grandfather house" adjacent to younger married children provides a transition into a valued, active, and responsibility-laden role-set which is bolstered by an ideology in which "old-fashioned ways" are revered and a knowledge of these ways is perpetuated by the older people (Hostetler and Huntington, 1971). Moreover, prestige resides with age because elders retain not only adequate economic resources (e.g., their own buggy to drive) but also purposeful community-wide religious roles, which end essentially with death. Tying these factors together is a strong value on the welfare of others, which overshadows self-absorption and preoccupation with personal needs and comforts. In these respects the distinct culture of the old order Amish provides an idyllic-supportive milieu for the aged that incorporates the three factors we have associated with beneficial conditions for the aged.

Moderate levels of ethnic distinctiveness. The Amish stand as a strong contradiction to the rule. Most other immigrant groups have not been able to maintain such a close integration of ideology, social organization, and economic tradition but rather key components of their sociocultural distinctiveness have dissipated under acculturative pressures. In the case of groups with middle/moderate levels of ethnic distinctiveness—Japanese, Chinese, and other Asian American groups, Mexican and other Hispanic American groups, Orthodox Jews, and segments of Black America—there remain strong religious and social components of tradition, while modes of integration with national cultural norms stem from attempting to become "good Americans," at least in the economic sense. We can assess the impact of this level of ethnic distinctiveness by examining data pertaining to Japanese and Mexican Americans.

The immigration pattern of first-generation Japanese Americans (*Issei*) mitigated many severe problems of extreme overt discrimination (except during World War II), an impoverished economic position, and life cycle dislocations suffered by other Asian immigrants, especially the Chinese (Kalish and Yuen, 1971). Arriving in smaller numbers, with a more balanced sex ratio than the Chinese, the Japanese were more likely to establish families here quickly than to wait until a return to their homeland. According to Kalish and Yuen (1971), this has had a significant impact on *Issei's* adaptation to the United States. The attachment of their children to their land of birth fostered a desire to remain here permanently and stimulated an interest in American culture and language (in part to protect themselves from its influences). Certain traditional values regarding responsibilities toward the aged were transmitted to offspring. Additionally, the greater acculturation of Japanese Americans stimulated high educational achievement and financial security of the second and third generations, which not only allows for much aid to flow through the child–parent tie but also has given the elderly a deep sense of pride in their childrens' accomplishments.

Much has been written about the high status and prestige accorded the elderly in traditional Japanese culture (Palmore, 1975; Benedict, 1945; Smith, 1961; Kiefer, 1974; Plath, 1972). Particularly, many have focused on the Japanese version of Buddhism and its linking of the aged and even the dead to a family system emphasizing filial devotion and an aged role infused with loving indulgence and an accepted dependence in this "second privileged period." Kiefer also stresses formal socialization into the retired role *(Inkyo)* with its greater freedom but also the expectation of increasing skill and wisdom. Maintenance of these ideals has not been possible in either modern Japan nor among Japanese Americans, yet studies of the latter group clearly show the salience of Japanese ethnicity for the elderly (Kiefer, 1974). In perhaps the only thorough qualitative documentation of cultural meaning of

ethnicity for the aged, Kiefer (1974) details how the *Issei* have handled
the problems of aging in the context of increasing Americanization of
their children and grandchildren.

Despite the significant generational differences noted by Kiefer
(1974) and Masuda, et al. (1970), most Japanese elderly still live with or
near their family, who importantly encourage the *Issei* to be involved
in family activities and outings. To a great extent their lives remain
focused on core Japanese values such as *Kansha* (gratitude), *Gaman*
(forbearance), *Makoto* (sincerity), and *Giri* (duty) which culminate in a
style of life Kiefer (1971) refers to as *structural intimacy*. This involves
valuing cohesiveness of the group over the benefit of membership and
many ritual obligations and privileges. Seen from the perspective of the
individual this means that psychological and material security are to be
achieved through the cultivation of mutually binding relationships
more than through the competitive pursuit of abstract ends. Here a
strong emphasis on productivity and activity by the *Issei* maintains a
self-esteem based not on egocentric self-worth but that of self-worth
perceived as group worth, with productivity related not to a material
impact on the world but to the building of intimate human bonds. Yet
the *Issei's* children have not fully accepted the premises of their parents' value system and aged parents will often refuse aid if it is not given
with the proper attitude and respect. A major compensating factor for
this source of disjuncture from the family is the solidarity of nearby *Issei*
age-peers, who through the Japanese language and similar early socialization patterns share a sense of mutuality which seems greater than
that *between* the generations. Indeed, Kiefer suggests that many *Issei*
have transferred their dependence needs to co-ethnic elders and that
high levels of reciprocal emotional and instrumental aid flow through
these nonkin informal social networks.

In sum, the practical meaning of ethnicity for *Issei* aged hinges on
core values which, while somewhat discontinuous through generations,
maintains the elderly in a nonstigmatized family role. More important,
however, much of their socialization into old age (Rosow, 1974) is provided by age peers who share these strongly held values and allow their
traditional basis of self-esteem to guide them through old age. This
latter aspect of Japanese ethnicity, linking the *Issei* into age-peer dependent mutuality may be more important for these aged than the
rules of filial piety most often alluded to.

For the Mexican American the impact of ethnicity on the aged is
less well documented, but also seems of great importance. The best
ethnographic materials come from the works of Margaret Clark (1959)
in a Mexican American *barrio* in northern California. Despite poverty,
the importance and care of the aged is provided for by an emphasis on

strong family ties, a strong fictive kinship system *(compadrazco)*, and the maintenance of folk-medical beliefs about which the elderly possess the greatest knowledge.[1] In the *barrio* studied by Clark, elders pride themselves on working as long as they are fit and contributing to the needs of the family. Although precise figures on elderly living with married children are not specified, contact with a large bilateral kin network seems quite impressive. One couple with just one child had 205 relatives in the surrounding country area, and Clark notes that the couple frequently visits with about two-thirds of the members of this extended kinship group and sees the others at least two or three times a year. For the elderly, ties with grandchildren were especially frequent and warm and children may be sent to live with grandparents for as long as a year's time.

An important formal institution providing extra support for the aged is the *compadrazco* system in which a couple will sponsor a Catholic ritual for a child (often a nonrelative) and thereby engender new enduring roles of "godparent" to the child and also a "co-parent" to the child's parents. Such a system cannot only strengthen kin ties (when relatives become co-parents) but also help compensate for failure of kin to live up to their responsibilities. Clark notes a case where a widower's co-parents took him into their house after they saw that the man's stepsons were not willing to do this.

Another resource seniors have is their retention of folk-medicinal knowledge concerning the cause and cure of ethnic-specific illnesses such as "magical fright" *(espanto)*. Grandparents are often the first resource used for many illnesses such as these. Even if a physician aided in the case, the cure is usually attributed to the healing knowledge of the local folk healer.

Yet one has to be cautious about the extent to which such traits effectively deal with problems of the aged in the diverse urban areas inhabited by the Mexican Americans and in light of the acculturation of their children. Moore (1971) in particular has cautioned about generalizing from the limited materials available and suggests that many of the patterns discussed have faded considerably in the last decade.

Low levels of ethnic distinctiveness. When we come finally to consider less clearly defined Euro-American ethnic groups that have blended large components of their traditional cultural system with mainstream American ideals, one finds a research wasteland dotted now and then with statistical demonstration of ethnic nonsalience. Thus, such people identified as members of various Euro-American

---

1. Yet this can be a double-edged sword as old women, especially those with weak kin networks, are also the ones most likely to be suspected of witchcraft.

ethnic groups—Italian, Polish, Jewish, and Irish Americans—are most often perceived as not having retained much cultural distinctiveness that might have an impact on the aged.

However, what does seem valuable to explore are important differences in value orientations related to the family and other social support systems and how this affects the elderly. The work of Cohler, Welch, and Lieberman (1975) studying Irish, Italian, and Polish Americans in Chicago give us an idea of the extent of such differences. Most instructive is their comparison of the latter two groups in terms of family and other interpersonal relations. While the statistical evidence showed that persons in both groups had roughly similar levels of social contact, structural and perceptual differences of these ties loom as important.

For the Polish it was found that they perceive a greater sense of isolation in that they are more likely to feel no one is available to them for aid in problematic situations. This greater degree of social isolation is related to traditional Polish concerns for privacy, self-containment, and much formality in social relations. The authors suggest that what appears to be a greater social isolation among the Polish American respondents may be a reflection of their preference for formal rather than informal relationships and a tendency to look to the community rather than to the family for support. Hence, they argue that there is a tendency here to undervalue informal relations of the family as a source of support in deference to resources through formal links to the community. In contrast, the Italians who emphasize a traditional value of "family centerness" (stressing survival of the small nuclear family unit over all other segments of society) and use chain migration to link up fellow townspeople in the same American urban neighborhood have put an inordinate stress on family relationships. Thus, in contrast to Polish respondents, Italian aged were more willing to seek out family and close friends in crisis situations. In this case, Italian women were noted as rising in status with age as they were much in demand to mediate problems in the family network. However, there are costs attached to this "mediating madonna" role. The same research reports that for aged females an overload of demanding family ties may lead to psychiatric stress with a positive correlation existing between an increasing number of family ties and *low* life satisfaction.

While ethnic differences are apparent, the ultimate questions remains: Do the differences make a difference? Cohler, Welch, and Lieberman (1975) in fact suggest that for the groups mentioned above, ethnic saliency for explaining variant patterns of behavior *decreases* in old age with middle-age cohorts more distinct than aged ones. Nonetheless, this does not mean that cultural differences of the non-aged ethnics will not have an impact on their elders. This can be especially important in socially patterning decisions about caring for one's aged parent. An indication of this is a study by Fandetti and Gelfand (1976) comparing Italians and Poles for attitudes toward institutionalization of the elderly. As one might predict from the previous discussion, the authors note "Italian respondents expressed a significantly stronger preference for using family arrangements than their Polish counterparts." Here is an ethnic difference which not only directly impacts on differential treatment of the aged but may also argue for awareness of such differences at some level of policy-making.

Ethnicity and identity. Especially for Euro-American ethnics the values of family and community integration may not be particularly effective buffers against the problems of old age in the reality of modern America. The strong family orientation among Italian Americans has not stopped the pervasive devaluation of the aged, a process embedded in our industrial occupational role status system (Gans, 1962). In this context an overdependence for one's identity on self-terminating occupational roles is a major aspect of alienation of the aged. While we have posited some aspects of cultural distinctiveness that might forestall such problems, we have to this point ignored the question of ethnic identity, that is, the subjective or emblematic use by a group of any aspect of culture in order to differentiate themselves from others (DeVos, 1975, p. 36).

The ethnic revival, so far as it is currently being manifested by third-generation Euro-Americans, centers on subjective identity markers (food, clothes, "roots," etc.) and a sense of belonging to a historically known past. What does this mean for the elderly? Perhaps most important is that a positive valuation of ethnicity as a nondenigrating component of identity can be a more continuous basis of self-esteem than an occupational identity, which suffers greatly through retirement. This can be especially crucial for urban elderly abandoned by their upwardly mobile children. A particularly good example of this has been noted for a group of isolated Eastern European Jews living in rooming houses and hotels in Los Angeles (Kessler, 1976). Culturally dispossessed from their families and their village environment of early socialization, "Their social world is built upon their search for continuity in their lives, a continuity they find in their common Jewish heritage. . . ." It is important to note here that most have never been strongly religious Jews but rather share a passionate *Yiddishkeit* (Jewishness) which more than anything links them, through retention of Yiddish and the occasional performance of religious ritual, to a venerated cultural past that survived even the Holocaust. It is implied here that such identity mechanisms are crucial for generating strong kin-like ties with a surrounding community of age-peers, yet the importance and validation of this assertion waits further research.

Another aspect of ethnic identity is its linkage to the ethnic revival model in providing a living bond to the historical "roots" of ethnic pride. In this, the crucial transaction flows *between* generations especially linking adolescent and elderly age cohorts. This is particularly clear in the third-generation ethnic renaissance emerging as a social and political movement. It is emerging not only as a rediscovered mode of local political organization but as a search by young age cohorts for a new sense of self. While a renewed "repository of wisdom" power resource may thus be gained by the ethnic elders, their roles must extend beyond storytelling, or it will be the *young* who gain more in the exchange.

Aging, Ethnicity, and Social Policy

There are several forces that favor an ethnically conscious social policy toward aging. First, the aged in American society have increasingly become the object of national, state, and local policy initiatives. There are many reasons for this, including several demographic trends. Suffice it to say that, as the number and proportion of older people has increased, their needs have become more visible and they have become more demanding of public recognition. Each of these has in turn forced an examination of our institutional arrangements vis-à-vis the aged. More recently there has been a growing recognition that the aged are a heterogeneous category of individuals, the search for the sources of this diversity occurring simultaneously with the "ethnic revival," calling attention to cultural heritage as an important source of attitudinal and behavioral differences. Finally, there is what Daniel Bell (1975) has called the "revolution of rising entitlements"—the increasing tendency for groups with common interests to turn to the government to solve problems. This has, according to Bell (1975), altered our political economy.

> The major conflicts increasingly are not between management and labor within the framework of the economic enterprise but between organized interest groups claiming their share of government largess. The political cockpit in which these battles are fought is the government budget. These battles have become the "class struggles" of the present and the future.

Since the 1960s, age and ethnicity in addition to race and sex have become dimensions of this conflict. In short, age has increasingly become the basis for special social entitlements as the aged have become a special interest group.

The preceding section of this chapter has demonstrated the complexity of the relationship between aging and ethnicity and emphasized that our knowledge about culturally distinct traits which influence aging and their presence or absence in various ethnic groups is uncertain. This by itself could render an ethnic-conscious policy problematic. While it is clear that among those groups presumed to be low on a continuum of ethnic distinctiveness ethnicity can be important to our understanding of aging in diverse social contexts, there is no clear relationship between ethnic distinctiveness and benefits to the aged. Ethnic patterns can be either functional or dysfunctional for the aged. Where they are functional and where ethnic solutions to the problems of aging are sufficient, as with the Amish or Hasidic Jews, an appropriate policy is to protect ethnic distinctiveness or at least to ensure that some of the latent consequences of public policy do not undermine functional patterns. At the levels of moderate or low levels of distinctiveness, however, where acculturative pressures are apparent or have perhaps prevailed, appropriate policy is less clear. In general, even when ethnic patterns are functional, all three of the supportive cultural components identified earlier may not be present. And even if all three conditions prevail, they might not be sufficient in themselves to help minority and ethnic elderly deal with the severe problems they face in American society.

The complexity of the relationship between aging and ethnicity nothwithstanding, whether or not ethnic differences alone constitute a sufficient basis for differential entitlements and treatment is problematic for several other reasons as well. Indeed, whether or not such a policy is possible will depend largely upon receptivity of the sociopolitical context. Although the growth of the aging population, the recognition of cultural diversity, and the changing context of political struggle favor an ethnically conscious policy, other forces do not. First, the articulation of policy to support ethnic culture is problematic in the context of a fundamental ideological trend. Whereas the shared sense of peoplehood that is the basis of ethnic identification was once roughly coterminous with a rural land space and common culture, historical change has lead to progressively larger political groups and the realization that the lives of individuals are increasingly linked to an international community. Accompanying these changes there have developed ideologies that are at most only tolerant of ethnic differences. Gordon (1978) notes

> In the modern industrialized urban state, such an ideological model, stemming from classic eighteenth and nineteenth century liberalism blended with nationalism, views the huge nation as "the people." The remnants of

former types of ethnicity are then regarded as inconvenient vestiges—to be tolerated if the state is democratic—but not to be encouraged. In the more extreme rationalist-liberal "oneworld" or "federation of nations," "world government" ideological systems, the ultimate point is reached: even nations are regarded as outmoded sociopolitical entities and the projected ideal sense of peoplehood is one which embraces the entire population of the world—the "brotherhood of man" knowing no boundaries, national or otherwise. Ethnicity, as representing a sense of special ancestral identification with some portion of mankind, has in this conception, disappeared entirely.

Second, Bell (1975) notes that "the government has made a commitment, not only to create a substantial welfare state, but to redress all economic and social inequalities as well." This commitment has included efforts in the areas of civil rights, housing, environment policy, health care, and income support. Insofar as the existence of injustices and inequalities have sustained both the cultural distinctiveness and identity of various groups, the success of this national commitment threatens to further obscure ethnic distinctiveness. For example, as more housing alternatives become available to ethnic minorities, ethnic concentration will be diluted as an important basis of ethnic distinctiveness.

While an ethnically conscious social policy toward the aged is improbable in the context of the above discussion, the ethnic factor may be expected to emerge occasionally in the debates of our political economy. For example, where a social policy conceived to redress injustices is ethnicity conscious, as in affirmative action programs, it can be anticipated that short-term ethnic consciousness may be increased. An example can be found in the relationship of Blacks to the Social Security system. In short, it has been submitted that elderly Blacks are discriminated against by the Social Security system for they, more often than whites, do not live long enough to collect benefits. As a result it has been suggested that Social Security benefits be adjusted to take account of these ethnic related differences in life expectancy. Jackson (1970), for example, suggested:

> ... it is now the case that (a) most Negroes die earlier, (b) perceive of themselves as being "old" earlier and (c) are in fact, *old* earlier than are whites. Hence this serious and highly pragmatic proposal: The minimum age-eligibility for retirement benefits should be racially differentiated to reflect present racial differences in life expectancies.

To the degree that the lower life expectancy of Blacks is related to poverty, the national commitment to reduce poverty should reduce the need for a specific policy for the ethnic aging.

Third, public policy by its nature tends to be destructive of group and individual differences. Policy and planning themselves are related to political centralization and the notion that peoplehood transcends the local distinctiveness and parochial interests of various groups. Further, the administrative structures that emerge as vehicles for the implementation of policy tend to be insensitive to individual differences. In a large complex industrial society, the need to rationalize and control services make it difficult to recognize minor cultural variations, although major cultural differences may be evident. For example, Supreme Court rulings have recognized the Amish practice of withdrawing children from school prior to age 16. Cain (1974) has described this with regard to age. In most societies, for example, until recently, old age was identified by the evidence of declining physical ability. As the aged have become the object of social policy and old age has become a separate legal status, however, chronological age has become the basis for identifying old age. Hence the Social Security Act of 1935 designated old age as a separate legal status and reduced the importance of individual variation in aging. In short, one of the latent consequences of centralized planning is often the undermining of the importance of individual differences and local distinctiveness, whether regional, ethnic, or other.

Finally, it has been argued that the problems of aging are in fact very similar in all ethnic groups. While ethnic differences do exist, and a particular problem such as poverty may be more or less prevalent in a given group, Kent (1971) has argued that treating the group as a policy referent rather than the problem amounts to "treating symptoms rather than causes."

When social class is controlled, very little evidence exists suggesting that various ethnic groups have specific needs, although there may continue to be life expectancy differences between whites and Blacks and other life chances may be somewhat differentially distributed. Rather, as was shown earlier, the needs of elderly appear to be essentially similar regardless of ethnic background. What does vary is the way ethnic groups respond to these needs. Further, it has been hypothesized that age exerts a leveling influence on some ethnic variation over time (Kent and Hirsch, 1969). Dowd and Bengtson (1978), using data from a large multistage probability sample of middle-aged and aged Blacks, Mexican Americans, and Anglos, presented data that supports, at least in part, this hypothesis.

In summary, given the uncertainty about the future of ethnic distinctiveness and identity, the close association between class position and ethnic-related life chances, the effect of modernization, and the existence of strong counterideologies, it is difficult to imagine an enduring social policy for the aged focused upon ethnic status.

This does not imply that the ethnic factor can or should be ignored in the implementation of established policies. The implementation and administration of policy can appropriately be ethnically conscious to the degree that cultural differences are related to the need for and the utilization of services. In other words, the bureaucratic structures designed to implement an ethnically blind policy may be sensitive to cultural differences. The training of service providers regarding cultural differences, the employment of indigenous workers, and the use of outreach mechanisms, to note just a few possibilities, have all been used as means of tailoring services to the special characteristics of beneficiary groups and can be part of the implementation of a national policy on aging.

References

Bell, D. The Revolution of rising entitlements. *Fortune,* April 1975. *91* (4), 98–103.

Benedict, R. *The Chrysanthemum and the Sword: Patterns of Japanese Culture.* Boston: Houghton-Mifflin, 1945.

Benet, S. *Abkhasians: The Long-Living People of the Caucasus.* New York: Holt, Rinehart and Winston, 1974.

Cain, Leonard D. The growing importance of legal age in determining the status of the elderly. *The Gerontologist,* April 1974, *14,* (2), 167–174.

Chin, H. H. The Chinese concept of face. *American Anthropologist,* 1944, *46,* 45–64.

Clark, M. *Health in the Mexican American Culture.* Berkeley: University of California Press, 1959.

Clark, M., and Anderson, B. G. *Culture and Aging: An Anthropological Study of Older Americans.* Springfield, Ill.: Charles C. Thomas, 1967.

Cohler, B., Welch, L., and Lieberman, M. Social relations and interpersonal relations among middle-aged and older Irish, Italian and Polish American women. Unpublished manuscript, 1975.

Cottrell, F. *Aging and the Aged.* Dubuque, Iowa: William C. Brown, 1974.

Cowgill, D. A theory of aging in cross-cultural perspective. In D. Cowgill and L. Holmes (Eds.), *Aging and Modernization.* New York: Appleton-Century-Crofts, 1972.

Cowgill, D. Aging and modernization: A revision of the theory. In J. Gubrium (Ed.), *Later Life: Communities and Environmental Policy.* Springfield, Ill.: Charles C. Thomas, 1974.

DeVos, G. Ethnic Pluralism: Conflict and accommodation. In *Ethnic Identity: Cultural Continuities and Change.* Palo Alto: Mayfield Publishing Company, 1975.

Dowd, J. J., and Bengtson, V. L. Aging in minority populations: An examination of the double jeopardy hypothesis. *Journal of Gerontology*, 1978, *33*(3), 427–436.

Erickson, R., and Eckert, K. The elderly poor in downtown San Diego hotels. *The Gerontologist*, 1977, *17*, 440–446.

Fandetti, D., and Gelfand, D. Care of the aged: Attitudes of White Ethnic families. *The Gerontologist*, 1976, *16*(6), 544–49.

Friedman, M. (Ed.) *Overcoming Middle Class Rage*. Philadelphia: Westminster Press, 1971.

Gans, H. *The Urban Villagers: Group and Class in the Life of Italian-Americans*. New York: Free Press, 1962.

Gerontologist, 1971, *11*(1), part II.

Glazer, N., and Moynihan, D. P. *Beyond the Melting Pot*. Cambridge, Mass.: The M.I.T. Press, 1963.

Glenn, N. D., and Grimes, M. Aging, voting and political interest. *American Sociological Review*, August 1968, *33*, 563–575.

Gordon, M. M. *Human Nature, Class, and Ethnicity*. New York: Oxford University Press, 1978.

Guttman, D. Alternatives to disengagement: Aging among the highland druze. In R. Levine (Ed.), *Culture and Personalities: Contemporary Readings*. Chicago: University of Chicago Press, 1964.

Harner, M. J. *The Jivaro: People of the Sacred Waterfalls*. New York: Double-day-Natural History, 1972.

Holmberg, A. R. *Nomads of the Long Bow: The Sirionó of Eastern Bolivia*. Garden City: Natural History Press, 1969.

Holmes, L. *Samoan Village*. New York: Holt, Rinehart and Winston, 1974.

Hostetler, J., and Huntington, G. *Children in Amish Society: Socialization*. New York: Holt, Rinehart and Winston, 1971.

Jackson, J.J. Aged Negroes: Their cultural departures from statistical stereo-types and rural-urban differences. *The Gerontologist*, 1970, *10* (2), 140–145.

Kalish, R., and Yuen, S. Americans of East Asian ancestry: Aging and the aged. *The Gerontologist*, Spring, 1971, *11*, 36–47.

Keifer, C. Notes on anthropology and the minority elderly. *The Gerontologist*, 1971, *11*, (1, pt 2), 94–8.

Keifer, C. Lessons from the Issei. In J. Gubrium (Ed.), *Late Life: Communities and Environmental Policy*. Springfield, Ill.: Charles C. Thomas, 1974.

Kent, D. P., and Hirsch, C. Differentials in need and problem solving tech-niques among low income Negro and white elderly. Paper presented at the 8th International Congress of Gerontology, Washington, D.C., 1969.

Kent, D. P. Changing welfare to serve minorities. In *Minority Aged in America*. Occasional Paper, #10, Institute of Gerontology, University of Michigan, Wayne State University, Ann Arbor, 1971, 25–34.

Kessler, J. B. Aging in different ways. *Human Behavior*, 1976, *5*, 56–59.

Masuda, M. et al. Ethnic identity in three generations of Japanese Americans. *Journal of Social Psychology*, 1970, *81*, 199–207.

Maxwell, R. J. The changing status of elders in a Polynesian society. *Aging and Human Development*, 1970, *1*, 137–146.

Maxwell, R. J., and Silverman, P. Information and esteem: Cultural considerations in the treatment of the aged. *International Journal of Aging and Human Development*, 1970, *I*, 361-92.

Moore, J. Mexican Americans. *The Gerontologist*, 1971, *11*, (1, part II), 30–35.

Palmore, F. *The Honorable Elders.* Durham: Duke University Press, 1975.

Plath, D. Japan: The after Years. In D. Cowgill and L. Holmes (Eds.), *Aging and Modernization*, 1972, 133–50.

Pospisil, L. *Kapauku Papuans and Their Law.* New Haven: Human Relations Area File Press, 1971.

Press, I., and McKool, M. Social structure and status of the aged: Toward some valid cross-cultural generalizations. *International Journal of Aging and Human Development*, 1972, *3*, 297–306.

Rosow, I. *Socialization to Old Age.* Berkeley: University of California Press, 1974.

Schweitzer, M. Cultural solutions to the problems of aging in two Oklahoma Indian communities. Unpublished manuscript, 1979.

Sheehan, T. Senior esteem as a factor of socio-economic complexity. *The Gerontologist*, 1976, *16*(5), 433–440.

Shelton, A. Igbo aging and eldership: Notes for anthropologists and others. *The Gerontologist*, 1965, *5*, 20–23.

Simmons, L. W. *The Role of the Aged in Primitive Society.* New Haven: Yale University Press, 1945.

Smith, R. Japan: The later years of life and the concept of time. In R. Kleemeier (Ed.), *Aging and Leisure: A Research Perspective into the Meaningful Use of Time.* London: Oxford University Press, 1961.

Sokolovsky, J., and Cohen, C. Measuring social interaction of the urban elderly: A methodological synthesis. *Aging and Human Development* (in press).

Spencer, P. *The Samburu.* Berkeley: University of California Press, 1965.

Trela, J. E. Age structure of voluntary associations and political self-interest among the aged. *The Sociological Quarterly*, Spring, 1972, *13*, 244–252.

7

Politics of Aging and Ethnicity

William Bechill

This is an effort to examine the responses made by the Administration on Aging (AOA) over the years to the needs of minority and ethnic aged. The AOA is generally recognized as the foremost agency at the federal level for identifying and responding to the interests of the nation's older population. It is therefore important to see how the agency has performed in this area.

This chapter is divided into four parts. First, the concept of AOA serving as a "social support" system for the nation's elderly is discussed. The idea of a governmental organization that is created to serve the interests of a particular group in the population is not all that new or novel, but in the light of some of the known serious needs of older people in our society, it is important to emphasize this particular conceptual view of one of the fundamental missions, if not the main mission, of the AOA.

The second part of the chapter sets forth some general views as to the relevancy of racial, ethnic, and cultural factors in the planning and provision of human service programs. Here, the position is taken that such factors are indeed central and ought to be respected in the organization and delivery of services to the older population.

Third, an admittedly speculative review is presented of some of the strategies that the AOA has used to respond to the needs of the minority aged and the ethnic aged. The final section of the chapter suggests some additional strategies that ought now to be considered by the AOA, particularly as the agency attempts to move in the direction of giving more priority in the future to the needs of low-income older persons and the so-called frail or more socially vulnerable elderly.

AOA as a Support System

The Administration on Aging was established under the provisions of Public Law 89–73, the Older Americans Act of 1965. The original act authorized a five-year program of grants to the individual states for community planning and services in the field of aging. The Act also assigned to AOA several other functions; these include serving as a national clearinghouse on the needs of older people, advising the Secretary of HEW on all matters pertaining to aging, directly administrating project grants for research and development, training personnel in the field of aging, and providing technical assistance and consultation to State and local governments on the problems of older people. (See U.S. Department of Health, Education, and Welfare, 1966, for a general history of the Older Americans Act.)

As an organization, AOA has undergone a remarkable transformation since its inception in October 1965. The initial authorizations for the first year for all of the existing grant programs of the Older Americans Act was a modest $6 million for the entire nation. In its formative period the agency was not viewed as one that would assume large-scale responsibility for the direct operation of service programs. Contrast these amounts and perspective with the present and proposed authorizations under the existing Older Americans Act! The current annual agency budget is well over $500 million dollars. The pending 1978 Amendments to the Act would provide for even further expansion of the various programs of the Act, as well as expand the roles of the AOA, state agencies on aging, and area agencies on aging. As an example, H.R. 12225, recently passed in the House of Representatives, would authorize a three-year extension of the Older Americans Act with specific authorizations over that period totaling over $4 billion. In a comparatively short period of time, the Older Americans Act has become one of the largest and most significant social service programs around.

The present status of the agency represents an amazing reversal over what was the case just seven years ago, in 1971. At that time the total budgets of AOA and the Older Americans Act program were just over $40 million. In the summer of 1971 there were many in the field of aging who were convinced that the AOA was being downgraded as an organization expected to be the central focal point in aging at the federal governmental level. Through a series of events that involved a decision by the Nixon Administration to provide more adequate funding for the Older Americans Act during the 1971 White House Conference on Aging, and strong leadership throughout the 1970s by key Democratic and Republican members of Congress (notably Congressmen John Brademas of Indiana, Claude Pepper of Florida, and William

Stieger of Wisconsin and Senators Frank Church of Idaho, Thomas Eagleton of Missouri, Ted Kennedy of Massachusetts, and Charles Percy of Illinois), the role of the AOA and the Older Americans Act has been dramatically expanded over this seven-year period.

The real breakthrough for AOA came in March 1972 when the Congress enacted the national Nutrition Program for the Elderly by adding a new title VII to the Act. The Congress authorized $100 million for the first year of the nutrition program, $150 million for the second year. The title VII program has become the most popular program of the Older Americans Act, featuring as its central focus the provision of congregate meals and related services to older persons in a wide range of community settings that are used as sites for the program. The nutrition program marked the first time that the AOA had been given responsibility for the administration nationally of a large-scale program of direct services. The 1972 legislation also contained provisions that indicated that priority attention in the program should be given to the needs of the low-income elderly as well as members of minority, Indian, and limited English-speaking groups (U.S. Congress, 92nd Session, P.L. 92–258).

The growth of the AOA continued under the Older Americans Comprehensive Services Amendments of 1973. Under this legislation, several new features were added to the programs of the Act. The most significant were those that authorized the development of comprehensive and coordinated systems of services for older persons in every state, the establishment of area agencies on aging with a related emphasis on area planning, a new grant program for the development of multipurpose senior centers, and the permanent establishment of an Older Americans Community Services Employment program to provide part-time public service employment for unemployed low-income persons age 55 and over (U.S. Congress, 93rd Session, 1973). These twin pieces of legislation, enacted in 1972 and 1973, were the turning points in the transition of the AOA from a small and struggling agency at the federal level to one that now has both major resources and authority, if not influence, that can be used at the national level to improve the conditions of the nation's older population.

Today the AOA may properly be viewed as a social support system for older people in the United States. It is a "system" that involves planning, provision of services, and advocacy in their behalf. The AOA has now begun to acquire the level of authority and resources that it needs to be responsive to its very broad constituency, the older people of our nation. It should fully "support" the people that it purports to serve through direct responsibility (in partnership with others working at a state and community level) for the planning and delivery of a wide spectrum of basic services needed by older persons. It must also have the ability to influence the channeling of other kinds of services to older people such as income support, health care, and housing.

The Relevance of Cultural, Racial, and Ethnic Factors

As a social support system, the organizations that operate under the Older Americans Act ideally must attempt to represent and serve *all* of the older population. From this perspective, one of the most difficult questions such organizations now face in the provision of their services is the extent to which they should take into account cultural, racial, and ethnic factors.

There appears to be a growing consensus that such factors should be respected. The question seems to be not whether race or cultural factors should be respected or considered, but how they should be respected and used by program planners and program managers. To what degree, for example, should ethnic factors be respected in the operation of a congregate meal program for older persons? in the operation of nursing homes serving both a multiracial and multinational population? Are ethnic factors important in the provision of services by agencies such as public welfare or a family service agency whose principal clientele may be either Black, Hispanic, Polish American, or Italian American? These are difficult questions. The point is that such questions should be the focus of debate in the human services area today, not whether such factors should be considered merely secondarily or at all.

In a background paper prepared for the National Institute on Aging, Professor Mary Wylie of the University of Wisconsin School of Social Work commented that public and private programs in the human services area often fail to perform well because they fail to understand their beneficiaries' culturally determined attitudes, beliefs, and values (Wylie, 1976). Wylie noted that programs designed for a primarily white, middle-class, urban population are often barely workable or capable of implementation by agencies working with other populations. When the same programs are applied "unchanged" to the poor, the widowed, members of minority groups, residents of rural areas, or citizens of other countries, the results are often disappointing and frustrating (Wylie, 1976).

In her excellent critique, Wylie stressed the importance of understanding cultural factors in programs affecting the aging. She noted that, "aged populations are heterogeneous (in terms of education, class, race, income, health, and so on) . . . and aging itself is a cultural, as well as a biological process. Culture invests the aging process with particular meanings and defines the appropriate relationships of the aged to themselves, to others, to social institutions, and to their environment" (Wylie, 1976, p. 2).

In the field of aging, experience dictates that the diversity of the older population should always be respected in program planning and program administration and that sensitivity is important in service delivery approaches that are designed to guarantee access to services to all groups in the older population entitled under various public laws and policies. That experience also should have provided some perspectives about the various strengths often associated with peoples' cultural, ethnic, or racial background, and how these can be respected and used in program planning, development, and operations.

Specific Responses of AOA

The organizational responses of the AOA to the needs of the minority and the ethnic aged have varied over the years. In large part, whatever responses were made in this area have been influenced by events experienced by the agency during various stages of its history.

The responses made during the formative years of the organization, a period roughly from 1965 through 1969, were minimal. During this stage, the AOA was mainly involved in the initial building of itself as an agency at the federal level and in the administration of the original grant programs of the Older Americans Act. The agency was beset with a number of serious questions, raised both within and without the federal government, as to what its actual role and scope of responsibilities were as an organization representing the interests of the nation's older people. The agency, and the budget of the Older Americans Act, was small by national standards. The AOA during this period was struggling, not only for an expansion and clarification of its legal mandate, but for its very organizational survival as well.

During these years the major organizations that represented Blacks, Mexican Americans, and other minority groups in American society devoted their primary attention to the implementation efforts of the federal government taking place with regard to the Civil Rights Act of 1964 and large-scale programs that were the cornerstones of the Great Society program of the Johnson Administration: Medicare, Medicaid, the Elementary and Secondary Education Act. At that time, the interest of the Department of Health, Education, and Welfare was largely centered on taking steps to insure that Black aged and other minority aged had access to hospitals, nursing homes, and other health care providers under both Medicare and Medicaid.

During these initial years, the AOA did give some limited attention to the minority aged. In 1966 and 1967, research and development grants were made to Louisiana State University for a study of cultural factors in adjustment to aging; to the Pennsylvania Department of Public Welfare for a comparative study of the needs and uses of services among Black and white aged in the Philadelphia area; and to Professor Helena Lopata, in Chicago, for a study of widowhood that included some material relative to the role of culture as a factor in the adjustments made by older widows.

Possibly the most significant contribution during this 1965–1969 period came with the implementation by AOA of a $2 million national demonstration in food and nutrition services for older persons. The program, which operated in 22 projects around the nation, is generally acknowledged as the forerunner of the present National Nutrition Program for the Elderly (Bechill and Wolgamot, 1973). The importance of cultural, racial, and ethnic factors in the development of the meals, supportive services, nutrition education, and outreach that were part of such projects were particularly underscored in projects operated in Chicago, Cincinnati, Denver, Detroit, Jackson, Mississippi, New York City, Phoenix, Walthill, Nebraska, and Washington, D.C. (U.S. Department of HEW, 1970).

The second stage development of AOA as an organization was from 1970 until the passage of the Comprehensive Older Americans Act Amendments in May 1973. During these years the agency's total budget grew to over $200 million. The AOA was active in the implementation of several new provisions of the Older Americans Act, including those that involved broader statewide planning, coordination, and evaluation of programs by state agencies on aging, the development of a National Older Americans Volunteer Program (authorized by amendments in 1969), and the already mentioned Title VII nutrition program.

During this time, the agency also became the target of a considerable amount of criticism by organizations and individuals representing various minority group interests. The most notable development was the formation of the National Caucus on the Black Aged in 1970 by Black gerontologists and others who were concerned with the lack of attention or priority being given to the needs of the Black aged by AOA and other federal agencies. The focal point of the Caucus's early concerns became the planning process that was then underway for the 1971 White House Conference on Aging. In the view of the Caucus leadership, the planning was being handled in a way that prevented any focus on the needs of Black or other minority aged. It was not until the appointment of Dr. Arthur Flemming, and Flemming's subsequent agreement to many of the objectives of the Caucus, that the 1971 White House Conference structure began to reflect any major concern for the interests of the minority group aged (Jackson, 1974).

The final 1971 Conference structure had separate sections and recommendations on Black, Spanish-speaking, Asian American, and native American elderly. The Conference marked the beginning of a highly visible approach in the field of aging with regard to minority aged.

From a social policy perspective, there were some immediate gains for the minority aged following the 1971 White House Conference on Aging. As one illustration, the 1972 Title VII Older Americans Act nutrition program highlighted the needs of the minority elderly. It also gave some attention to the ethnic elderly. Section 705 of the original Title VII provisions reads, in part, "that preference shall be given to projects serving low-income individuals and provide assurance—that grants will be awarded to projects operated by and serving the needs of minority, Indian, and limited English-speaking eligible individuals in proportion to their numbers in the State" (U.S. Congress, 92nd Congress, P.L. 92-258). Section 706 of the same Act reads, in part, "to provide special menus, where feasible and appropriate, to meet the dietary needs arising from the health requirements, religious requirements, or ethnic backgrounds of eligible individuals."

The priorities regarding the low-income elderly and the minority group elderly are well known. Reference to the limited English-speaking elderly as a priority target population in the Title VII program and the reference to ethnic background in regard to special menus are much less known. To our knowledge, the AOA has not singled out the limited English-speaking elderly for much attention in the day-to-day implementation of the Title VII nutrition program. The one exception is the Spanish-speaking elderly, who are recognized as a minority group by the AOA.

The third stage development of AOA dates from the passage of the 1973 legislation through 1978. Over this five-year span the programs of the Older Americans Act have expanded dramatically. The cumulative effects of major amendments made by the Congress to the Older Americans Act in 1973 and 1975 have been to increase the agency's budget to well over $500 million annually and to see the agency begin to wield major influence at the national level.

Social policy is often determined by events and individuals as much as it is by basic social and economic conditions. Accordingly, the key role played during most of this period by Arthur Flemming must be mentioned. Dr. Flemming served as the U.S. Commissioner on Aging

throughout most of this period and provided outstanding leadership to
the AOA. A skilled organization builder and public administrator,
Flemming stressed the importance of creating the viable "aging network" that has become the centerpiece of the 1973 Comprehensive
Services Older Americans Act legislation. This aging network consists
of some 56 state agencies on aging, some 560 area agencies on aging,
over 1,100 Title VII nutrition projects, an estimated 1,500 multipurpose
centers that receive funding under the Title V provisions of the Older
Americans Act, and a number of national organizations in the field of
aging that derive considerable support for their operations from grants
made by the AOA (U.S. Senate Special Committee on Aging, 1978).

Besides a commitment to the building of a network, Flemming also
brought to his position a strong commitment in the area of civil and
human rights. During most of his tenure as Commissioner, Dr. Flemming also served as the Chairman of the U.S. Civil Rights Commission,
a position that he still occupies. His commitment to and concern with
the needs of the minority aged were given great visibility during his
service as Commissioner on Aging.

Two particular strategies were followed by Flemming and the
AOA during this period of mid-1973 until Flemming's departure in
February 1978. No doubt there were other efforts in this area made by
the agency as well, but these stand out.

First, there is little question that the AOA has made a major effort
to assure that priority attention be given to the needs of the low-income
and minority group aged in the implementation of the various programs under the Older Americans Act, particularly the Title III state
and community service program and the Title VII nutrition program.
In the process, the AOA has defined the "minority" aged to include four
groups: Black, Spanish-speaking, Asian American, and native American.
These four groups make up the agency's major concerns with respect
to racial and ethnic groups in the population. For the moment at least
there is no comparable interest within AOA for more activity in the
examination of the socioeconomic situations of various white ethnic
older populations, their need for services, and for some priority attention. Three such groups whose needs might be important to explore
would be the Italian American elderly, the low-income Jewish elderly
urban population, and various of the Eastern European elderly.

A second strategy employed by AOA during this stage was to create
a coalition of national organizations that now represents the interests
of the various minority aged at the national level. The AOA supports
the work of four such organizations in substantial financial terms. For
instance, the National Center for the Black Aged, an offshoot of the

National Caucus of the Black Aged, was initially created in 1973 under an AOA model projects grant. The Center has subsequently become a national research and training center on the needs of the Black aged.

Similar model project grants led to the establishment of the Asociacion Nacional Pro Personas Mayores representing the Hispanic elderly in 1975, of the Pacific Asian Elderly Research Project with regard to the needs of the Asian American aged in 1976, and of the National Indian Council on Aging in 1977 (U.S. Senate Special Committee on Aging, 1978).

These organizations act as a coalition on the national policy scene in behalf of the minority aged. In a very short time, they have been able to develop specific data relative to the needs of the minority elderly, and also to become active in lobbying and social action efforts.

Each was active to some extent in the legislative hearings on the 1978 Older Americans Act legislation. This legislation, incidently, includes provisions that give emphasis to racial and ethnic factors in programs for older persons. As passed by the House of Representatives, H.R. 12255 would give a clear priority to the low-income elderly under a restructured Title III program that would consolidate the present state and area comprehensive services and planning, national nutrition program, and multipurpose center program into one title of the Act. The bill also would create a separate program of grants for social and nutritional services for individual Indian tribes, rather than have such programs operate through the usual state agency and area agency arrangements. A provision of the Model Project program part of the Act would give priority to projects designed to improve the delivery of services to "low-income, minority, Indian, and limited English-speaking individuals and the rural elderly." And, significantly, the bill would also authorize a study of racial and ethnic discrimination in any federally assisted programs and activities affecting older persons. This latter provision no doubt will involve a study by the U.S. Commission on Civil Rights that will be similar to a study recently completed by the Commission on age discrimination in various federally assisted programs under a 1973 Older Americans Act provision (U.S. Senate Special Committee on Aging, 1978).

Conclusion

One could speculate that the Administration on Aging might have adopted other strategies regarding minority and ethnic aged than those actually followed in recent years. Perhaps as an alternative to the creation of separate national organizations for the minority elderly, AOA might instead have built a program of public policy that would have directly involved the existing leadership structure of various minority and civil rights organizations. It is also conceivable that AOA might have utilized significant amounts of its discretionary project funds to establish national or regional centers on the Black elderly, the Hispanic elderly, and other groups at major universities throughout the nation. As another strategy, the AOA could have moved into a strong advocacy position and, through the use of its already existing authority, highlighted the serious needs of the minority elderly and called for new and major social policy initiatives and innovations by federal, state, and local governments, as well as a wide range of private organizations to improve the well-being of the minority aged. Such an effort would have emphasized the serious needs of the minority aged in such areas as income, health care, housing, employment, and social services.

Regardless of past strategies, one approach that AOA should now pursue is to expand the concern it has demonstrated toward the minority elderly to various of the white ethnic elderly. The Eastern European American elderly, the Italian American elderly, and the Jewish elderly are three groups in the older population whose present situation needs to be better understood in the development and provision of programs and services. In this writer's view a concern with these groups would be a useful point of departure for a broad concern with ethnicity in the administration of the various Older Americans Act programs.

It would seem important for AOA and other Federal agencies and departments to have information on the extent to which certain white ethnic elderly populations, for whom there may be serious questions of accessibility, are receiving services under such programs as Medicare, Medicaid, the Supplemental Security Income program (SSI), the Title XX social services program of the Social Security Act, and the various subsidized housing programs under the National Housing Act. It would be useful to know what, if any, obstacles to services under these and other programs are being experienced by the elderly of Eastern European, Italian, Jewish, and other ethnic backgrounds. To what extent, for example, has the SSI program reached the large European ethnic elderly population living in Baltimore, Chicago, Cleveland, Detroit, and New York City? To what extent is the elderly poor Jewish population located in Baltimore, Chicago, Los Angeles and New York City benefiting from SSI, Medicare, or Medicaid? To what extent are the various programs of the Older Americans Act reaching the large numbers of Italian American elderly living in urban areas in New York, New Jersey, and Pennsylvania? These and similar questions are legitimate and need to be investigated. The results of such studies should be acted upon in the future by those responsible for the planning of programs for older persons at the national, state, and community levels.

Another area where opportunities exist for the creation of a meaningful national agenda of concern with ethnicity and ethnic backgrounds is in the field of housing and community development. It should not take too much imagination to see the logical linkage between the needs of older persons in our large central cities and the present effort by the Department of Housing and Urban Development, under the leadership of Assistant Secretary Gino Baroni, to revitalize and retain the physical and social identity of urban neighborhoods. One aspect of this effort is the retention of the cultural and ethnic identities of such neighborhoods as a means of promoting the stability of the neighborhood, and of the city, as a social unit.

Finally, it is understood that the AOA will launch over the next year or so a major effort to build various advocacy assistance services into the present "aging network" of public and private organizations. The purpose of such an effort will be to help insure that older persons have both access and availability to the wide range of services that are offered under various public laws. As part of such a useful effort, organizations who work at the community levels, and who know the interests of various ethnic groups, should have a role in program formulation. White ethnic aged elderly should not be served by separate types of delivery systems; what is being proposed is that public and private organizations who provide services to the elderly do so in ways that respect and utilize, when feasible, the knowledge, the relationships, and possibly the facilities of organizations representing various ethnic groups to improve and enhance delivery of services to older persons.

References

Bechill, W., and Wolgamot, I. *Nutrition for the elderly: The AOA experience.* U.S. Department of Health, Education, and Welfare, Administration on Aging. Washington, D.C.: U.S. Government Printing Office, 1973.

Jackson, J. NCBA, Black Aged, and Politics. *The Annals,* September 1974, *415,* 138–159.

U.S. Congress, 92nd Session, Public Law 92–258. *National nutrition program for the elderly act,* 1972.

U.S. Congress, 93rd Session. *1973 comprehensive older Americans services act,* 1973.

U.S. Congress, 95th Session, U.S. Department of Health, Education, and Welfare, Administration on Aging. *Food and nutrition older Americans act projects—Title IV research and development.* Washington, D.C., July 1970.

U.S. Department of Health, Education, and Welfare. *1965 year of legislative achievements.* HEW, Office of the Secretary, Washington, D.C., 1966.
U.S. House of Representatives, 95th Congress. *H.R. 12255,* 1978.
U.S.Senate Special Committee on Aging. *Part I developments in aging: 1978.* U.S. Government Printing Office, Washington, D.C., 1978.
Wylie, M. *Research on human services and delivery systems.* Unpublished background paper prepared for the National Institute on Aging, 1976.

Part II
Ethnic Families and the Aged

In recent years, the family has been a focus of sociological study as well as of general mental health, social work, and medical practice. It is now also becoming a focus of gerontological study and professional practice among those serving the aged. Overall concern with the family during the last several decades by social scientists and helping professionals has been largely concerned with the evident problems of the family, particularly the high rate of dissolution and the impact this has on family members. Since most of the aged no longer live under the same roof as their married children, however, they have not been included in these studies.

Although the myth persists that these self-contained younger nuclear and older subnuclear families are typical of contemporary American society, empirical research has demolished this position, finding that these supposedly isolated entities are interrelated. This approach requires that we examine modified extended families rather than nuclear families. The discovery that adult children generally continue to assist their aged parents (and vice versa) after forming a new family-of-procreation, however, by no means resolves the issue of adequate provision for the aged, for at present millions of low-income and single-parent families cannot even provide adequately for their young children, much less for the greatly increased numbers of aged family members.

In addition, the needs of the economically and socially displaced elderly for subsistence and emotional support from relatives has increased despite growing extrafamilial assistance of various kinds, and it is clear to those aware of demographic trends that in the coming decades many families will have two generations of aged members to cope with—80- and 90-year-olds as well as 60- and 70-year-olds—along with a more than double burden of problems caused by the greater physical and mental debility of the very old.

Despite growing concern, our understanding of the ways in which families support their aged members and the role relationships involved is minimal. Once-popular notions such as the belief in "role reversal" have been largely discarded, but the actual relationships and forms of assistance between generations is still not well understood. It is therefore not suprising that the different ways in which families of ethnic groups view and treat their aged members has received practically no attention. The interrelationships within ethnic families is the focus of this section. While the chapters point out differences among ethnic groups, they also highlight similarities, chief among which is the generosity of the modified extended family whose adult members assist one another.

Cantor compares a large number of Black, white ethnic, and Spanish-speaking families as regards the interaction and mutual assistance between their aged and non-aged members. Her findings that white families have about the same levels of such interaction and assistance as Black ones should revise the prevailing underestimation of the strengths of the former and overestimation of the strengths of the latter. It also should help correct unfounded assumptions concerning the supposedly nuclear character of white families and extended character of Black ones, since both are found to be predominantly of the modified extended type. On the other hand, Spanish-speaking groups include a large proportion of extended families and have significantly higher levels of aged–non-aged interaction and assistance. Despite its methodological sophistication, Cantor's study does not touch on ethnic differences within the white population, as do Mostwin and Guttman in Part III.

Chapters 9, 10, and 11, on minority group families, come to many expected conclusions along with several problematical or novel findings. Maldonado stresses the well-known familism of Mexican Americans, although his view of the limited nature of their kin relationships conflicts with the generally accepted view of this group's still-prevailing traditional family, including even godparents. While he finds family structure changed, Maldonado also reports a continuing high level of respect and strong commitment to familial care for the aged, despite their decreasing functional importance within and outside the family. This suggests that support of aged relatives may be one positive component of the much-maligned "macho" role of the non-aged Mexican American male.

Block marshals the sparse available data in her discussion of native American elderly. In addition to documenting the disgraceful conditions and lack of services which characterize their existence, she cites evidence that separation from their ethnic group in nursing homes distant from their communities undermines the health and even hastens the death of aged American Indians.

The positive effects of participation in their ethnic group by the elderly is more clearly outlined by Montero's findings. His analysis of Japanese American aged is based on a national study. Only 1% of Montero's respondents report being lonely and very high stable rates of churchgoing and visiting by Japanese immigrants in their 70s and 80s contradicts the disengagement hypothesis.

Finally, Gelfand and Olsen examine and compare American Jews and Mormons, characterized as religio-ethnic groups, in their orientations toward their aged. The different approaches to what is appropriate care for the aged are shown to derive from the cultural traditions of these two groups. This analysis adds a dimension absent from the rest of Part II by reviewing the history of these groups as a means of gaining insight into their present orientations.

8

The Informal Support System of New York's Inner City Elderly: Is Ethnicity a Factor?

Marjorie H. Cantor

In planning services for the elderly as well as in studying the aging process, there has been a tendency to view older people as a homogeneous group set off from the rest of society by virtue of a single determinant—age. But elderly people do not, upon reaching 65, shed their identity as members of racial, ethnic, or socioeconomic subgroups. Rather, it may well be that subgroup membership as such is the crucial factor conditioning how people grow old, socially, psychologically, and even physically.

At the present time the population of New York City is made up of three dominant ethnic subgroups: white, Black and Spanish-speaking (principally though not exclusively Puerto Rican). Unquestionably, important socioeconomic variations exist within each subgroup, but certain conditions of status, culture, and history have tended to distinguish white, Black and Hispanic New Yorkers from one another.

Therefore in 1970 when the Department for the Aging undertook its comprehensive study *The Elderly in the Inner City* (Cantor, 1973), race, ethnicity, and socioeconomic status were conceptualized as key variables in the attempt to understand the life of New York's older

Data reported herein are from the New York City Department for the Aging study *The Elderly in the Inner City* (Marjorie H. Cantor, Principal Investigator). This research was supported by a grant from the Administration on Aging, No. AA-4-70-089-02.

residents. The findings to be presented in this chapter are from this study and concern subgroup analysis in one important area of the lives of the elderly—the informal social support system, particularly the family.

Study Hypotheses Relating to Ethnicity

Among the several hypotheses of *The Elderly in the Inner City* study were the following pertaining to the issue of ethnicity and aging:

1. Due to effects of discrimination and minority group status, Black and Spanish-speaking elderly enter the period of old age with greater social, economic, and physical deficits than do their white elderly peers. As a result their needs for community services in the areas of income maintenance, health, and housing will be greater than among white elderly.

2. However, the cultural patterns of the Black and Hispanic communities, particularly the extended or augmented family structure and value system, tend to mitigate role loss and social isolation. Thus, Black and Spanish-speaking elderly will be more likely than whites to possess an informal social support system of greater magnitude offering more concrete support.

The increased jeopardy of older inner city Blacks and Hispanics in the areas of income, housing, and health has been documented by research findings from *The Elderly in the Inner City of New York* as well as by other researchers (Cantor, 1976b; Cantor and Mayer, 1975; Kent and Hirsch, 1971–1972; Dowd & Bengtson, 1978).

Our focus here is on the second hypothesis regarding the greater viability of the informal support network of Black and Spanish-speaking elderly. Before presenting the findings in the area of informal supports, a brief overview of the study sample and methodology might be helpful.

The Study Sample and Its Characteristics

The universe for the study *The Elderly in the Inner City* included all persons 60 years and over living in the inner city of New York. Unlike other central cities, New York's inner city is not an easily identifiable core area of decay surrounded by concentric circles of newer communities to which the more affluent have fled. On the contrary, each of the five boroughs has its own blighted areas interspersed amidst middle- or upper-class neighborhoods. The inner city of New York was therefore defined for study purposes operationally rather than geographically as the 26 areas of the city having the highest incidence of crime, infant mortality, welfare case load, deteriorated housing, and environmental decline. These conditions clearly duplicate those found in the inner or central cities of other urban areas in the United States.

The inner city was purposely chosen as the focus for the study because of its heavy concentration of low-income elderly considered most in need of services and because virtually all of the Black and Hispanic elderly live in inner city neighborhoods. It was thereby possible to insure sufficient minority group representation in order to make meaningful cross-ethnic comparisons.

A replicated probability sample was employed, embodying five randomly selected, stratified, interpenetrating matched samples. Through a two-step enumeration process, 2,180 households were identified as having one or more older persons. Six call-backs ultimately yielded 1,552 interviews, a completion rate of 71%. The final sample 1,552 respondents proved to be highly representative of the approximately 400,000 older persons living in the inner city neighborhoods in 1970, the time of interviewing.

Interviews conducted in the home covered most aspects of an older person's life as well as standard measures of morale, anomie, and functional ability utilized with other elderly populations here and abroad. Space precludes a full discussion of the sample characteristics (see Table 8-1), but a few important points need to be made. The inner city elderly of New York are principally a low income, urban population; 49% of the sample were white (N=767), 37% Black (N=580), and 13% Spanish-speaking (N=205), principally of Puerto Rican origin.

Among the white elderly population (N=767), slightly less than one-half (47%) were born in the United States. Of those born overseas, Eastern Europe is most strongly represented (18%), followed by Italy (13%), other parts of Western Europe (9%), Great Britain and Ireland (6%), Asia (2%), and Greece, Turkey, and Cyprus (2%). Of additional note, moreover, is the fact that approximately 41% of the *parents* of the total elderly sample population were themselves born in the United States. Thus, over 40% of the elderly in the inner city are second-generation Americans.

The vast majority of the study population, 91%, said that they lived in their own households; 39% were found to be living alone. Although there was considerable occupational and class spread in the total sample, particularly among the white respondents, the vast majority were classified in the two lowest categories of the Hollingshead Index of Social Position and during their working years were involved in skilled or semi-skilled occupations. At the time of interview, most were retired

Table 8–1. Major Demographic Characteristics of Inner City Elderly Respondents

	Percent			
	Total	White	Black	Spanish
Age				
60–64	22.0	15.2	26.2	35.8
65–69	28.2	25.1	31.8	30.0
70–74	22.1	22.3	23.5	17.2
75+	27.2	36.9	17.9	17.0
Sex				
Male	41.0	45.2	35.2	41.9
Female	59.0	54.8	64.8	58.1
Ethnicity				
White	49.4	49.4		
Black	37.4		37.4	
Spanish	13.2			13.2
Religious affiliation				
Protestant	43.5	18.3	86.0	17.4
Catholic	35.3	43.2	9.6	78.7
Jewish	14.9	29.5	0.8	0.4
Socioeconomic status				
Hollinghead's ISP (IV and V: working and lower class)	74.7	63.8	85.3	85.3
Income: under $2,500/yr. (est. per capita)	63.8	55.6	71.3	73.6
Occupation: manual	67.6	57.3	79.4	72.4
Education: 8th grade or less	59.9	50.1	65.3	80.4
Marital status				
Married	34.3	35.9	29.3	42.6
Widowed	42.0	39.9	45.2	41.1
Never married	13.4	17.3	10.8	6.1
Separated or divorced	10.3	6.8	14.8	10.3
Living arrangements				
Live alone	39.2	47.4	33.1	26.2
Live with spouse	33.4	34.7	29.0	41.0
Live with others (not spouse)	27.4	17.9	37.9	32.8
Health				
Have health problem(s)	67.3	62.8	72.1	70.6
Self-perceived health as poor	23.8	20.6	25.2	31.4
Incapacity-Index: severely impaired or incapacitated	15.4	13.6	15.5	22.2
Nativity				
Born on U.S. mainland	53.3	46.5	80.2	3.4
Total respondents	(1,552)	(767)	(580)	(205)

and lived on incomes significantly below city-wide levels for all elderly and far below an adequate income standard for a city with high costs.

The majority of the sample reported frequent face-to-face and telephone contacts with their children, who gave as well as received assistance. Where children were not available, neighbors, young as well as old, acted as substitutes for absent primary social supports. Most inner city elderly have a primary support system made up of family and neighbors. But 8% of the sample (or approximately 86,000 older persons in the inner city) appeared to have no informal support system and were entirely on their own. Some few of these were in touch with community or religious institutions but the absence of any significant others suggests that they were likely to be among the true isolates.

The Concept of a Social Support System

In urban industrial society, the support system of the elderly increasingly involves an amalgam of informal services provided by family, friends, and neighbors and formal services offered by large organizations, both governmental and voluntary. As Litwak has noted (1965, 1976), kinship structures have gradually evolved from the traditional extended family to the modified extended family in which a coalition of separately housed, semi-autonomous nuclear families operates in a state of partial dependency with shared family functions. Accompanying this evolution in family structure has been a shift in the nature of the role of family and society with respect to the elderly. Thus, today the United States government provides the floor of basic services for older people in such crucial areas as income maintenance, housing, health, safety, and transportation. But the family and significant others retain considerable importance in meeting the more idiosyncratic social support needs of the individual.

A social support system can be broadly defined as encompassing those informal and formal activities as well as personal support services required by the elderly in order to remain independently in the community. Such a support system, including both its informal and formal components, is seen as enabling an older person to fulfill three major personal needs: opportunities for socialization, the carrying out of the tasks of daily living, and the provision of personal assistance during times of illness or crisis. The informal support system is distinguishable from the formal or organizational component by virtue of its individualistic and nonbureaucratic nature and by the fact that members of the informal network are selected by the elderly principally from among kin, friends, or neighbors.

Three levels of the informal personal support system of older people can be identified, kin, close friends or intimates, and neighbors, each with a complementary role to play. These three levels comprise six separate elements: four are part of the kinship structure—spouse, child, sibling, and other relatives; and two, friends and neighbors, involve unrelated individuals usually living in geographic proximity to the elderly inner city New Yorkers. The emphasis here is on the family, particularly children, and on the extent and type of relationship that occurs between older people and their kin.

Gibson (1972), in an article critical of the current positive claims about the viability of the kinship structure, suggests the need to delineate and empirically examine the following relevant subdimensions of family interaction: the availability of kin, the proximity of kin, the frequency of kin contact, and the functionality of kin. He notes that the availability of kin is of particular importance since the traditional measures of kin interaction, *viz.* proximity, frequency of contacts, etc., usually fail to take into account the pool of relatives actually available for interaction.

Because our basic concern is to determine the extent to which older people in the inner city receive meaningful support from those around them, merely having a living child or friend does not seem in and of itself to be enough. Is that support element really functional or operable? Or to put it another way, does the respondent in fact have a steady and ongoing relationship with significant others that renders meaningful social support even a possibility? To address this issue the concept of functional support is herein proposed to be operationalized in our research as follows: a functional spouse is defined as one with whom one lives; a functional child, sibling, or friend is someone whom the respondent sees at least monthly or is in phone contact with at least weekly; functional relatives are those living within the confines of the city who are seen or heard from regularly; and functional neighbors are those persons in the immediate neighborhood whom the respondents know well and who help out respondents either a great deal of the time or at least in emergencies.[1]

Naturally, these stricter definitions with the emphasis on availability and ongoing interaction reduce the number of children, friends, and neighbors in an older person's informal support network. Nevertheless, they sharpen the focus of the analysis to include only persons in a position to offer meaningful support to the respondents both in times

1. The conceptual definition of a functional member of the social support system refers to a person upon whom one can depend in times of need. Thus, a person with whom one lives, e.g., spouse, child, or even sibling, most likely fits this definition and is therefore subsumed under the concept of functionality.

of crisis and on an ongoing basis. In the findings which follow, the concept of functionality will be employed.

Data Analysis: Methodology

The focus of this chapter is the relationship of ethnicity to the likelihood of an older inner city New Yorker having an informal support system and to the nature of the helping relationships. A series of multiple regressions was therefore performed. This technique was chosen because it allows an evaluation of both the independent effect of ethnicity and the relative importance of ethnicity as a predictive factor while simultaneously controlling for the effects of other significant independent variables such as sex, social class, health. In essence the questions addressed can be stated as follows: Are Black and Hispanic elderly, simply by virtue of their ethnic identification, more likely than white elderly to have a support system? Furthermore, are there differences in the nature and level of interaction between the elderly and their support network, particularly children, which can be ascribed principally to ethnicity or are other variables, such as social class, perhaps the overriding and more strongly determining factors?

The distinction between ethnicity and social class is purposely emphasized because the study findings indicate that these emerge as the principal differentiating determinants with respect to the informal support system of older New Yorkers.

Independent and Criterion Variables

Based upon previous knowledge of the data, six independent variables were selected as having potential influence on the extent and nature of the informal support system of the elderly. The six variables encompassed four major domains: ethnicity, sex, socioeconomic position, and health status. Race/ethnicity was accounted for by two variables, Black and Hispanic, with white utilized throughout as the constant reference group. Socioeconomic status was measured first by the Hollingshead two-factor Index of Social Position (ISP) and second by a measure of current income.[2] With respect to sex, a value of 1 was assigned to females, 0 to males. The final independent variable, health status, was

2. Hollingshead's two factors include occupation at age 50 and education, while the current income was determined on a per capita basis by dividing the amount of household income by the size of the household. Five ordinal categories of ISP were arrived at (5, 4, 3, 2, 1), with 5 representing the lowest position on the continuum. Income categories were: under $1,500, $1,500–2,499, $2,500–4,499, $4,500 and over. Values range from 1 to 4 with 1 being the lowest level.

represented by the Townsend Index of Functional Ability in which higher scores indicate greater impairment and more restricted ability to carry out functions of daily living.

In the regression equations, ethnicity was purposely entered as two dummy variables rather than as a single variable in order to make possible the analysis of similarities and differences among the three dominant ethnic groups in the inner city, white, Black, and Hispanic. In addition this two-variable method provides a more conservative measure of significance than if ethnicity had been combined into a single variable.

A series of criterion variables was selected to describe the extent and operation of the informal support system. Examples of such measures are the likelihood of living with spouse, total number of functional relatives, total number of functional children, frequency of seeing child, amount of help parent gives child, types of help given by parents to children and by children to parents. (Criterion variables used in the analysis are displayed in Tables 8-2 through 8-7.)

Again, although these separate variables could perhaps have been combined into single measures of the extent of the informal support system and the degree of interaction between the elderly and the various support components, a fuller picture is derived by keeping them separate. Use of a composite index too frequently obfuscates important relationships, although it could increase somewhat the amount of variance shown.

Findings

The Functional Elements of the Family Network

A closer examination of the operation of ethnicity with respect to the informal kinship network requires looking separately at each of the potential functional elements—spouse, children, siblings, and other relatives—in terms of level of interaction and the division of functional tasks, particularly between children and their older parents (see Table 8-2).

Spouse. Only one-third of the inner city elderly sample still have a living spouse. On first glance it appears that the Hispanic elderly are the most likely of the three groups still to be living with a spouse, and this greater tendency among the Spanish-speaking elderly still to have a spouse persists when the effects of the relevant independent variables of sex and class are controlled for. However, because the Hispanic are the youngest of the three groups studied, it is important to control for age as well. When age is entered into the regression equation, the

Table 8–2. Respondents Having Each Type of Functional Social
Network Component, by Ethnicity

Functional Component	Percent			
	White (N = 767)	Black (N = 580)	Spanish (N = 205)	Total (N = 1,552)
Spouse	34.7	29.0	41.0	33.3
Child	54.0	53.2	72.5	56.1
Sibling or relative	56.2	57.6	43.8	55.1
Friends and/or neighbors	54.2	59.1	47.5	55.1
None	6.6	4.3	4.6	5.4

significance of ethnicity as a predictive factor disappears, leaving as the contributors to the likelihood of still having a spouse in the house, in order of importance, sex, age, social class, current income, and level of functional ability (See Table 8-3). In fact, as one would expect, those elderly who are younger, male, of higher social class, and with greater functional ability are most likely still to be living with spouse regardless of their race or ethnicity.

Children. Children are certainly next in importance to any informal support system of an older person, both in terms of the potential for psychological support and concrete assistance in tasks of day-to-day living. Spanish-speaking elderly as a group are the most likely to have children with whom they are in ongoing contact. Seventy-three percent of the Hispanic respondents had at least one functional child, while among both Black and white respondents only slightly over half had at least one functional child (see Table 8-2). It is possible, however that the introduction of other key independent variables such as sex, socioeconomic status, or functional ability may eliminate this seeming advantage of the Spanish-speaking elderly.

A series of multiple regressions in which the six key independent variables were regressed upon the eight child-oriented criterion variables of the study indicates that this is not so. Thus, as can be seen by the Betas in Table 8-4, even after controlling for sex, social class, income, and level of functional ability, the Hispanic elderly consistently have a greater potential for support from children than whites or Blacks. Moreover, they have a higher level of interaction with their children.[3]

3. Although this closeness may be somewhat related to the Spanish having *more* functional children, the fact remains that they do have a higher potential for social support and a higher level of interrelatedness. Spanish and Black elderly are significantly more likely than whites to have a child in the household, but all three groups have a similar proportion of other children living within walking distance (13% white, 11% Black, and 12% Spanish).

Table 8-3. Multiple Regression Analysis of the Existence of Interaction with Spouse and with Other Relatives (Standardized Partial Regression Coefficients and Zero-Order Correlations)

Independent Variables	Likelihood of Living with Spouse[a]				Other Relatives[a]			
	Age not Included in Regression Equation		Age Included in Regression Equation		Total Number of Functional Relatives[b]		Likelihood of Having at Least One Functional Relative	
	Beta	r	Beta	r	Beta	r	Beta	r
Black	.010	-.053	-.028	-.053	.001	.001	.056[c]	.055
Spanish	.056[c]	.039	.021	.039	-.006	-.011	-.015	-.038
Sex (female)	-.358[d]	-.368[d]	-.377[d]	-.368[d]	.029	.026	.045	.047
ISP	-.105[d]	-.092[d]	-.122[d]	-.092[d]	.005	-.012	.001	-.014
Current income	-.044	.053	-.084[d]	.053	.062[c]	.050	.102[d]	.077[c]
Level of functional ability	-.102	-.157[d]	-.056[c]	-.156[d]	.033	.025	.070[d]	.053
Age	—	—	-.182[d]	-.151[d]				
Multiple R	.384		.429		.069		.132	
Multiple R^2	.147		.184		.005		.017	

[a]N = Total sample
[b]Functional relative = relative in New York City seen or heard from regularly
[c]$p \leq .05$ level
[d]$p \leq .01$ level

Table 8-4. Multiple Regression Analysis of the Existence and Degree of Interaction with Children (Standardized Partial Regression Coefficients and Zero-Order Correlations)

Independent Variables	Existence of Interaction[a]				Degree of Interaction[b]							
	Total No. of Functional Children Seen[c]		Likelihood of Having at Least One Functional Child		Frequency of Seeing Children		Frequency of Being in Phone Contact		Closeness to Children		Desire to See Children More Often	
	Beta	r	Beta	r	Beta	r	Beta	r	Beta	r	Beta	r
Black	−.022	−.036	.006	−.027	.026	.006	−.034	.020	.001	.021	−.070[d]	−.094[e]
Spanish	.129[e]	.151[e]	.108[e]	.114[e]	.160[e]	.179[e]	.012	.039	.169[e]	.195[e]	.077[d]	.109[e]
Sex (female)	.014	.020	.052[d]	.071	−.024	−.022	.029	.028	−.005	−.004	.000	.018
ISP	.075[e]	.103[e]	−.058[d]	−.003	.165[e]	.194[e]	.092[e]	.089[e]	.145[e]	.180[e]	−.022	.009
Current income	−.048	−.091[e]	−.106[e]	−.115[e]	.006	−.076[d]	−.007	−.043	−.034	−.021	−.064	−.077[d]
Level of functional ability	.013	.043	.032	.066	−.012	.015	−.016	.003	−.059	−.017	−.055	.072[d]
Multiple R	.182		.174		.246		.102		.253		.154	
Multiple R²	.033		.030		.061		.011		.064		.024	

[a]N = Total sample
[b]N = Those respondents having one or more child
[c]Functional children = children seen at least monthly or in phone contact with at least weekly
[d]p ≤ .05 level
[e]p ≤ .01 level

Thus, Spanish-speaking elderly have more functional children and are more likely to have at least one functional child (see Table 8-4). They not only see their children more often and receive more help from them, but also give more help in return (see Table 8-5). When asked to evaluate the degree of closeness to children and the desire for increased contact, it is the Spanish who report a significantly greater sense of closeness with children and would, if given a chance, prefer even more contact with their offspring. Only in the area of frequency of phone contact with children does being Spanish fail to make a unique contribution; but since more Hispanic elderly live with or near children this finding is not surprising. It should be noted that in all cases in which being Hispanic makes a significant contribution to the amount of variance, the significance is at the $p<.01$ level.

These findings appear to substantiate the hypothesis regarding the positive effects on the informal support network of still being part of an extended family culture. What is somewhat surprising, however, given the evidence of an extensive system of mutual interdependency between generations in the Black community (Cantor, Rosenthal, and Wilker, 1975; Stack, 1974), is the absence of similar findings with respect to elderly Blacks in the sample. The regression results (Table 8-4) suggest no substantial difference between Blacks and whites with respect to the number of functional children, the likelihood of having at least one functional child, the frequency of seeing and phoning children, the amount of help received from children, or feelings of closeness to children. However, Black and Spanish elderly both tend to give a greater amount of help to their children than do whites (Table 8-5), probably a correlate of greater need on the part of offspring. This greater sharing of more limited economic and social resources on the part of Hispanic and Black elderly suggests a positively adaptive method of meeting the pressures of poverty and unemployment within a functional family system.

In addition to ethnicity as a predictive factor governing parent–child relationships, the independent contribution made by the social-class position of the respondent should be noted.[4] The lower the social class position and/or current income, the greater the extent of supportive relationships between parents and children, while the higher the

4. In the study *The Elderly in the Inner City,* respondents were asked questions pertaining to both social class (as defined by Hollingshead's two-factor ISP) and current income. Social class is seen as having long-range determinants while current income involves the actual amount of money the older person has to live on at the current time. Although in younger populations class and income tend to be highly correlated, this is not necessarily so in older age. In the present study ($N=1,552$) the correlation coefficient of class and income was only .33. However, since both measures address the issue of socioeconomic status, they have been dealt with together in the discussion of the findings.

Table 8–5. Multiple Regression Analysis of Flow of Assistance from Parents to Children (Standardized Partial Regression Coefficients and Zero-Order Correlations)

Dependent Variables	Total Amount of Help Given		Help When Ill		Help with Chores of Daily Living		Giving Advice		Giving Gifts	
	Beta	r	Beta	r	Beta	r	Beta	r	Beta	r
Black	.130[b]	.078[a]	.005	-.010	.059	.052	.124[b]	.053[a]	-.035	-.042
Spanish	.170[b]	.109[b]	.048	.026	.062	.039	.213[b]	.165[b]	-.076[a]	-.118[b]
Sex (female)	.015	.018	.063[a]	.020	.068[a]	.038	-.025	-.038	-.051	-.108[b]
ISP	.020	.023	.006	-.027	.055	.050	.059	.073[a]	-.113[b]	-.199[b]
Current income	.085[a]	.078[a]	.044	.074[a]	.012	.013	.121[b]	.064[a]	.103[b]	.219[b]
Level of functional ability	-.152[b]	-.154[b]	-.209[b]	-.204[b]	-.189[b]	-.159[b]	-.009	-.019	-.206[b]	-.260[b]
Multiple R	.242		.367		.207		.237		.338	
Multiple R²	.059		.134		.043		.056		.115	

[a] $p \leqslant .05$ level
[b] $p \leqslant .01$ level

socioeconomic indicators the less involved the relationship. Thus, ISP, either separately or together with income, makes a difference with respect to the total number of functioning children, as well as to the likelihood of having at least one such child.

Socioeconomic status factors also affect the frequency of interaction and the amount of help given and received, although interestingly enough neither class nor income influences parents' desire to see children more often (see Table 8-4). It would appear that as social class rises, nuclear families in a kinship network maintain a greater distance between themselves, and that elderly parents are less intensely involved on a day-to-day basis with their adult children. But, as will be seen when the various types of help given are examined, higher socioeconomic status elderly are not forsaken by children. Rather it appears that assistance and intervention is considered appropriate and is in fact given in time of crisis, but socialization with peers, rather than with children, is expected to fill the void of intensive parent–child interaction.

Siblings and other relatives.   Because of increased age and greater likelihood of geographic dispersion, siblings and other relatives are probably a less important source of concrete assistance in the tasks of daily living than spouse or children. Nevertheless, they can play a psychologically supportive role in the informal support system of the elderly.

Two-thirds of the respondents report having one or more living siblings; there is no significant difference ethnically in the likelihood of having at least one living sibling. But the less important role of siblings in the support network of the inner city elderly is suggested by the fact that only 37% of all living siblings reside in New York City and are in regular enough contact to be considered functional. Spanish are over half again as likely as white or Black elderly to have a sibling nearby (see Table 8-6).

With respect to both the likelihood of having a functional sibling and the level of interaction with a functional sibling, ethnicity contributed independently to the amount of variance only in the case of the Spanish-speaking elderly. They were found to be significantly less likely to have functional siblings and to interact less frequently with their siblings than either whites or Blacks (Table 8-6). However, the factor that appears to make more difference in relation to ongoing relationships with siblings is income. (Beta is .129 in case of total number of functional siblings, .142 with respect to frequency of seeing, and .115 for phoning, all significant at the $p<.01$ level.) The higher the income, the greater the likelihood of having a functional sibling and the greater the frequency of seeing and phoning a brother or sister. Women are also significantly more likely to maintain a relationship with a sibling

Table 8-6. Multiple Regression Analysis of the Existence and the Degree of Interaction with Siblings (Standardized Partial Regression Coefficients and Zero-Order Correlations)

Independent Variables	Existence of Interaction[a] Likelihood of Having at Least One Functional Sibling[c]		Degree of Interaction[b] Frequency of Seeing Siblings		Frequency of Phoning Siblings	
	Beta	r	Beta	r	Beta	r
Black	-.001	.011	.014	.025	.026	.036
Spanish	-.060[d]	-.081[e]	-.081[e]	-.113[e]	-.139[e]	-.182[e]
Sex (female)	.099[e]	.074[d]	.123[e]	.093[e]	.131[e]	.101[e]
ISP	-.013	-.067[d]	-.036	-.095[e]	-.111[e]	-.168[e]
Current income	.129[e]	.138[e]	.142[e]	.153[e]	.115[e]	.162[e]
Level of functional ability	-.050	-.068[d]	-.048	-.068[d]	-.065[d]	.093[e]
Multiple R	.185		.222		.288	
Multiple R^2	.034		.049		.082	

[a] N = Total sample
[b] N = Those respondents who have a sibling
[c] Functional sibling = sibling seen at least monthly or in phone contact with at least weekly
[d] $p \leq .05$ level
[e] $p \leq .01$ level

than men, a finding not surprising when one considers the central role in maintaining family relationships assumed by so many inner city elderly women, both Black and Spanish.

With respect to relatives other than spouse, children, or sibling, only 42% of the sample had one or more such functional relatives. If respondents did have a functional relative they rarely had more than two.

There was no significant difference among ethnic groups with regard to the total number of relatives with whom respondents maintained a functional relationship (see Table 8-3). Blacks, however, were more likely than either Hispanics or whites to have at least one functional relative (Beta is .056, $p<.05$ level). In addition, the level of functional ability provides a significant independent contribution to the variable. Thus, the more functionally able and mobile an older person, the more likely he or she is to keep up with at least one other relative (Beta is .07, $p<.01$ level). Again, however, the preeminent predictor variable is one of socioeconomic status: the higher the income, the greater the number of functional relatives and the higher the level of interaction.

Several times in this discussion the importance of social class, either alone or in conjunction with ethnicity, as a determinant of the nature of the familial support system of the elderly has been seen. These findings reinforce the notion that the measures of socioeconomic status are the more stable and overriding predictors of both the span or comprehensiveness of the social support system of an older person and the number of distinct functional components in that system. On the other hand, however, there is a negative relationship between class and the number of and the level of interaction with functional children. Thus, the crucial issue for older people at the upper end of the income and class continuum is whether having more potential support elements (who are not children) to draw upon can compensate for the decreased likelihood of support from and constant interaction with children.

Patterns of Assistance between Children and Parents

There are several types of mutual assistance that occur within the family network and the role ethnicity plays in the patterning of relationships. Our data mainly concern children and parents because, as noted, it is children rather than siblings or other relatives who are the basic ingredient of familial support; neighbors and friends appear to be the other significant support element when the informal support network is looked at in its totality.

Mutual assistance between parents and children. Respondents are given a list of common types of assistance and asked which they performed for their children and which their children did for them, and the frequency of assistance given. Ten types of assistance from parent to child were listed and 11 types from child to parent. Based on these, the following four broad categories of help were established:

1. Crisis interaction—help during illness
2. Assistance with chores of daily living—baby-sitting, shopping, keeping house, fixing things in the house, meal preparation, chauffering, and taking on vacation
3. Advice giving—child-rearing, home management, major purchases, jobs, business and money matters
4. Gift giving—monetary and nonmonetary presents

Before going into the details of the assistance provided by children to elderly parents and whether or not the hypothesis regarding greater support in the case of Hispanic and Black elderly is substantiated, it is important to note the tendency when considering intergenerational assistance to think of older people primarily as recipients of aid. This is far from the case. On the contrary, our data underscore the reciprocal nature of the relationship between the two generations. For example, three-fourths of the inner city elderly who had at least one child reported helping children in some manner. The most frequently reported form of assistance to children was gift giving (67%), but older parents also often helped in crisis intervention during times of illness (51%), with helping in chores of daily living and giving advice less common.

To what extent does ethnicity contribute to this picture of parent-to-child assistance? When the six independent variables (Spanish, Black, female, ISP, current income and functional ability) were regressed upon the total amount of help and the specific types of help, it appeared that ethnicity does contribute significantly to the total amount of help given by parents and is important with respect to two of the four types of help (see Table 8-5). Both Black and Hispanic elderly are more likely to be involved in the lives of their children than are the white elderly. This higher level of total assistance probably reflects both the greater presence of the extended family in the Hispanic community and the greater need among low-income minority groups for intergenerational assistance as a means of offsetting the effects of poverty and discrimination.

An examination of the standardized partial regression coefficients of the six independent variables shows that both income and functional ability are also determinants of the total amount of help given by parents to children. Thus, elderly who are functionally impaired give less help, while the higher the income level, the greater the likelihood that parents will give help, particularly in the form of gifts.

Although the total amount of parental help is affected by ethnicity in the case of Spanish-speaking and Black elderly, with regard to the specific forms of assistance ethnicity is important in only two areas: giving advice, a greater likelihood in the case of both Black and Spanish; and giving gifts, least likely among Hispanic elderly—the poorest of the three groups. Ethnicity, however, does not significantly affect the likelihood that parents assist in chores of daily living or crisis intervention when someone is ill. With respect to assistance in these two important areas, white elderly are found to be as likely to help children when needed as are Spanish-speaking or Black elderly.

Children to parents. While the level of assistance from parents to children is high, the reverse flow is even higher. In this study 87% of the respondents reported receiving help from their children.

Gift giving again ranks first (82%), followed by help in times of illness (66%). Assistance with chores of daily living is given somewhat less frequently, and the proportions of children involved range from 50% in the case of shopping to around 20% in meal preparation or housekeeping. Advice giving is the least frequently reported form of assistance from children to parents, just as it was in the case of parents to children. Ours is a society that stresses independence, and there appears to be a growing tendency for the various units of even extended family networks to reserve decision making for themselves except in the cases of major economic matters.

We now come to the crux of our inquiry regarding the role of ethnicity in the support system of the elderly. As hypothesized, do Black and Hispanic elderly receive more help from children and in a greater variety of areas than their white peers? Our analysis indicates that ethnicity is indeed a significant determinant in the case of the Hispanic elderly, but being white or Black is not significantly related to the level of help received from children or to the forms the help takes (see Table 8-7). Being Spanish is also a nearly consistent predictor with respect to the types of help—including the greater likelihood of receiving gifts (including money) from children, help with chores of daily living, and assistance when ill. These findings are consistent with the data that Spanish elderly have more functional children and interact more frequently in person with their children.

However, although being Hispanic is likely to increase the chances of receiving help from children, the parent's functional ability, sex, current income, and social class position are, if anything, even more important determinants of amount and patterns of help. Thus, if an older person is ill, he or she is far more likely to receive assistance, regardless of ethnic background, while there is a negative relationship between income and class factors and the amount of help received. Elderly from working-class backgrounds and those with limited incomes are more likely to receive assistance from children than are those

Table 8–7. Multiple Regression Analysis of Flow of Assistance from Children to Parents (Standardized Partial Regression Coefficients and Zero-Order Correlations)

Dependent Variables	Total Amount of Help Given		Help When Ill		Help with Chores of Daily Living		Giving Advice		Giving Gifts		Ratio of Total Help Child to Parent to Total Help Parent to Child	
	Beta	r	Beta	r	Beta	r	Beta	r	Beta	r	Beta	r
Black	.049	.043	-.007	-.005	.056	.057	.011	-.001	.053	.033	-.038	-.022
Spanish	.102b	.132b	.073a	.115b	.077a	.108b	.061	.069a	.131b	.140b	.002	.064a
Sex (female)	.086b	.135b	.062a	.101b	.054	.109b	.047	.058	.144b	.168b	.036	.110b
ISP	.085b	.173b	.095b	.154b	.084a	.176b	.018	.047	.054	.120b	.033	.116b
Current income	-.107b	-.210b	-.070a	-.164b	-.117b	-.217b	-.032	-.064a	-.067	-.146b	-.129b	-.222b
Level of functional ability	.155b	.215b	.147b	.193b	.181b	.235b	.026	.049	.048	.106b	.313b	.355b
Multiple R	.313		.263		.316		.106		.256		.385	
Multiple R²	.098		.069		.100		.011		.066		.148	

a $p \leq .05$ level
b $p \leq .01$ level

171

with higher socioeconomic status. This inverse relationship between income/class and help holds true even in the case of assistance when ill and help with the chores of daily living—two vital types of informal support. We do not know whether the decreased likelihood of assistance on the part of children as socioeconomic status increases is a response to the greater financial ability of the parent to provide for his own needs or whether it reflects the greater geographic and psychological distance often associated with upward mobility and higher social status. It should be noted that many of the white elderly in the inner city came from immigrant backgrounds, so that social distance between them and upwardly mobile children is undoubtedly present in many cases.

Implications

What does this all mean in the case of the elderly? First, it is obvious that many myths or stereotypes regarding the role of ethnicity are unfounded. Certainly we cannot smugly assume that although minority group elderly may suffer social deficits of income, health, and housing, they are nonetheless in a stronger position than the white elderly with respect to assistance from family and other kin. Although the Hispanic elderly, at this time at least, are significantly more likely to have functional children with whom they interact more frequently and from whom they receive a greater amount and variety of help, it is impossible to predict how long this will last. From other data in our study and from practical experience in the Hispanic community, it appears that the impact of the dominant culture on Hispanics is considerable and that the role of the family may be in jeopardy. And, as we have seen, the hypothesis with regard to the Black elderly having greater potential for support from kin does not appear to be verified. Thus, it is likely that since even now socioeconomic status and health appear to be the more powerful underlying and long-range determinants of aid from children to parents, it may well be that in the future ethnicity as such will diminish in importance as an independently significant predictor of informal social support. Nevertheless, it is possible that the family-oriented value system of the Hispanics will survive despite the acculturation process.

On the other hand, it is apparent that white elderly New Yorkers, the majority of older people now and for sometime to come, have not been forsaken by their children. Even middle- and upper-class white elderly receive assistance from children, particularly when their physical conditions deteriorate. Furthermore, white parents report feeling as close to their children as do Black elderly who, in turn, are more likely to live within close geographic proximity of their children.

Furthermore, there is the crucial role of class with respect to the nature and structuring of the informal support system. Black, Spanish-speaking, and other poor and working-class families are more likely to have highly developed patterns of child–parent interaction arising out of economic and social necessity than is the case among the more well-to-do elderly. Thus, children of the lower socioeconomic groups can be characterized as potentially more ever-present and involved in a sustained manner in the lives of their parents. But the question must be raised as to the duration and extent of the supportive role they can maintain, given their own economic pressures. To what extent and in what manner should society assist such families in the maintenance of viable kinship networks with mutual assistance between genera-tions?

And what about older people from the middle and upper strata? As class and current income rise, the spread of the social support system increases. Such older people, if they are still mobile, are more likely to continue functional interactions with siblings, other relatives, friends, and neighbors. However, the role of children seems to undergo a change as class rises. Although children are still involved during crisis and illness and provide parents with gifts and financial assistance, the closer, more frequent interaction characteristic of lower socioeconomic groups diminishes. This puts a greater burden on elderly parents to find other sources of ongoing socialization and daily emotional sustenance. If elderly from middle-class backgrounds are fortunate enough to have a circle of friends or are comfortable in group activities, these may compensate. But for those no longer able to get around easily, social isolation and inability to obtain assistance in chores of daily living may become a real problem. In addition, we must remember that many elderly who are characterized as middle-class based on education and occupation at age 50 and who carry with them middle-class values regarding independence and self-sufficiency are the very group found living at incomes just slightly above the poverty level and who are therefore ineligible for many services. The community must find a way to help such older people compensate for the absence of functional kin and for the consequent dearth of social interaction.

Above all, the varied and sometimes almost contradictory data presented here with respect to the roles of ethnicity and social class in the informal support systems suggest that there are no easy answers or pat generalizations that apply to entire groups of older people. This must be kept in mind especially in efforts to insure that the elderly get the services they need and richly deserve.

References

Cantor, M. H. Effect of ethnicity on life styles of the inner city elderly. In M. P. Lawton, R. J. Newcomer, and T. O. Byerts (Eds.), *Community planning for an aging society*, Stroudsburg, Pa.: Dowden, Hutchinson and Ross, 1976, 41–58. (b)

Cantor, M., and Mayer, M. Factors in differential utilization of services by urban elderly. Paper presented at 28th annual meeting of the Gerontological Society, Louisville, Kentucky, 1975.

Cantor, M., Rosenthal, K., and Wilker, L. Social and family relationships of Black aged women in New York City. Paper presented at 28th annual meeting of the Gerontological Society, Louisville, Kentucky, 1975.

Dowd, J. J., and Bengtson, V. L. Aging in minority populations: An examination of the double jeopardy hypothesis. *Journal of Gerontology*, 1978, *3*, 427–436.

Gibson, G. Kin family network: Overheralded structure in past conceptualizations of family functioning. *Journal of Marriage and the Family*, 1972, *34*, 13–23.

Kent, D. P., and Hirsch, C. *Needs and use of services among Negro and White aged.* Vols. I and II, Penn State University, 1971–1972.

Litwak, E. Extended kin relations in an industrial democratic society. In E. Shanas and G. Streib (Eds.), *Social structures and the family: Generational relations.* Englewood Cliffs, N.J.: Prentice-Hall, 1965, 290–326.

Litwak, E. Retirement, migrants and tasks of organizations and families. Grant proposal, 1976.

Stack, C. B. In M. Z. Rosaldo and L. Lamphere (Eds.), *Woman, culture and society.* Stanford University Press, Stanford, Calif., 1974.

9
Aging in the Chicano Context

David Maldonado, Jr.

To understand the Chicano elderly, the Chicano context and experience need to be understood as well. This is not to disassociate the Chicano elderly from certain universal experiences shared with other elderly groups, but rather to emphasize the significance of being a Chicano and especially being an elderly member of this ethnic community. A basic premise in this chapter is that the ethnocultural factor is indeed a significant element in the lives and experiences of the elderly, especially for the ethnic minorities of color. Their experiences can best be analyzed along two broad areas: (1) the influences of ethnocultural factors and (2) the *minority* ethnic social experience. Both hold important consequences for growing old in the Chicano context.

Why the Chicano Elderly?

The elderly among the Chicanos would probably refrain from using the term *Chicano* as a term of self-identity. Rather, they seem to prefer *Mexicano* or *Mexican*. Other acceptable terms are *Mexican American* or *Spanish speaking*. This is not meant to disassociate them from those who call themselves Chicanos, but rather is a reflection of the older persons' relatively high foreign birth rate, their strong sense of Mexicanness, and the relative newness of *Chicano* as a general term of identification. Nevertheless, for present purposes the term *Chicano elderly* will be used.

As a whole, Chicanos, along with other Hispanic groups (Puerto Ricans, Cubans, etc.) have historically been ignored or considered as insignificant by social scientists and policy makers. However, current population trends indicate that in the not too distant future, the Hispanic population will become the largest ethnic minority group in the nation. Nonetheless, the Chicano elderly remain overlooked. At least two circumstances possibly account for this oversight. First, it is argued that their numbers are relatively insignificant to merit much attention. Second, it has been assumed that the Chicano elderly are properly cared for by the Chicano family, which has been romanticized as an extended system. Recently, these two positions have attracted critical attention.

Arguing for the significance of the Chicano elderly, Dr. Leo Estrada (1977) reports that the Spanish-origin elderly population (inclusive of all Hispanic population, of which about 50% are Chicano) has tripled in the last two decades, and from 1970 to 1975 this group has increased by approximately 23%. More significantly, the Mexican-origin elderly increased by 47.6% in the same period! It is also important to note that the Spanish-origin elderly population tends to be younger; for example, 70.2% were between 65 and 69 years of age. These figures indicate that, indeed, the Spanish-origin elderly population is significant and increasingly so. When these statistics are combined with those of the overall youth of the Spanish-origin population, the significance of their elderly in the future becomes more evident. The recognition that the large undocumented Mexican immigrant population is adult further strengthens the argument that the Chicano elderly is an increasingly important population to recognize and address.

Data released by the Bureau of the Census and analyzed by Estrada (1977) likewise raise serious questions concerning the extended family concept, i.e., multigenerational households. Alfredo Mirande (1977), in reanalyzing the Chicano family, argues that the ideal, extended family, in which the elderly would play a functional role of leadership, is not dominant in the Chicano community, but rather that the nuclear structures appear to be increasing. (Interestingly, he views the elderly as important sources of "warmth and support rather than authority figures.") That this shift to nuclear families has affected the state of the elderly is a reality that must be confronted and analyzed.

Who Are the Chicano Elderly?

The Chicano elderly are older persons of Mexican origin. These include those born in Mexico who immigrated into the United States. These represent about 58% of the present Chicano elderly population. Many immigrated as children or youth between 1910 and 1930 as a result of the Mexican revolution and the need for labor in the United States. These immigrants compose an important element of today's Chicano elderly. That they arrived in their youth and were nurtured by adults who were adult products of Mexican Society has certain cultural consequences for these Chicano elderly. That they were reared by poor aliens has had tremendous socioeconomic consequences as well.

Another subgroup of the foreign-born Chicano elderly are those who immigrated as adults. Undocumented immigration has been difficult to measure; however, legal immigration statistics indicate a significant increase of Mexican immigration beginning in 1953. Since most of the Mexican immigration is labor oriented, it can be assumed (data are extremely limited) that adults constitute a very important proportion of this immigrant population. Just what their proportion is among the Chicano elderly foreign-born population is unknown, but it is not expected to be near that of the young arrivals. Nevertheless, this subpopulation would tend to be culturally quite different from those who arrived decades earlier. Socioeconomically, these elderly have also had less time to prepare for their old age in this society, including less time for socialization and building the economic and cognitive base.

The third subgroup of Chicano elderly are those who were born and reared in this country and are thus natives; they represent about 42% of today's Chicano elderly population. Many of these constitute a third generation and trace their roots to the original settlers. This phenomenon is especially true in New Mexico, California, Texas, Arizona, and Colorado, where the vast majority of the Chicano population is concentrated.

The Ethnocultural Factor

Ethnocultural factors are elements of one's ethnic and cultural being. A basic premise of this chapter is that all persons are cultural beings— that is, that all persons are born into, shaped by, and nurtured in an environment (family, peer groups, community, and certain other significant social conditions such as religion) that is itself a function of certain cultural values, traditions, practices, and world views. These factors have a great influence on accepted and expected behavior, roles, relationships, and self-understanding. This is not to argue that culture is constant or unchanging, but rather to emphasize the great impact that it has on any particular community, family, and individual.

There are those, however, who suggest that the influence of ethnocultural variables is more significant during the early and formative stages of the life span and of less consequence at both ends. It is argued that at the extremes (infancy and old age) physiological factors and the more immediate physical environment play more dominant roles. Thus, it is argued that for the elderly, the cultural variable would be deemphasized as the aging process becomes more evident and as the physiological factors become more crucial (Gaitz, 1974). Again, this chapter is not arguing against the significance of certain physiological processes that influence human behavior in old age nor denying their overall importance, but, rather, is calling attention to the key roles that the ethnocultural factors play in the lives of the elderly.

The Chicano Ethnocultural Context

Attempts to grasp and present the Chicano culture have not been overly successful. Those individuals writing before the 1960s, especially non-Chicano writers, tended to perpetuate or initiate stereotypes unfavorable to the Chicano community. During and after the 1960s many Chicanos produced equally biased, romanticized notions about Chicano culture. Thus, the quest for the essence of Chicano culture continues, but hopefully more objectively by all parties. In spite of the risks involved, this chapter will identify and present some of the more generally accepted notions of the Chicano culture as the context for the Chicano elderly.

The Family

Most students of Chicano life tend to agree that the family holds the key to Chicano culture and that a better understanding of that unit can lead to increased enlightenment in regard to Chicano culture in general. In spite of variations in interpretation, there is considerable consensus that the following are key characteristics of the Chicano family: (1) familism, (2) age hierarchy, (3) male leadership (Alvarez and Bean 1976), and (4) mutual aid and support. A fifth characteristic—the extended structure —has recently come under considerable criticism.

The first characteristic attributed to the Chicano family is that of *familism,* which refers to the centrality of the family for the Chicano. It is the family that surrounds and nurtures the highly dependent infant, that provides the social and value foundations for the developing child, and that serves as the introductory vehicle for relationships outside the family. Through it, the individual is introduced to the kinship system, the community, and the church.

It is within the context of the family that the young Chicano also develops his-her sense of being—the person's self-identity. The individual's self-identity, especially in the context of the ethnic community, is closely related to his/her membership in a certain family. Thus, self-identity is intimately tied to family identification. The individual is known and knows himself as a member of a particular family. His social status is determined by the family's status.

This notion has been expanded further to note that the needs of the family unit supersede those of the individual. Those who come from a rugged individualistic perspective take a negative view of Chicano adults as dependent to an almost pathological degree (Montiel, 1973). A more empathetic interpretation views this phenomenon simply as a cultural difference and as an excellent system for mutual assistance and emotional support. Whatever the interpretation, the practice is there. Chicanos, regardless of their age, strongly identify with their parents and siblings.

A second characteristic closely related to familism is the practice of mutual aid within the family. The family is viewed as a life-long system of emotional support and, at times, material assistance. This is especially true in regard to the expected obligations toward the parents and the elderly. Although Chicano parents tend to deemphasize their dependency upon their children, a cultural value is that the offspring will provide for the parents when they reach old age. With the changing family structure, however, this type of cultural value becomes increasingly difficult to implement and is the root of serious intergenerational and intrapersonal stress. Nevertheless, the values are maintained, lagging behind some practice patterns.

Another related characteristic is the age hierarchy—the status associated with age. As an individual matures, he/she increases in status. The younger children must respect and obey the older siblings, who at times play parental roles. Adults are always to be respected, especially the elderly. To a large extent respect was associated with the authority that rested in the older person, but was also related to the continuing functional role that the elders played in the extended family. However, with the decline of extended families, the isolation of the elderly, and the widening of the socioeconomic differences between generations, the elderly are increasingly playing lesser roles and holding less authority. Nonetheless, *respect* has continued, but more for traditional cultural reasons than as part of any actual practice.

A fourth family characteristic that has been identified as significant for Chicano culture in general concerns sexual roles. The traditional observation is that of male leadership. Many have referred to this phenomenon as male "dominance"; in fact, *machismo* is the most popular term used to describe the Chicano male role. The literature and recent history, however, have effectively shown that this observation is not unique to Chicano culture and that its application to the Chicano male has been unfair and certainly overdone. What is considered to be a "man"—*un hombre*—in the Chicano context is quite contrary to the popular notion of machismo. To be a man means to be responsible, protective, and caring for his family—providing materially for the family and protecting it from external threats. Internally he heads the decision-making hierarchy, which at times is modified to take into consideration the age variable. With recent social change and mobility, such roles tend toward the culturally symbolic. For the Chicano male elderly, as a multigenerational household declines and as his functional roles decrease, his leadership based on his sex is also deemphasized. However, this situation has to be qualified by the continuing value placed on respect for the surviving elder, regardless of age or sex.

If the family serves as the core and vehicle of Chicano culture, then from the foregoing discussion it can be seen that the cultural context of the Chicano elderly has been going through some rapid change, especially in the last three decades. This is not to suggest that Chicanos will eventually become more Anglo-like or that ultimately this cultural gap will disappear. What appears to be occurring is that Chicano culture is changing to reflect and adapt to other social dynamics—in short, it is modernizing. However, certain values are maintained, for example, the importance of the family, the expected mutual aid among family members, and the respect for the elderly. These values, based on certain historical situations of the past, are maintained in new settings and new forms.

For the Chicano elderly of today, this requires an adjustment in regard to their expectations. Although they cannot expect to continue in multigenerational households in which they make functional contributions and in which they hold ultimate authority, they are nonetheless highly respected and serve as the hub of family activity and communications, remaining as living bridges to the Chicano past and culture.

The Ethnically Different Experience

In order to understand the Chicano elderly, their ethnocultural background has to be understood because it holds the key to their value systems, self-understanding, behavior patterns, and social structures. However, it is vital to recognize that because the Chicano elderly are culturally different from the general population, their life situation takes on additional dimensions not reflected among those elderly who share a culture with the majority of the population.

The experience of being culturally different and especially of having one's culture being a minority culture (minority in the sense that it is not the culture of the dominant population) holds significant implication for any individual, but especially for those most dependent upon social and public institutions as in the case of the elderly. Several aspects of that experience can be identified: (1) high sense of ethnic self-identity, (2) ethnocultural centrism, and (3) cultural incongruence with public institutions.

Ethnic self-identity. One of the significant aspects of the ethnic minority experience is the development of an ethnic self-identity. This refers to the centrality of the person's ethnicity to his/her self-understanding. For the ethnically different, and especially for those who are ethnic minorities, it does not take long to recognize and to become overtly conscious of the presence of cultural differences and their impact on one's life. As the individual develops and experiences intergroup contacts, and especially as differences are noted and their impact felt, the individual's ethnic self-identity takes shape. This is reinforced from within by the ethnic group as well as externally by the dominant and other minority cultures. To be aware of one's culture, to identify with that culture, and to have these as components of one's self-identity are important dynamics to recognize among the ethnic populations.

Ethnocultural centrism. A second aspect of the ethnic minority experience is that of ethnocultural centrism. Ethnocultural centrism refers to the attitude that one's culture or ethnicity is superior to all others and that other cultures and other ethnic lifestyles are inferior. The most extreme ethnocultural centrism is encountered among the dominant population; the strength of its criticism of other cultures is enhanced by the sociopolitical and economic forces associated with it. The ethnocentrism of other minority groups is of less immediate consequence; however, it may contribute to and reaffirm the notion that certain ethnic groups are indeed inferior.

Ethnocultural centrism can be understood as a pathological extreme of ethnic pride. However, ethnic group identity and ethnic pride in themselves are not pathological; they become so only when viewed as superior to others, thus defining others as inferior. The experience of the ethnic minorities is to confront the notion that their culture and lifestyles are inferior and worthy of discarding. When an ethnic group such as the Chicanos is growing in numbers and is in close proximity to its cultural source, it cannot be expected to discard its culture and to lose its group identity; from all indications it will remain an ethnic group in the future. Nevertheless, its maintenance is sometimes viewed as resistive and thus as being against the normative cultures of the majority. The poverty of its members is considered further reason for criticism. Thus, for various reasons, Chicanos have been the target of ethnocultural centrism among the majority population. For the Chicano elderly, this has been a lifelong struggle.

Cultural incongruence. The third aspect of minority experience concerns cultural incongruence in social and public institutions. Because the dominant population holds the socioeconomic and political powers and is able to control the major social institutions, it is not surprising that these systems reflect the culture, values, traditions, and practices of the dominant population. History has shown that these institutions (educational, legal, human services, etc.) have not been very responsive to minority cultures. These cultures are viewed as exceptions or as temporary stages of those on their way to acculturation, the presumed ideal goal of most social and public institutions. Therefore, these systems have made very little effort to address ethnic minority persons in and through their own cultural forms. This cultural incongruency has resulted in large-scale misunderstandings, ineffectiveness, underutilization, and human suffering.

The Ethnic Minority of Color

For a significant number of ethnic elderly persons, their experiences go beyond ethnicity to color. In addition to ethnocultural centrism and cultural incongruity, these persons, because they are black, brown, red or yellow, tend to confront dynamics that are strictly racial in nature. The Chicano elderly have been viewed as racially different, and because of this difference, they have experienced negative differential treatment. Racism has been confronted at both the interpersonal and institutional level. History well records the personal attitudes, institutional practices, and community traditions that have treated Chicanos as racially different and, thus, as inferiors and less deserving.

In conclusion, the Chicano elderly of today have overcome great social and economic obstacles during their lives. Today they stand as survivors of personal and group struggles. They have survived, and, in surviving, they have reaffirmed the belief that there is some source of strength within themselves and within their culture. The task remaining is to discover these sources of strength so that others may also reach old age.

References

Alvarez, D., and Bean, F. The Mexican American family. In C. H. Mindel and R. W. Habenstein (Eds.), *Ethnic families in America*. New York: Elsevier, 1976.

Estrada, L. F. The Spanish origin elderly: A demographic survey, 1970–1975. Manuscript partially published in *Aging Research Utilization Report*, 1977, *1*, 13–14.

Gaitz, C. M. Mental health of Mexican Americans: Do ethnic factors make a difference? *Geriatrics*, 1974, *11*, 103–106, 109–110.

Mirande, A. The Chicano family: A reanalysis of conflicting views. *Journal of Marriage and the Family*, Nov. 1977. 747–756.

Montiel, M. The social science myth of the Mexican American: In O. I. Romano (Ed.), *Voices*. Berkeley: Quinto Sol Publications, 1973.

10

Exiled Americans:
The Plight of Indian Aged
in the United States

Marilyn R. Block

The social science literature on various ethnic and racial minority groups has traditionally ignored the aged. While considerable information has been published on American Indians in general, there is little information available on Indian elderly. This is due in part to the fact that, as a racial group, Indians have a small population and the smallest number of elderly among all minority groups.

The Indian elderly compose the most deprived group of individuals in the United States. They exist on little or no income. "The aged Indian lives in a state of grinding poverty, the scope and impact of which is unknown to any other population group in the U.S." (Benedict, 1971, p. 52). For most, the poverty of old age is the result of a lifetime of deprivation. American Indians, from the time of birth, have experienced substandard housing, limited education, inadequate income, poor health, malnutrition, a lack of urgently needed services, and the emotional problems inherent in a changing culture. With advancing age, the severity of these conditions is intensified.

The needs of this segment of the population have been largely ignored because its members are a statistically insignificant minority group. American Indians have been effectively exiled.

Selected Demographic Data

Although any attempt to reach a definitive understanding of the plight of the aged native American[1] requires a firm statistical foundation, there currently exists an appalling lack of available data. Where data do exist, the information is largely inadequate and inaccurate. There are several reasons for the gross disparities in available data. First, census figures have been collected by non-Indians who are unable to speak the indigenous language and so have trouble locating the living quarters of Indians. Second, Bureau of Indian Affairs (BIA) figures usually reflect only those numbers of Indians eligible for services and so are not reflective of the entire Indian population. Third, various agencies, programs, and other groups use different criteria in establishing a definition of who is an Indian (Advisory Council, 1971), and the different definitions affect data. This lack of reliable figures results in a great degree of confusion. When figures from different sources are examined, the confusion is compounded.

Langone (1969) finds that "data is [sic] simply not available with respect to American Indians. Information compiled on a reservation basis was more adequate a hundred years ago than it is at present." Of the approximately 18,000 file cards in the Library of Congress Main Catalog, there are only 16 cards under the subheading Indian *Statistics,* 11 under *Census,* and none under *Population,* while the subheadings *Pottery* and *Legends* show 417 entries (Advisory Council, 1971; Langone, 1969).

If data are inaccessible and incomplete for Indians in general, the problem is even more acute when seeking specific information on elderly Indians. There is a paucity of information about the Indian population by age, and there are no reliable estimates as to the number of elderly Indians (Advisory Council, 1971; Doherty, 1971). In addition, the data are scattered and fragmentary and come from a variety of sources. Despite this problem, a summary of statistical information on elderly Indians will be presented to lay the groundwork for a discussion of the relationship of the elderly Indian to the Indian family.

1. The term *native American* refers to members of the aboriginal peoples of the Western Hemisphere, who are of Mongoloid descent. For purposes of data collection, native Americans are often subdivided into the following three major groups: *American Indian:* a member of any of the aboriginal peoples of the Western Hemisphere, except the Eskimos, constituting one of the divisions of the Mongoloid stock; *Eskimo:* a member of a group of peoples of northern Canada, Greenland, Alaska, and eastern Siberia; *Aleut:* a member of a people of the Aleutian and Shumagin islands and the western part of Alaska peninsula (*Webster's Seventh Collegiate Dictionary,* 1965). Where the terms *American Indian, Eskimo,* or *Aleut* appear in the text, information refers to that group only. Where the term *native American* appears, information applies to all three subgroups.

Population.   Approximately 45,000 American Indians are aged 65 and over. The designation of Indians as "old" at that age has caused a great deal of dispute. Because the average life expectancy of the American Indian is only 44 (compared with 72 for the total population), Indians can be considered "older" at a younger chronological age, thus increasing the overall number of those who should be termed "elderly." Tables 10-1 depicts the distribution of Indians in the population by age.

Table 10-1.   Indian Population by Age, United States, 1960

Years	Total	Male	Female
All ages	546,228	273,526	272,702
45–49	21,711	10,878	10,833
50–54	20,767	10,310	10,457
55–59	31,560	15,066	16,494
60–64	11,830	6,080	5,750
65–69	9,975	5,181	4,794
70–74	6,857	3,524	3,333
75 and over	8,765	4,443	4,322

Source: Public Health Service, IHS Statistics Branch, 1971.

Geographic distribution.   More than 90% of American Indians reside in 27 states (Advisory Council, 1971). The majority of older Indians are located west of the Mississippi River on or near reservations (see Table 10–2). Approximately one-third of American Indians leave the reservation, but well over half of those who do so return (Doherty, 1971). Those who do move off the reservation appear to be younger Indians, not the elderly. The majority of older American Indians reside on or near reservations: 56.4% of those over 55 and 57.1% of those over 60 (Williams, 1977). As younger Indians leave the reservations and become increasingly assimilated into urban settings, the percentage of elderly Indians on reservations should begin to decrease.

Table 10–2.   American Indians 55 Years of Age and Over, by Region, 1970

Region	55 and Over		65 and Over	
	No.	*%*	*No.*	*%*
United States	88,809	100	63,823	100
West	37,228	41.9	26,533	41.6
South	27,686	31.2	20,267	31.8
North Central	16,644	18.7	11,643	18.2
Northeast	7,251	8.2	5,380	8.4

Source: Blanch S. Williams, Older American Indians, 1970. *Facts and Figures*, No. 9, Administration on Aging, 1977.

Health and mortality. Indians are the victims of inferior health status and inadequate health care throughout life. Lack of basic sanitary facilities, poor and crowded housing, inadequate nutrition, impoverished economic status, and limited education are all factors contributing to poor health. These deficiencies translate into an average life expectancy of 44 years (average life expectancy is slightly higher for native Americans—45.7 years as of 1967; Hill, 1970). While over 60% of the general population live to age 65 or over, only 33% of native Americans can expect to reach age 65 (Advisory Council, 1971; Benedict, 1971). Those native Americans who do survive to age 65 "are eight times as likely as whites to die from tuberculosis, twice as likely to die of gastritis and cirrhosis of the liver and twice as likely to die of influenza and pneumonia" (Benedict, 1971, p. 56).

Indian Aged and the Family System

Any remarks about the elderly Indian within the family structure must be approached with caution. Generalizations about 266 Indian tribes, bands, villages, pueblos, and groups spanning a 30-state geographic area in the continental United States, as well as 216 native Alaskan commu nities, are no more reliable than are generalizations about Europeans which fail to distinguish among Norwegians, Germans, Dutch, and French. Just as each European nationality has its own social and familial conventions, so does each Indian tribe.

Tribal differences have long existed regarding the status of the elderly. Historically, this status has been predicated upon the economic position of the tribe. Thus, among largely nomadic tribes and in areas where life was severe, instances of abandonment, neglect, suicide, and even sanctioned murder occurred. In sharp contrast were those tribes with an extended family situation, where maintenance of the elderly was the norm, since they continued to perform definite and useful functions (Doherty, 1971).

In addition to these traditional differences, the culture of the 1970s has created its own disparity. The United States has four distinct Indian populations—reservation Indians, rural Indians, migrant Indians, and urban Indians (Jeffries, 1972). Because each of these four groups lives in different areas and maintains different lifestyles, it is wrong to identify a particular familial pattern and ascribe it to all Indians.

With these caveats in mind, some description of the aging Indian's status within the family can be offered. The reader must be aware that these are extremely broad characterizations.

Indians traditionally have identified not only with the nuclear family, but also with the extended family, clan, and the tribe (Advisory Council, 1971).[2] This identification resulted from the respect and reverence offered the elderly within the family, clan, and tribal structure. Reverence for the aged, however, is fast eroding, a process abetted by Federal emphasis on younger Indians in most assistance programs. The aged have been pushed to the periphery of tribal existence, and increasingly excluded from the social dynamics of both tribal and familial life.

Doherty (1971) finds that this emphasis on the young, which has contributed to the destruction of the extended family, has also considerably aggravated the loss of status and esteem of elderly persons. Levy (1967) supports this view:

> . . . the shifting economy has produced hardships for the young at the same time that it has almost completely destroyed the productive roles and economic holdings of the other traditionalists. More uncomfortable perhaps has been the resultant destruction of the education and advising functions of the experienced older person [p. 225].

The need to adapt to a materialistically oriented society has strongly subverted traditional Indian values regarding family. The evidence indicates that

> the shift to wage work has encouraged the development of the nuclear family at the expense of the extended family. Old people are a burden to young couples operating in a cost economy with the low incomes of unskilled workers. The domestic skills of the aged are less important in a small household [Levy, 1967, p. 225].

Younger Indians are often forced to leave the reservation if they are to realize any sort of job opportunity. Wages are often minimal, barely covering basic needs. Unable to support additional family members, and equally unable to send money back to the reservation, the young Indian leaves his aging parent with no economic base. Older family members sometimes receive welfare grants, but these are usually inadequate to cover basic needs. The traditional kinship support system of the family structure is unfeasible when the family has no resources (Butler and Lewis, 1973), and the tribe is unable to assume the responsibility and care of the elderly because economically it is no better off.

2. The term *clan* refers to a unilateral kin group, based on either matrilineal or patrilineal descent. The term *tribe* refers to a nonliterate community or a collection of such communities occupying a common geographic area and having a similar language and culture (Theodorson and Theodorson, 1969).

Institutionalization. The decision to enter an institutionalized living arrangement is difficult for any aged individual and his or her adult children. Institutionalization tends to be isolating, even when such elderly have strong family systems.

For the aged Indian, the isolation previously experienced is exacerbated when medical intervention of any type is required. Few reservations have medical facilities near at hand. Generally, when health or nursing home care is required by an Indian, he must travel a great distance from the reservation.

The need for hospitalization or nursing home care often causes the aging Indian to lose touch with friends and relatives who are unable to travel the distance (sometimes 100 miles) for even infrequent visiting. The lack of easy access to medical and nursing home facilities near reservations serves to further erode ongoing family interaction. Limited resources prevent any possibility of senior day care centers or visiting home health services, alternatives that have been successful in maintaining the aged within their family structures in urban and suburban settings.

Those programs designed to assist Indians have failed to account for the maintenance of the aging Indian within his or her family. The Indian aged continue to be forgotten Americans. As long as they are ignored by those professing to help, their plight and the prospects for their children and grandchildren as they age will not improve.

Directions for Policy

There can be little doubt that Indians, and especially elderly Indians, require strong and immediate intervention by local, state, and federal agencies and programs if their predicament is to be resolved. Intervention strategies must not, however, be implemented at the expense of the family system; strategies must be designed to buttress the kin network.

One such area that requires reexamination is health. Those health services currently available to the elderly Indian contribute to neither physical and emotional well-being nor to maintenance of the family system. Adequate medical services are not easily accessible; these are generally located at such a distance from the reservation that only the most severely ill attempt to overcome the lack of transportation and avail themselves of required assistance.

There is an overwhelming need for several types of health support services that will maintain the aged Indian within the family system as long as possible: in-home services, day care centers, and nursing homes.

In-home services. Increasingly, more Indian elderly "are being left alone in their homes without being fed or cared for and without access to emergency services" (National Tribal Chairmen's Association, 1976, p. 17). While a number of special services have been available to needy elderly for many years, these same services have not been incorporated into programs for Indians.

One such needed service is the assistance provided by the visiting home nurse, who provides a minimal level of health care for those people not ill enough to require hospitalization. This form of assistance is unavailable on reservations where care of the elderly Indian within the home has never been considered a priority by government programs.

Additionally, an elderly Indian residing off-reservation and requiring 24-hour care must pay for it out of a meager pension or do without (National Tribal Chairmen's Association, 1976). There should be programs to pay for such live-in care. The burden has often been placed on younger family members; forced to work long hours in order to earn enough money on which to subsist, children of the elderly Indian cannot afford the expense of providing 24-hour maintenance, nor are they able to afford the expenditure of time necessary for 24-hour maintenance, since this would entail leaving the labor force.

Programs geared to meeting the health and nutritional needs of aged Indians would contribute to their emotional well-being as well as to their physical condition, since these would permit the aged to remain within a family and/or tribal system that otherwise might not have the resources to aid the aged.

Day care centers. Day care centers should be made available and accessible to the Indian elderly in their local areas. Two kinds of day care centers would provide benefits for the elderly. Visitation day care service would enable the elderly and their families to meet with health personnel on the reservation when assistance was necessary. Of greater impact perhaps would be the availability of the senior day care center, which maintains the elderly on a daily basis. It provides a positive alternative to institutionalization since the aged are able to spend evenings and weekends with their families. This service allows adult children to spend days working or pursuing other activities instead of forcing them into an either-or decision.

Nursing homes. According to the National Tribal Chairmen's Association (1976)

> Many Indian elderly suffer emotional shock in nursing homes far from their familiar environment and integrated with patients from other ethnic groups. This often accelerates health problems and may lead to premature death due to a feeling of isolation from loved ones who are too far away to pay regular visits (p. 17).

Nursing homes located on the reservations would permit elderly to maintain ties with various social networks: immediate family; extended family members; friends; and tribal members. Food and leisure activities offered in such institutions would not be strange, but could develop out of the culture of the particular tribe, eliminating much of the isolation that currently accompanies the nursing home experience for a great many Indians.

The present federal funding system, however, refuses to authorize money for nursing home facilities unless these are licensed by the state. Certain states refuse to license nursing homes on reservations because jurisdiction over the home becomes an issue (National Tribal Chairmen's Association, 1976).

The Future Role of Government

Most existing policies regarding the situation of Indians are predicated on quantitative issues rather than on qualitative concerns. Policies are implemented in a manner designed to serve the most Indians for the least number of dollars, regardless of the impact of or desire for such services. Existing programs and services have failed to take into consideration the social and emotional needs of the Indian people. In serving a group that culturally has valued the family and the tribe, programs and services geared to the individual are doomed to failure. A system of advocacy for *elderly* in need of special services should be established and maintained, but such a system must consider the elderly in relation to a family and a tribal network.

The elderly Indian has long been neglected, even though he is considered a valuable resource by Indian tribes, who fear that their cultures are dying. Without local, state, and federal policy decisions aimed at family and tribe, rather than at individual support, the Indian elderly will probably be unable to become again a valued part of the Indian community. This situation will not be remedied until health services designed to maintain the elderly at an optimal level are made available within the Indian community.

References

Advisory Council on the Elderly American Indian. Working paper prepared for the Special Committee on Aging, U.S. Senate, Nov. 1971.

Benedict, R. A profile of Indian aged. In *Minority aged in America.* Ann Arbor: Institute of Gerontology, University of Michigan–Wayne State University, 1971.

Butler, R. N., and Lewis, M. I. *Aging and mental health: Positive psychosocial approaches.* St. Louis: C. V. Mosby, 1973.

Doherty, R. P., Growing old in Indian country. In *Employment prospects of aged Blacks, Chicanos, and Indians.* Washington, D.C.: National Council on the Aging, Inc., 1971.

Hill, C. A., Jr. Measures of longevity of American Indians. *Public Health Reports,* 1970, *85,* 233–239.

Jeffries, W. R. Our aged Indians. In *Triple jeopardy . . . myth or reality?* Washington, D.C.: National Council on the Aging, Inc., 1972.

Langone, S. A. A statistical profile of the Indian: The lack of numbers. In *Toward economic development for native American communities,* Vol. I. Washington, D.C.: U.S. Government Printing Office, 1969.

Levy, J. E. The older American Indian. In *Older Rural Americans: A Sociological Perspective,* E. G. Youmans (eds.). Lexington, Ky.: University of Kentucky Press, 1967.

National Tribal Chairmen's Association. *Summary report: National Indian conference on aging.* Phoenix: National Tribal Chairmen's Association, Inc., 1976.

Theodorson, G. A., and Theodorson, A. G. *Modern dictionary of sociology.* New York: Thomas Y. Crowell, 1969.

Williams, B. S. Older American Indians, 1970. *Facts and figures, No. 9.* Washington, D.C.: Administration on Aging, 1977.

11

Disengagement and Aging among the Issei

Darrel Montero

Although there is now a developing body of literature that examines the social context of aging among racial and cultural minorities, there is still a paucity of literature on the aging process among Japanese Americans. This may be explained in part by the relatively small numbers of Japanese in the United States. The 1970 Census reports that there are fewer than 600,000 Japanese Americans, of which two-thirds live in Hawaii or the Pacific Coast region. This geographic clustering has served to insulate this ethnic group, and in particular those aged 65 or over, who constitute less than 10% of the total Japanese American population (U.S. Bureau of the Census, 1973, p. 24). Thus, they are not visible to the majority of Americans and have been less likely to be the subject of funded research. Sue and Kitano (1973) have commented upon the stereotypical view of the Japanese in this country as a model minority; that is, they appear to have achieved socioeconomic success and are not perceived by the majority of Americans as a group that needs public

The study upon which this paper is based was made possible through grants from the Japanese American Citizens League, the Carnegie Corporation of New York, and the National Institute of Mental Health (Grant No. 5 RO1 MH12780-04). Computing assistance was obtained from the Health Sciences Computing Facility, UCLA, sponsored by NIH Special Research Resources Grant RR-3, and the Computer Science Center, University of Maryland. I especially want to thank Gene N. Levine, the principal investigator of the Japanese American Research Project, for use of survey data collected under his direction. I am indebted to Donald E. Gelfand, Judith McDowell, Larry McLaughlin, Tara McLaughlin, and Judith Treas for their extensive comments, and to Claudia Burns and Chris Turner for assistance in data processing.

assistance. This may also serve to explain why they have escaped the attention of so many social scientists.

This chapter focuses upon the Issei, the immigrant first-generation Japanese Americans, who are a unique subgroup within this American minority. It is convenient to divide Japanese Americans into three distinct generations: the Issei, who immigrated to this country between 1895 and 1924; their American-born children, the Nisei; and the Sansei, who are children of the Nisei and grandchildren of the Issei (Kitano, 1972). The main thrust of Japanese immigration began around 1900 and ended with the Exclusion Act of 1924. This Act effectively cut off any further immigration from Japan, a state of affairs that continued until 1952. This Act served, however unintentionally, to define a unique and relatively homogeneous ethnic subgroup.

Although there is a developing general social science literature which summarizes research on Japanese Americans (Kitano, 1976; Lyman, 1970, 1977; Petersen, 1971), there are few recent research monographs (Connor, 1977; Kiefer, 1974a; Montero, 1978). While these works do not specifically focus upon the process and problems of aging among the Issei, they do report upon the socioeconomic status and demographic characteristics of this population. Thus, they offer some perspective for placing elderly Japanese Americans in a broader socio-historical context.

Social gerontologists have focused much attention on Cumming and Henry's (1961) social disengagement theory, which suggests that older people often do not wish to maintain the same level of immersion in social relations as in their earlier years. They theorize that a voluntary mutual withdrawal takes place on the part of the elderly and the rest of society. Following Cumming and Henry's (1961) thesis, this chapter examines the relationship between age and social participation. Employing data from a national sample of Japanese Americans, we examine a series of indicators of the Issei's social participation—visiting patterns with friends and relatives and membership in voluntary associations—to determine whether in fact there is a differential level of social participation by age or sex of the elderly.

Method

The sample. The data for the present study are derived from a sample of 1,047 first-generation Japanese American respondents (the Issei). This sample is part of a larger sociohistorical, three-generational, national study of Japanese Americans conducted by the Japanese American Research Project at UCLA. A complete description of the design of the sample has been given elsewhere (Montero, 1978). Since the design for the larger study serves as the context for the present study, it is outlined briefly below.

One of the early purposes of the study was to sample and interview surviving members of the first generation (the Issei) on the U.S. mainland, most of whom were becoming quite elderly. In 1963 an attempt was made to list every Issei immigrant still living in the United States, excluding Hawaii and Alaska. The listing was largely derived from Japanese association membership lists and supplemented by lists from Buddhist and Christian churches; it totaled approximately 18,000 persons.

During 1964–1966, interviews with a random sample of listed Issei were carried out by specifically recruited and trained bilingual Japanese American interviewers. With a respondent refusal rate of less than 1%, this yielded a sample of 1,047 Issei. Of these, 45, or 4.3%, were under 60 years of age and were excluded from the present analysis. Our effective sample is thus 1,002 Issei.

Sampling comparisons.   We suspect a sampling bias which is hard to confirm. We believe we have sampled too many Issei respondents who are immersed in organized Japanese American life and too few who are unaffiliated. The bias is inherent in the original Issei listing procedure. Undoubtedly, our original lists of Issei were incomplete, leaving out people who had failed to join an organization. We have, in effect, probably undersampled peripheral and unaffiliated persons and taken a disproportionate share of the better educated and better off. The Japanese immigrant community, however, was one of the most highly organized of immigrant groups (Park and Miller, 1921), and the error is not nearly as great as it would be for some other immigrant nationalities.

The Issei Immigrant: A Brief History

The Japanese came to this country as sojourners; that is, they intended to stay for a time, build a nest-egg, and then return to their homeland (Miyamoto, 1939). Many of the men were younger sons who could not inherit land under Japan's system of primogeniture and who viewed working in the United States as a reasonable way to establish themselves financially (Connor, 1977, p. 64). After several years of hard work their natural inclination was to marry and continue the family line, a matter of considerable importance in Japanese culture. In order to save the expense of going home to marry, or because they lacked the necessary funds to do so, many of the men sent for spouses to join them in this country. Often the couples knew of each other only through letters and photographs, and the wives in these arranged marriages came to be known as picture brides (Gee, 1976; Levine and Montero, 1973). In most cases there was a substantial age difference between the two partners, and the typical immigrant Japanese family consisted of a middle-aged man with a young wife and small children. This arrangement encouraged the established pattern of traditional Japanese culture, which bestowed prestige and authority upon older men. Because of this difference in ages, the elderly Issei who survive today are apt to be women (Kalish and Moriwaki, 1973). There were virtually no unmarried Issei women, and those Issei men who remained bachelors appear to have the greatest problems of adjustment among this aging ethnic group (Kitano, 1976).

Traditionally, old people in Japan have held a respected position within the community and the family. They were sought out for guidance and wisdom, and ideally aging parents would live with their oldest son and his wife. Among the poor of Japan, the labor of the elderly was often necessary for the maintenance of the family, and those who were physically unfit for more strenuous duties were still able to mend tools, sew, and care for the grandchildren. Thus, the elderly Japanese had a strong sense of being needed. Even after death they maintained a function within the family by being a source of emotional security (Plath, 1964a).

In the United States, of course, the Issei grow old and face death in an entirely different environment. Here the prestige of the elderly is not nearly so great as in traditional Japan (Kitano and Sue, 1973). Even so, Kiefer (1974b) sees the Issei, for the most part, enjoying a healthy and comfortable old age. This conclusion is based on an analysis of four factors: companionship, authority and autonomy, productivity, and acceptance of death.

Companionship. Because the Issei constitute such a small, homogeneous group, they have many opportunities for social contact with each other. The language barrier prohibits them from much social intercourse with the Anglo community, and because of traditional Japanese reserve they do not make friends easily. Nonetheless, their own tightly knit group provides a satisfying social context and appears to meet their needs.

Authority and autonomy. Traditionally, dependent Japanese elders are not considered subordinate to their children, but are simply being repaid for their life's work. This outlook has changed somewhat in the United States, particularly since many Issei fathers were forced to forfeit their positions of authority prematurely due to World War II relocation. Placed in camps in the interior of the country, they lost businesses and property and faced added insult when governmental authorities would deal only with their children, the native-born Nisei. After the war, many Issei were too old to start over, and some could survive only by working with or for their children. Nevertheless, the traditional Japanese family unit was strong enough in most instances to survive such trauma, and today most Issei see themselves as more autonomous than their children see them.

Productivity. In Japanese culture the worth of the individual is measured by what he contributes to the group (Plath, 1964b), and as we have seen, the elderly Japanese believe that, even after death, they will continue to be needed and worthwhile members of the family. Even those who cannot work in later years can feel productive in a spiritual and philosophical sense by their very presence.

Acceptance of death. Likewise, the belief that one's life is but part of a larger thread may account for the philosophical acceptance of death typical of the Issei. The Japanese traditionally view death as an inevitable, natural event. One who loves nature does not fear it; thus he does not fear death.

Hendricks and Hendricks (1977) have described those aged who are poor and also members of racial or ethnic minorities as being in triple jeopardy. This description would seem to indicate that such people have three strikes against them. Is this in fact the case with aging Japanese Americans, or do the Issei themselves view their condition in a different light?

Being a member of a minority may even be an advantage for the elderly (Kiefer, 1974b). The Issei, who are few in number and live near each other, have no sense of anonymity, which the majority of elderly may feel. They have a unique identity, and while they may be an invisible minority as far as the rest of society is concerned, within their own tightly knit community they know each other well. In spite of the hardships and prejudice they have faced in this country, most Issei are glad they came (Kitano, 1976).

On the other hand, those with problems are not as apt to admit to that fact as others might be, and being wary of governmental authorities they do not seek help until the situation is desperate (Kalish and Moriwaki, 1973). In an effort to shed some light on these important questions, we turn now to an examination of the findings from our national sample of Japanese Americans.

Findings

Demographic characteristics. Our sample of 1,002 Issei includes 66% men and 34% women, whose median ages are 76 and 71 years, respectively. The Issei's median number of school years completed in Japan is approximately 8 years. One-quarter (26%) of the Issei live with their spouse, another 58% live with their spouse and/or other family members, whereas only one in seven (14%) lives entirely alone and fewer than 2% live with people who are not relatives. The Issei's living arrangements suggest the opportunity for the existence of a close network of family support systems.

The Issei were asked what difficulties they still face since their arrival in the United States. Nearly a majority (46%) state that they face no difficulties. One-third of the Issei report that the English language has proven to be the greatest difficulty. Remarkably, less than 1% of the Issei report that they currently experience loneliness.

In order to determine the potential for the presence of a strong family support system, we asked the Issei to report the number of relatives living in the United States. We find that our typical respondent has nearly five relatives residing here, and four in ten of our respondents report that they have one or more siblings in this country. This would appear to represent an excellent opportunity for the continuation of strong bonds of kinship for these Issei. On the other hand, one in three Issei has only one relative currently living in the United States, and a plurality (43%) have no relatives in this country.

In order to determine the extent to which the Issei feel they have achieved their goals in life, we asked our respondents: "Have you achieved the place in life that you wanted for yourself and your family?" Three in four Issei report that they have in fact achieved their goals. When asked what factors had contributed to their success, three-quarters of the Issei report that diligence, hard work, honesty, and thrift were responsible. Other reasons for the Issei's success, (in order of frequency) included health, good luck, and shrewdness.

In order to determine how the Issei are faring economically, we asked if they were financially dependent upon their children for support. Six in ten of our respondents report that they are completely financially independent of their offspring. In contrast, almost one-fifth report that they receive over one-half of their financial support from their children.

Following this brief demographic sketch of the Issei, we turn now to an examination of such indicators of the Issei's social participation as: visiting patterns with friends and relatives and membership in voluntary associations. These findings will help us to determine whether in fact there is a differential level of social participation by age, as suggested by Cumming and Henry's (1961) of social disengagement thesis.

Issei Visiting Patterns

Table 11-1 reports upon the relationship between age, sex, and social participation as measured by the Issei's visiting patterns with other Issei, Nisei, and Caucasian friends, and with their own children.

Visiting with other Issei.   Table 11-1 reports that age is inversely related to frequency of visiting with Issei friends. That is, the oldest Issei (81 years or older) are less likely to visit their Issei friends than are their youngest counterparts (60–65 years of age). Regardless of sex, approximately six in ten of the youngest Issei visit other Issei friends at least once a month. As age advances, the frequency of visiting drops fairly systematically for both men and women.

There are at least two tentative explanations for this relationship. First, with advancing age the oldest Issei may simply not have the physical and psychological wherewithal to engage in social visiting. A second explanation suggests that the older the Issei, the greater the possibility that more of his cohorts have died. The findings that follow may shed some light on which of the two explanations is more accurate.

Visiting with Nisei friends.   We next report upon the relationship between the Issei's age and visiting patterns with Nisei friends. The results show the same general pattern of decreasing frequency of visiting with advancing age. In this relationship, however, there is a difference by sex. Approximately one-half of the youngest men (60–65) visit Nisei at least once a month, whereas only one-third of the youngest women visit that frequently. This difference by sex persists even through the oldest cohort of Issei, where frequency of visiting decreases to one in four of the men and fewer than one in five of the women. Thus, this finding that frequency of visiting Nisei friends as well as Issei friends declines with age tends to support our second explanation offered above. That is, it appears that shrinking numbers of fellow Issei to visit is not as important a factor as the Issei's decline in physical and psychological wherewithal to engage in social visiting that comes with advancing years.

Visiting with Caucasian friends.[1]   We found two general patterns when we asked our Issei respondents how frequently they visit with Caucasian friends. First, we found that for men, visiting with Caucasians is inversely related to age, whereas the findings for the women reveal no systematic relationship with age. Second, regardless of age

1. For visiting with Caucasians, we dichotomized visiting into "ever visit" and "never visit" in order to maximize cell frequencies, because so few Issei ever visited Caucasians regularly. For visiting Issei and Nisei friends and Issei's children, frequent visiting is defined as once a month or more often.

Table 11-1. Issei Visiting Patterns with Friends and Relatives by Age and Sex

Age	Percentage of Issei Who Visit Frequently[a]							
	Issei		Nisei		Caucasian		Children	
	Male[b]	Female	Male	Female	Male	Female	Male	Female
60–65	62	59	48	34	50	34	68	66
(N)	(82)	(37)	(63)	(21)	(64)	(21)	(32)	(18)
66–70	61	49	35	31	44	43	76	78
(N)	(65)	(54)	(36)	(34)	(46)	(47)	(35)	(29)
71–75	58	54	28	25	56	38	70	73
(N)	(50)	(51)	(24)	(24)	(48)	(34)	(28)	(16)
76–80	54	52	31	27	42	20	64	71
(N)	(90)	(25)	(51)	(13)	(70)	(10)	(51)	(10)
81+	48	41	24	18	39	33	68	71
(N)	(76)	(9)	(38)	(4)	(61)	(8)	(39)	(5)

[a]Frequent visiting is defined as monthly or more often for Issei, Nisei, and children; for Caucasians frequent visiting is defined as one or more times annually.
[b]Male and female categories refer to the sex of the Issei respondent.

women visit Caucasians less frequently than their male counterparts. For the youngest Issei cohort (60–65) one-half of the men and one-third of the women visit Caucasians in their homes. For the oldest cohort (age 81 and over) this pattern of visiting declines to approximately 40% of the men, whereas the visiting rate for the women remains unchanged.

   Visiting with children. We next asked the Issei how frequently they visit their children. Regardless of age the data reported in Table 11-1 reveal that approximately two-thirds of the Issei visit their offspring at least once a month. Interestingly, we also find no difference in visiting patterns by sex, whereas for our other indicators of visiting (with Issei, Nisei, and Caucasian friends) we found a consistently lower rate of visiting by Issei women.

Community and Organizational Participation

Table 11-2 reports upon the relationship between age, sex, and social participation as measured by the Issei's neighborhood friendship patterns, frequency of religious attendance, and membership in voluntary associations.

   Neighborhood friendships. In order to determine the extent to which our Issei respondents are immersed in their neighborhood, we asked the Issei: "Of all your friends, what percentage live in your immediate neighborhood?" Regardless of sex, approximately 40% of the youngest Issei (age 60–65) report that a majority (50%) of their friends

Table 11–2.　Issei Community and Organizational Participation by Age and Sex

Age	Percentages					
	Neighborhood Friendships[a]		Religious Attendance[b]		Organizational Membership[c]	
	Male	Female	Male	Female	Male	Female
60–65	41	39	31	40	42	14
(N)	(54)	(24)	(39)	(25)	(53)	(8)
66–70	42	28	28	42	29	10
(N)	(44)	(31)	(29)	(46)	(30)	(10)
71–75	37	36	51	54	27	6
(N)	(31)	(34)	(43)	(51)	(23)	(5)
76–80	27	31	46	58	16	9
(N)	(44)	(15)	(76)	(28)	(25)	(4)
81+	32	29	40	46	18	0
(N)	(50)	(6)	(61)	(10)	(27)	(0)

[a] Neighborhood Friendships refers to those respondents who report 50% or more friends living in the neighborhood.
[b] Religious Attendance is defined as twice monthly or more.
[c] Organizational Membership refers to membership in one or more voluntary associations.

live in the immediate confines of their neighborhood. Among the oldest Issei this figure declines to one-third. In brief, age is inversely related to the percentage of friends in the Issei's neighborhood. Controlling for age, women report fewer neighborhood friendships than men.

These findings are consistent with those reported in Table 11-1, which reveal that frequency of visiting declines with age. This decline in visiting may be explained by the fact that our oldest cohort of Issei report that they have fewer friends residing in their immediate neighborhood (Table 11-2), thus making visiting more difficult. On the other hand, the finding that approximately six in ten of the Issei have friends outside their immediate neighborhood has implications for the degree of social integration of the Issei. Thus, while frequency of visiting may depend upon physical proximity, actual friendships do not.

Religious attendance. When we asked our respondents how frequently they attend religious services, we find a somewhat inconsistent pattern. Approximately one in three of the men and four in ten of the women in the two youngest cohorts (60–65 and 66–70) attend frequently (twice monthly or more). Regardless of sex, the frequency of religious attendance increases to a majority in the next cohort (aged 71–75), and then decreases again to four in ten of both men and women in the oldest cohort (aged 81 and over). In general we do find a consistently higher level of religious attendance for Issei women of all ages than for their male counterparts.

It is interesting to note that data reported earlier (Table 11-1) reveal that on every indicator of frequency of visiting with Japanese and Caucasian friends, the women visit less frequently than the men. Yet in an institutionalized setting of organized religion the women consistently attend religious services more frequently. One possible explanation for this finding may be that the Issei's parents may have differentially socialized their sons and daughters regarding the importance of religion. Also, the men may have been encouraged either by socialization or necessity to navigate in wider occupational and social waters.

Organizational memberships. For our final indicator of social participation, we asked the Issei if they currently belong to an organization. Four in ten of the youngest Issei men and only one in seven of the youngest women report that they are currently a member of a voluntary association. This level of membership declines fairly systematically with age. The oldest Issei cohort, for example, reports that only one in five of the men and none of the women belong to an organization. Regardless of age, women report a lower rate of membership in organizations than men. Because organizational associations are often related to one's occupation, and because fewer Issei women were employed outside the home than Issei men, it is not too surprising that the women belong to fewer organizations.

Summary and Conclusions

The intent of this chapter has been to examine Cumming and Henry's (1961) social disengagement hypothesis as it applies to one generation of Japanese Americans, the Issei. Employing data from a national sample of Japanese Americans, we examined a series of indicators of the Issei's social participation.

We divided our indicators of social participation into two analytical categories: visiting patterns with friends and relatives and participation in voluntary associations. The findings suggest a general pattern of age being inversely related to social participation. However, within this general pattern we find several important exceptions. Regarding visiting patterns, on the one hand we find that the Issei's frequency of visiting with Issei, Nisei, and Caucasian friends is inversely related to age and is lower for women than for men. On the other hand, the frequency of the Issei's visiting with their own Nisei children is unrelated to age or sex.

Regarding Issei participation in community and organizational affairs, the data reveal a particularly inconsistent pattern. Age is in-

versely related to percentage of friends residing in the Issei's immediate neighborhood. On the other hand, the Issei's church attendance
generally increases with age and is consistently higher among women
than men.

On the matter of organizational affiliation, the data reveal that age
is again inversely related to membership. Moreover, membership in
voluntary associations is consistently lower for women regardless of age.

Thus, we find partial support for the social disengagement thesis,
which suggests that social participation decreases with age. This is in
contrast to Kiefer (1974b), who seems to see little evidence of such
disengagement among the Issei. Kiefer (1974b) argues that the Issei
retain close ties with friends and family, although perhaps not with the
larger American community, and remain socially active within their
ethnic group. Our findings indicate that age is inversely related to social
participation, as measured by frequency of visiting with friends and
relatives and participation in community and organizational activities.
We find one notable exception to this general pattern which is of theoretical interest: that is, visiting with the Issei's children did not decline
with age.

Hochschild's (1975) comprehensive discussion has probably laid to
rest any attempt to develop a disengagement approach into a comprehensive theory of aging. This does not mean, however, that the concept
of disengagement should be discarded. We need to know what activities
or interactions are granted the highest priorities by the elderly as their
life space narrows because of deaths or chronic illnesses, and how these
preferences are carried out. These data are crucial in understanding the
process of aging among various ethnic groups, as well as in assessing
current and proposed programs.

The findings reported here indicate the disengagement of elderly
Japanese Americans from many social and organizational ties, but the
continued existence of a strong family system. The bulwark of this
system appears to be the adult children with whom the elderly Issei
continue to visit on a regular and frequent basis. These children may
thus be placed in the position of providing the major support network
for the elderly. If the Japanese American family is changing under a
variety of acculturative and assimilative pressures from the majority
American society, providing social support may prove increasingly difficult for the family. We need to focus intensively on the degree to which
traditional features of Japanese American family structure can be maintained and mobilized to meet the needs and demands of the Issei elderly. Despite the difficulties in studying racial and ethnic groups
(Montero and Levine, 1977), we also need to foster further research on
concepts such as disengagement using comparative data from a variety

of such groups. This information will aid in developing an effective balance between informal support networks based on family and friends and formal services for the aged.

References

Connor, J. W. *Tradition and change in three generations of Japanese Americans.* Chicago: Nelson-Hall, 1977.

Cumming, E., and Henry, W. *Growing old: The process of disengagement.* New York: Basic Books, 1961.

Gee, E. Issei women. In Emma Gee (Ed.), *Counterpoint: Perspectives on Asian America.* Los Angeles: University of California Asian American Studies Center, 1976.

Hendricks, J., and Hendricks, C. D. *Aging in mass society.* Boston: Winthrop Publishers, 1977.

Hochschild, A. Disengagement theory: A critique and proposal. *American Sociological Review,* 1975, *40,* 553–569.

Kalish, R., and Moriwaki, S. The world of the elderly Asian American. *Journal of Social Issues,* 1973, *29*(2), 187–209.

Kiefer, C. *Changing cultures, changing lives.* San Francisco: Jossey-Bass, 1974(a).

Kiefer, C. Lessons from the Issei. In Jaber F. Gubrium (Ed.), *Late life, communities and environmental policy.* Springfield, Ill.: Charles C Thomas, 1974(b).

Kitano, H. Japanese-Americans on the road to dissent. In J. Boskin and R. Rosenstone (Eds.), *Seasons of rebellion.* New York: Holt, Rinehart and Winston, 1972.

Kitano, H. *Japanese Americans: The evolution of a subculture* (2nd ed.). Englewood Cliffs, N.J.: Prentice-Hall, 1976.

Kitano, H., and Sue, S. The model minorities. *Journal of Social Issues,* 1973, *29,* 1–9.

Levine, G., and Montero, D. Socioeconomic mobility among three generations of Japanese Americans. *Journal of Social Issues,* 1973, *29*(2), 33–48.

Lyman, S. *The Asian in the West.* Social Science and Humanities Publication No. 4, Reno: University of Nevada, 1970.

Lyman, S. *The Asian in North America.* Santa Barbara, Calif.: CLIO Press, 1977.

Miyamoto, S. Social solidarity among the Japanese in Seattle. *University of Washington Publications in the Social Sciences,* 1939, *11*(2), 57–130.

Montero, D. The Japanese-American community: A study of changing patterns of ethnic affiliation over three generations. Unpublished doctoral dissertation, University of California, Los Angeles, 1978.

Montero, D., and Levine, G. (Eds.). Research among racial and cultural minorities: Problems, prospects and pitfalls. *Journal of Social Issues,* 1977, *33,* 1–222.

Park, R., and Miller, H. *Old world traits transplanted.* New York: Harper, 1921.

Petersen, W. *Japanese Americans: Oppression and success.* New York: Random House, 1971.

Plath, D. Where the family of God is the family: The role of the dead in Japanese households. *American Anthropologist,* 1964(a), *66*(2), 300–317.

Plath, D. *The after hours.* Berkeley: University of California Press, 1964(b).

Sue, S., and Kitano, H. (Eds.). Asian Americans: A success story? *Journal of Social Issues,* 1973, *29*(2), 1–209.

U.S. Bureau of the Census. *Japanese, Chinese and Filipinos in the United States: Subject report PC (2)-1G.* Washington, D.C.: U.S. Government Printing Office, 1973.

12

Aging in the Jewish Family and the Mormon Family

Donald E. Gelfand and Jody K. Olsen

The family has drawn increasing attention as a unit of analysis in American society, but it is only within the past few years that social scientists have been paying attention to the relationships between the family and their elderly parents. Unfortunately, some of this attention has resulted from the additional demand for long-term beds and the need of service providers to ascertain whether there are alternative modes of accommodating elderly parents. As the life expectancy for both men and women extends over the next 50 years, knowledge of the family and its makeup and functioning will be ever more crucial to prevent the projected increase in long-term care beds from becoming a reality.

Knowledge of aging and its relationship to the family is still limited and is especially weak in terms of the ethnic family. In this chapter we will initially outline some of the important demographic and structural issues that are affecting the aging individual within the family unit, and will then apply our framework to two major ethnic populations—Jews and Mormons.

The Aging Family

It has become popular to discuss the "graying" of the population. This phenomenon—an increase in the number of aged generally—has an impact on the major social institutions of the society, including the family.

Clearly the family has become a social unit characterized by older individuals. This aging of the family, however, does not represent the total extent of the changes. The importance of the graying of the population is not only the extent to which the individuals in the family will be older but the increasing presence of two generations of aging individuals in the family. Our projection, based on a number of indices from census data, indicates that not only will there be two generations of individuals over 55 as we move into the 21st century, but these two generations will be part of an increasingly prevalent four-generation family. The projected configuration of the four-generation family in 50 years is indicated in Table 12-1. As column (c) indicates, the four-generation family will be common in the early years of the 21st century.

These estimates are based on an increasingly late date of first marriage for white women, which accounts for the decline in the number of four-generation families by 2027 (see Gelfand, Olsen, and Block, 1978, for a detailing of these estimates). A reduction in the tendency toward late marriages would increase the prevalence of the four-generation family with two elderly generations.

We can hypothesize about the effects of this demographic configuration. At the least, we can expect that families with a large number of elderly in their 80s will experience strains resulting from the needs of these elderly for assistance of various kinds. This includes assistance for ambulation, assistance in meeting monetary demands, and psychological support to withstand the devaluation of aged individuals that occurs in American society. These support demands may be complicated by the individual needs of the second-generation individual, aged 55 and above, who is attempting to cope with the social, psychological, and physiological changes of impending "old age." At worst, a family with this configuration may find the demands of the elderly first-generation

Table 12–1.   **Configuration of White American Family by Age and Generation in 2002 and 2021**

(a) Year of Birth of Women	(b) Age of Women in 2002	(c) Age of Child in 2002	(d) Age of Women in 2027	(e) Age of Child in 2027
1892	110	83	—	—
1919	83	57	108	82
1945	57	32	82	57
1970	32	4	57	29
1998	—	—	29	—

Note: Adapted from Gelfand, D., Olsen, J., and Block, M. "Two generations of elderly in the American family: Implications for family services." *The Family Coordinator*, 1978, *27* (4), 395–404.

parent too difficult and resort to a strategy of finding long-term care organizations that will relieve them of the perceived burden of caring for the elderly parent.

The degree to which this pattern of action will be evidenced in families may vary on a large number of dimensions. Socioeconomic and demographic variables such as ethnicity may affect the reactions of individuals to the problems of elderly members of their families. Before focusing on the factor of ethnicity by examining Jews and Mormons, it is worthwhile attempting a brief discussion of other variables that may intervene in this situation and mitigate or accentuate ethnic differences. These include geographic mobility patterns, health and mental health status, age differentials, and family roles.

Geographic mobility patterns. It has been believed that a major requisite of American social mobility is a willingness to engage in geographic mobility. There have been numerous articles on the massive amounts of geographical movement among Americans. More intensive analysis indicates that the major amounts of movement among Americans does not involve major distances but moves within county lines. The effect of both long and short distance movements on relationships within families is intensive. These intense effects are felt not only within the nuclear family, but on the relationships among extended family units. Extended family relationships may be of more importance to the aging individual than to an adolescent with a wide network of friends and acquaintances.

Health and mental health status. As indicated, health and mental health status are crucial variables in understanding the relationships among family members. Johnson and Bursk (1977) found attitudes toward elderly members to be strongly related to health and associated dependencies related to a deteriorating health status. Indeed, the belief in the field has often been that physical status is a major determinant of mental health among older individuals (Lowenthal, 1968; Simon, 1971).

Age differentials. Age differentials will be important determinants of the family relationships. This has often been noted in studies of siblings but must now be carried over into studies of relationships among adult generations, especially as the aging process moves people into the different roles and statuses connected with various ages in the society. Violations of age-graded statuses are still relatively exceptional, and we cannot expect that a change in the mandatory retirement age to 70 will drastically affect the ages at which marriage, child-bearing, and career development are expected to take place.

Family roles. The roles of family members may be varied among major groups according to such attributes as class and ethnicity. Expectations of filial responsibility and even interaction may thus vary widely among families from differing backgrounds. At this point, the research available only begins to tap the roots of these differences and the degree to which expectations are, or are not, being fulfilled among various substrata. With this background in mind we can examine the effects of aging on Jewish and Mormon families.

Jews and Mormons provide interesting comparison for both their similarities and their differences. Most obvious is the fact that they are both what is probably best termed *religio-ethnic* groups. The religious element cannot be separated out as easily as is possible in discussion of more nationality based ethnic groups such as Italians or Poles. Second, although both of these groups are now firmly rooted in the American social structure, they were both immigrant groups that fought against hostility, antipathy, and discrimination before they became established in the society. Overall, both of these groups have been successful at attaining the type of social mobility believed to be an intrinsic element of the American dream for new immigrants.

In choosing to look at these two groups we are thus limiting our analysis to basically middle-class American cultures, and to individuals with options about care for their aged that may not be open to poorer members of many southern European ethnic groups as well as racially based minority groups in this society. An examination of these two groups may thus help us to distinguish the trends that prevail among upwardly mobile populations and the possibility of religious values intervening in American middle-class expectations regarding care for the aged.

Jews and the Aging Family

Analyzing Jewish and Mormon families and their relationship to the aged necessitates an historical approach. Utilization of this approach enables the social scientist to avoid the trap of viewing ethnic groups as an undifferentiated mass. This is true not only of the two religio-ethnic groups discussed in this chapter, but of other groups that can and must be differentiated by class and ethnicity. Although some sociologists have adopted Gordon's "ethclass" (1964) as a construct, in this chapter we will continue to separate the concepts and statuses attributed to ethnicity from those of class.

In discussing many American ethnic groups, it is necessary to consider a number of distinct periods of immigration, which can be separated according to the background of the migrants who entered the United States during particular periods. These distinctive periods are

important in the effect on the attitudes of individuals toward a variety
of issues and problems. As Moore (1971) has noted, it is imperative that
we examine the life-history of present-day elderly to understand their
values, attitudes, and behavior.

Jews in Europe.   In the history of American Jews, the important
events are not only the initial immigration but the succeeding waves of
immigration that came to the United States during the late 1800s and
the holocaust of World War II. Most of the early Jewish immigrants to
this country were of west and central European origin. More educated
than the groups that followed, they were also more assimilated into the
cultures they had left. Since these cultures were close in their value
premises to those of the United States, the acculturation process facing
these immigrants was considerably reduced.

The mass immigration of the 1880s produced large numbers of
Jews from Eastern European backgrounds who approximated more
closely the peasants from Eastern Europe who were fellow immigrants
than their German co-religionists. The similarities of the Eastern European Jews to gentile peasant migrants should not be overstressed
since discriminatory laws prevented Jews from owning land or participating in general communal activities. Eastern European Jews lived in
separate areas and were subject to conscription into the army at young
ages.

Jews were also subjects of the infamous pogroms, which served as
tension release for the subjugated peasants of the society and turned
hostility away from the oppressive ruling regimes. The hostility of Eastern Europeans toward Jews also had a number of unanticipated consequences. Initially, it placed Jews into the undesired position in the
society of taking on unwanted jobs. These unwanted jobs later became
important in industrializing, commercial cultures. Second, conflicts
with the "outside" community helped maintain the boundaries that
have reinforced the feeling of separateness that has been seen as a
major bulwark in the maintenance of Jewish identity (Friedmann,
1967). The status competition of Jews in their villages was in contrast
to that in other ethnic communities, partly because of restrictions on
Jewish ownership of land. In Polish communities, Lopata (1976) asserts,
competition in the village for status placed family members into a
pattern of commitment to other family members. This made them
accountable for their contribution to the family.

The Jewish *shtetl* was a precarious environment for all of its members, and there was little chance of rising above the grinding poverty
that so many of its chroniclers have described. Status differentials were
not based on land ownership. Indeed, Kutzik (1967) has argued, stratification in traditional Jewish communities was based on the participation

of the individual in Jewish philanthropic groups. Alternatively the individual would leave the Jewish community, disguise to the greatest possible degree his/her Jewishness, and achieve prosperity in the hostile gentile world. Howe (1976) describes some touching scenes of families placing their children age 14 and 15 on trains in Russia in the hope that they would be able to travel to the United States.

Jews in America. The population of Jews who entered this country has now become aged and representative of the "young-old" or "old-old" of our society. Our knowledge about this group and their relationship with the family is less than optimal because of the lack of information about Jews obtainable from the census. Any analysis of elderly Jews must therefore be extrapolated from available studies of specific Jewish populations in metropolitan areas.

Although there is still some limited immigration of Jews into the United States, this group has little influence on policies and attitudes of American Jews. The immigration into the United States that ended in the 1920s has now produced a clear age differentiation between second- and third-generation Jews. The elderly in this population will thus be primarily first- and second-generation individuals. While this is comparable to other groups, the literature has suggested some factors that supposedly still differentiate Jews from Catholics and Protestants. This includes a lower rate of alcoholism, juvenile delinquency, and crime in general and, until recently, a lower divorce rate.

The divorce rate is especially crucial for an examination of the aged in the family since the stability of the nuclear family will affect the relationships and support systems available to the elderly family members. An examination of available data indicates that divorce rates among Jews have increased considerably in the last two decades. At a recent conference on American Jewish family life (Vescey, 1978), statistics were cited indicating that 40% of Jewish marriages were now ending in divorce. This high ratio of divorce represents a form of accommodation to American norms that is troubling individuals dedicated to the maintenance of traditional Jewish ties.

If the stability of the family is being threatened by a shakiness in Jewish marriages, the position of the elderly in these family units must then be reevaluated. Howe (1976) notes that the Jewish woman had low status in the *shtetl* of Eastern Europe and therefore lost no status coming to the United States. It has commonly been assumed that the respect and prestige in these communities was accorded to the scholar. While this may have been true, the type of learning prescribed by the Talmudic tradition did not necessarily benefit the scholar who emigrated seeking opportunities in the secular American society (Slater, 1969). There were thus major complaints among Jews living on the

Lower East Side of New York about the loosening traditions of respect and observance in the early 1900s. The elderly Jews, whether scholars or tailors, could pass on attitudes but not specific training or skills that would be valuable for the younger members of the family (Howe, 1976). Still, the Jewish family has been portrayed as providing a higher degree of support than comparable Catholic or Protestant families (Wake & Sporakowski, 1972).

Mormons and the Aging Family

Development of the church.   A historical perspective is essential in understanding the current attitudes and beliefs toward the family unit and the elderly among Mormons. The Mormon church was first organized with six members in 1830 in upstate New York. However, it grew to over 1,000 members by the end of the year, mainly because of the strong proselytizing efforts made by the new members. Proselytizing has remained an important church activity to the present time. Not only was proselytizing done in New York and the surrounding area, but missionaries were sent to England and the Scandinavian countries beginning in 1837. Many of the converts from these countries were urged during the early years to move to the United States and the West, and today many Mormons in the West can trace their ancestry to these early converts (Smith, 1950).

The church and its leaders attracted opposition from the beginning. Developing a collective system of community organization and espousing first allegiance to the "Kingdom of God," the group was little understood and much feared by others. The leader of the church, Joseph Smith, had already been arrested twice before the church was eight months old. The members of the church were forced to leave New York within a year and so moved to Ohio. At this time some of the members went on to Missouri, where they encountered continual opposition. (It should be noted that this was the 1840 period before the Civil War when Missouri was undergoing an internal struggle over the slavery issue.) Many Mormons were killed in mob action and the group was forced to change counties five times during the following ten years. The group in Ohio also had to move again, this time to a new city, Nauvoo, Illinois. Further violence, which included the killing of the church leader, made it clear to members that they should move further West. The trek West inflicted additional hardships, partly because of poor preparation for the journey and the bitter winter along the way.

Once in Utah (1847) the physical harrassment from outside groups decreased, but the display of hostility remained high. Difficulty regarding plural marriage began in 1852 and was a particularly sore point for national officials. Congress denied the Mormons their vote, and finally the church as a corporation was forced to dissolve in 1889. After the rescinding of the order of plural marriage by the church president in 1890, hostility began to subside and statehood was granted to Utah in 1896. As was true of the Jews, the persecution felt by the Mormons during the nineteenth century—first in the form of repeated loss of home, property, and life, and then in the form of hostile physical elements while working the soil of desert land for a livelihood—bound the families and communities together. The Mormon communities had to stay close for group survival. Poverty was difficult to measure, as Mormon groups distanced themselves from those around and shared what resources were available among the entire group. Getting ahead was a collective process rather than an individual one of someone making it on his own (Campbell and Campbell, 1976).

The family and the early church. In this setting early families were "large, close-knit, hard-working, and religious" (Smith, 1950). The families came largely from towns, not farms, and continually recreated a town structure with each move. The importance of the collective system was a natural outgrowth of this background. The family concept became extremely important during these times, as it gave everyone a place, a belonging, a group with which to identify. With the constant turmoil, this was important for survival. As new converts joined the church, the family concept was extended to them by adoption. New members would be adopted into already practicing Mormon families since many lost their own family through alienation at the time of conversion. The practice of plural marriage, which began as early as 1842 but was not officially endorsed until 1852, can be seen as an extension of this same concept. It was deemed as a method whereby "righteous men could bring many children into the world." It was also seen as a way whereby all women could have a husband, although census information does not bear out the contention that there were many more women than men. However, there are many examples of husbands taking sisters, widowed cousins, and occasionally widowed in-laws as second wives. The first wife remained the strongest one and was the one to give permission before others were married. Actually, only 10–15% of the men of the church practiced polygamy, and of that group two-thirds had only two wives (Campbell, 1976).

Family and the contemporary church. The importance of the family and of the sense of "connection" with a family unit has been carried into the present through church doctrine. The Mormon belief is that the post-mortal existence is based on an extended family kinship network. If one does not have an affiliation on this earth with such a system, progress after death cannot occur. The family is the basic social organization in the eternal Kingdom of God. Marriage is essential to eternal progression. The importance of this is further reinforced through "geneology" and "work for the dead." Members of the church are strongly encouraged to seek out their ancestors, carefully document their vital information such as births, marriages, and children, and then, through baptism, to bring them into the church family system, so that they can have the opportunities for continued progression after mortal life. Thus, through the research and ordination process, current members within the church are reinforcing for themselves the importance of the extended family unit.

With the emphasis on preserving the extended family unit after death, there is a greater acceptance of both the extended and nuclear family units during the mortal existence. For those couples married in the Mormon Temple for "time and eternity," the divorce rate is only 2%, although it is hypothesized that part of the low divorce rate is based on the fact that in meeting the standards for temple marriage, the couple has already established commonality on many issues. For those not marrying in the Temple, the divorce rate approaches the national average.

Changes in family demography. It is interesting to note that, despite church doctrine and the continuance of a community structure through the Ward (congregation), the rate of fertility in the church is dropping, as it is nationally. Mormon families, however, are still larger (2.89) than the national average of 1.87 (Campbell, 1976). The drop is greater for those Mormon families living outside Utah than for those in the state, a reflection of the effect of their geographic distance from the central Mormon community. This change as well as others is expected to continue as more Mormons leave Utah to advance economic and professional careers.

Results of the relatively scanty research on the Mormon family and aging show that there is family involvement for the older church members. It is natural that the church should reinforce the importance of support for older members through the family since it is seen as an eternal unit and "the cornerstone of the society." The importance of this is stressed repeatedly. For example, at a worldwide church conference a general authority stated, "The church is not without its fault in the care of the aged. This is not due to the principles or teachings of the church, but rather to the shortcomings of its members" (Featherstone, 1974). The speaker went on to observe that the responsibility for caring for aged parents rests strongly with the offspring.

Family attitudes toward the elderly. In a study of elderly Mormons and their contact with adult children in two rural counties of

Utah, only 58% of the respondents had personal contact with their children, as opposed to the national average of 65%. However, both counties included had experienced several decades of population decline resulting from young people leaving because of the poor job opportunities. This was affirmed in a question which indicated that 88% of the sample had contact at least once a month by letter or telephone if not personal contact. This study also showed that most of the elderly parents interviewed expressed very close feelings toward their children. Of those interviewed, 98% felt they were close to their children. Less than 4% of the total indicated feeling less close than during the years when their children were growing up at home, thus offering some support for the argument that the Mormon family remains close, even when physical distances intervene.

This closeness was affirmed as part of the pilot project on children's attitudes toward the elderly. As part of this study, 35 Mormon children living on the East Coast were tested as to the attitudes and knowledge of the elderly, similar to a study done by Seefeldt and co-workers (1977). Although the test scores were not significantly different from those obtained by Seefeldt et al. (1977), the children expressed through anecdotal comments an active knowledge of and interest in their grandparents, most of whom lived in the West. The children talked of regular phone calls, special letters they had written, and annual summer trips to their grandparents' houses. These children knew a great deal about their grandparents even if they had seen them only five or six times in their life, information that was generated largely through the church program of "family home evening," a time each week when the family meets together. The family home evening program talks about the family and the importance of each family member.

Elderly in the church. There are two functions within the church setting that are most commonly fulfilled by older people and could provide specific role-taking opportunities.

One of these functions is Temple work. There are 14 Mormon Temples, each of which houses the performance of special ordinance (mainly to the dead) work every day except Sunday. Adult church members are asked to attend the Temple regularly and participate in the ordinance work conducted there. This activity is highly encouraged, and the congregational normative structure rewards this activity. To help assist in the ordinance work and to assist other members, "Temple workers," who are church members, are assigned by the congregation leader to work approximately seven hours a day, four days a week in the Temple. Age is not necessarily a criterion for the selection of Temple workers, but because of the time requirements and lack of financial compensation, Temple workers are usually older retired active church members. Therefore, for those older members who (1) live within close proximity of a Temple, (2) are full believers in the Church doctrine, (3) are retired with an adequate income, (4) are educationally competent to read, understand, and memorize the programs of activity, and (5) are reasonably healthy (the physical demands are too great for one in poor physical health) there is a non-family role system within the church. Only a very small percentage of older church members are active Temple workers.

A second function commonly filled by older people is that of geneology work. As indicated, this work is the systematic researching of family history. The work is to be completed on carefully designed forms and each member involved is to provide adequate verification of the key ancestral information. The work is time-consuming, particularly if the family history is being researched for the first time. This work must be completed before Temple work can be done, since most ordinance work completed in the Temples is based on the information supplied through geneology work. Although each family member is encouraged to research his or her own lineage, the task is usually assigned to an older member of the family, who completes the work for the entire family. For those older people who involve themselves in geneology work, two rewards are usually forthcoming. First, they acquire a sense of their own place in their family history, enhancing the value of the family structure. Second, they become experts in their family history and thus of great value to other family members. The other, and usually younger, family members rely on the family geneology expert for information they need to show their own congregations that they are involved in geneology work. Many times, because of this knowledge, these older people are also called upon to organize family reunions and to prepare informal family histories.

It is difficult to identify other defined functions for older members within the church structure. This is ironic, since the church leadership itself is determined by seniority, a factor that encourages a positive correlation between age and top leadership positions. The President of the church and his two counselors are 82, 75, and 78, respectively. As reported in a recent paper (Peterson, 1977), there is an informal tendency to retire people from congregation leadership activity. All congregation positions are lay, and administrative responsibilities are shared by congregation members. Seldom are older men called as bishops or stake presidents (who govern local membership wards) or older women as Relief Society or Primary (a children's organization) presidents. The emphasis on youth activity in the Mormon church means a lack of emphasis on activities for the aged. As one person indicated in the Peterson interviews, "It seems that the older members are retired from church jobs when or about the time they are forced to retire from their employment jobs. Many continued to attend their meetings but only to listen. It is easy to lapse into inactivity if there is nothing for you to do." The most common concern expressed by the 185 older Mormons interviewed by Peterson was that of finding a place to live when they might find it difficult to care for themselves. "There was the hope, the desire that in the future, when they might find it difficult to care for themselves, there would be established a retirement village, a rest home, or a nursing home that would be for them, for Mormons, run by Mormons or sponsored by the Mormon church with Mormon standards." (1977). This is an interesting response in that it indicates little faith that the family unit will be available to play a significant role in the care of the older person. Peterson found, in fact, that despite the family orientation in the church and the continued emphasis on strong family unity, "the familistic orientation was not referred to very frequently during the interviews." As was indicated early through the leadership statement, the church sees the responsibility of caring for the elderly as a family responsibility, one that will continue to strengthen the extended family ties. Yet despite expressions of regular contact and closeness to younger family members, older members of the church do not see this family tie as the solution to the problems of being old. Thus, they are caught without adequate service and housing options within the church setting. If the church made efforts to provide these services, it would be countering a component of its theological base, that of family responsibility.

It is questionable whether or not most older people within the Mormon church fare any better, on the average, than older people in general. The family unit is the basis of the church and is emphasized through all facets of church activity. This can bring a sense of belonging to a unit and a closeness not easily established outside the church setting. However, this same emphasis on the family unit and its need to support members of the family is a great inhibitor to the development of needed services if the family unit is not able to provide the services.

Conclusion

On the basis of the history described in this chapter, strong similarities could be expected in the relationships of Mormons and Jews to aged family members. There are, however, some important differences in this history that impinge on these apparent similarities and deserve examination.

The clearest commonality between Jews and Mormons is the persecution each group has suffered throughout its history, although overt persecution of Jews was stronger in Europe than it has ever been in the United States. The reality of threat of continued persecution has served as a bond for members of both of these groups. For Jews, the threat of discrimination and the need to be free of reliance on non-Jewish institutions fostered the growth of a complex network of social and health services. These service delivery systems can be found in major urban centers which contain an appreciable number of Jewish residents.

Mormon-affiliated social and health services are concentrated primarily in Utah. This difference reflects the relative degree of geographic dispersion among these two groups. Jews coming from small European communities associated farming with the peasantry that they blamed for much of their European persecution. In the United States, they concentrated on becoming workers and entrepreneurs in growing businesses and industries, many of which were marginal at that time. Whatever their occupational efforts, Jews made few attempts to stay together as a group within one specific territory. Indeed, common territoriality probably connoted for many the area in which Eastern European immigrants were forced to live together under the Czarist governments in Russia. The freedom to move individually to any area of the United States without obtaining permission was a precious right enjoyed by the new immigrant.

In contrast, the history of Mormon persecution shows a group trying to stay together and find an area where they could practice their religious-cultural beliefs without interference. While some Mormons stopped in Independence, Missouri, the major body of Mormons continued westward to Utah after their flight from Nauvoo, Illinois. The establishment of the major Mormon colony in a bounded area gave the term *community* a geographic meaning not applicable among Jews. The continuation of an agricultural tradition also helped to maintain the cohesion of an extended family. The marginal, commercial industrial occupations entered into by Jews in many urban areas required geographical changes not demanded of Mormons. Among Jews, the extended family thus encountered threats to its ties and its ability to provide mutual assistance.

The traditional respect for learning in the traditional European Jewish community was not associated with financial rewards. Respect for scholarship did, however, provide the base for an equivalent regard for expertise in other areas. Jews thus became major American consumers of services and professionals, moving quickly themselves into professional service occupations such as medicine and law.

The roles available for an older person in both of these groups is limited, although more so among Jews than among Mormons. More assimilated into the general American culture, Jews have adopted the attitudes toward aging associated with modern industrialized commercial societies. This has weakened the ability of Jewish families to deal with aging parents. As Simos (1973) indicates, many Jewish adult children indicate little comprehension of how to deal with aging parents exhibiting social, physical, and psychological problems.

"In the world, but not of the world," Mormons have maintained some roles for the elderly intrinsic to their culture. These roles provide some degree of status and prestige for an elderly individual. They include Temple work, missionary work done by older couples, and geneology work. All of these roles are church-related and limited to relatively few individuals. Given the pervasive normative quality of their religious beliefs, it is not surprising that Mormon elderly express a desire to have service provided for them by Mormons. Among Jews, church-related roles do not guarantee any degree of prestige in the community, taking a back seat to communal service efforts. This may include the philanthropic efforts, a difficult task for elderly individuals surviving on fixed incomes.

The Mormon preference for extensive church-affiliated services does not fit the Mormon belief that responsibility for personal problems remains with the family. In this regard, Mormon families may be exhibiting attitudes closer to those found among Southern and Eastern non-Jews than among Jews. In a recent study, a strong reliance on the family to provide at least the first level of assistance to the elderly was found among Italians and Poles (Fandetti and Gelfand, 1976). The point at which families in different ethnic and religio-ethnic groups turn to professional assistance remains to be determined, but a delay in seeking professional assistance for problems in a number of areas, including mental health, have been correlated with increased severity of these problems (Horwitz, 1977).

Both Mormon and Jewish families are facing severe tests. An urbanized population, Jewish families have, and expect to have, expert professional social and health services available to them in major metropolitan areas. It is as yet unclear whether these services can fill the gaps left by the loss of roles for the elderly in the family and the lack of culturally prescribed roles for the aged. More traditional, agrarian-based Mormon culture has maintained church-related roles for the elderly that are, unfortunately, not able to fulfill the needs of all elderly Mormons. Despite this deficiency, the church's emphasis on the responsibility of the family for mutual assistance implies a lower degree of service availability for the elderly whose families cannot bear the strains imposed by any appreciable physical or mental decrements.

As the family with two generations of elderly becomes more common, the demands placed on both the family and service agencies may become more severe (Gelfand, Olsen, and Block, 1978). With their lesser degree of preparedness and ideological commitment to the family, to the general exclusion of formal services, elderly Mormons may find their resources more limited than Jews. Gauging the weaknesses and strengths of ethnic groups such as Mormons and Jews and attempting to support family structures in cultures that emphasize the family will be one major aspect of future programs in gerontology.

References

Campbell, L., and Campbell, E. Emergence of the Mormons as a minority group. In Mindel, C. H., and Habenstein, R. W. (Eds.), *Ethnic families in America*. New York: Elsevier, 1976.

Fandetti, D., and Gelfand, D. E. Care of the aged: Attitudes of white ethnic families. *Gerontologist,* 1976, *16*(6), 544–549.

Featherstone, V. J. The Savior's program for the care of the aged. Presentation at the Semi-Annual General Conference of the Church, Salt Lake City, October, 1974.

Friedmann, George. *The end of the Jewish people?* New York: Doubleday, 1967.

Gelfand, D. E., Olsen, J. K., and Block, M. R. Two generations of elderly in the American family: Implications for family services. *The Family Coordinator* 1978, *27*(4), 395–404.

Gordon, M. *Assimilation in American life.* New York: Oxford University Press, 1964.

Horwitz, A. Social networks and pathways to psychiatric treatment. *Social Forces,* 1977, *56*(1), 86–105.

Howe, I. *The world of our fathers.* New York: Harcourt, Brace, Jovanovich, 1976.

Johnson, E., and Bursk, B. Relationships between the elderly and their adult children. *Gerontologist,* 1977, *17*(1), 90–96.

Kutzik, A. The social basis of American Jewish philanthropy. Unpublished doctoral dissertation, Brandeis University, 1967.

Lopata, H. *Polish-Americans.* Englewood Cliffs, N.J: Prentice-Hall, 1976.

Lowenthal, M. *Aging and mental health in San Francisco.* San Francisco: Jossey-Bass, 1968.

Moore, J. Mexican-Americans, *Gerontologist,* 1971, *11*(1), 30–36.

Peterson, E. T. The elderly among the Mormons. Unpublished manuscript, 1977. Available from Brigham Young University, Provo, Utah 84602.

Peterson, E. T. Intergenerational contact and alienation in elderly Mormon families. Unpublished manuscript, 1975. Available from Brigham Young University, Provo, Utah 84602.

Seefeldt, C., Jantz, R. K., Galper, A., Serock, K. Using pictures to explore children's attitudes toward the elderly. *The Gerontologist,* *17*(6), 1977, 506–512.

Simon, A. Mental health. In *1971 White House Conference on Aging: Physical and mental health.* Washington, D.C.. White House Conference on Aging, 1971.

Simos, B. Adult children and their aging parents, *Social Work,* 1973, *18,* 75–85.

Slater, M. My son the doctor: Aspects of mobility among American Jews. *American Sociological Review,* 1969, *34*(3), 359–373.

Smith, Joseph Fielding. *Essentials in church history.* Salt Lake City, Utah: Deseret Book Company, 1950.

Vescey, G. Confronting crisis in the orthodox Jewish family. *New York Times,* February 3, 1978, A14.

Wake, S., and Sporakowski, M. An intergenerational comparison of attitudes towards supporting aged parents. *Journal of Marriage and the Family,* 1972, *34,* 42–48.

Part III

Research on Ethnicity and Aging

The need for expanded research on ethnicity and aging is enormous. The authors in this section provide a glimpse of the many attitudinal and behavioral issues that need to be explored. From a variety of disciplinary backgrounds, they explore the role of ethnicity in the life satisfaction, general and neighborhood support systems, economic and physical well-being, and physical and mental health of the aged. It should be clear to the reader that the practical implications of these chapters are extensive. The type of theoretical and research sophistication shown here needs to be carefully translated by practitioners into a variety of assistance programs for the aged.

Cohler and Lieberman's research focuses on aged of Italian- Irish, and Polish descent and identifies psychological characteristics that allow differentiation among these three groups. Their work has major implications for the crucial issue of the continued role of ethnicity among future generations. The focus on personality factors related to ethnicity is a major step in a difficult research area. Its continuation will provide an opportunity to further delineate differences among ethnic groups which affect the individual's aging processes.

The vast majority of elderly who maintain residence in the community face serious problems. Guttmann's research is dedicated to exploring the supports white ethnic aged utilize. He differentiates the utilization of formal service networks, informal family, and non-family assistance mechanisms among eight ethnic groups of European origin. The finding of little use of existing social services raises additional ques-

tions about the effectiveness of the programs now available to the ethnic aged. Guttmann's work is closely related to Cantor's (Chapter 8) and
Biegel and Sherman's focus on mental health resources in Baltimore
and Milwaukee ethnic neighborhoods (Chapter 19).

Utilizing the same sample, Mostwin focuses on the elements involved in providing a sense of fulfillment for the aged. The differences
among the eight ethnic groups are provocative. This is especially true
of Mostwin's finding of differences between Poles in Baltimore and in
Washington, D.C. These differences reflect the need for more detailed
analyses of the interrelationship of class and ethnicity among the aged.

McAdoo examines the fear of physical violence that plagues the
Black elderly in Washington, D.C., and other major urban areas. The
omnipresent threat of personal violence reported by McAdoo may be
one of the major reinforcers, if not the cause, of the fatalism that Varghese and Medinger note among minority aged (Chapter 6). McAdoo's
work is a contribution to the increased discussion about the effects of
feared or actual violence on the lives of the elderly.

Physical security must of course be matched by the requisite economic resources that would allow the elderly to maintain a desired
lifestyle. As Snyder points out, Black elderly who have personal security
and have worked steadily for many years may still find themselves
lacking adequate income to meet their retirement needs. He shows that
recent pension reforms do not sufficiently narrow the income gap that
will continue to exist for many years between white and Black elderly.

Health services are also inadequate in meeting the needs of many
ethnic and minority elderly. The evaluation of Zambrana, Merino, and
Santana of the existing institution-based physical and mental health
services now available to Puerto Rican elderly of East Harlem leads
them to advocate an "intracommunity" approach. Central to this approach is the use of aged Puerto Rican community health workers to
facilitate Puerto Rican involvement in home-based health and social
services as well as adult day care services for the ambulatory elderly.
The authors suggest that this type of approach is suitable for any ethnic
elderly population.

Biegel and Sherman's study of ethnic neighborhoods leads them to
conclude that substantial natural as well as professional mental health
resources exist within these communities. Being fragmented and
largely unrecognized by service providers, these resources are un-
derutilized. The authors present an approach for coordinating and making such resources available, particularly to the aged. This chapter is the
first published report of a National Institute of Mental Health project,
which is already in the process of developing mental health services in
ethnic communities based on the model outlined.

The last chapter, by Markson, is based on a study of the over-65 population of two state mental hospitals in New York. The research revealed that Central and Eastern European ethnics, including Jews, are heavily overrepresented in proportion to their presence in the population. Her conclusion that placing the aged of different ethnic backgrounds in the same mental institution does them a disservice raises questions about the supposedly democratic, health-promoting policy of "integrated" and "nonsectarian" facilities.

13

Personality Change across the Second Half of Life: Findings from a Study of Irish, Italian, and Polish-American Men and Women

Bertram J. Cohler and Morton A. Lieberman

Findings from a growing number of studies have shown that personality continues to change across the life cycle, from earliest childhood through old age (Block, 1971; Maas and Kuypers, 1975; Vaillant, 1977; Neugarten, 1973). Significant transformations in personality can be observed in middle and old age. Personality change, however, is not independent of social and cultural context. This chapter considers the impact of ethnicity—cultural identity—in shaping the course of personality change across the second half of life.

Background of the Present Research

Aging and personality. While the concept of personality is one which has been subject to much criticism in the behavioral sciences (Mischel, 1973; Shweder, 1975), it is also clear, as LeVine (1973) has

This research was supported in part by AOA Grant 93-P-57425 and by NIA Grant HD MH-07521. The authors wish to thank Professors Bernice Neugarten and David Gutmann for their comments and advice throughout this research.

noted, that we cannot do without some concept of psychological processes or dispositions organized in a coherent manner, functioning to promote adaptation in ways that differ systematically across human groups.

Previous research concerning the impact of aging upon personality (Neugarten, et al., 1964) has shown that, accompanying the transition from middle to old age, both men and women show "measurable increases in inward orientation, and measurable decreases in cathexes for outer-world events" (Neugarten, 1973, p. 321). The rather unfortunate term *disengagement* was coined from this work. referring to this shifting cathexsis of the inner world with decreased energy available for social relations (Cummings and Henry, 1961). Hochschild (1975) has carefully reviewed the meanings attributed to this concept and distinguishes between two aspects of social disengagement: diminished social bonds between persons, and the person's subjective definition of the significance of these diminished social bonds. This social disengagement may be contrasted with psychological disengagement, which Neugarten (1973) refers to as interiority:

> Different modes of dealing with impulse life became salient with increasing age. Preoccupation with inner life became greater; emotional cathexes toward persons and objects in the outer world seemed to decrease; the readiness to attribute activity and affect to persons in the environment was reduced; there was a movement to persons in the environment was reduced; there was a movement away from outer-world to inner-world orientation. This change was described as increased *interiority* [Neugarten, 1973, p. 320].

In her 1964 report on aging and personality change, Neugarten and her colleagues provided a variety of dimensions and types based on different instruments, all pointing in the direction of increased interiority with age.[1] Among older men, interiority was expressed as increased passivity and oral-sensual longings, while among women, interiority was expressed as increased egocentrism and aggression; however, in both sexes there was evidence of increased introversion together with increased concern with satisfaction of personal needs. Interiority provides a useful means for organizing findings from a variety of other studies. Looft (1972), Looft and Charles (1971), Chown (1961), and Angeleitner (1974) report findings showing increased egocentrism and intolernace of divergent opinions and attitudes with age. Schaie (1959) and Chown (1968) found increased introversion with age.

1. For a critique of the typological approach to the study of personality and aging, see Livson (1973).

Brim (1976) reports a decrease in the sense of personal control with age, while results from the national survey study of Veroff and co-workers (1960) show a decrease with age in both the need for achievement and the need for affiliation.

While interiority appears to be a useful means for understanding personality change across the second half of life, the explanation for this change is somewhat less clear. In a series of papers beginning with the Kansas City research, Gutmann (1966, 1969, 1977) has interpreted these changes in terms of parental role-transitions across adulthood. Gutmann views the increased interiority accompanying aging as a part of a shift from active mastery of environmental challenges through energetic attempts to resolve problems in the world, to a more passive means of responding to such challenges through accommodation of self to environment. He suggests that, at least among men, becoming a parent leads to a sense of emergency. This results in actions designed to insure the safety and care of these offspring and determines the active mastery style of younger men. Later in adulthood, as children become adults and no longer require as much care, this sense of emergency disappears, and men adopt an increasingly passive and accommodating stance toward the environment, together with lessened emphasis upon stereotypical sex-role interests.

Gutmann's cross-cultural research has primarily involved personality changes among men. However, findings from the small-group literature (Bales, 1950), as well as from cross-cultural studies of the organization of sex roles within the family (Parsons. 1955; Zelditch, 1955), suggest that just as assumption of the parental role leads to increased efforts at active mastery among men, among women it leads to increased concern with resolving family tensions and increased preoccupation with issues of nurturance and caretaking. When their children enter adulthood, women are freed from their roles as mother and housewife and are able to devote greater time and energy to the task of realizing their own needs. This leads to increased emphasis on an active mastery style at just about the same time that men adopt more passive attitudes towards mastery.[2] However, no systematic research exists regarding changes in mastery style with aging among women.

Culture and personality change across adulthood.   Increased interiority is presumed to be a function of the aging process, independent

2. Gutmann's findings regarding the increased reliance upon passive mastery styles among older men, and preliminary observations by Gutmann and the present authors regarding increased reliance upon more active mastery styles among older women, are consistent with earlier formulations of interiority. Women appear to be more active outside the home, much of this action in the service of increased concern with realizing women's own needs in a more "egocentric" manner. On the other hand, women with dependent children emphasize primarily meeting the needs of others.

of culture. Gutmann (1977) reviews a variety of findings supporting this assumption among cultures as diverse as the Guatemalan Highland Maya and the Druze of the Middle East. Gutmann's paradigm for understanding the impact of culture on aging is based on the assumption that the personality changes he has studied are universal; cross-cultural comparisons become mere replications of the basic "experiment."

However, viewed as a system of meanings providing answers for fundamental human problems, culture is transmitted across generations and becomes the orientation of successive actions as the internalized dimensions of action of individual members of the culture (Parsons, 1951). From this perspective, different meaning systems lead to the development of quite different personality types (Weber, 1957).

Ethnicity represents the perceived continuation, among a group of persons, of meaning systems transposed from a "homeland," where the meaning system is shared in common, to another culture with a different meaning system, in which the previous world-view is no longer normative, but only one among many competing alternative solutions. To the extent that we can speak of culture as determining observed differences in behavior (including the characteristic modes of responding to personality measures), leading to differences in modal personality (Inkles and Levinson, 1954; Inkles, 1961) or in ethnic personality (Devereux, 1975), these differences can be observed across successive generations within diverse ethnic groups in pluralistic societies such as our own (Cohler, 1976; Cohler and Lieberman, 1978). Transmitted through both pre-adult and adult socialization (LeVine, 1973; Greeley, 1974; Greeley and McCready, 1974), ethnic personality is further enhanced by such structural factors as residential propinquity.[3]

From this perspective, the question addressed in this chapter is of the impact of ethnicity upon the course of personality change across the second half of life. Specifically, the extent to which ethnicity influences the expression of interiority, assessed using measures of interpersonal dominance and assertiveness, achievement, perception of locus of control as in environment or self, characteristic masculine and feminine preferences, and the Gutmann mastery style measures. It was expected

3. This propensity for immigrants and their offspring to live in residentially segregated housing (Lieberson, 1963; Heiss, 1966) has led Yancey et al. (1976) to claim that ethnicity is a pseudo-phenomenon and merely a reflection of this residential segregation. However, as Breton (1964) has noted, even these so-called ethnic communities vary in their structural characteristics, including extent of residential segregation. The poverty which Yancey et al. have noted to be associated with such ethnic communities may not be a function merely of residential segregation but of a more pervasive conflict in values as well, in which previous modes of adaptation are no longer effective, leading to what Wallace (1956) has described as "mazeway disintegration."

that, within each ethnic group, middle-aged men would display greater reliance upon active mastery and more characteristic masculine preferences than their older counterparts, while middle-aged women would be characterized by increased reliance upon passive mastery and more characteristic feminine interests than older women.

Method of Study

The Groups

Using a survey research format and a quota-sampling procedure, 386 men and women, 40 to 80 years of age, and either first- or second-generation Irish, Italian, or Polish respondents within the Chicago Standard Metropolitan Area (SMSA), were interviewed.[4] Within this group of urban respondents, the initial refusal rate was 10%, even prior to screening for eligibility in the study. Among those respondents who qualified, appointments were made for subsequent interviews, which required approximately 2½ hours of the respondent's time. More than 65% of these appointments were kept, leading to a total completion rate among eligible respondents of about 70%. The design of this study is shown in Table 13-1.

It should be noted that there were significant differences among these three ethnic groups, both in total family income (mean family income for Irish respondents = $10,058; for Italian respondents = $8,-759; for Polish respondents = $9,161; $F = 7.38$, $p < .001$; 2/316 df) and in socioeconomic status, based on education of respondent and occupation of head of household ($x^2 = 28.84$, $p < .001$, 8 df), with the social status of the Irish respondents markedly greater than that of the Italian or Polish respondents. These latter two ethnic groups were nearly identical on these measures of education and occupation.

Measurement

A number of measures were selected for this study which, on the basis of previous research, were believed to show changes with aging in the direction of increased interiority and introversion. These measures were taken from a larger survey instrument, which included self-report, thematic apperception, and other structured and semistructured approaches to personality measurement.

4. In the present study, the terms Irish, Italian, and Polish ethnic groups refer to the first- and second-generation Irish American, Italian American, and Polish American groups. In order to increase readability, the two-word term is not used, but all findings are understood to refer to these three ethnic groups.

Table 13-1. Design of the Study and Number of Persons within
Each Age, Sex, Ethnic Group[a,b]

Cell of Design		Ethnic Group						Total
		Irish		Italian		Polish		Total
		%	N	%	N	%	N	N
Sex	Age							
Men	40–49	12	(15)	10	(15)	12	(15)	45
	50–59	12	(15)	15	(21)	12	(15)	51
	60–69	12	(15)	12	(17)	13	(16)	48
	70–79	12	(15)	10	(15)	12	(15)	45
Total men:		50	(60)	47	(68)	50	(61)	189
Women	40–49	15	(17)	13	(19)	12	(15)	51
	50–59	12	(15)	15	(21)	12	(15)	51
	60–69	11	(14)	15	(21)	12	(15)	50
	70–79	12	(15)	10	(15)	12	(15)	45
Total women:		50	(61)	53	(76)	50	(60)	197
Total in study			121		144		121	386

[a] Due to rounding, column percents do not always total 100.
[b] Value of x^2 for association between age and ethnic group: 1.63 (NS; 6df). Value of x^2 for association between sex and ethnic group: 0.30 (NS; 2df). Value of x^2 for association between age and sex across groups: 0.25 (NS; 3df).

The self-sort. The measure of dominance is one of two summary measures derived from the respondent's self-sort of 48 items based on Leary's (1957) theory of personality, as modified by Rosner (1968) for use with older persons. Rosner reports both satisfactory internal consistency and stability over time for this measure of perceived interpersonal assertiveness.

Questionnaire measures. The shortened form of Rotter's (1966) measure of locus of control was based on Kuyper's (1972) item analysis of responses of older persons. We selected four items that showed satisfactory internal consistency and stability over time.

Sources of life-gratification were also derived from a questionnaire measure in which respondents selected from a list of 56 sources of gratification those which they believed to be characteristic of themselves. Much of the work on life-gratification has been reviewed by Gordon and Gaitz (1976), who follow Kleemeier's (1961) pioneering research on leisure time activity. In the present study, the concept of life gratification was broadened to include a large number of intrinsically rewarding activities. Using cluster analytic procedures, 13 scales were constructed, of which four were selected for their relevance to interiority and introversion: seeking stimulation, achievement orientation, preferred feminine activities, and preferred masculine activities. The "feminine interests" scale has 8 items correlating at least .70 with the total scale, and an internal consistency value (Cronbach's 1951 alpha) of .93. The "masculine interests" scale has five items correlating at least .66 with the full scale score, and an alpha of .90. The ten items composing the scale of seeking stimulation correlate at least .60 with the total score and the internal consistency figure of .94 shows that this scale too is unipolar. The scale of responsible achievement or achievement orientation has six items, each of which correlates at least .65 with the total score and an alpha of .91.

Thematic apperception technique. Card 17BM from Murray's (1943) Thematic Apperception Test (TAT) was administered to all respondents. This picture is described as follows by Murray: "A naked man is clinging to a rope. He is in the act of climbing up or down." These stories were scored in terms of Gutmann's (1969) scale of mastery styles, with inter-scorer reliability determined in consultation with Gutmann. Overall, 87% reliability was established (+1 scale point) across an 8-point scale later recorded to a 3-point scale, which is regarded as an ordinal scale from active, autonomous striving, to passive striving in compliance with external demands, to "autistic" mastery achieved through fantasy alone.

Speech samples. Interpersonal assertiveness was rated from a five-minute free or unstructured speech sample, using the manual developed by Gottschalk and Gleser & Winget (1969). In the present study, the speech samples contained less fluent segments than those originally employed by Gottschalk and Gleser, and the minimal acceptable sample was reduced from the 100-word segment employed by these investigators to 70 words. Analysis of the relationship between scales scored using the method developed by Gottschalk and Gleser with the 100- and 70-word minimum limits yielded measures of association and correlation with other measures which were approximately the same. However, since the 70-word minimum permits inclusion of virtually all respondents, this word limit provided the most economic use of the information from the free speech samples. Repeated studies of interrater reliability using the Gottschalk and Gleser manual yielded virtually identical correlations between rates of .80 to .83 across samples containing as many as 500 and as few as 70 words.

Findings and Discussion

While it is impossible to document personality changes over time in a cross-sectional study of the second half of life, it is possible to determine whether, in contrasting groups differing in age, personality differences may be found which are consistent with the concept of increased interi-

ority with aging. However, before considering the results from a multivariate examination of this concept, it is useful to consider the correlations among the personality measures themselves, as well as with
relevant demographic factors including age and generation in the
United States, separately for men and women within each of the three
ethnic groups; these correlations are shown in Table 13-2. Among men,
the several measures of interiority appear to be largely independent;
correlations significant at the conventional .05 level are primarily
among the measures of life-gratification. Across the three ethnic groups,
achievement orientation is the one personality measure most correlated with age among men although, within the group of Irish men,
achievement concern *increases* with age. Among women, within each
ethnic group, there is a positive correlation between achievement concern and age, suggesting a pattern of increased active mastery, a striking contrast to the decreased involvement in achievement with age
among Italian and Polish men.

There is little relationship between generation of residence in the
United States and the personality measures used in this study among
either Irish men and women or Polish men. However, among Italian
men, first-generation residence is associated with increased belief in an
external locus of control and with increased expression of feminine
interests. Among both Polish and Italian women, increased concern
with achievement is associated with first-generation residence in the
United States.

In order to study personality change across the second half of life
which previous research has suggested, these measures of interiority
were included in a discriminant analysis, contrasting middle-aged (age
41–59 years) and older (age 60–79 years) men and women within each
ethnic group. The findings from this discriminant analysis are shown in
Table 13-3, and are generally consistent with prior expectations, although varying somewhat across the three ethnic groups.

The discriminant analysis is least successful in explaining differences between middle-aged and older Italian women and Polish men.
Overall, however, this analysis correctly predicted group membership
for more than 77% of respondents. Particularly striking is the finding,
running counter to developmental predictions, that an active and assertive stance toward the environment is more characteristic of older than
of middle-aged Irish men. Older Italian and Polish men show the expected transition from active to more passive styles of mastery and
increased interiority. For women, there is a shift with age toward increasingly active mastery styles within each of the three ethnic groups,
and, with the exception of Irish women, also an increased concern with
achievement.

Table 13–2. Correlations among Personality Measures and with Age and Generation in the United States among Men and Women within the Irish, Italian, and Polish Groups[a]

Personality Measures	(1)	(2)	(3)	(4)	(5)	(6)	(7)	(8)	(9)	(10)
Irish Group (52 men; 35 women)										
Dominance (1)		-.26	-.21	.15	.20	-.32b	.09	-.15	-.13	-.20
Locus of control (2)	-.44c		.20	-.12	-.35c	.07	.16	.18	-.16	.09
Mastery style (3)	.05	.08		-.02	.07	-.20	-.00	.09	-.09	.00
Seeking stimulation (4)	-.02	-.12	-.16		-.04	-.35c	.20	.19	.16	-.08
Achievement orientation (5)	.15	.19	.19	-.12		-.05	-.09	-.07	-.24	.38c
Masculine interests (6)	-.07	-.02	.18	-.39b	-.19		-.14	-.13	.02	.19
Feminine interests (7)	.18	.13	.04	.15	.25	-.09		.12	.14	-.25
Assertiveness (8)	-.24	.16	-.17	-.02	.00	.15	.04		-.01	-.03
Generation in U.S. (9)	.05	-.12	-.05	-.01	.12	.03	.17	-.15		.07
Age in years (10)	.09	-.02	.23	-.15	.34b	.11	-.29b	-.03	-.07	
Italian Group (61 men; 54 women)										
Dominance (1)		-.01	.02	.12	.12	.11	.13	-.13	-.04	-.12
Locus of control (2)	-.23b		-.01	-.04	-.17	.11	-.17	-.13	.30b	.27b
Mastery style (3)	.02	.13		-.07	-.05	.04	-.04	-.28b	.18	.20
Seeking stimulation (4)	.38c	-.04	-.07		-.13	-.01	-.25b	.15	.05	.02
Achievement orientation (5)	.11	.01	-.12	-.06		.18	.21	.12	.21	-.45d
Masculine interests (6)	-.08	.00	.07	-.42c	.29		-.13	.08	.04	-.13
Feminine interests (7)	.25	-.17	-.32b	.00	.50d	-.25		-.16	.34c	-.27b
Assertiveness (8)	.08	.09	.06	.08	.07	-.13	.02		.14	-.20
Generation in U.S. (9)	-.08	.02	-.42c	.07	.19	-.22	.39c	.22		-.54d
Age in years (10)	-.05	.17	.43c	-.10	.24b	.27b	-.37c	.02	-.29b	
Polish Group (51 men; 38 women)										
Dominance (1)		.05	.08	-.24	.00	.09	.12	-.09	.16	-.02
Locus of control (2)	-.03		.24	-.18	-.28	.40c	-.31b	.17	-.16	.21
Mastery style (3)	-.05	.21		.04	.11	-.05	.20	.12	.00	-.08
Seeking stimulation (4)	.03	.41c	.06		-.01	-.30b	-.23	-.05	.04	-.13
Achievement orientation (5)	.29	.31	-.24	-.15		-.32b	-.03	-.06	-.14	-.47c
Masculine interests (6)	.02	.13	.21	.04	-.28		-.26b	.00	.07	.23
Feminine interests (7)	.14	-.22	-.17	-.27	.35b	-.30		.14	-.01	-.17
Assertiveness (8)	.07	.16	.23	-.03	-.07	.15	-.08		-.18	-.13
Generation in U.S. (9)	-.09	-.34b	-.23	-.23	.34b	-.03	-.28	-.22		.15
Age in years (10)	-.24	.33b	.10	.02	.42c	.17	-.51c	.00	-.41c	

a Correlations for men are shown above the diagonal and for women below the diagonal.; b p < .05; c p < .01; d p < .001

235

Table 13–3. Discriminant Analysis of Personality Measures Using Middle-aged and Older Men and Women within the Three Ethnic Groups[a]

Personality Measure	Irish		Italian		Polish	
	Men (N = 52)	Women (N = 37)	Men (N = 61)	Women (N= 54)	Men (N = 51)	Women (N = 38)
Canonical correlation	.57	.63	.59	.42	.49	.72
% Variance explained	32%	40%	35%	18%	24%	52%
% Group correctly predicted	67%	84%	80%	67%	75%	86%
Dominance: Self-sort		.98 (1)				
Locus of control scale		−.72 (3)		.49 (3)		.55 (3)
Mastery style: TAT	−.35 (3)	−.90 (2)				
Seeking stimulation			−.55 (3)	.57 (2)	−.35 (3)	
Achievement orientation	.91 (1)		−.83 (1)	.83 (1)	−.84 (1)	.83 (1)
Feminine interests	−.36 (2)		.59 (2)		.42 (2)	
Masculine interests						.71 (2)
Assertiveness: Speech sample						

[a]Standardized coefficients based on discriminant analysis using middle-aged (41–59) and older (60–79) men and women. Rank of coefficient within three highest coefficients for each discriminant analysis are shown in parentheses. Except as noted, all measures are based on personality questionnaire items.

The three highest ranked discriminant coefficients for each group are shown in Table 13-3. Concern with achievement is the single most powerful factor differentiating between the middle-aged and older groups, appearing as the first ranked discrminating factor for five of the six groups, followed by the measure of feminine interests. Feminine interests were found to increase with age among both Polish and Italian men, but appear to be more characteristic of younger than of older Irish men. Older Irish men emphasize active mastery styles to a greater extent than younger men and are more concerned with achievement and less interested in typically feminine pursuits. Older Irish women are more dominant than their younger counterparts, and both prefer explanations of actions based on self rather than environment and emphasize an active mastery style to a greater extent than middle-aged Irish women.

Older Italian men avoid external stimulation, rely to a greater extent on passive mastery, and emphasize more typical feminine pursuits to a greater extent than middle-aged Italian men, while older Italian women are more concerned with achievement and with seeking stimulation than their younger counterparts, but also rely to a greater extent on an explanation of actions based on the environment rather than the self.

The pattern for Polish men is identical with that among Italian men. Older Polish women tend to be more concerned with achievement than their younger counterparts and prefer, to a greater extent, more typically masculine interests. However, as among Italian women, the older group tends to emphasize an external locus of control to a greater extent than the younger group. Among women, overall, there is evidence of increased concern with achievement and with an active and assertive challenge to the environment. This pattern, found consistently across the three ethnic groups, fits well into Gutmann's (1975, 1977) theory of the "parental imperative," for it is only after the middle years that women are freed from the care of dependent offspring.

The findings from this comparative cross-sectional analysis of three ethnic groups provides some confirmation for a theory of personality change across the second half of life based on the closely related concepts of interiority and mastery styles. At the same time, ethnicity appears to have an impact upon this process of personality change across the second half of life.

The clearest effect of ethnicity was found among the men studied. While older Italian and Polish men show increased passive mastery, and accompanying preferences for more sensual and regressive forms of satisfaction said to accompany the transition to old age among men (Gutmann, 1969, 1977), the reverse pattern differentiates middle-aged from older Irish men.

Two not unrelated factors, social status and cultural background, may account for the different pattern of personality change accompanying aging among Irish men, as contrasted to the Italian and Polish men. Consistent with the higher mean income level reported for the Irish ethnic group, Cohler and Lieberman (1977) have reported that the mean social status of Irish respondents is significantly greater than that of respondents in the two other groups ($p < .001$). Such economic success may lead to increased concern with achievement among Irish respondents when contrasted with those in the two other ethnic groups.

European immigrants who decided to migrate to America may have been more ambitious than their counterparts who chose to remain at home (Kleiner and Parker, 1963), leading to increased desire for achievement in the new society; such a propensity is particularly marked among Irish immigrants (Greeley, 1974). Such selectivity may be understood in the particular migration history of the Irish. The characteristic pattern of land inheritance among rural Irish families is for the father to select one adult child, not necessarily the eldest son, particularly interested in maintaining the family farm (Arensberg, 1959; Arensberg and Kimball, 1968; Humphreys, 1966); this child inherits the land by general family agreement.

Another alternative, existing even before the introduction of large-scale potato cultivation in the 18th century, was for the Irish father to break up the farm into smaller units among each of the children wishing to remain with the land. Potato cultivation increased the yield possible from small land holdings over that which could be realized from grain crops and made this pattern of land distribution even more viable (Lees and Modell, 1977). However, as Freeman (1957) has noted, over a period of time, farms became so small that many farmers were reduced to a status akin to that of a day laborer.

The more discontented and achievement-oriented of these farmers sought to leave the land, but neither Dublin nor London was a possibile site for relocation. As a result of a series of economic reversals, including the inability of Irish textiles to compete with those manufactured more efficiently and at lower cost by English mills, there was little work available in the depressed Irish cities. London was hardly receptive to Irish migrants, leaving little alternative for ambitious Irish countrymen but to migrate to the United States or to join the Church. The result was selection in favor of increased achievement motivation among those who choose to emigrate.[5]

Further, in contrast with members of the Polish or Italian ethnic groups, Irish immigrants tended to migrate alone rather than as a part of a family group. This solo migration was due in part to the rather late age at which marriage takes place among both men and women in rural Ireland (Arensberg and Kimball, 1968), in turn due in part to the fact that living apart from the larger village unit, communication with other villagers was less complete. As a result of both the absence of other close family members and less detailed knowledge of the New World, the Irish immigrant arrived by himself, responsible to a greater extent than among Eastern and Southern immigrant groups for making his own way in the New World.

In contrast with the Irish pattern of inheritance, Italian families did not actually own family farms. but rented a number of land parcels from large landowners and lived in agro-villages often separated from these land plots by many kilometers (Chapman, 1971; Boissevain, 1966; Cronin, 1970). There is no property to transmit to the next generation and, given the degree of poverty and lack of opportunity for economic sources which continues to characterize southern Italy and Sicily, and an entire family might decide to emigrate to the United States, helped along by other villagers who have already settled in the United States, a process described by the McDonalds (1964) as *chain migration*. The

5. While the Great Famine of the 1840s gave new impetus to emigration, it did not appear to alter the process leading more ambitious countrymen to emigrate; those more ambitious were simply given additional reason to emigrate to the United States and, to some extent, Canada and Australia as well.

fact that Italian peasants live in villages rather than on isolated family farms increases communication about such possibilities of greater success in the New World and thus facilitates migration. In contrast with the Irish countryman, who usually moved alone to the United States, the pattern in southern Italy and Sicily was for the nuclear family unit to move to the New World, continuing the social structure of the village in residentially segregated communities in the United States (Gans, 1962; Suttles, 1968; Cohler, 1976).

The Polish pattern of immigration is intermediate between the extremes of the Irish and Italian patterns, for there is a family farm tradition in rural Poland, with transmission of land to succeeding generations, principally through the eldest son. Reports such as the classic study of Thomas and Znaniecki (1918–1920) and the more recent comparative ethnographic study by Bloch (1976) suggest that men and women choosing to immigrate from Poland to the United States, as contrasted to those who remain at home, do show increased desire for achievement. On the other hand, migration from Poland to the United States is supported by local parish of the Church and is more of a corporate decision than among Irish immigrants, who seek their fortune largely on their own, without the support of other family members or fellow villagers (Lopata, 1976; Kantowicz, 1977). The more independent and autonomous actions required of the Irish countryman in deciding to immigrate are consistent with the concern with independence, achievement, and active mastery which subsequently becomes an important part of ethnic personality.

In addition to the role of the immigration process itself in fostering this increased emphasis upon initiative and mastery, the very nature of social relations in the Old World affects the extent to which active mastery is represented as an important aspect of ethnic personality among members of these three ethnic groups in America. Schooler (1976), notes that the "legacy of serfdom" was represented to a different extent in Northern Europe, including Ireland, and in Eastern and Southern Europe. The fuedal system, which encourages passive responses to problems and dependency in social relations, never took hold in Ireland (Greeley, 1972), and even English rule, which began with Henry II in 1156, had little impact upon Irish society; rebellion and strife between the Irish and the English in Ireland was pervasive until the realization of Irish independence after the first World War.[6] In

6. While in at least some counties Irish farmers worked land owned by English landlords, this was not a truly feudal system and the farmer was not regarded as a serf; therefore, in contrast to their Continental counterparts, Irish countrymen did not suffer the psychological consequences of fuedalism.

contrast with this Irish quest for independence, the feudal land-tenure system, which was pervasive in Eastern Europe until the 19th century and which continued in southern Italy until quite recently, has had a quite different psychological impact. As Schooler notes, the effect of living in a society in which decisions about land and the produce of one's own labor are made by others is that there is a loss of feeling of autonomy and capacity for rational planning, together with increased feelings of subjugation to control by external forces.

Schooler's formulation and the accompanying presentation of preliminary findings from a cross-ethnic study in the United States are consistent both with results of other systematic research and with ethnographic reports showing the increased preference among Southern and Eastern European immigrants and their descendants for a present-oriented, concrete, and passive stance toward the environment, which is in such contrast to the striving for autonomy and a capacity for rational planning characteristic of Western European and American society (Weber, 1957; Covello, 1972; Moss and Cappannari, 1960a,b; Kluckhohn and Strodtbeck, 1961; Gans, 1962; Spiegel, 1971).

It is interesting to note that Schooler's findings of increased emphasis upon an external locus of control among persons from Eastern and Southern European cultures, most closely identified with the "legacy of serfdom," as contrasted with Northern European societies, were replicated in the present study, at least among the women.[7] For both Italian and Polish women, although the transistion from middle to old age was in other respects marked by increased assertiveness and more active efforts at mastery, it was also marked by increased emphasis upon perception of the environment as the source of control of supplies and satisfactions, which is usually more characteristic of passive mastery. This emphasis upon external locus of control is in marked contrast with the emphasis upon both increased active mastery and internal locus of control characteristic of older Irish women, who are from a culture in which the legacy of serfdom has been much less pronounced, and shows once more the continuing influence of ethnicity upon the nature of personality change across the second half of life.

7. It should be noted that the findings reported here and the conclusions reached on the basis of these findings refer to a quite specific cohort of European immigrants and their direct descendants. Different historical events and different pathways to migration among more recent immigrants, even from within these same ethnic groups, may well lead to quite different patterns of personality changes with aging. As Ryder (1965), Riley (1973), and Elder (1974), have noted, successive generations are affected by such historical circumstances in quite different ways (but also see Rosow, 1978, for a lucid critique of the use of cohort analysis).

Summary and Conclusion

Findings from studies of personality change across the second half of life have shown that the transition from middle to old age is accompanied by increased preoccupation with self and increased introversion which, among men, appears as increased passivity in responding to challenges from the environment, together with increased interest in provision of basic sustenance for self. Among women this transition from middle to old age is characterized by greater egocentrism and assertiveness, which is reflected in increased concern with active mastery, although primarily in order to provide for one's own needs rather than those of others.

Most previous research in this area has focused upon personality change among men and has been concerned primarily with the attempt to demonstrate the universality of this personality change across cultures. The present study was concerned with the impact of cultural processes, represented by ethnicity, as a factor influencing the course of personality change across the second half of life. While findings were much as expected among the Italian and Polish ethnic groups, with increased reliance upon passive mastery differentiating middle-aged from older men, and increased emphasis upon achievement and active mastery differentiating middle-aged from older women (a finding also reported among Irish women), quite contrary results were reported among Irish men. In contrast to their counterparts in the two other ethnic groups, older Irish men can be differentiated from middle-aged men by greater concern with active mastery and with achievement.

This difference in mode of personality change with age among Irish men as contrasted with men in the two other groups, and to a certain extent among Irish women as contrasted with women in the two other groups, may in part be explained by ethnic differences growing out of patterns of land tenure in the Old World together with patterns of migration to the New World: Italian and Polish respondents came from a tradition of serfdom in which individual initiative and responsibility were discouraged and in which migration to the United States was undertaken by family units embedded in a complex set of relations with relatives and villagers who had previously emigrated. Irish respondents came from a culture in which this tradition of serfdom was much less important and in which the prevailing pattern of land inheritance emphasized individual initiative and achievement; life careers among those not choosing to remain with the land were left largely up to individual initiative with little choice available for the most ambitious except migration to the New World. This emphasis upon individual achievement, together with an emphasis upon delaying marriage until middle-age, and upon living as a part of an isolated family unit outside the village support system, led to a pattern of individual rather than collective-family migration among Irish immigrants, which promoted increased rather than decreased concern with active mastery among older men and women within the Irish group. The findings of the present study show that personality change across the second half of life is not independent of cultural context and that aging may accentuate differences in modal or ethnic personality.

References

Angeleitner, A. Changes in personality of older people over a 5-year period of observation. *Gerontologica,* 1974, *20,* 179–185.

Arensberg, C. *The Irish countryman: An anthropological study* (1936), Gloucester, Mass.: Peter Smith, 1959.

Arensberg, C., and Kimball, S. *Family and community in Ireland* (1940) (Second Edition). Cambridge, Mass.: Harvard University Press, 1968.

Bales, R. F. *Interaction Process analysis: A method for the study of small groups.* Reading, Mass.: Addison-Wesley, 1950.

Boissevain, J. Poverty and politics in a Sicilian agro-town. *International Archives of Ethnography,* 1966, *1,* 198–236.

Bloch, H. Changing domestic roles among Polish immigrant women. *Anthropological Quarterly,* 1976, *49,* 1–10.

Block, J. *Lives through time.* Berkeley, Calif.: Bancroft Books, 1971.

Breton, R Institutional completeness of ethnic communities and the personal relations of immigrants. *American Journal of Sociology,* 1964, *70,* 193–205.

Brim, O. Life-span development of the theory of oneself. In H. Reese and L. Lipsitt (Eds.), *Advances in child development and behavior,* Vol. II. New York: Academic Press, 1976, 241–251.

Chapman, M. (Gower-Chapman). *Milocca: A Sicilian village* (1935). Cambridge, Mass.: Shenkman Publishing Co., 1971.

Chown, S. Age and the rigidities. *Journal of Gerontology,* 1961, *16,* 353–362.

Chown, S. Personality and aging. In K. W. Schaie (Ed.), *Theory and methods of research on aging.* Morgantown, West Virginia: The University of West Virginia Library, 1968.

Cohler, B., and Grunekaum, H. *Mothers and Grandmothers: Personality and Childcare in Three Generation Families.* Chicago: The University of Chicago, Committee on Human Development, 1976.

Cohler, B., Lieberman, M., and Welch, L. *Social Relations and Interpersonal Resources among Middle-aged and Older Irish, Italian, and Polish-American Men and Women.* Chicago: The University of Chicago, Committee on Human Development, 1977.

Cohler, B., and Lieberman, M. Ethnicity and personal adaptation. *International Journal of Group Tensions,* 1977, *1* (3–4), 22–41.

Covello, L. *The Social Background of the Italo-American School Child* (1944). Totowa, New Jersey: Rowman and Littlefield, 1972.

Cronbach, L. Coefficient alpha and the internal structure of tests. *Psychometrika*, 1951, *16*, 297–334.

Cronin, C. *The Sting of Change: Sicilians in Sicily and Australia.* Chicago: The University of Chicago Press, 1970.

Cumming, E., and Henry, W. *Growing Old.* New York: Basic Books, 1961.

Devereux, G. Ethnic identity: its logical function and its dysfunctions. In G. De Vos and L. Romanucci-Ross (Eds.), *Ethnic identity: Cultural Continuities and Change.* Palo Alto, Calif. Mayfield Publishing Company, 1975, 72–70.

Elder, G. *Children of the Great Depression.* Chicago: The University of Chicago Press, 1974.

Gans, H. *The Urban Villagers: Group and Class in the Life of the Italian-Americans.* New York: The Free Press-Macmillan, 1962.

Gordon, C., and Gaitz, C. Leisure and lives: Personal expressivity across the life-span. In R. Binstock and E. Shanas (Eds.), *Handbook of Aging and the Social Sciences.* New York. Van Nostrand Reinhold, 1976, 310–341.

Freeman, T. W. *Pre-Famine Ireland.* Manchester: The University of Manchester Press, 1957.

Gottschalk, L. and Gleser, W G. & Winget, C. Manual of instruction for using the Gottschalk & Gleser content analysis scales. Berkeley, Ca: Univ. of California Press, 1969.

Greeley, A. *That Most Distressful Nation.* Chicago: Quadrangle Books, 1972.

Greeley, A. *Ethnicity in the United States.* New York: Wiley, 1974.

Greeley, A., and McCready, W. Does ethnicity matter? *Ethnicity,* 1974, *1*, 89–108;

Gutmann, D. Mayan aging: a comparative TAT study. *Psychiatry,* 1966, *29*, 246–259.

Gutmann, D. In the country of old men: Cross-cultural studies in the psychology of later life. *Occasional Papers in Gerontology,* Number 5. Ann Arbor: Institute of Gerontology, University of Michigan-Wayne State University, 1969.

Gutmann, D. Parenthood: A key to the comparative study of the life-cycle. In N. Datan and L. Ginsberg (Eds.), *Life-Span Developmental Psychology.* New York: Academic Press, 1975, 167–184.

Gutmann, D. Notes toward a comparative psychology of aging. In J. Birren and K. W. Schaie (Eds.), *Handbook of the Psychology of Aging.* New York: Van Nostrand-Reinhold, 1977, 302–326.

Heiss, J. Residential segregation and the assimilation of Italians in an Australian city. *International Migration Review,* 1966, *4*, 165–171.

Hochschild, A. Disengagement theory: A critique and a proposal. *American Sociological Review,* 1975, *40*, 553–569.

Humphreys, A. *New Dubliners: Urbanization and the Irish Family.* London: Routledge-Kegan Paul, 1966.

Inkles, A. Personality and social structure. In R. K. Merton, L. Broom, and L. S. Cottrell (Eds.), *Sociology Today: Problems and Prospects.* New York: Basic Books, 1961, 249–278.

Inkles, A., and Levinson, D. National character: The study of modal personality and socio-cultural systems. In G. Lindzey (Ed.), *Handbook of Social Psychology*, Vol. II. Reading, Mass.: Addison-Wesley, 1954, 977–1020.

Kantowicz, E. Polish Chicago: Survival through solidarity. In M. Holli and P. D. A. Jones (Eds.), *The Ethnic Frontier.* Grand Rapids, Mich.: Eerdmans Publishing Company, 1977, 179–210.

Kleemeier, R. *Aging and Leisure.* New York: Oxford University Press, 1961.

Kleiner, R., and Parker, S. Goal striving and social status, and mental disorder. *American Sociological Review,* 1963, *28,* 189–203

Kluckhohn, F., and Strodtbeck, F. *Variations in Value Orientations.* New York: Harper and Row, 1961.

Kramer, S., and Masur, J. *Jewish Grandmothers.* Boston: Beacon Press, 1976.

Kuypers, J. Internal locus of control, ego functioning, and personality characteristics in old age. *The Gerontologist,* 1972, *12,* 163–173.

Leary, T. *The Interpersonal Diagnosis of Personaltiy.* New York: The Ronald Press, 1957.

LeVine, R. Behavior and Personality. Chicago: Aldine Publishers, 1973.

Lieberson, S. *Ethnic Patterns in American Cities.* New York: Free Press-Macmillan, 1963.

Livson, N. Developmental dimensions of personality: a life-span formulation. In P. Baltes and K. W. Schaie (Eds.), *Life-Span Developmental Psychology: Personality and Socialization.* New York: Academic Press, 1973, 98–123.

Looft, W. Egocentrism and social interaction across the life span. *Psychological Bulletin,* 1972, *78,* 73–92.

Looft, W. & Charles, D. Egocentrism and social interaction in young and old adults. *Aging and Human Development*, 1971, 2, 21–28

McDonald, J., and McDonald, L. Chain migration, ethnic neighborhood formation, and social networks. *Milbank Memorial Fund Quarterly,* 1964, *42,* 82–97.

Lees, L., and Modell, J. The Irish countryman urbanized: A comparative perspective on the famine migration. *Journal of Urban History,* 1977, *3,* 391–408.

Lopata, H. *Polish-Americans: Status Competition in an Ethnic Community.* Englewood-Cliffs, N.J.: Prentice-Hall, 1976.

Maas, H., and Kuypers, J. *From Thirty to Seventy.* San Francisco: Jossey-Bass, 1975.

Mischel, W. Towards a cognitive social learning reconceptualization of personality. *Psychological Review,* 1973, *80,* 252–283.

Moss, L., and Cappannari, S. Patterns of kinship, comparaggio, and community in a south Italian village. *Anthropological Quarterly,* 1960, *33,* 24–32 (a).

Moss, L., and Cappannari, S. Folklore and medicine in an Italian village. *Journal of American Folklore,* 1960, *73,* 95–102 (b).

Murray, H. *The Thematic Apperception Test.* Cambridge, Mass.: Harvard University Press, 1943.

Neugarten, B., and associates. *Personality in Middle and Late Life.* New York: Atherton, 1964.

Neugarten, B. Personality change in late life: A developmental perspective. In C. Eisdorfer and M. P. Lawton (Eds.), *The Psychology of Adult Development and Aging.* Washington: American Psychological Association, 1973, 311–338.

Parsons, T. *The Social System.* New York: Free Press-Macmillan, 1951.

Parsons, T. Family structure and the socialization of the child. In T. Parsons and F. Bales (Eds.), *Family Socialization and Interaction Process.* New York: Free Press-Macmillan, 1955, 35–131.

Riley, M. Aging and cohort succession: Interpretations and misinterpretations. *Public Opinion Quarterly,* 1973, *37,* 35–49.

Rosner, A. Stress and Maintenance of Self-Concept in the Aged. Unpublished doctoral dissertation, The University of Chicago, 1968.

Rosow, I. What is a cohort and why. *Human Development,* 1978, *21,* 65–75.

Rotter, J. Generalized expectancies for internal versus external control of reinforcement. *Psychological Monographs,* 1966, *80,* No. 1, whole No. 609.

Ryder, N. The cohort as a concept in the study of social change. *American Sociological Review,* 1965, *30,* 843–861.

Schaie, W. The effect of age on a scale of social responsibility. *Journal of Social Psychology,* 1959, *50,* 221–224.

Schooler, C. Serfdom's legacy: an ethnic continuum. *American Journal of Sociology,* 1976, *81,* 1265–1285.

Shweder, R. How relevant is an individual difference theory of personality. *Journal of Personality,* 1975, *43,* 455–484.

Spiegel, J. *Transactions: The Interplay between Individual, Family and Society.* New York: Science House-Aronson, 1971.

Suttles, G. *The Social Order of the Slums.* Chicago: The University of Chicago Press, 1968.

Thomas, W. U., and Znaniecki, F. *The Polish Peasant in Europe and American* (two volumes). New York: Alfred Knopf, 1918–1920.

Vaillant, G. *Adaptation to Life.* Boston: Little-Brown, 1977.

Veroff, J., Atkinson, J., Feld, S., and Gurin, G. The Use of thematic apperception to assess motivation in a nationwide interview study. *Psychological Monographs,* 1960, *74*(499), 12.

Wallace, W. Revitalizing movements *American Anthropologist,* 1956, *58,* 264–281.

Weber, M. *The Protestant Ethic and the Spirit of Capitalism* (1904–05) (tr. Talcott Parsons). New York: Charles Scribners, 1957.

Yancey, W., Erickson, E., and Juliani, R. Emergent ethnicity: a review and formulation. *American Sociological Review,* 1976, *41,* 391–403

Zelditch, M. Role differentiation in the nuclear family: A comparative study. In T. Parsons and F. Bales (Eds.), *Family, Socialization and Interaction Process.* New York: Free Press-Macmillan, 1955.

14

Use of Informal and Formal Supports by White Ethnic Aged

David Guttmann

In recent years there has been a decline in "melting pot" theories of racial and ethnic assimilation. At the same time, the notion of American society as a pluralistic system of "unmeltable ethnics" (Novak, 1973) has been gaining ground. Even though ethnicity continues to be an important determinant of human behavior and a necessary condition for meaningful living for millions of American citizens, scholars have given little or no serious consideration to its effect upon the lives of the aged. Thus, despite increased research activity on aging, we know relatively little about the aged within the various ethnic groups, their current patterns and conditions of living, or the factors that promote (or hinder) wholesome and meaningful living.

The purpose of this chapter, therefore, is to examine the relationship of several ethnic communities to aging and the aged. Specific attention will be given to support systems used by white ethnics from Eastern, Central, and Southern Europe. In addition, this study assesses the extent and impact of support of the ethnic communities on the overall well-being of the elderly. That is, the study looks at whether elderly ethnics are provided with the kind of help they seek in order to cope with their problems, whether they have opportunities for personal growth and enrichment, and whether they participate in cultural and social organizations and in group activities. Equally important, the study seeks to discover how the support systems used may be maximized and what is needed to make these support systems amenable to the elderly's need for optimal conditions of living. An integral part of this effort is to study stated preferences for services by ethnic elderly and to provide a basis for strategy in utilizing support systems by government agencies and by ethnic communities in planning and in service delivery.

Significance and Rationale

Discovering the use of support systems by the elderly in various ethnic communities is in line with Kaplan's (1975) recommendations concerning research about the elderly of different ethnic groups. Kaplan stresses the need to recognize the range of behavior within each group and to determine whether it is best to use similar means to meet what appear to be the same wishes in different ethnic groups. Encouraging the study of ethnic elderly, Kalish (1971) notes that almost nothing has been written about ways in which ethnic communities may ease life for the aging person (or make it more difficult). Our analysis of the unique cultural patterns of various ethnic groups follows Moore's (1971) suggestion of studying minority group elderly in order to gain knowledge about the functioning of aging individuals in small groups, as well as in larger and more distinctive collectivities.

Further justification for undertaking this research is based on continued requests by social scientists to assign high priority to ethnic factors in studies about the elderly. In social work, for example, Kolodny (1969) notes that there has been a general lack of systematic appraisal of ethnic factors in relation to people's needs and use of services. Current understanding of the process of aging and attempts to provide programs for the older segment of society suggest that this population is as heterogeneous as society in general (Crouch, 1972). A historical examination of intergroup relations in the United States reveals the pervasiveness of ethnic tensions and suggests the large extent to which ethnicity must be taken into account in social planning.

While the situation of the ethnic aged in American society is still largely in the stage of early exploration, some headway has been made in research with regard to racial minorities. Several aspects of this research are applicable to studies of cultural differentiation in the aging process and to the aged. There is still, however, insufficient recognition of the specific problems of white ethnic groups in general. From the viewpoint of society, the main questions center around the formal and informal support systems that exist within the various American ethnic groups and the relationship of these supports to efforts by the general society to deal with the problems of the aged.

Theoretical Framework

The wide variability and complexity of both "ethnicity" and "aging" make it necessary to adopt a theoretical framework broad enough to embrace all the relevant structural and dynamic elements. Therefore, this study was based on the symbolic interaction theory of Mead (1934) and Parsons (1968). This theoretical framework encompasses both the sociological and psychological aspects of human behavior.

The symbolic interaction theory, with its emphasis on social interaction as a base for the interpretation (meaning) of the surrounding world, seems to be applicable to the problems of aging persons in cultural groups in relation to the diverse, patterned, and sociocultural aspects of the aging individual's life (Kolm, 1977). Within this framework, "ethnic factor" or "ethnicity" is defined as the cultural bond of a given social group. However, the "cultural content" of the bond (i.e., unique patterns of values, beliefs, traditions, languages, and behavior) has been derived historically and transmitted from generation to generation, perhaps in a modified form but still recognizable as belonging to that group. These patterns form the basic elements of a group's broadest identity which, in turn, provides the basis for the organization of the individual identities of the members of a group. Thus viewed in the framework of the interrelationship of cultural content, social structures, and personality, old age may be perceived as a phase of the individual life-cycle. Like all other such phases, aging is subject to normative patterns (cultural and social) developed by the group in its history (Kolm, 1977).

In this study it is assumed that the nature of participation in one's ethnic group will reflect the previous patterns of behavior and lifestyle of that group. If a certain lifestyle has proven to be satisfying in adulthood, the same type of behavior will most likely continue into old age as well. Yet the nature of satisfaction will vary according to culturally induced values and attitudes toward life and toward the aging process.

Formulation of the research problem. The principal question underlying this study was: In decision making concerning services to the aged, what do we have to know about the ethnic component in the aged's utilization of support systems within various communities? In formulating the research problem, attention was focused on four major questions emerging from the theoretical framework and from the review of the literature:

1. What are the particular problems and needs of the elderly in different ethnic groups?

2. What are the ethnic support systems which meet these needs?

3. What is the relationship of the services provided by the general community and society to these particular ethnic support systems?

4. Could ethnic support systems be utilized and reinforced within the existing framework of assistance provided by society?

Research Design and Hypotheses

The research design in this exploratory study was based on an ethnographic survey of specific ethnic groups. Ethnographic surveys, as Cuellar (1974) points out, enable the researcher to gain knowledge about specific populations, such as selected ethnic subcommunities in a metropolitan area. The idea here is not to select a representative sample of the elderly citizens in a given city, but rather to study more intensively various subgroups of aged who are most likely to have different lifestyles and probably different needs. This idea, in turn, was translated into the following formal hypotheses:

1. There will be significant differences in use of the support systems by the ethnic elderly with regard to emphasis on formal and informal supports used.

2. The main variables differentiating the use of support systems among the ethnic groups will be their immigration status, income, occupation, and level of education.

3. There will be a difference between concentrated and dispersed ethnic communities in use of particular support systems.

Population and sampling. Eight white ethnic groups in the Washington/Baltimore area were selected as the universe for the study: Estonians, Greeks, Hungarians, Italians, Jews, Latvians, Lithuanians, and two groups of Poles. In order to test the differences between concentrated (Baltimore) and dispersed (Washington) types of ethnic communities, we added the second group of Polish elderly. These groups include both old immigrants (those who came to this country prior to World War II) and new immigrants (those who emigrated after World War II). All of the groups were assumed to be ethnically strong and well organized. We also assumed that, in addition to their pronounced cultural differences, the groups would differ in terms of religion, time of migration to the United States, patterns of settlement in this country, and socioeconomic status.

Instruments, Data Collection, and Analysis

In the absence of an available standardized scale to measure the support systems utilization by the elderly in ethnic groups, we formulated, constructed, and validated our own instrument—a questionnaire consisting of 102 items. In creating the research tools, we relied on the expertise of nationally known gerontologists[1] and the assistance of an advisory council of representatives of the ethnic groups studied.[2] The final version of the questionnaire included measures on (1) ethnic awareness and participation in community life; (2) demographic background, including socioeconomic data; and (3) use of support systems.[3]

The questionnaire was translated into seven languages: Estonian, Greek, Hungarian, Italian, Latvian, Lithuanian, and Polish.[4] Interviewers were selected on the basis of their knowledge of the ethnic community and the ethnic language and were trained in the proper administration of the questionnaire. A follow-up survey on the extent of ethnic language used in interviews revealed that for over half of the sample, use of the ethnic language with the elderly subjects was either a necessity or a convenience. Therefore, we may conclude that knowledge of the ethnic language and translation of the instruments are important preconditions for successfully reaching the ethnic elderly.

Data were analyzed both descriptively and inferentially. Frequencies, means, and percentages for the total sample and for each specific ethnic group were the first steps in data analysis. These steps were followed by cross-tabulations of selected variables such as sex, education, income, and length of stay in the United States in order to identify the statistically significant differences among the groups according to immigration patterns—whether the subjects were old immigrants who came to this country prior to 1939, new immigrants who came after 1939, or U.S. born—and by analysis of variance.

1. We wish to acknowledge the assistance and valuable suggestions of Drs. Helen Lopata, Robert Habenstein, and Lewis W. Carr.
2. We also wish to thank members of the Advisory Council in Washington, D.C., and Baltimore, Maryland.
3. The questionnaire, along with the coding instruments, is available upon request.
4. We were assured by the spokespersons of the Jewish community that the Jewish elderly have no difficulty in speaking English. For this reason we did not consider it necessary to translate the questionnaire into Yiddish.

Results

Use of Formal Supports

Differences among the ethnic groups emerged in both the number and type of formal services used by ethnic elderly:

1. Jewish elderly used more services than any other of the ethnic groups.

2. Almost 75% of the Hungarians did not use any of the formal services.

3. *Medicaid* was used by 20% to 25% of the elderly in the Greek, Jewish, Hungarian, and Polish (Washington) groups, and to a considerably less degree by the other groups.

4. Use of *food stamps* was minimal.

5. Little or no use was reported for *meals on wheels*.

6. Only a small percentage of Italian and Jewish elderly used the *hot lunch* program.

7. *Housing subsidies* were utilized by 11.3% of the Jewish group and by extremely small percentages of the other groups.

8. Estonians led the rest of the groups in using *clinics* (15%) and *police* (13.8%).

9. Close to 40% of Jewish elderly (more than three times the average) used *community centers*.

10. *Counseling* was seldom used by any group.

11. *Visiting nurses* were used by a small percentage of the population.

12. *Escort services* were not used at all.

13. A little over 50% of Greeks used *church-provided services* (51.3%), followed by Italians (37.5%), and by 20% each of the Estonian and Jewish elderly.

In general, it is important to note that all of these formal supports were utilized by only a small portion of the respondents.

Further analysis of the data was done by using cross-tabulations. Specifically, we assessed whether the use of the support systems by the ethnic groups studied was significantly different by immigration status.

Only six of the 16 services listed were significantly different in terms of their use by old immigrants, new immigrants, and U.S.-born ethnic elderly. New immigrants used more health clinics and Medicaid than the other two groups. U.S.-born elderly used significantly more senior citizen centers, while the old immigrants used the church and visiting nurses as important formal supports. Overall, between 71% and

85% of all elderly in the eight ethnic groups reported that they did not use any services.

These findings indicate that formal services either do not reach a large segment of the ethnic elderly or that the elderly in these white ethnic groups have less need for government-offered services. That the latter may be the case is implied in the characteristics of the population. As a combined group, over 80% of the respondents were between 60 and 79 years of age. Of the respondents, 75% indicated that they have no important social problem, 82.8% listed no important physical problem, and almost all of them (94%) claimed to have no important psychological problem. In addition, 22% of the respondents felt that their health is better than the health of other people in their age group. Only 13% had incomes of less than $200 per month, while close to half of the respondents considered their monthly income adequate for their needs. Of the subjects, 25% reported no special economic burden. Therefore, we may conclude that a low level of utilization of formal support systems may be related to the relatively healthy economic, social, and psychological condition of the respondents.

Use of Informal Supports

Who helps ethnic elderly in need? What help do they receive from their children? What help do they receive from the ethnic community, from outside of the family? Are ethnic elderly really "taken care of" by their families? Our findings indicate that on the average, a little more than 25% of the respondents reported that they received help from their children. The highest frequency of help received from children was reported by the Greeks (38.8%), while the lowest was in the Estonian group (20%). As for the kind of help given by the children, small proportions of the respondents listed shopping, translation of English documents into ethnic languages, regular checking on the situation of the elderly parent, transportation, and a combination of several types of help.

Help outside the family. Other sources of help used by ethnic elderly include ethnic friends, non-ethnic friends, ethnic organizations, non-ethnic organizations, and other (unspecified) sources of help. The average frequency reported for help by ethnic friends was 29.4%. However, there were variations among ethnic groups with regard to availability of ethnic friends for help. Whereas close to 50% of all Italians listed ethnic friends for support, only 11.3% of the Hungarians had similar help. More than 27.5% of the Hungarians listed other (non-ethnic) friends for support, exceeding three times the average for the combined groups. The Jewish group relied on Jewish ethnic organizations for help to a far greater extent that did other groups (12.5%). The Italians did not list any help from other (non-ethnic) organizations. On the average, less than 5% of the elderly reported that they were helped by the ethnic community.

Cross-tabulation of the immigrant status with variables related to use of the informal supports revealed significant differences among the three groups. New immigrants are helped by their children twice as much as old immigrants. U.S.-born elderly are helped by a combination of various family members significantly more than the other two groups. New immigrants also have significantly more ethnic friends to call on for help than either U.S.-born or old immigrants.

Supporting others. The respondents were also asked whether they themselves support other people (particularly their families and friends) and whether they give unspecified help to others. This analysis was undertaken in the realization that support is a "two-way street." On the average, 50% of all the respondents reported that they helped others with money. The Polish elderly in Washington exceeded the average considerably (72.6%), whereas the Jewish elderly have the least reported amount of help with money (36.3%). Among those who were helped with money were the family for 33.% of the respondents, friends (6%), and a combination of friends and others (10.8%). Of the respondents, 40% helped others with shopping or running small errands. The Greeks exceeded this average considerably. Once again, the family was helped to a greater extent than friends or unspecified persons.

Respondents also helped others with transportation. The major help was given to friends, exceeding help given to family or to others. Close to 33% of all the elderly reported that they provide babysitting for their families. (The Italians did the most babysitting, while the Washington Polish group reported the least.)

Almost half of the respondents reported that they helped other people with household repairs. The Greeks reported more help in this regard than did the rest of the groups. A little over half of the respondents cared for a sick person. (The Washington Polish led the rest of the groups in this category of help to others.) Finally, almost 33% of all the respondents said that they provided some unspecified help for someone else.

In addition to the support given by the elderly to others, over 25% of the respondents also reported that they were engaged in volunteer work. Greeks and Jews were the most frequent volunteers (over 40% each), while the Italians reported the lowest amount of volunteer work (19%).

Significant differences by immigrant status were revealed in cross-tabulations performed with relation to the help given by ethnic elderly to other people. New immigrants and U.S.-born elderly gave significantly more help to others than did old immigrants.

Sociodemographic Variables and Immigration Status

Significant differences by immigrant status did emerge with regard to education, income, adequacy of income, living arrangements, perception of life in the near future, and life satisfaction.

New immigrants and U.S.-born had significantly higher education than old immigrants. U.S.-born ethnic elderly had significantly higher income in general and considered their incomes as more adequate than both old immigrants and new immigrants. Overall, less than 25% of the respondents had some kind of socioeconomic burden, but there were no significant differences among the three groups with regard to this variable. As for living arrangements, new immigrants live significantly more with their spouses and children than do either U.S.-born or old immigrants. This finding may be due to the fact that the old immigrants came to this country as individuals (usually as a single person or married without a family) to establish the economic conditions necessary before bringing the family from overseas (Mindel and Habenstein, 1976). The new immigrants, on the other hand, came largely with their families and continued to use the family as their natural base for support with living arrangements. Additional differences by immigration status were noted with regard to perception of life in the near future. U.S.-born elderly had three times more positive ratings for life in the near future than the other groups. Close to half of all respondents had made preparations for handling a future financial problem. However, the differences among the groups were not statistically significant on this variable.

Views and Attitudes

Preferences in service provision. The preferences for social services by governmental or nongovernmental agencies was also studied as part of the effort to identify the views and attitudes of ethnic groups to formal and informal support systems. The findings indicate that close to half of all the respondents (48.9%) have a clear preference for government-provided social services. However, 25% of the respondents have no stated preference for social services to be provided either by the government or by other public and private agencies. An additional

13% would prefer to have services provided in a combination of public and ethnic agencies. Greek elderly indicated preference for government-offered services at more than twice the rate of the Jewish group. The Italians, on the other hand, were almost twice the average for the combined groups in favor of no special differentiation. Among the reasons cited for preferring government-offered services was that the respondents were taxed for these services. Interestingly, the Polish elderly in Washington had the highest rate of those who did not see any need for services (16.3%). Preference for services to be provided by the ethnic community and by the church was relatively small, not exceeding 10% for any one group. However, the Jewish group indicated the highest preference for services by a combination of synagogue and ethnic community (8.8%).

Nearly 66% of all respondents preferred to have ethnic staff in nursing homes in case they needed to use this institution. The Greeks, however, exceeded this average, 75% of them favoring their own ethnic group members as staff in these institutions.

Treatment of the aged. Treatment of aged people by American society and by the ethnic community was also assessed along a continuum ranging from well to badly. Of the respondents, 25% perceived the elderly in the United States as being treated either well or badly, while almost 20% of the respondents' opinions fell into middle categories. The Italians perceived the treatment of the elderly in the most positive terms. The Jewish group's perception was in the least positive terms. The Greeks, on the other hand, fell between these two perceptions and maintained a somewhat neutral position. Only small percentages of each ethnic group thought that elderly in general are treated with respect and consideration in society; yet more than 20% of the respondents indicated that they need better care. Less than 10% felt that the elderly are isolated.

There were, however, very important differences in the perception of the treatment given the aged by the ethnic community. Well above 50% of all the elderly in the study thought that they were treated well (Italians and Greeks rated as high as 75%). Only an extremely small minority perceived the treatment of the elderly by the ethnic community as bad (2.2%). When we looked into the specifics of the treatment given the elderly in the ethnic community, we found great variations among the ethnic elderly's perceptions of the various groups. For example, 26.3% of the Greeks thought that the elderly are treated with respect and consideration, in contrast to 2.5% of the Jewish group. The Greeks reported recognition of the elderly's wisdom. The Jewish group, on the other hand, indicated that elderly need better care and are not respected in the community.

What future concerns do ethnic elderly have and what preparations do they themselves make to deal with their future concerns? The
leading concern in this regard by close to 20% of the population was
worry about being sick and being alone. However, 33% of the respondents thought that their situation would not change for the worse in the
near future. Interestingly, 18% thought that their conditions would
become better in the future. Aside from concern about their health,
financial security was the biggest problem shared by all ethnic groups.
A strong indication of a wish to remain independent was expressed by
over 80% of the respondents, who said that they would rely only on
themselves in dealing with various problems and concerns. Only an
insignificant minority (1.5%) indicated that they would turn to government for assistance. Family, church, and ethnic organizations combined
were named by less than 6% as sources of support in dealing with future
problems. A small percentage considered spouse, relatives, and friends
in combination with church as sources for future support. Of those who
did not make any specific preparations for dealing with future problems, almost 40% indicated that in case of a problem they would turn
to their children for help. Over half of the respondents had made
preparations for serious illness. These preparations included the use of
private insurance by close to 40%. The church was singled out as the
most important source of help in dealing with a serious illness.

Using a one-way analysis of variance, significant differences in life
satisfaction emerged among the ethnic groups studied ($F = 12.21$, $df = 8.691$, $p = 0.0000$). The Polish elderly, both in Washington and in
Baltimore, had the highest scores on life satisfaction, whereas the Latvi-
ans had the lowest scores. Immigration status, feelings about ethnicity,
activities, and health were significantly related to life satisfaction of the
ethnic elderly. For example, the old immigrants among the Greeks
were less satisfied with their lives. On the other hand, these respondents had significantly higher satisfaction with their family relationships than either new immigrants or U.S.-born. This finding indicates
that the family for the old Greeks is still the most important support
system. Life satisfaction by immigration status for each ethnic group
and for the combined groups is presented in Table 14-1.

Discussion

As these findings indicate, there is very little use of the formal services
by ethnic elderly. However, when services are used, differences in
immigration status do play a significant role in service utilization. U.S.-
born and new immigrants use significantly more services than do old

Table 14–1. Summary of One-way Analyses of Variance of Life Satisfaction by
Immigration Status for Each Ethnic Group and
All Ethnic Groups Combined

Ethnic Group	MS	F	df_1/df_2	Significance of F
Jewish	13.862	0.376	2/72	0.688 (n.s.)
Greek	125.044	3.723	2/77	0.02
Hungarian	131.846	4.881	2/77	0.01
Polish (Washington)	156.725	5.296	2/77	0.007
Latvian[a]	—	—	—	—
Estonian	19.427	0.763	2/77	0.385 (n.s.)
Lithuanian	96.978	2.958	2/76	0.05
Italian	104.524	4.303	2/77	0.01
Polish (Baltimore)	91.607	3.116	2/75	0.05
All groups combined	387.686	12.214	8/691	0.000

[a]All Latvians were in one group, that is, new immigrants.

immigrants. It is possible, of course, that many ethnic elderly do not use a certain service for which they display an apparent need because they are unaware of its existence. Therefore, innovation and creativity are needed in educating the less knowledgeable about community services. As we have shown, over half the ethnic elderly studied did not speak English well enough to be interviewed in this language. On the other hand, use of the ethnic language in communication with significant others was very high for all the groups. In both the Estonian and Latvian groups, 100% of the elderly speak their native language. Similarly high ratios were noted for both reading and writing in these languages. Moreover, the ethnic language is still used to a large degree (particularly by the Baltic and the Greek elderly) at meetings. Literature in ethnic language is heavily used by new immigrants, who subscribe to ethnic publications significantly more than the others ($x^2 = 105.23$, df $= 6$, $p = 0.001$). It seems likely that language plays a significant role as a cultural barrier to knowing about services in using them as needed. Another possibility is that many elderly ethnics do not use government-offered services because of the stigma attached to their use. Support for this contention comes from studies of Asian American elderly and their underutilization of government services. As Fujii (1976) notes, exclusion from public social and health services has been attributed to barriers such as language, culture, and the structure of the delivery systems. Exclusion from services may be externally imposed upon the aging by service-providing institutions through insensitivity to cultural differences. It may also be self-imposed by the elderly because of their particular value system (which inhibits the use of services) and because of the lack of familiarity with the processes and procedures of the formal supports. This may be particularly true for the old immigrants, who came to this country before services were instituted on a large scale and who identified with the self-reliance philosophy prevalent in the majority's culture. These old immigrants most likely have never learned to rely on government services and "looked down" on those who had to use them. The new immigrants, on the other hand, with their superior education and previous exposure (in their countries of origin) and experience in use of public services accept, we assume, the formal services as a matter of course. Moreover, at present very few health and welfare agencies have bilingual staff, and no documents relating to provision of services are translated into various languages. Thus, services may not be accessible for large numbers of needy ethnic people. It is also possible that the location of services outside of the immediate neighborhood is an additional factor in service underutilization by ethnic elderly.

The findings of the study also indicate that the church as a source of support for the ethnic elderly is used less intensively than reported by Fandetti and Gelfand (1976). Activities related to church work by the elderly on a frequent basis ranged from a high of 53.8% by Greeks to a low of 16.3% by Italians. Nevertheless, the variations among the ethnic groups with relation to use of the church indicate that this source of support still plays a significant role in the emotional well-being of the respondents. Therefore, in planning services for the aged, the current and potential importance of the churches as supports needs to be considered. This approach is especially true for Catholic and Greek Orthodox elderly, for whom the church has traditionally been a major support system within the ethnic community.

Importance of informal supports. The most important source of support for older adults is their families. Even though older adults may live by themselves, family contacts for most of them are frequent and supportive. Our findings are in line with those reported by the Harris Poll (1975), indicating that the great majority of ethnic elderly are supported by their living children; support is given voluntarily without law or compulsion. The importance of this finding in terms of service provision is that services to older ethnics (or to older people in general) need to be operated with great sensitivity to family ties. It is important to have reliable information about the older ethnics in the community who have no family resources to draw upon, since these are most likely the socially isolated and lonely people for whom services by the ethnic community and by public agencies are the most important. But even when the family constitutes the main barrier against physical and mental deterioration, there is a need for supportive services to enable and to enhance intergenerational living. As Winston (1976) notes, central to the provision of extensive in-home service is a deep commitment to the philosophy that the most stable and desired place for individuals of all ages to life is in their own homes as long as appropriate types of care can be provided.

In addition, ethnic friends and to a large degree ethnic organizations are preferred by ethnic elderly to any other support systems. Various researchers (Mindel and Habenstein, 1976; Mostwin, 1972; Giordano, 1973) have emphasized the importance of the ethnic factor for mental health and have called for keeping knowledge regarding ethnic group differences in the forefront in assessing individual and group needs. Mostwin (1976) in particular calls attention both to differential values and attitudes among families of Eastern and Central European background toward outsiders and to the implications of these values and attitudes in the provision of mental health and social services. Since the findings of this study have shown that the majority of the ethnic elderly in the study are relatively well-off economically, the support system needed for further improvement in the overall well-being of the ethnic elderly must enhance the emotional aspects of their lives. This approach is particularly true with regard to the approximately 10% of the population who are the most socially isolated and lonely and who participate minimally in the cultural, social, and political life of the ethnic community.

Theoretical and Practical Implications

The findings presented so far have been strongly supportive of the basic assumptions upon which the study is based. That is, the significant differences found in use of both formal and informal support systems among the ethnic groups have substantiated the major hypotheses of the study. Furthermore, use of the support systems was also differentiated by immigration status.

The importance of the ethnic group as a major support for the ethnic aged has been demonstrated by this study. The great majority (over 95%) of the elderly in all the groups studied felt very proud of their ethnic backgrounds and felt very close to their ethnic groups. There was also a clear preference by the respondents for association with their own ethnic groups. The overwhelming majority of the respondents (93.8% and over) indicated that the ethnic culture should be preserved. Maintaining the ethnic heritage was cited as the leading reason for preserving ethnic culture. As the findings indicate, ethnic elderly maintain frequent participation in ethnic organizations, prefer ethnic staff in institutional services, continue friendship associations with fellow ethnics, and observe ethnic/national holidays. These findings may be perceived as evidence of strong interaction among members of a given ethnic group. They are closely tied to the elderly's feelings of well-being and life satisfaction and constitute a major informal support. Therefore, this support system is important in promoting positive aspects of living for older ethnics.

From the practical perspective, the significant differences found in support utilization among the elderly in various culturally different ethnic groups underline the need for professionals to become sensitive and informed about the differences in perception and attitude toward service use by older members of distinct ethnic communities. These differences must be taken into account and respected in service delivery and in planning of services to ethnic aged.

The dependence of older persons on services provided through state and federal programs has been documented and needs no further elaboration here. What needs to be stated, however, is the means by which the well-being of ethnic elderly can be enhanced. Despite the differences found in ethnic groups with regard to services utilization, and despite the ethnic variations in attitude toward services provided by the government, the fact remains that elderly ethnics might use more formal services if their fellow ethnics would sanction such use. Therefore, we recommend that social welfare agencies use indigenous community workers as "gatekeepers" to assist the elderly to benefit from available services. These gatekeepers, as Barg and Hirsch (1972) have demonstrated, are persons living and working within the community who are informed of the supportive services and of the procedures used for obtaining social, economic, and health supports. More important, they are in touch with the elderly in their day-to-day living.

Experimentation with locating social work services in local physicians' offices (with the full cooperation of the physicians) was reported by Linstrom and associates (1970) to be successful. These sources of information were trusted, and the elderly in the immediate neighborhood benefited.

Staffing major service agencies with bilingual professionals who are aware, knowledgeable, interested, and well-motivated to respond to the cultural needs of the elderly in a given ethnic community can lead to far greater utilization of services as well.

Going beyond increasing utilization is the need for improved quality of services. We need to devise and define standards against which the adequacy of service to be offered to elderly ethnics will be measured. We believe that the ethnic communities should play an important role in developing standards based on real knowledge of the situation of their own elderly and that the elderly themselves should be involved actively in this process. The *Bicentennial Charter for Older*

Americans (1976) lists two basic rights for all older Americans in the area of services: the right to the best level of physical and mental health services and the right to ready access to effective social services. These services should enhance independence and well-being yet provide protection and care as needed. Translating these rights into actions on behalf of all older Americans (not just to those in ethnic communities) will be a formidable task for professionals and lay leaders upon whose decisions the welfare of the aged largely depends.

References

Barg, S., and Hirsch, C. A successor model for community support of low-income minority aged. *Aging and Human Development,* August 1972, 243–252.

Bicentennial Charter for Older Americans. Washington, D.C.: The Federal Council on the Aging, January 1976.

Crouch, J. Age and institutional support: Perceptions of older Mexican Americans. *Journal of Gerontology,* October 1972, 524–529.

Cuellar, J. On the relevance of ethnographic methods: Studying aging in an urban Mexican-American community. In V. L. Bengston (Ed.), *Gerontological research and community concern: a case study of a multidisciplinary project.* Los Angeles, Calif.: Andrus Gerontology Center, University of California at Los Angeles, 1974.

Fandetti, D. V., and Gelfand, D. E. Care of the aged: Attitudes of white ethnic families. *The Gerontologist,* 1976, *16*(6), 544–549.

Fujii, S. M. Elderly Asian Americans and use of public services. *Social Casework,* March 1976, *57*(3), 208–218.

Giordano, J. *Ethnicity and mental health—research and recommendations.* New York: Institute on Pluralism and Group Identity, 1973.

Guilford, J. P. *Fundamental statistics in psychology and education* (4th ed.). New York: McGraw Hill, 1965.

Harris, L., and Associates. *The myth and reality of aging in America.* Washington, D.C.: National Council on the Aging, 1976.

Kalish, R. A. A gerontological look at ethnicity, human capacities, and individual adjustment. *The Gerontologist,* Spring 1971, Part II, *11*(1), 78–87.

Kaplan, J. The family in aging. *The Gerontologist,* October 1975, Part I, 385.

Kolm, R. Ethnicity in social work and social work education: some theoretical considerations. In Richard Kolm et al. (eds.), *Appreciation of ethnic pluralism in education for social work.* Washington, D.C.: The Catholic University of America, 1977.

Kolodny, R. Ethnic cleavages in the United States. *Social Work,* January 1969, *14*, 13–23.

Linstrom, R. C., et al. A linkage point for health and social services. *The Gerontologist,* Summer 1970, 107–110.

Mead, G. H. *Mind, self and society.* Chicago, Illinois: University of Chicago Press, 1934.

Mindel, C., and Habenstein, R. W. The American ethnic family: Protean or adaptive? In C. Mindel and R. W. Habenstein (Eds.), *Ethnic families in America.* New York: Elsevier, 1976.

Moore, J. Mexican Americans. *The Gerontologist,* Spring 1971, Part II, *11*(1), 30–36.

Mostwin, D. In search of ethnic identity. *Social Casework,* May 1972, *53*(5), 307–316.

Mostwin, D. Differential values and attitudes among the families of Eastern and Central European background: implications for mental health and social services. Paper presented at the Conference on Ethnicity and Social Welfare, Baltimore, Maryland. Institute on Pluralism and Group Identity, January 1976.

Novak, M. *The rise of the unmeltable ethnics.* New York: Macmillan, 1973.

Parsons, T. *The social system.* Glencoe, N.Y.: The Free Press, 1968.

Winston, E. *Aging in America: Implications for service providers.* Washington, D.C.: National Council on the Aging, 1976.

15

Emotional Needs of Elderly Americans of Central and Eastern European Background

Danuta Mostwin

In the domain of human emotional needs, three stand out as basic: (1) the need for love, (2) the need for survival, and (3) the need for creativity. These needs differ in expression and intensity depending on the individual's personality, socieconomic status, and cultural heritage. In old age, "which brings no lessening of the family influence and no safety from the perils of its emotional climate" (Howells, 1975), the needs for love, survival, and creativity continue and their lack of fulfillment are at the roots of biopsychosocial difficulties of the elderly.

This chapter addresses what is assumed to be a vital aspect of these needs and their fulfillment: the cultural or ethnic heritage of the older person. Too often the ethnic heritage of the elderly is disregarded, although it is essential to understanding and meeting their basic needs. Another assumption is that, particularly for the elderly, these needs are largely directed toward and fulfilled through the family.

In light of these assumptions, the three basic needs identified above can be further defined and described as follows:

1. The need for love. Love for the elderly means care, respect, and intimacy. It involves the immediate and extended family and, to a greater or lesser extent, the ethnic community.

2. The need for survival. As with people of all ages, the need for survival is expressed in the wish to be part of a totality larger than oneself. In the case of the elderly, this often expresses itself in a desire to perpetuate one's values, beliefs, and life philosophy by transmitting them to the younger generation.

3. The need for creativity. As with people of all ages, creativity means self-expression, individuation, and striving for self-sufficiency which brings satisfaction. The need to be creative and yet close to one's own family in a give-and-take relationship differs from the need for love and for survival in its emphasis on personal independence.

The orientation of this chapter is ecological: It proposes to examine the needs of the older person within a frame of his or her life space. The life space (Lewin, 1935) includes the person, his or her family, important others, and all other elements that have emotional meaning for the individual at a given time.

The population selected for this analysis are elderly American Estonians, Latvians, Lithuanians, Hungarians, and both American and Polish Poles. The sources of data are two studies: "Informal and Formal Support Systems and Their Effect on the Lives of The Elderly in Selected Ethnic Groups" (Guttmann et al., 1978); *The Place of the Elderly in the Family and Society* (Piotrowski, 1973).

The focus of this chapter is on the Polish elderly (1) because they are represented by three different samples: a sample of 80 Polish elderly from the Washington, D.C., area, a similar sample from the Baltimore area, and one of 2,845 elderly Poles in Poland, and (2) because of my familiarity with the Polish ethnic group.

Demographic Characteristics

The U.S. sample includes 480 persons 60 years of age and over of five nationalities. These include 80 Estonians and the same number of Latvians, Lithuanians, and Hungarians. There are 160 Poles: 80 from Washington, D.C., and 80 from Baltimore, Maryland.

The respondents are classified into three different groups according to place of birth and time of arrival in the United States: (1) those who came before World War II—*the old immigrants;* (2) those who arrived after World War II—*the new immigrants;* and (3) persons *born in the United States.* The Estonians and the Latvians are mainly European-born new immigrants. One-third of the Lithuanians were born in the United States, less than one-third are old immigrants, and the remainder are new immigrants. The Hungarians as a group are fairly recent arrivals. Although some of them came to this country before World War II and nearly 9% were born in the United States, the majority (67%) are new immigrants who came to the United States after the abortive Hungarian Revolution of 1956.

The sample represents first- and second-generation immigrants. The largest number of second-generation are among the Poles in Baltimore. The Poles in Washington, D.C., have nearly equal amounts of first and second generation, while one-third of the Lithuanians are second generation.

Both sexes are well represented, although Washington Poles and Hungarians have somewhat more men than women. It is possible either that more men than women are interested in ethnic issues and therefore more were available for the interviews or that among the old immigrants the pattern of single-men immigration prevailed.

The majority of the respondents were between 60 and 69 years of age. The Latvians had the largest number over 70 years of age, and the Poles the largest proportion of those between 60 and 69 years of age. The sample's education was overwhelmingly limited to either grade school or high school, with a very small percentage of persons having an education beyond college. Hungarians were the most educated group, with over 32% of the respondents having more than 18 years of schooling. In contrast, nearly 48% of the Poles in Baltimore had attained only one to eight years of education. However, in the Washington sample, twice as many Poles have more than 16 years of education than in the Baltimore group (for the high proportion of university educated among Washington, D.C., Poles see Mostwin, 1951).

The Need for Love

The loss of contact with the family, i.e., the unsatisfied need for love, is considered to be one of the major problems of old age (Piotrowski, 1973). More than 75% of our respondents have children, but only a small fraction reside with their children or grandchildren. The majority live with their spouses and about 30% live alone.

In Poland, 67% of persons over 65 make their homes with their children and only 17% live independently. Out of those classified as "in agriculture," 76% live together with their children, but only 55% of white- collar workers make their homes with their children.

The ethnic elderly in the United States appear to be more independent, and this may be a sign of less need for family contacts. According to our findings of high interaction of aged and non-aged relatives living in separate households, the ethnic elderly typically practice "intimacy at a distance." The frequency of contacts differs with different ethnic groups, as Table 15-1 illustrates.

According to these findings, the Hungarians have considerably fewer contacts with their children than other ethnic groups. They are

Table 15–1. Contacts with the Children (%)

Ethnic Group	Have Children	Living with Children	Contacts		Frequency of Contacts Combined
			Daily	Frequent	
Estonian	78.8	23.3	33.8	32.5	66.3
Latvian	76.3	36.4	42.5	21.3	63.8
Lithuanian	72.5	20.0	41.3	22.5	63.8
Hungarian	77.5	30.1	37.5	18.8	56.3
Polish in Washington	72.5	35.1	51.3	15.0	66.3
Polish in Baltimore	78.8	25.1	58.8	15.0	73.8

also, as we know from the demographic characteristics, the most educated group. The Poles in Baltimore retained the characteristics of an
agricultural, traditional family. While generally not living with their
children, they nevertheless retained a strong tendency for daily contact
with them.

We can hypothesize that two key variables determine the degree
of need for intimacy with one's own children: tradition and education.
Tradition stems from history and location of the country of origin. The
dependency of most Europeans on the land, for example, necessitated
reciprocal dependency of the old and the young: the old provided the
wisdom of experience, the young vitality and physical strength. These
complementary roles became a national tradition, still to some extent
held by American ethnic groups of peasant background.

Since education provides extra-familial channels of emotional satisfaction, it was considered necessary to ascertain the influence of education on the traditional patterns of family life and the need of an older
person for family closeness. Some indications are provided by examining the group of Poles in Washington, D.C. This group is interesting in
that about half of the respondents were born in Poland and immigrated
to the U.S. after World War II and half of them were born in this
country. These new immigrants had, upon entering the U.S., relatively
more education than those who were born in America of old immigrant
parents. According to our findings, of the Poles in Washington, those
born in the United States have significantly more daily contact with
their children than those born in Poland. However, those born in Poland also have frequent (but not daily) contact with their children. We
can hypothesize that the difference in educational level is responsible
for this intragroup difference. Those who are satisfied with the frequent
but not daily contacts do not need the daily assurance of their children's
love. For them, the interaction with the children is probably more an
intellectual than a physical, face-to-face exchange.

We may wonder why, of all the ethnic groups, the Hungarians have considerably less contact with their children. Is the degree of education the main reason for this? Or is it possible that the generation gap, more intensified in this group of new immigrants, is the reason? An in-depth study of the Hungarian American family can possibly answer these questions and provide information leading to better delivery of services, including those providing emotional support, to elderly Hungarian Americans.

The majority of all respondents consider their relations with their family to be highly satisfactory. The most satisfied are the Poles in Baltimore, the least are the Latvians and Estonians. The latter two groups are largely newcomers to the United States. Their lesser degree of satisfaction with the family relations as compared with other groups may have its roots in the ongoing process of adjustment, aspects of which interfere with intrafamilial relations.

The help received from children is an indication of the need for help and the degree of parental expectation of help from their children. Interestingly enough the Hungarians, who have considerably less contacts with their children, have a higher frequency of help received (35%), than the Lithuanians (33%), the Poles in Baltimore (17%), or the Latvians (16%). The Hungarians stress "love" as a kind of help received from the children, while the Poles in Baltimore do not even mention "love." Poles in Washington include "love" but less so than Hungarians and Lithuanians. There exists a certain embarrassment among Slavic ethnic groups in relation to "love" as an ingredient of parent–child relationships, since love is expressed in action rather than in words and reserved for the expression of tenderness toward small children or the expression of sexual feelings (Mostwin, 1976).

The need for care and the confidence invested in one's own children are expressed in the responses to the question: Who can help the elderly when in need and to whom would they turn for financial help? The children were the first choice of the majority of the respondents. They were listed as a definite preference over governmental help.

This corresponds with the findings from the study done in Poland, where 70% of the respondents never requested help from public assistance either because there was "no need for it" or because "it is a disgrace to apply for help when one has children and there are others more in need" (Piotrowski, 1973).

About half the respondents are not satisfied with the way the elderly are treated in the United States and think that their ethnic communities provide them with more care and respect. Only some of the Hungarians (15%) believe they are treated with more respect and con-

sideration by other Americans than by their Hungarian community. It
is possible that the Hungarians, who have the largest percentage of
highly educated respondents, have become well integrated into America's educated class, and that the respect they receive is an appreciation
of their educational achievement rather than the expression of reverence for their old age. However, Hungarians also have the highest
frequency (40%) of those who desire "better care" for the elderly in the
United States.

While the majority of our respondents gave priority to "family life"
as an activity that made them happy, rating the greatest achievements
in life vary among the groups. For Hungarians, the priority is on professional achievements; for Lithuanians and the Poles in Baltimore, the
family has priority over professional or occupational satisfaction; and
among the Poles in Washington, the ratings are equally divided.

The need for love in terms of the need for care, respect, and
intimacy is felt by all respondents. It varies in its expression depending
on the education of the respondents, their rootedness in the United
States, and the traditional valuation of the family in the country of
origin. The majority of all six groups considered their need for care,
respect, and intimacy as best satisfied by their own immediate family,
extended family, and ethnic community.

The Need for Survival

The need for survival exists in all of us. It becomes stronger and more
conscious with the coming of age and the realization of the approach
of death. The desire not to vanish completely, but to leave a part of
one's inner self behind, was expressed by the Roman poet Quintus
Horatius Flaccus in his ode "Non omnis moriar." In our modern society
this need has long been ignored.

Our analysis of the need for survival examines (1) survival as a force
in the ethnic life space and (2) survival as an intervening variable between the cultural heritage of the ethnic elderly viewed as an independent variable as well as certain symptoms viewed as a dependent
variable. According to Murray, "A need is an intervening variable,
hidden in the head, the operation of which can only be inferred on the
basis of certain symptoms. Hence, the task of identifying an active need
is not that of labelling the kind of behavior that is observed, but making
a diagnosis" (Murray, 1967, p. 455).

The following symptoms will serve as the basis for the diagnosis of
the elderly's need for survival: (1) involvement in socialization of children and grandchildren to one's cultural values; (2) feelings about one's

ethnic heritage; (3) participation in the social life of one's ethnic group; and (4) attitudes regarding transmission of cultural values, norms, language, etc., to the younger generation.

Survival as a Force in the Life Space of the Ethnic Elderly

The life space of an elderly Polish American is more complex than the life space of his contemporary in Poland. Polish Americans are the subject of pressure from within because of their own inner loyalty, and from without because of their ethnic community, to perpetuate the cultural heritage of Poland. But they are also indirectly, and to a certain extent through their children, the subject of pressure to perpetuate American norms and values to which they are also loyal.

Elderly Poles in Poland are supported in their desire to pass down their cultural heritage to the younger generation by a uniform pressure from the total environment: friends, relatives, schools, and institutions. The forces in the community support this position.

It is obvious that the life space of an elderly individual in his/her native country and that of an ethnic American are, in spite of the same basic human needs, quite different. The need for survival is felt by both of them, but the symptoms of this need are not the same. Consequently, we cannot understand the behavior of an elderly ethnic American by assuming that he/she is like the elderly in his/her country or origin, or even that he/she is partially Polish and partially American, or partially Hungarian and partially American, etc.

The unique constellation of the three environments—the heritage of the country of origin, the ethnic community, and American society —combine to create a Polish American subculture. The values of this subculture and not the "pure values" of the country of origin constitute the acting force in fulfilling the need for survival.

For example, an immigrant Polish American who had worked all his life as a steelworker provided in his will that his life savings support young relatives on condition that they enter professional schools. The value of education, which was not part of Polish peasant culture, had become part of his outlook in this country. In the letters to relatives in Poland, he expressed a view of life that reflected major American values (businesslike approach, matter-of-fact appraisal of reality, competition, right to equality and free expression) which had become woven into the fabric of his Polish heritage. By transmitting this in the form of advice and admonition to his young relatives in Poland, he was unconsciously acting as a sociocultural bridge between the two distant countries (Mostwin, 1965).

Symptoms of the Need for Survival

Language.   Efforts by the elderly to maintain and transmit their ethnic language is here viewed as a major aspect of personal and group survival. These efforts can be assessed by ascertaining the fluency in English of those born in Europe and knowledge of the ethnic language of those born in America.

Responses to our questions concerning immigrants' fluency in English bring out different levels of attachment to their ethnic language by elderly of Central and Eastern European background. Latvians and Estonians most fluently speak their respective ethnic languages. Hungarians, although they are mostly new immigrants (over 90%), are less competent in their native tongue. The Hungarians had to overcome more difficulties in learning English since more than half of them spoke no English on arrival to the U.S. Currently, only 40% of the Hungarians "usually" speak their native language with their wives or husbands. Surprisingly, the Latvians have a rather low frequency of "usually" speaking with their spouses (28.8%) in their ethnic language, and only about half of the Estonians communicate with spouses in Estonian. The frequency of the communication among spouses in their ethnic language is nearly equal for the remaining three groups: 35% for Poles in Baltimore, 35% for Poles in Washington, and 32.5% for Lithuanians.

Older immigrants, like Poles in Baltimore, retained relatively high frequency of good or fair spoken Polish (over 92%). They exceed in this respect the Poles from Washington (83.8%) in spite of about 50% of this group being new immigrants.

The great majority of our respondents believe that their children should learn the ethnic language. Leading in this respect are Estonians and Latvians (98.8% for each group), followed by the Lithuanians (97.-5%), Poles in Baltimore (97.5%), Hungarians (95%), and the Poles in Washington (87.5%). The significant difference between Baltimore and Washington Poles may reflect the intragroup difference discussed previously, related to the agricultural and nonagricultural backgrounds of the respondents.

Asked why the children should learn the ethnic language, the majority of the respondents pointed to the practical benefits of knowing the language, for communicating with fellow-ethnics and use in visiting the ancestral homeland. This was most cited by the Poles in Baltimore (72.5%), least cited by the Poles in Washington, who expressed their interest in the cultural and traditional value of the ethnic language. The Lithuanians consider the knowledge of their language as a perpetuation of cultural tradition, but only 20% of the Hungarians share this attitude.

We may assume that, while all the ethnic elderly emphasize the importance of transmitting their language to their children, those who were born in the United States and who have acquired the American values of thriftiness and businesslike approach may have a more practical and less idealistic view of the advantage of learning the ethnic language.

Feelings about ethnic heritage. Feelings about ethnic heritage depend on a variety of factors including in-group loyalty, level of education, and the availability of alternatives to ethnic channels of expression. Sandberg in his study of the Polish Americans of Los Angeles (1977) differentiates among three dimensions of ethnicity: religion, culture, and nationality.

1. *Cultural ethnicity* consists of the "values, beliefs, and practices usually passed down from generation to generation [which] includes key indicators of Polish-American cultural life" (Sandberg, 1977p.).

2. *Religious ethnicity* is practiced by the Polish immigrants who regarded their national parish as both a religious and a community center.

3. *National ethnicity* includes the feeling of kinship, mutual responsibility, sense of belonging with others of similar background, and attitudes toward the country of origin.

In our study, new immigrants are characterized more by national ethnicity than the old immigrants or those born in the U.S. The latter two groups identify more with cultural and religious aspects of ethnicity.

Over 95% of the respondents believe that their respective cultures should be preserved. The Lithuanians and the Poles in Baltimore are 100% in agreement, while the Hungarians have the lowest frequency of all six groups (93.8%). The responses to the question, "How do you feel about your ethnic background?" indicates that the Lithuanians (93.8%) are proudest of their ethnic identities. The Estonians, who are possibly more reserved or more critical of themselves than the others, expressed the least pride in their ethnic heritage. Over 50% of them consider themselves "very proud" while about 30% of the group responded that they are "proud" of their Estonian background. The correlation between the years of education and the feeling of being very proud were statistically significant for the Polish group in Baltimore: the higher the frequency of "very proud," the lower the education of the respondents. This tends to support the finding of Sandberg's study (1974) that social class is inversely related to the salience of ethnicity.

Our findings should be regarded with caution and tested against variables other than the direct verbal expression of pride in a person's heritage. These other variables should include active contributions on behalf of the ethnic group.

In summary, the respondents feel strongly about the preservation of their ethnic heritage. In our diagnostic appraisal, this might be considered one of the symptoms of the need for survival of an elderly ethnic person.

Transmission of ethnic values. Why should the ethnic culture be preserved? The most important reasons expressed by the majority of the respondents is the continuation of heritage. The Estonians (33.8%) and the Hungarians (18.8%) emphasize music and art. For Poles in Baltimore (22.5%) and in Washington (15%), Polish cooking is a skill they wish preserved. This clearly relates to why the Hungarians more than other groups want their children to maintain their ethnic music, art, and crafts and appears to contribute to why Poles in Baltimore (65%) consider the observance of festal holidays a custom they want to pass down to their children. This is true, but to a lesser degree for the Poles in Washington, D.C. (35%). Observance of holidays, which involves family, religion, customs, rituals as well as the preparation and sharing of food, is an interesting differential. Only 5% of Latvians, 7.5% of the Hungarians, 10% of the Estonians, and 11% of the Lithuanians named observance of holidays as a custom they want their children and grandchildren to maintain.

As shown in Table 15-2, every group considers its culture to be important and unique, but the Poles in Washington, who are either more modest or more restrained in this respect, differ considerably from the group of Poles in Baltimore. On the other hand, the Poles in Washington express the strongest desire of any of the groups to enrich U.S. culture with Polish values.

Table 15–2. Why Should Ethnic Culture be Preserved? (%)

Group	Enrich U.S. Culture	Continue Heritage	Disseminate Information about Culture	Prevent Assimilation	Other	Unique, Important Culture
Estonian	2.5	38.8	1.3	0.0	8.8	25.0
Latvian	11.3	52.5	0.0	1.3	6.3	21.3
Lithuanian	3.8	52.5	2.5	2.5	7.5	23.8
Hungarian	10.0	26.3	6.3	0.0	23.8	26.3
Polish in Washington	22.5	26.3	5.0	5.0	15.0	7.5
Polish in Baltimore	6.3	38.8	1.3	0.0	15.0	28.8

We may consider this finding an example of different expressions of the same or similar feelings. This difference between the two groups can be accounted for by such factors as education and place of birth. The old immigrants and the U.S.-born ethnic elderly tend to give preference to cultural and religious customs, while the new immigrants are more sophisticated about the art and music (and, I assume, science and literature) of their countries of origin and, as mentioned before, are more nationalistic in their ethnicity.

The need for survival is directed toward the next generation. It is wider in its scope than the need for love since it reaches not only the family and the ethnic group, but also the country of origin. This need is expressed in the feeling of importance attached to one's ethnicity and in the concern for the preservation of one's cultural heritage.

The Need for Creativity

The need for creativity is conceptualized for the purpose of this paper as a need for "self-actualization" (Maslow, 1968). According to Maslow, creativity is the universal heritage of every human being and shows itself in everyday living. It is, we may assume, one of the leading conditions for the emotional health and happiness of an elderly person.

About 50% of the respondents in the American study expressed satisfaction with their current life. The degree of satisfaction varies with the age of the respondent and with the amount of income (which implies the amount of independence). The Latvians, who are older and have considerably lower monthly incomes, are the least satisfied of all the groups. The Estonians, who are in the same income bracket as Latvians, have a higher frequency (51.3%) of those who think "things get better when you get older." The most optimistic, but also the youngest, are the Poles in Baltimore (70%) in spite of their income, which is wider in range than among the other groups. Therefore income, while essential, cannot be seen to be the only thing responsible for the feeling of satisfaction.

Our study of the ethnic elderly provides us with some insight into the activities of our respondents. From this, we may deduce what makes them happy and what enhances their emotional health and fulfills their needs for self-actualization.

Some of them are working past retirement age (Hungarians, 26.-3%; Poles in Washington, 22.5% and Latvians, 25%). We can probably assume that the first two of these groups, which have the highest frequency of professionals, continue past their retirement work in professions. But what about Latvians? They have only 10% of the professionals and the highest frequency (16.3%) of laborers. Do they work for pleasure or because, having the lowest income, they are forced to work?

The Latvians, of all the groups, like crafts and hobbies, but not the indoor hobbies that are the preference of the Estonians (65%—the highest frequency of all the groups), who are famous for their needlework.

The Poles in Baltimore tend not to work past retirement. They and the Hungarians (more than others) find happiness in family life while Poles in Washington and Estonians tend more than others to find satisfaction in doing things for their friends. Some of the elderly are most satisfied in helping others, according to Guttmann (1978), "one-half of all the respondents reported that they helped others with money. The Polish elderly in Washington exceed the average considerably (72.-6%)." He also reports that "caring for the sick is the activity of over one-half of the respondents. The Washington Poles led the rest of the groups in this category of help to others" (Guttmann, 1978, p. 11).

It is possible that the Poles in Washington, half of whom are new immigrants, are relating to "others" and to "friends" as members of the extended family that they do not have in this country. It is also possible that their centralized location in the capital makes them more accessible to visitors than the Poles in Baltimore, who are residentially dispersed and concentrate more on their own families and local community than on any exchange with nonrelatives.

The church is important for the Poles with 83.5% of those in Baltimore and 80% of those in Washington attending church frequently. But only one-third of the Latvians go frequently to church.

In the Polish study (Piotrowski, 1973) creativity was approached through a focus on work: the amount of work and the attitudes of the elderly toward work. Asked how long they wanted to work, the respondents "in agriculture" answered, "Until the end of my days," or "As long as I am strong enough to work." Asked what they would miss most after ceasing to work, the Polish elderly identified the following reasons: contact with people, the feeling of being useful, the respect of the environment, participation in life, satisfaction from work itself, income, and independence. Income had the highest frequency of response. Next was satisfaction from work itself and the feeling of being useful.

In our study of the ethnic elderly, the primary focus was not on work itself, but on life satisfaction. Employment and income were two of the many components. It is significant, however, that the seven reasons listed by the Polish elderly in Poland had their counterparts in the findings of the American study.

Conclusion

Three basic emotional needs of elderly Americans of Central and Eastern European background have been presented in ecological perspective. The elderly ethnic persons have been analyzed in their interaction with their environment: the family, the ethnic community, and American society.

Of the three needs, the need for love is directed primarily toward their own family, the need for survival reaches beyond family into the ethnic group and as far as the country of origin, and the need for creativity brings the elderly into interaction with others.

This chapter inquires into the meaning of cultural heritage in the life of elderly ethnic Americans. The conclusion might be formulated as follows:

1. "Intimacy at a distance" seems to be the preferred choice of our respondents gratifying their need for love. Although only a small fraction of respondents reside with their children, the need for family closeness is expressed in the high frequency of contact with children. The confidence in, and need for care from, children is expressed in the preference for help from children rather than from governmental assistance.

The findings imply the importance of family ties for the ethnic elderly. They also emphasize the importance of a familiar milieu for an ethnic elderly individual to fulfill his need for love.

2. The need for survival expresses itself through the continuation of cultural heritage. Nearly all of our respondents (95%) believe that their ethnic cultures should be preserved. They speak their ethnic languages and feel their children should continue to do so. Some groups emphasize music and art (Hungarians and Estonians), others, customs and holidays (Poles), but every group considers its culture worthy of preservation and transmission to the younger generation.

3. The need for creativity, or self-actualization, is primarily expressed by engaging in crafts and hobbies or by working past normal retirement time. But it also can be considered to be involved in such widespread activities as visiting others and attending church services.

It is significant that practically all these activities require both independence and sharing oneself with other persons. The individuals whose childhood memories of the "old country" or old neighborhood become more vivid with age will find interaction with others similar to themselves more meaningful and gratifying. This implies the need for an ethnic support system, including but going beyond the family. By providing a warm, supportive climate of acceptance, ethnic institutions from friendship cliques to formal organizations promote the process of self-actualization, one of the requisites for emotional health of the ethnic elderly.

References

Guttmann, D., et al. *The impact of needs, knowledge, ability and living arrangements on decision making of the elderly.* Washington, D.C.: Catholic University of America, 1977.

Guttmann, D., et al. *Informal and formal support systems and their effect on the lives of the elderly in selected ethnic groups.* Washington, D.C.: Catholic University of America, 1978.

Howells, J. G. (Ed.). *Modern perspectives in the psychiatry of old age.* New York: Bruner & Mazel, 1975.

Lewin, K. *A dynamic theory of personality: Selected papers of Kurt Lewin.* New York: McGraw-Hill, 1935.

Maslow, A. H. *Toward a psychology of being.* New York: D. Van Nostrand, 1968.

Mostwin, D. The last will of Blaise Twardowski *(Testament Blazeja).* In *Asteroids.* London: The Polish Cultural Foundation, 1965.

———. *The transplanted family, a study of social adjustment of the Polish immigrant family to the United States after the second World War.* Doctoral Dissertation, Columbia University, 1951.

———. Differential values and attitudes among the families of Eastern and Central European background. A paper presented at the University of Maryland Conference on Ethnicity, January 16, 1976.

Murray, H. A. Toward a classification of interaction. In Parsons and Shils (Eds.), *Toward a general theory of action.* Cambridge, Mass.: Harvard University Press, 1967.

Piotrowski, J. *Miejsce Czolowieka Starego w Rodzinie i Spoleczenstwie.* Warszawa: Panstowe Wydanie Naukoew, 1973. (Translation: *The Place of the elderly in the family and society*).

Sandberg, N. C. *Ethnic identity and assimilation: The Polish-American community. Case study of metropolitan Los Angeles.* New York: Praeger, 1977.

16

Well-Being and Fear of Crime among the Black Elderly

John Lewis McAdoo

Just as individuals can be clearly distinguished from one another by physical, social, and psychological characteristics, so can groups of people be differentiated by virtue of their shared culture, ethnicity, and socioeconomic status. As we move toward a greater recognition of our pluralistic society, the importance of identifying and understanding ethnic differences becomes critical in environmental and social planning for the elderly (Cantor, 1976). This need is most crucial in large urban areas with their high population density and ethnic diversity that are affected by crime, poverty, and other social ills. It is important that we study the effects of crime and the consequences of crime on the social activities and psychological well-being of older Americans of all ethnic groups.

A review of the gerontological literature reveals a paucity of studies about the consequences of crime for Blacks and other ethnic groups. The aged are portrayed in the literature as a homogeneous group who tend to be affected by the aging process in the same way, regardless of race, socioeconomic status, or environmental influences. Jackson (1968) and others have pointed out that we need to study the subgroups within the aged community. However, as was noted in a recent literature review, most of the subgroups studied were made up of samples of white middle-class aged respondents living in medium-sized cities or suburban communities (Cantor, 1976). This study was designed to fill the gap in the literature regarding the consequences of crime for urban ethnic groups. The goal of the study was to explore the effects of fear of crime on one ethnic group living in the community, the Black elderly.

The study was designed and carried out while the author was a gerontological fellow placed with the National Caucus of the Black Aged in Washington, D.C. The National Caucus of the Black Aged (NCBA) is attempting to identify the types of problems that these ethnic elderly groups have as a result of crime in their areas, provide safety tips, aid in securing their premises, provide transportation to stores, banks, and clinics, and offer counseling and referral services where appropriate. This study is a result of NCBA's need to get a better understanding of the way in which fear of crime has affected the social fabric of the area.

This chapter reports the findings of an exploratory, descriptive investigation into the effects of fear of crime on the social and psychological well-being of the Black aged in the Shaw area of Washington, D.C. We explored the effects of the fear of crime on those elderly persons who live in public and private housing, and upon both victims and nonvictims of crime. The results of this study will be used to develop a larger study dealing with the differential effects of fear of crime on various ethnic groups.

Recently there has been a shift in victimization studies dealing with the urban elderly. Previous research efforts focused on the amount of property lost, risk of being a victim, and failure to report crimes to the police (Hinderlang, 1976; Gottfredson and Hinderlang, 1976). Other studies focused on types and numbers of crimes experienced by the elderly (Biderman, Johnson, and McIntyre, 1967), and residents' attitude toward police. Many of these studies suggest that older people are less likely to be victims of crimes than younger people. There have been several studies suggesting that we look at the consequences of victimization among the elderly. One of the major consequences of criminal victimization among the elderly is that fear of possible victimization may cause reduction in social activities (Sundeen and Mathieu, 1976; Gubrium, 1973; Clements and Kleiman, 1976).

Gubrium (1973) found that fear of crime existed in 70% of over 200 older people questioned. Cunningham (1973) noted that 45% of 860 elderly in Kansas City victimized by burglary reported that, as a result of their experiences, they did not go to certain places and engage in social activities for fear of further victimization. Similarly, Middleton's (1976) study noted that 76% of 766 elderly in Cleveland felt that fear of victimization limited their mobility and community involvement.

Clements and Kleinman (1976) noted that aged residents in cities over 50,000 show significantly greater fear of crime than their younger counterparts or older inhabitants of the suburbs, small towns, and rural areas. A national survey of people 65 years and older (Harris, 1975) noted that fear of crime was rated by 23% of the respondents as being their most serious problem. A similar study by the National Council on Aging found that for people over 65, crime in the streets was among their greatest fears (National Council on Aging, 1975).

Sundeen and Mathieu have reviewed most of the earlier studies related to fear of crime and its consequences among the urban elderly. They note that fear of crime varies in intensity according to social characteristics such as race, sex, and income level. Black women were found to have the highest degree of anxiety, followed closely by Black men, white women, and white men, and that older persons of low socioeconomic levels have higher anxiety levels than those in higher socioeconomic groups.

Bild and Havighurst (1975) found that 41% of their Chicago sample 65 years or older rated fear of crime as their most serious problem. Similarly, Schooler (1970) found that elderly people were more concerned with their safety than with social interaction with their peers. The result of this fear is lowered morale and self-imposed house arrest (Goldsmith and Tomas, 1974).

It was also found that urban elderly tended to have fewer connections with individuals or community support systems, perceived that they were vulnerable to becoming victims during the day as well as in the evening, had greater fear of the four most common crimes, had lower estimates of the likelihood of being able to depend upon informal networks of control and protection, and had a lower evaluation of the police. When comparing central city elderly with suburban elderly and those in a retirement community, it was found that all three communities had similarly high levels of fear of crime (Sundeen and Mathieu, 1976).

In summary, most of the studies reviewed noted that the closer we move toward the center of a city, the higher the level of fear of victimization becomes, even when actual crime rates against the elderly are dropping. Because of poor economic conditions the minority elderly are forced to live in urban dwellings where crime among all groups is high. The urban elderly observe or hear about crimes committed against others and recognize that they are more vulnerable. It is this group of elderly on which fear takes its toll. The minority elderly are forced to curtail social activities, stay home from church, or abandon shopping trips for fear of being robbed. They are also afraid of a strange adult, terrified of two or three youths on the street, and frightened by a dimly lit elevator (Clements, and Kleiman, 1976).

Research Design

One hundred and twenty Black senior citizens living in the Shaw area of Washington, D.C., were randomly selected from 2,000 residents to participate in our study. The 120 subjects were interviewed by trained Black males and females supervised by the author. The major variables used in the study were: (1) victim status (victimized or not); (2) residence (public or private housing); (3) age status (under or over 70 years of age); and (4) sex.

The data were collected using a questionnaire developed by the author, on the dependent variables of fear of crime, vulnerability of self, activity level in social and religious groups, frequency of contact with friends, and state of health. Background information related to occupation, length of retirement, education, geographic mobility, and income was also obtained.

The Rosenberg (1965) self-esteem inventory was administered as part of the questionnaire. This scale was designed to measure attitudes toward the self along a favorable-to-unfavorable dimension. The scale refers to how the individuals respect themselves, feel about their self-worth, and recognize their limitations with growth expectations. The scale is not an intensive assessment tool like that found in more detailed psychological measures. It was selected because it has been used extensively on adults in nationwide surveys and because of its ease of administration.

The Rosenberg self-esteem measure, composed of 10 Likert-type items, allows for one of four responses of agreement or disagreement. Reliability of the scale was established using the Guttmann procedure, with a reproducibility of 92% (Robinson and Shaner, 1971). Validity was established using National Institute of Mental Health employees with independent psychological ratings.

Results

Sample

As noted above, the sample was composed of 120 Black elderly people randomly chosen to participate in the study. Thirty-seven (31%) were men and 83 (69%) were women. When the sample was examined for victim status, 57 (48%) of the respondents reported that they had been victims of crime and 63 (52%) reported they had not. Fifty-eight (48%) of the elderly lived in public housing and 62 (52%) of them lived in privately owned dwellings (see Table 16–1).

Table 16–1. Frequency and Percentage of Subjects by Groups for Total and Crossed by Victim Status and Residence

| Group | Total | | Victim Status | | | | Residence | | | |
| | | | Victim | | Nonvictim | | Public | | Private | |
	f	%	f	%	f	%	f	%	f	%
Victimization										
Victim	57	48								
Nonvictim	63	53								
	120	101								
Residence										
Pub. housing	58	48	29	51	29	46				
Priv. housing	62	52	28	49	34	54				
	120	100	57	100	63	100				
Sex										
Male	37	31	18	32	19	30	14	24	23	37
Female	83	69	39	68	44	70	44	76	39	63
	120	100	57	100	63	100	58	100	62	100
Age Level										
Under 70	57	48	28	49	29	46	22	38	35	56
Over 70	63	52	29	51	34	54	36	62	27	44
	120	100	57	100	63	100	58	100	62	100
Marital Status										
Married	32	27	15	26	17	27	20	35	12	19
Widowed	61	51	28	49	33	62	7	12	20	32
Single	13	11	14	25	13	21	31	53	30	49
Separated/ Divorced	14	11								
	120	100	57	100	63	100	58	100	62	100

Age. The ages ranged from 50 to over 85, with 48% below 70 years and 56% 70 or older. The proportion of those who had been victims was about the same in both age groups: 49% of those under 70 and 51% of those over 70. There also was no significant age difference in the place of residence, nor were there income differences between the two age groups (see Table 16–1).

Marital status. Of all the subjects, 51% were widowed, 27% were married, 11% had never been married, and 11% were separated or divorced. Significantly more women were widowed than men ($p = .001$). Those subjects under 70 years tended to have more divorces and separations, while those over 70 had more married and widowed ($p = .0002$). Subjects who lived in public housing tended to be separated or divorced ($p = .02$).

Living arrangements closely matched marital status for this sample. Of the respondents, 51% lived alone, 27% were with spouses, 12% lived with friends, and 5% lived with their children.

Income. Of the 106 (88%) subjects who answered this question, the incomes ranged from $1,500 (16%) to $6,500 (1%); 50% earned between $2,000 and $3,000, with a mean income of around $2,160. No income differences were found for victim status, nor for the two age groups. However, the expected income difference was found in residence. Those living in the projects had significantly higher incomes (p = .006). Of those living in the projects, 86% earned between $2,000 and $4,000, while only 68% of those subjects who lived in private dwellings fell into this range.

Occupation and retirement. Thirty-one percent had been retired less than 6 years, 33% between 6 and 12 years, and 33% had retired over 12 years ago. When they worked, 72% worked as laborers, 10% as clerks, 14% as semiprofessionals or professionals, and 3% as housewives.

Education. Over half of the sample had less than a sixth-grade education, 19% had between first and third grade, 35% between fourth and sixth grade, 27% had attended junior high, 8% had gone to high school, and 10% had some advanced training or classes beyond 12th grade.

Geographic mobility. Almost all (99%) had lived in the Washington, D.C., area longer than 10 years: 62% had lived in their present neighborhood more than 10 years, 17% between six and nine years, and 22% less than six years. Before they moved into the area, 44% had lived in the South and 25% had come from the mid-Atlantic states; 22% had always lived in the District. Those in private housing had remained in the neighborhood significantly longer (p = .02).

Fear of Crime

Almost all of the elderly subjects (91%) indicated that they feared crime. This was true regardless of their victim status. Living in private or public housing also made no difference, nor did their age group. While they all were very afraid of being the victims of crime, the males were significantly more afraid than females (see Table 16–2).

How fear changed their lives. Of the respondents, 95% felt that they and other elderly people in their community had been forced to change their activities because of victimization and fear of crime. This opinion was held across age, sex, place of residence, and victim status. Of the sample, 66% indicated that they were reluctant to go out alone during the day unless it was necessary because of their fear of crime.

Only 33% of the sample indicated that they went out regularly during the day in spite of their fear of victimization. Of the total sample, 88% indicated that they were afraid to go out alone at night.

Extent of fear of crime. Of those who responded to this question, 47% felt their neighborhood was more dangerous than others, 48% felt it was the same as other neighborhoods, and only 4% felt it was safer. Of the sample, 49% felt crime had increased and 9% felt crime had decreased in their neighborhood; 35% felt it was at the same high level. Again, no significant difference in attitudes was found among all groups.

Fear of being robbed was widespread: 41% felt their chances of being robbed had increased. Those who had been victimized had significantly different opinions on their chances of being robbed ($p = .05$). The majority of those who were victims (51%) felt that the chances of being robbed had increased, while only 32% of the nonvictims felt this way; 18% of the victims and 38% of the nonvictims felt their chances

Table 16–2. Significant Chi Squares of Fear, Background, Variables, and Activity Level by Victim Status, Residence, Sex, and Age

Group	Variable	x^2	df	p	Direction of Difference	
Victim status						
Victim	Chances of being robbed	9.46	4	.05	V > NV	
Nonvictim	No. groups members of	6.19	2	.05	NV > V	
	No. groups active in	6.53	2	.03	NV > V	
	How often go to meetings	4.08	1	.04	NV > V	
Residence						
Pub. housing	Crime worth reporting	4.04	1	.04	Pri > Pub	
Pri. housing	How often see friends	17.62	3	.0005	Pub > Pri	
	How often contact friends	11.87	4	.02	Pub > Pri	
	No. groups active in	13.02	2	.002	Pub > Pri	
	How often go to meetings	8.46	1	.004	Pub > Pri	
	Marital status	8.15	2	.02	Pub > Pri / Pri > Pub	Mar., Wid. / Sep., Divor.
	Length in neighborhood	9.91	3	.02	Pri > Pub	
	Yearly income	12.43	3	.006	Pub > Pri	
Sex						
Male	How often contact friends	23.37	4	.001	F > M	
Female	No. groups belong to	11.43	2	.003	F > M	
	No. groups active in	9.26	2	.01	F > M	
	Marital status	18.29	2	.0001	F > M / M > F	Mar., Wid. / Sep., Divor.
Age						
Under 70	Crime worth reporting	4.83	1	.03	−70 > +70	
Over 70	Marital status	16.93	2	.0002	+70 > −70 / −70 > +70	Mar., Wid. / Sep., Divor.

of being robbed were similar to what they had always been. It appears that once the person has been made a victim, the fear becomes more specific about being robbed again. While they all had a generalized fear of crime, once they were victims they felt that their chances of being victimized had increased (see Table 16-2).

To our question regarding the extent to which crime in their neighborhood was greater or less than that reported on TV for the rest of the country, the majority (74%) of the sample felt that the actual crime was worse than portrayed on TV. Only 5% of the sample felt it was less and 18% felt it was the same.

Reporting crime. In spite of the fear of crime of the subjects in this sample, and the profound changes in their lifestyle brought about by this fear, 87% felt that crimes were not worth reporting to police. Only 10% of all of the subjects responded that crimes should be reported to the authorities. Those subjects who lived in private housing felt more positive about reporting crimes than those who lived in public housing ($p = .04$). Those subjects under 70 felt more positive than those over 70 ($p = .03$) about reporting crimes. The respondents living in public housing and those subjects over the age of 70 seemed to have developed a sense of powerlessness based upon their past experiences with crime in the community. These two groups, public housing residents and aged 70 plus, appeared to be emotionally victimized by their fear of crime, feeling trapped in their dwellings at night without a sense that those in authority would help them.

Activity Level

The impact of fear of crime on the lives of the subjects in this sample could be shown through their level of activity with friends and in social and religious groups. While almost all had indicated that the fear of crime had caused a change in lifestyle and a dread of leaving their homes at night, some were maintaining a fairly high social activity level. We wanted to see whether the independent variables had impact on this social activity level. The extent of involvement in social groups, frequency of contact with friends, and involvement in their church were all used as measurements of activity levels (see Table 16-2).

Contact with friends. The majority of the subjects (57%) reported that they had few (between three and four) close friends, 34% had many friends, and 9% had very few friends. No differences were found between age, sex, residence, and victim status in reporting the number of friends they had.

Most of the Black aged reported that they saw their friends regularly. As a group 31% reported seeing them several times a day, 30%

saw their friends once a day, and 14% saw them several times a week; 26% saw their friends once a week or less. There were differences found between the sexes and place of residence on how often they saw their friends. However, no differences in age and victim status were found in contact with friends (see Table 16–2).

The women in the sample contacted their friends much more than men ($p = .001$): 37% of the women but only 3% of the men contacted their friends several times a day, while 42% of the men versus only 14% of the women contacted them only once or twice a week. Those who lived in public housing had significantly more contact with their friends ($p = .02$) and actually saw them more ($p = .0005$) than those in private dwellings. No significant age differences were found in the different groups.

Church activity. Of the sample, 65% indicated that they were active in their church's affairs and 34% indicated that they were not. Most of the subjects limited their activity to attendance at religious services. However, 47% of the sample reported that they were not members of any church group; 26% of subjects were members of one church group and 18% were very active in two or more church groups. No age or sex differences were noted in amount of church activity reported.

Of those in the sample who were active in church, few held any leadership roles as represented by being officers of the groups. Only 3% reported that they were chairmen, 3% were secretary-treasurer of their group, and 5% were leaders of a committee in the church; 62% of the sample indicated their only involvement was that of a member.

Group activity level. The social group activity level was measured by their responses to a question about the number of groups they had joined, the number of groups in which they were active, and their frequency of meeting attendance.

The majority (66%) did not belong to any organized groups, 19% belonged to one or two, and only 14% were members of three or more. When the groups were compared, nonvictims were members of significantly more groups than victims ($p = .05$). Women were again members of more groups than men ($p = .003$). No age differences were found.

While one may have a membership in a group, it is not an indication of one's involvement in that group. Therefore an additional question was asked relative to the number of groups in which they were actually active: 69% were not active in any group and 31% were active at some level; 16% in one or two groups and 15% in three or more. Nonvictims were significantly more active in social groups than victims ($p = .03$). Nonvictims also went to meetings more frequently ($p = .04$).

Those in public housing had a significantly higher activity level than those in private units ($p = .002$) and they went to meetings significantly more than the subjects in private dwellings ($p = .004$). Women were more active in groups than men ($p = .01$) and went to many more meetings ($p = .005$). No age differences were found (see Table 16–2).

The picture that emerges of this sample of elderly Blacks and their involvement with social groups is one in which most have only a few friends, are not active in social groups, and tend to live alone. They appear to be living more in isolation than gregariously interacting with others. However, those who have not been victims, women, and people in public housing were much more active in more social groups than victims, men, and private dwellers. It should be remembered that the same proportion of men and women lived in public housing; therefore, these findings are not the result of an interaction between sex and residence. In other words, women were more active than men regardless of residence and both men and women in public housing were more active than either group in private homes. The age of the respondents was not an important variable in activity level. The important factor may be the higher life-long social involvement of the women and the close proximity of the elderly to each other in public housing. Their lack of active involvement may be a direct result of the state of health: 51% indicated that they were just in fair health and 18% said that their health was poor. Only 28% were in good health and 3% in very good health.

Age

Comparisons were run on all variables between those over and under 70 years of age. The respondents felt positively about themselves regardless of their age level. No significant age differences were found on their activity level, church involvement, involvement with friends, and income. The respondents also had similar attitudes about their fear of crime. The only exception was that those under 70 felt that crimes were worth reporting more than those over 70 ($p = .03$). The backgrounds of both of these groups were similar with the one significant exception in marital status. Those who were single, separated, or divorced occurred more in the under-70 group and those who were married or widowed were in the over-70 group.

Self-esteem

Self-esteem was scored on the seven-point Rosenberg (1965) scale, with the low score indicating positive self-concepts. The mean score for the total group was 2.49, indicating positive feelings of self-worth. There were no significant differences found in the scores of the victims and nonvictims, nor between those residing in public or private housing. Significant self-esteem differences also were not found between those under 70 or over 70 years of age.

The only significant differences in self-esteem were found between the men and women. The men were significantly lower than women in self-esteem ($p = .01$). The women felt themselves to be more worthy and showed a greater sense of satisfaction with themselves and their social relationships. This would be consistent with our earlier finding of the higher level of social interactions and greater contact with friends of the women. The men were much more isolated than the women (see Table 16–3).

Conclusion and Implications

Our purpose was to explore the effects of fear of crime on one ethnic group to fill gaps in the literature. We found that the total group expressed great fear of crime. It did not matter whether they lived in public or private housing. Black men seemed more afraid of the consequences than Black women. As a result of this fear, many of the subjects reported that they were more cautious about activities, have cut down on their visits to friends and relatives, limited their participation in

Table 16–3. Summary of Anova (Analysis of Variance) on Self-Esteem Run on Victim Status by Residence and *t* Test on Self-Esteem by All Subgroups

F test	df	MS	F	p
Source				
Victim (v)	1	.06	.04	ns
Residence (R)	1	.91	.67	ns
V X R	1	4.91	3.09	ns
Error b	3	1.71		
Error w	112	1.36		

t test	N	M	SD	t	df	p
Group						
Victim	57	2.51	1.09	−0.19	115	ns
Nonvictim	60	2.55	1.24			
Public housing	56	2.63	1.04	0.85	115	ns
Private housing	61	2.44	1.27			
Male	36	2.94	1.39	2.63	115	.01
Female	81	2.35	1.00			
Under 70	56	2.63	1.32	.85	115	ns
Over 70	62	2.44	1.01			

church and social groups, and tended to live a life of relative isolation, rarely venturing out of their homes at night.

Crime for these 120 residents in Washington, D.C., was seen as worse in their area than portrayed on TV. The subjects reportedly felt powerless to the extent of believing it was futile even to report crimes. The above findings on the lack of age differences regarding feelings of victimization indicate that the commonality of being poor and Black was more important in attitudes held than that of being over or under a certain age. The subjects took certain precautions because this was part of their inner city lifestyle. However, in spite of this generalized fear, respondents did not have depressed self-esteem. In spite of having limited resources and feeling vulnerable to crime, they still were able to maintain feelings of dignity and self-worth.

Those interviewed who were more socially active tended to feel better about themselves than those who were more isolated. If lack of isolation and involvement with people is conducive to the maintenance of sound mental health, it would appear that women, nonvictims, and those in public housing may be at an advantage. The association between frequent personal interactions, active social contacts, and maintenance of positive mental health would indicate that social programs community activities, and work programs should be planned and implemented that would decrease the fear of crime and increase the level of social activities and feelings of well-being of these elderly. However, unless some means of security for their movements are provided, and they are able to have a sense of protection against crime, these inner city aged Black residents will tend to continue their isolated existence because of the fear of crime.

While the people in this sample appear to have compartmentalized their fear of crime and maintained adequate self-esteem, much can be learned about studying both those who have extremely low self-esteem and high anxiety regarding crime and those who have high self-esteem and relatively low fear of victimization and relationships of these differences to satisfaction with life. Social workers, as well as mental health and other professionals need to learn more about the range of normal aging behavior as it relates to ethnicity, fear of crime, or mental health to help develop treatment strategies for those elderly who succumb to the effects of fear, isolation, and loneliness.

For those elderly who succumb to the pressures of isolation due to fear of crime, there seems to be a strong need for an approach that provides services to them in their homes. This service should include providing encouragement for the elderly person to participate in group meetings (church, community social groups, etc.) where social workers and mental health or other professionals would facilitate interaction and the development of new friends. There may need to be some intervention in the kin-network system to facilitate more communication, emotional support, and social interaction by the members. This may include the kin-network system developing strategies for helping the elderly person feel safer about leaving his/her home and attending social events.

Social workers and mental health and other professionals may need to break new ground in their treatment strategies. For example, they may help those who are isolated to develop communication and group skills leading to multi-ethnic coalitions around common community problems. If the fear of crime is a major problem, the coalition could learn new skills needed for influencing the political process so as to obtain better protection. Activity of this type could help the elderly perceive themselves as important members of the community.

The NCBA's pilot project to provide safety information such as effective methods of securing doors and windows, as well as NCBA's outreach programs, which provide transportation to and from stores, clinics, and meetings, should go a long way toward providing prevention of mental illness for the Black elderly persons in the Shaw area who feel isolated and dehumanized by the social forces around them. However, it is felt that it is time that other agencies got involved in providing services that tend not to "blame the victim" but that provide the kind of environment and support system that will allow the older person to live in an environment relatively free of crime. The team approach to multi-ethnic, multi-age coalitions may provide the best opportunity for that kind of environment.

Finally, there is a need for research into the consequences of fear of crime on various ethnic and cultural groups living in large urban areas. We need to learn if the consequence of fear of crime is different for different social classes across ethnic and cultural groups. This type of research would allow us to compare similarities and differences in various ethnic groups of the effects of fear of crime and coping strategies used by each group to control such fear. This research has moved to meet this need by providing a descriptive picture of how low-income Blacks living in an urban area cope with the effects of fear of crime in their social lives. Further, research should be done in other cities to verify these results on a larger sample, to examine how different ethnic groups cope with the consequences of crime. From such research we can develop public policy that takes into consideration the needs of different ethnic groups. The effectiveness of service delivery systems for the aged, across ethnic groups, can be implemented only if they are based on research and policies that accurately reflect life experiences of the elderly.

References

Biderman, A., Johnson, L., and McIntyre, Report on a pilot study in the District of Columbia on victimization and attitudes towards law enforcement. Washington, D.C.: U.S. Government Printing Office, 1967.

Bild, B., and Havighurst, R. Senior citizens in great cities: the case of Chicago. *Gerontologist*, 1975, *16*(1), 47–52.

Cantor, M. H. Effects of ethnicity on lifestyles of the inner city elderly. In M. P. Lawton, R. J. Newcomer, and T. O. Byerts (Eds.), *Community Planning for an Aging Society*. Stroudsburg, Pa.: Dowden Hutchinson and Ross, 1976, 41–59.

Clements, F., and Kleiman, M. B. Fear of crime among the aged. *Gerontologist*, 1976, *16*(3), 207–210.

Cunningham, C. *Crimes against aging Americans, the Kansas City study*. Kansas City, Mo.: *The Midwest Research Institute*, 1973.

Goldsmith, J., and Tomas, E. Crimes against the elderly: a continuing national crisis. *Aging*, 1974, *236–7*, 10–13.

Gottfredson, M. R., and Hinderland, M. J. An analysis and classification of injury and theft in personal victimization. Albany, N.Y.: Criminal Justice Research Center, 1976.

Gubrium, J. F. Victimization in old age: available evidence and three hypothesis. *Crime and Delinquency*, 1973, *20*(3), 245–250.

Harris, L., and Associates. *The myth and reality of aging in America*. Washington, D.C.: National Council on Aging, 1975.

Hinderlang, M. J. *Criminal victimization in eight American cities*. Boston, Mass.: Ballinger Corp., 1976.

Jackson, J. Negro aged and social gerontology: critical evaluation. *Journal of Social and Behavioral Sciences*, *33*, 1968, 42–47.

Middleton, F. *Analysis of statistics, senior safety and security program*. Cleveland, Ohio, 1976.

National Council on Aging. *Myths and Realities of Aging in America*. Washington, D.C.: National Council on Aging, 1975.

Robinson, J., and Shaner, P. *Measures of social psychological attitudes*. Ann Arbor, Mich.: Institute for Social Research, The University of Michigan, 1971.

Rosenberg, M. *Society and the adolescent self image*. Princeton, N.J.: Princeton University Press, 1965.

Schooler, K. Effects on environment and morale. *Gerontologist*, 1970, *10*, 194–197.

Sundeen, R. A., and Mathieu. The fear of crime and its consequences among the elderly in three urban communities. *Gerontologist*, 1976, *16*(3), 211–219.

17

Future Pension Status
of the Black Elderly

Donald C. Snyder

Recent studies of the relative position of Blacks in the U.S. labor market following passage of the Civil Rights Act of 1964 have focused on earnings, unemployment, and other related labor market indicators. These studies have ignored Black–white pension differentials in their analyses, a serious omission in light of the growing share of compensation taken by fringe benefits. Pension contributions represent an important source of both current and future income, and changes in the distribution of those contributions are useful indicators of future trends in retirement income of Blacks.

Likewise, public debates about the ability of the Social Security system to provide the elderly with an adequate retirement income have concentrated the public's attention on the economic well-being of the elderly. While these analyses provide strong evidence that poverty among the aged is disproportionately high, that many more elderly can be classified as "near poor," and that there are significant disparities in the distribution of income between Black and white elderly, they ignore the role that the pension status of Black workers plays in explaining the disparity of income between Black and white elderly. For example, among those receiving retirment income, Blacks are less likely to receive pension benefits than whites by a factor of 1:2. Thus,

Support for this research was provided by the Computer Science Center of the University of Maryland and by the U.S. Administration on Aging, Department of Health, Education and Welfare. Any errors or omissions are my own.

one of the major causes of the disparity of income between Black and white elderly is the different treatment accorded them by the private pension system.

By reviewing trends in the industrial distribution of Black employment and pension contributions, and by examining Black employment in a sample of large firms providing pension coverage to their employees, we gain an understanding of the changes in the relative labor position of Blacks during the last decade. We can use our knowledge of past changes in Black participation in the private pension system to anticipate the timing of future changes in the distribution of pension benefits between newly retired Black and white elderly. In addition to explaining more about the relative gains of Blacks, an accurate estimate of this time horizon will enable policy makers to better understand the income needs of elderly Blacks over the remainder of the century.

Some of the questions addressed in this study are:

• What are the trends in pension-covered employment of Black male workers in the U.S. labor market?

• Has the pension-covered employment status of Blacks improved since 1960?

• What is the age distribution of Black workers across industries with high per worker pension contributions? Any trends?

• Have there been Black employment gains in firms with pension plans? If so, what are the nature and extent of these gains?

• Is there any evidence of the effects of the 1964 Civil Rights Act on Black employment?

• What do aggregate and firm experiences portend for the future pension status of newly retired Blacks?

It should be pointed out at the start that this chapter does not attempt to analyze the effects of the Civil Rights Act on employment of Blacks; rather we assume that this Act has had a favorable impact on Black employment opportunities (and provide strong evidence that it has). Our purpose is to assess the nature and extent of (any) employment gains in pension-covered industries or firms. This assessment then serves as the foundation for projecting *changes* in the future pension status of newly retired Blacks.

The chapter first describes pension coverage in the U.S., then reviews the current distribution of Social Security and pension benefits by race and sex of recipients. Following this documentation of current racial disparities in pension benefits received, the next section describes the distribution of pension contributions and Black employment (by age cohort) across industries in 1960 and 1970. This description emphasizes the importance of considering non-wage compensation as an element in labor market studies and of analyzing the age distribution of employment changes. We then analyze employment gains of Black males in a sample of 72 of the largest firms in the United States. This analysis serves to demonstrate that employment gains of Black workers during the 1960s have been significant; total Black employment in these firms rose by 41%, for example. However, we find the greatest gains in employment and pension status concentrated among younger workers. The last section builds on this analysis and projects changes in the future pension status of newly retired Black males. The chapter concludes that the results of our investigation suggest that there will be a considerable delay before the ratio of Black/white pension-eligible retirees significantly increases.

Pension Coverage in the United States

Pension income received by retirees is determined by their employment history: pension benefits vary by occupation, industry, union status, length of service on the longest job, and earnings. Nearly all unionized, white-collar, durable manufacturing, and government employees are covered by pension plans. Southern workers, however, are less likely to be covered by pensions and Blacks are less likely to have been employed in those occupations covered by pensions or in unionized jobs. Currently, elderly Blacks are less likely to receive private pension benefits because their employment was concentrated in industries offering little pension coverage, e.g., agriculture or nondurable manufacturing in the South.

　　　Private pension coverage in the U.S. has grown from 12.2% of the labor force in 1940 to 49.3% in 1973 (Ture and Fields, 1976). Over 65% of private nonfarm workers were employed in establishments offering pensions to at least some employees in 1972 (Bell, 1975). Not all these employees will collect benefits, however, as some are excluded from company plans (e.g., do not meet an earnings requirement or are blue-collar or part-time employees and are thus excluded from participating) and others will leave the firm without qualifying for benefits.

　　　The duration of employment with an employer is a crucial element determining pension benefits. Short-service workers (e.g., those with less than 10 years of continuous service) hardly ever qualify for vested benefits, and if separated from employment, benefits available at retirement are small. Vesting gives a worker a right to a pension benefit at retirement age if he voluntarily quits or is laid off, based on years of service and the benefit formula in effect at the time of separation. The Employees Retirement Income Security Act of 1974 (ERISA) required all firms to offer vesting beginning in 1976, typically after 10 years of service. A review of the distribution of job tenure across Black and white male beneficiaries reveals that nearly one-half of white workers have 25 years of service on their longest job, while only one-third of Blacks experienced such a long association. Further, 28% of Black males had less than 15 years of service on any job, compared to 20% of white males. Other evidence, however, suggests that Blacks quit pension-covered employment less frequently than whites (Schiller and Snyder, 1978). This may imply that they are faced with fewer opportunities to change jobs or that they value pensions highly. These results may also reflect a trend toward greater job stability (and tenure) among Black males. If this is the case, their continued high rates of firm attachment in pension-covered employment would generate a growing share of private pension benefits in the future.

Pension Income of Elderly Blacks

The results of a survey of newly entitled Social Security beneficiaries aged 62–65 during 1968–1970 illustrate the disparities in pension coverage of older Blacks and whites. Not only is the Primary Insurance Amount (PIA)—the monthly benefit paid—which Blacks receive lower than that received by whites, but the frequency of pension income is lower at both high and low PIA values. Table 17-1 shows that 82% of newly entitled Black males applying for Social Security were not expecting a pension benefit, while only 65% of whites relied solely on Social Security benefits. At the other extreme, 26% of white males were entitled to a PIA of $150 or more *and* a pension benefit, while only 10% of Black males were so fortunate. These figures mask the low retirement income of Blacks because they exclude noncovered workers, who are disproportionately Black.

A further insight gained from a review of these data is that pension status and Social Security benefits are lowest for Blacks who are employed in the private sector. Table 17-2 shows a significant proportion of newly entitled beneficiaries who did not expect to receive any pension benefits even though their longest job was in a private sector firm. Only 22% of Blacks employed in the private sector were eligible for a pension, while 36% of white beneficiaries were so entitled. This relative experience is reflected in the retirement income of the elderly population, with only 8% of elderly Black households receiving pensions from the private sector in 1971, compared to 19% of whites. We must look to trends in employment in pension-covered establishments in the private sector, therefore, as a potential source of improvement in the income status of the Black elderly.

Table 17–1. Pension Coverage of Newly Entitled Beneficiaries, 1968–1970

Pension Status and PIA	Blacks	Whites
Not receiving or expecting second pension	82	65
PIA under $150	71	43
PIA $150 or more	11	22
Receiving or expecting second pension	18	35
PIA under $150	8	9
PIA $150 or more	10	26
Total percent	100	100

Source: Rubin, L. *Reaching Retirement Age*, Table 15.5, p. 220.

Pension Contributions and Black Employment 1960–1970

The distribution of pensions by industry.   Pension contributions per worker vary across industries, as we see in Table 17-3. These Department of Commerce unpublished National Income Accounts data show a growth in fringe benefit payments from 1960 to 1970 and at the same time show that relative pension benefit contributions vary across industries. Most expenditures are concentrated in manufacturing, principally durable goods industries, as we see in Table 17-3. Manufacturing, as a whole, accounted for 59.9% of all expenditures in 1970, down slightly from 61.5% in 1960. An example of concentrated fringe benefits is provided by looking at two manufacturing indus-

Table 17–2. Sector of Employment of Beneficiaries, 1968–70

Sector of Longest Job	PIA and Pension Status			
	No Pension		Pension	
	<$150	>$150	<$150	>$150
Blacks				
Private	61	16	6	15
Federal government	40	18	53	4
State or local government	49	2	16	23
Total percent	62	16	8	14
Whites				
Private	24	35	4	36
Federal government	20	6	61	12
State or local government	18	12	24	46
Total percent	32	32	7	29

Source: Rubin, L. *Reaching Retirement Age*, Table 15.7, p. 222.

Table 17-3. Private Sector Compensation and Black Male Employment by Industry 1960–70

Industry	Average Wage and Salary Compensation		Average Pension Contribution		1970/60 Ratios		
	1960	1970	1960	1970	Average Wage	Average Pension Contribution	Average Black Male Employment
	(1)	(2)	(3)	(4)	(5)	(6)	(7)
Farms	$1,555	$ 3,296	$ .89	$ 6.42	2.12	7.21	.74
Agricultural services	2,961	4,744	.68	4.10	1.60	6.03	.53
Metal	6,116	9,095	5.76	13.90	1.49	2.41	1.13
Coal	5,307	9,568	313.00	807.00	1.80	2.58	.70
Crude petroleum	5,859	9,456	96.30	128.00	1.61	1.33	2.86
Mining quarrying	5,347	8,491	90.90	20.00	1.59	.22	.11
Continuing construction	5,443	9,323	16.50	90.40	1.71	5.48	.93
Manufacturing	5,352	8,149	155.90	328.38	1.52	2.11	1.20
Nondurable goods	4,817	7,382	153.30	322.60	1.53	2.10	1.38
Food	4,930	7,568	111.00	330.00	1.54	2.97	1.08
Tobacco	4,054	6,888	377.70	885.00	1.70	2.34	1.16
Textile	3,720	5,803	48.00	110.30	1.56	2.30	1.80
Apparel	3,317	5,034	36.90	74.20	1.52	2.01	1.07
Paper	5,554	8,538	137.70	251.50	1.54	1.83	1.22
Printing	5,617	8,275	85.00	193.30	1.47	2.27	1.32
Chemicals	6,413	9,745	354.50	660.60	1.52	1.86	1.07
Petroleum	7,063	10,661	1,072.00	2,465.00	1.51	2.30	.93
Leather	3,594	5,521	44.70	125.00	1.54	2.80	1.39
Durable goods	5,767	8,704	159.90	338.60	1.51	2.12	1.15
Lumber	3,801	6,349	22.90	89.00	1.67	3.89	.86
Furniture	4,376	6,451	50.00	122.50	1.47	2.45	1.00

Stone, clay, glass	5,328	8,182	118.70	286.20	1.54	2.41	.87
Primary metals	6,340	9,206	262.00	485.80	1.45	1.85	1.04
Fabricated metals	5,696	8,387	84.30	305.00	1.47	3.62	1.19
Nonelectrical machinery	6,079	9,280	158.70	352.00	1.53	2.22	1.40
Electrical machinery	5,675	8,485	167.50	260.00	1.50	1.55	1.67
Transportation equipment	6,640	9,932	85.30	266.80	1.50	3.13	1.26
Motor vehicles	6,596	9,998	290.00	575.00	1.52	1.98	1.30
Instruments	5,920	8,865	—	—	1.50	—	—
Miscellaneous manufacturing	4,463	6,752	88.60	142.60	1.51	1.61	1.91
Transportation	5,690	9,032	60.70	197.80	1.59	3.26	1.11
Railroads	6,214	10,014	63.60	117.50	1.61	1.85	.79
Local passenger	4,585	6,344	—	—	1.38	—	—
Trucking	5,263	8,366	27.40	150.50	1.59	3.49	1.22
Water transportation	5,910	9,670	123.80	362.50	1.64	2.93	.89
Air transportation	6,639	11,414	175.00	547.40	1.72	3.13	1.30
Pipeline transportation	6,957	10,765	300.00	1,100.00	1.55	3.67	2.00
Transportation service	5,159	7,838	83.30	—	1.52	—	1.14
Communications	5,319	8,307	277.40	660.90	1.56	2.38	1.80
Electric, gas	6,007	9,674	475.50	876.40	1.61	1.84	1.80
Wholesale trade	5,719	8,884	78.70	192.60	1.55	2.45	1.02
Retail trade	3,366	4,880	23.00	56.30	1.45	2.45	.96
Finance, insurance, Real Estate	4,640	7,380	171.10	368.70	1.59	2.15	1.18
Banking	—	—	—	—	—	—	—
Services	—	—	—	—	—	—	—

Source: U.S. Bureau of the Census. The National Income and Product Accounts of the U.S., 1929–1974 Statistical Tables and unpublished National Income data.

tries, employing approximately 3.6% of all males in the private sector force in 1970. Autos and primary metals alone made 71.5%, 23.0%, and 10.6% of expenditures on supplemental unemployment benefits (SUB), health and welfare, and pension plans, respectively (17.7% of the total of fringe benefits in 1970, up from 15.7% in 1960).

In columns 3 and 4 of Table 17-3 we see that pension contributions per worker ranged from lows of $.68 per worker in 1960 and $4.10 in 1970 to highs of $1,072 and $2,465, respectively, demonstrating the effects of being employed in different sectors on the probability of receiving and the relative size of pension benefits. Column 6 shows the percentage growth in contributions from 1960 to 1970. This figure is an important indicator of changes in the pension status of workers in each industry, but it must be interpreted with caution because it captures both increases in coverage and increases in contributions per covered worker. Also, some growth in contributions occurred during this period to fund prior obligations. For these reasons, the percentage growth may overstate (implied) increases in benefits. Contrary to these activities, many plans underfunded promised benefits, so actual contributions may understate implied benefits. We include both the level of contributions and the growth from 1960 to 1970 in Table 17-3 so the reader may observe these differentials.

When we look at compensation across industries it becomes apparent that per worker wages and pension contributions are unequally distributed. This makes it clear that the distribution of future pension benefits between Blacks and whites is sensitive to the distribution of Black employment across industries. For example, growth in pension contributions per worker has been high in durable manufacturing between 1960 and 1970, a sector that has also absorbed significant numbers of Black workers.

Changes in the distribution of Black employment. There is considerable evidence that employment opportunities of Black workers have improved in the last two decades (Vroman, 1974). Vroman's study identified changes in the industrial distribution of Black males between 1950 and 1970 that indicated improved earnings status of those workers as they moved from employment in agricultural and personal services to professional services and manufacturing and transportation. A more detailed breakdown of employment trends in each sector emphasizes these very different growth patterns. For example, oil and gas and pipeline transportation show the greatest gains, while agricultural services and coal evidence sizable declines, as we see in Table 17-4.

Employment growth of Black workers also varied across age cohorts (Table 17-5) as well as across age cohorts within industries, with some industries apparently "aging" and becoming Blacker, while oth-

Table 17-4. Black Industrial Deployment 1960-1970

Industry	Age Cohort				
	25-34	35-44	45-54	55-64	65+
Farms	.50	.46	.48	.62	.50
Agricultural services	.34	.34	.37	.48	.39
Metal	1.02	.92	1.10	1.08	.69
Coal	.18	.25	.61	.60	1.20
Crude petroleum	3.37	2.4C	3.13	3.69	90
Mining, quarrying	.85	1.15	1.23	6.13	.42
Continuing construction	1.08	1.08	1.29	1.53	1.56
Manufacturing	1.36	1.13	1.28	1.40	1.31
Nondurables	1.29	1.10	1.19	1.37	1.36
Food products	.86	.87	.93	1.14	.82
Tobacco	1.07	.75	.86	.68	.73
Textile mill products	2.11	1.32	1.34	1.59	1.80
Apparel products	1.07	1.07	1.29	1.47	1.70
Paper products	1.234	5.99	1.15	1.24	1.05
Printing, publishing	1.34	1.29	1.28	1.15	1.22
Chemicals	1.28	.98	1.00	1.23	.95
Petroleum	1.19	.54	.58	1.31	.43
Rubber	1.55	1.05	1.31	1.41	4.26
Leather	.72	1.16	1.23	.94	1.06
Durables	1.39	1.15	1.31	1.41	1.28
Lumber	.51	.66	.74	1.01	.95
Furniture	1.00	1.10	1.44	1.51	2.34
Stone, clay, glass	.98	.89	1.04	1.16	1.19
Primary metals	.92	1.00	1.08	1.01	.66
Fabricated metals	1.23	.98	1.15	1.36	.79
Machinery, nonelectric	2.41	1.27	1.35	1.41	.95
Electric machinery	1.89	1.47	1.45	1.72	1.18
Transportation equipment	1.90	1.21	1.45	1.50	1.30
Motor vehicle	2.07	1.23	1.50	1.51	1.28
Instruments	2.11	1.54	1.34	2.15	.67
Miscellaneous manufacturing	1.50	1.42	1.78	1.79	2.14
Transportation	2.26	1.55	1.56	1.53	1.47
Railroads	.87	.39	.51	.69	.54
Local passenger	2.15	1.37	1.37	1.42	1.46
Motor freight	1.51	1.34	1.56	1.40	1.73
Water transportation	.97	.87	.91	1.04	.75
Air transportation	2.60	1.61	2.62	1.90	1.60
Pipeline transportation	.37	1.63	.92	.60	.22
Transportation service	1.40	1.19	2.14	2.44	.95
Communication	2.91	1.91	1.51	1.42	2.78
Electric, gas	1.69	1.17	1.27	1.28	1.37
Wholesale trade	1.36	1.42	1.50	1.66	1.51
Retail trade	1.085	1.089	1.064	1.353	1.469
Finance, insurance	2.24	1.55	1.19	1.25	1.02
Banking	3.20	1.61	.95	1.35	.91
Services	1.300	1.313	1.237	1.411	1.352

Source: 1960 and 1970 Census of the Population, Special Reports.

Table 17–5. Ratio of 1970 to 1960 Male Employment by Age and Race

	All Males	Black Males
Total 25+	1.067	1.095
25–34	1.119	1.124
35–44	.968	1.026
45–54	1.108	1.100
55–64	1.134	1.192
65+	.956	1.027

Source: Subject reports of the 1960 and 1970 decennial censuses and *Employment and Training Report of the President, 1976*.

ers are becoming "younger" and Blacker. Nonelectrical machinery is an example of the latter and leather is an example of the former.

Aggregate pension coverage of Black males. Two sources of growth in pension-covered employment of Blacks can be identified. First, some industries that employed similar proportions of Blacks in 1960 and 1970 significantly increased contributions per worker. Second, other industries experiencing large gains in Black employment offered relatively high pension contributions in both years. For example, employment of Black workers grew slightly in the paper products industry (22%), but contributions per worker doubled. In contrast, the percent of Black employees in nonelectrical machinery grew by 40%, while at the same time pension contributions per worker more than doubled. Other examples of industries exhibiting high growth of Black employment and high per worker contributions are air transportation; electric, gas, and sanitation; and transportation equipment. In these industries, Black employment grew by 30%, 80%, and 39%, and pension contributions grew by 213%, 184%, and 122%, respectively.

Employment Patterns of Black Males
in a Sample of Firms 1959–1970

This section reviews the employment experiences of Blacks in our sample of pension firms during 1959–1970. After receiving the data base, we look at employment patterns of Blacks before 1964 and compare these experiences to those in the years following Civil Rights legislation. We then analyze the growth in Black employment during 1959–1970 across age cohorts and then assess the cyclical sensitivity of Black job attachment in pension-covered employment.

Longitudinal pension employee (LPE) file. The firm data we analyzed came from a match of private pension plan descriptions on file with the Labor Management Services Administration (LMSA) of the

Department of Labor (DOL). After determining benefit and nonbenefit plan provisions from this source, this information was matched with firm employment data from the Longitudinal Employer-Employee Data (LEED) file from the Continuous Work History Sample (CWHS) of the Social Security Administration (SSA). The consolidated sample of 72 firms, the Longitudinal Pension Employee (LPE) file, contains pension and employment histories of each firm for the years 1959–1970.

Growth of Black employment. Male workers employed in our sample firms numbered 2.2 million in 1959 and 2.3 million in 1970 (4.2% of all male employment in 1970). Overall growth in employment in these firms was below the national average over this 12-year period; however, Black employment in these sample firms increased by 7% during this time (Table 17-6). This growth was composed of two parts: one part represents increases in the number of Blacks employed in the 66 firms with some Black employees in 1959, the other part represents new hires of Blacks in six firms who had no record of Black males on their payroll in 1959 (Table 17-7). By 1965 all firms in the sample reported some Black workers. The youngest cohort (age 25–34 years) experienced the greatest gains in employment, as might be expected. When Black employment is analyzed by age cohort, we see that much of the growth was concentrated among workers under age 40 in 1970. The proportion of Black employees between ages 40 and 61 changed little between 1959 and 1970, but grew markedly for older workers.

The first column of Table 17-7 shows the number of Black employees (BEM: an employer with Black employment greater than .1% of cohort employment in a year) for each cohort in 1959 and 1970. The second column is the mean percent Black employment for all BEM firms. The distribution of Black employment varies across firms of different sizes in 1960 and 1970, as can be seen by comparing the percent of Black employees in the BEM firms in column 3 with column 2. Comparing the percent firm/employment values, we see that the

Table 17–6. Ratio of 1970 to 1959 Male Employment in a Sample of Firms by Age and Race

	All Males	Black Males
Total 25+	1.051	1.469
25–34	1.163	2.578
35–44	.815	1.03
45–54	1.148	1.216
55–64	1.186	1.161
65+	.489	.488

Source: Snyder, D. C. Longitudinal Pension Employee (LPE) file.

Table 17–7.   Black Employment in a Sample of Firms 1959–1970

	Firms with Black Employment (BEM) ('59–'70)	% Blacks per Firm	% of Employment in Firms with Blacks Present	% Change in Black Employment
All	66–72	.076–.101	.082–.114	139
25–34	54–71	.085–.149	.077–.151	196
35–39	52–56	.099–.118	.092–.124	135
40–44	45–53	.105–.117	.097–.108	111
45–54	48–64	.110–.102	.095–.096	101
55–61	41–45	.156–.105	.100–.098	98
62–64	21–26	.151–.158	.127–.129	102
65+	18–14	.315–.378	.161–.219	136

Source: LPE file

difference for all workers is not large in 1959 (.006) but grows to .013 by 1970. We can infer that growth in black employment was relatively greater in larger establishments. Additionally, the larger establishments in the sample increased the number of Black workers they employed by concentrating their hiring among the youngest workers. Rows 2 and 3 show this pattern; in both cohorts the employment/firm percent ratios were less than one in 1959 and greater than one in 1970. All other cohorts have lower employment/firm ratios in both periods, showing practically no employment gains for Black workers 40 and over in the larger sample firms. This point is made even more clearly in column 1, where we see that the number of BEM firms increased from 54 to 71, nearly a one-third increase in the number of establishments employing the youngest cohort. The ratio of the proportion of Blacks employed in each firm (in firms with any Black workers) in 1970 and 1959 is shown in column 4. Again, the concentration of employment gains among younger males is evident.

One of the most interesting findings from this exercise concerns differences in the firm attachment patterns of older Black males. Looking at rows 4–6, we see that the employment position of Black males aged 40–61 remained unchanged over the decade. When we look at rows 7 and 8, the proportion of Blacks remaining attached to our sample firm increased from .16 (18 firms) to .22 (14 firms) in 1970. The clear implication is that Blacks continue to work longer than whites (surprising in view of their shorter life expectancy). Furthermore, the ratio of Blacks to whites in the oldest cohorts is growing, implying that this trend is waxing. The change in the age distribution of Blacks in our sample firms can be seen in Figure 17-1. Both younger and older work-

ers are more prevalent in 1970 than in 1959. Hiring patterns probably
account for the employment of younger workers; nearly one-third of
our sample firms added Black workers in this age group, as we noted
above, but a growing proportion of older Blacks is difficult to explain,
particularly in light of the considerable early retirement incentives
contained in our firms' pension plans.

   A number of explanations for the higher firm attachment rates of
older Black males can be advanced. For example, Blacks are likely to
have shorter firm attachment than whites; therefore, retirement benefits are lower than for whites. The lower wage replacement rate of
Blacks would be expected to induce later retirement (longer firm attachment), as we observe. On the other hand, the assumption of fewer
years of service for Blacks over 65 in 1970 means that they would have
to have been initially employed after they were 45 years of age in 1950
(to have less than 20 years, a relatively modest benefit), though it seems
unlikely that so many Black workers over 40 or 50 would have been
initially employed during the Korean war years. Alternatively, this pattern of apparent delayed retirement of Blacks could be the result of
their late entry into firms, in which case we would conclude that em-

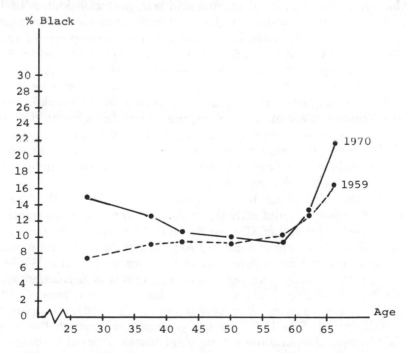

Figure 17–1. Distribution of Black Males in 1959–1970 by Age Cohort

ployment goals of firms were satisfied by hiring workers of all ages (the constant proportion of Blacks 40–51 during 1960–1970 contradicts this, however).

If firms did hire more older Blacks in the late 1960s (reflecting tight labor markets during the Vietnam War period), we would observe greater firm attachment among older Blacks in firms that do not impose automatic retirement at age 65. This hiring behavior of firms would be rational, due to the combination of higher age to qualify for benefits that would be required of late entrants and fewer years of life expectancy of Blacks. To test for the effects of automatic retirement on the employment patterns of Black males, we separately analyzed the employment experiences of Blacks in those firms without this restriction on older workers' employment opportunities within the firm. Of the 2,100 Blacks age 65 or over in 1970, over 90% were employed in firms without an automatic retirement (at age 65) provision. The implications of recent amendments to the Age Discrimination in Employment Act of 1965, which raised the minimum mandatory retirement age to 70, for older Black workers to acquire pension income are clear.

Cyclical sensitivity. Vroman's study noted the concentration of Black males in the manufacturing and transportation sectors in 1970 (1/3) and pointed out that employment in these sectors exhibits strong sensitivity to business conditions; thus, Black earnings would show a similar sensitivity. It is also true that pension credits earned by Blacks are affected by business conditions, since workers who are laid off stand to lose pension credit for that year and credit for all prior years if the layoff is permanent and they are not vested. Rigid break-in-service provisions, in effect in many plans, may disqualify separated workers who are not vested from ever regaining prior service credits, even upon recall to work. We examine the potential for pension losses by examining the cyclical sensitivity of Black employment in our sample of firms by computing the change in total and Black employment from 1969–1970. Total employment in our sample fell from 2,515,900 to 2,357,200 (a 5% decrease), significantly different from the minor contraction in Black jobs, which fell 268,000 to 267,400. This represents a loss of less than 1% of Black employment in 1969! If anything, Black employment appears insulated from recession in our sample of firms. While this experience probably does not extend to the rest of the economy, the patterns of continued Black firm attachment, in the face of sizable layoffs, is encouraging. The only group with positive employment growth during 1969–1970 was the youngest age cohort; this growth offset increased separations among older Blacks. This evidence must be viewed cautiously, however, since our data describe only a few firms and do not cover a full business downturn. Thus, any speculation about how Blacks fared as the recession deepened during 1973–1975 (particularly in autos, steel, and other manufacturing) would be premature.

Future Pension Status of Elderly Blacks

The concentration of employment gains in the younger cohorts means that an increase in the proportion of newly retired Blacks eligible for pension benefits from our sample firms will not occur for some time. The number of years before this increase could occur can be seen by a simple extrapolation into the future. A worker 30 years of age in 1970 will not reach normal retirement age until the year 2005 and will be eligible for early retirement some time after 1990, depending on the pension features of his firm's plan. If this experience were applicable to all employers, we would observe a significant increase in the percentage of Blacks applying for Social Security who were also expecting a private pension benefit. Workers who were 40 years of age in 1970 will reach normal retirement age in 1995 and will be eligible for early retirement in the 1980s. Some growth in the percentage of this cohort with pensions should be evident by 1990, presumably increasing through the remainder of the century. Very small employment gains were experienced by Black workers between the ages of 45 and 61 in 1970, so little change in overall pension status would be expected from this source. However, pension income of Blacks would be improved by more stable employment and longer job attachment.

After two decades have passed we should observe sizable and significant improvement in the pension status of the Black elderly who have been employed in our sample of firms. Beyond the turn of the century, greater numbers of Black workers in the economy will also be eligible for two retirement incomes; parity with the proportion of whites receiving pensions may even be achieved by this time.

Summary and Conclusion

Private pension coverage in the U.S. has grown at a phenomenal rate since World War II. The number of covered workers was 9.8 million in 1950 and had grown to 30.3 million by 1975 (Ture and Fields, 1976). During this time, benefits paid by pensions grew from $.37 million in 1950 to $14.8 million in 1975. Blacks, concentrated in the South prior to 1950 and mobile through the 1950s and 1960s, did not participate fully in the growth of the pension system. As a consequence, the pension status of older Black workers at retirement was noticeably inferior to that of whites as recently as 1970. However, this study has found that Black gains in employment in a sample of pension—covered establishments during the 1960s have been significant, indicating an improvement in pension status of future Black retirees. The employment growth of younger Black males between 1959 and 1970 attests to improved pension status for elderly Blacks in the future. Unfortunately, middle-aged and older Blacks did not share in this favorable employment growth in our sample of firms.

This analysis has made clear that equal access to jobs in pension-covered employment will elevate the relative pension status of non-whites in the future. However, at least two decades must pass before any increase in the proportion of Black employees receiving pensions will be apparent in our sample of firms. Other firms in the economy may have lagged behind these employers in hiring Blacks and not all offer pensions to their workers; hence, the pension status of newly retired Blacks will probably not improve in the aggregate until some time after that of Black workers in our sample firms. This means that other sources of retirement income to supplement Social Security benefits of older Blacks will have to be utilized to change the relative income status of newly entitled Blacks during the interim. To conclude, the potential for gains in pension income of the Black elderly seem assured. Gains in employment, wages, and pension coverage all bode well for a narrowing income gap between Black and white elderly who retire in the future, but many workers, both Black and white, will remain outside pension-covered employment and will have to rely on their own resources to supplement their Social Security benefits.

References

Bell, Donald R. "Prevalence of Private Retirement Plans." U.S. Department of Labor, Bureau of Labor Statistics, reprinted from *Monthly Labor Review,* October 1975, pp. 17–20.

Employment and Training Report of the President, 1976, Washington, D.C.: U.S. Government Printing Office.

Handbook of Labor Statistics 1974. U.S. Department of Labor, Bureau of Labor Statistics. Washington, D.C.: U.S. Government Printing Office.

Rubin, Leonard. "Economic Status of Black Newly Entitled Workers." *Reaching Retirement Age: Findings From a Survey of Newly Entitled Workers, 1968–70* (Research Report No. 47), Social Security Administration, Office of Research and Statistics, 1976, pp. 215–232.

Schiller, Bradley, and Snyder, Donald. "Pension Plan Changes and Quit Behavior: A Longitudinal Analysis" (mimeograph) College Park: The University of Maryland, 1978.

Snyder, D. C. Longitudinal Pension Employee File. Unpublished data.

Ture, Norman, and Fields, Barbara. *The Future of Private Pension Plans.* Washington, D.C.: American Institutes of Research, 1976.

U.S. Bureau of the Census. The National Income & Product Accounts of the U.S. 1929–1974 statistical Tables and unpublished National Income Data. Washington, D.C.: U.S. Government Printing Office.

U.S. Bureau of the Census. 1960 Census of the Population Special Reports. Washington, D.C.: U.S. Government Printing Office, 1961.

U.S. Bureau of the Census. 1970 Census of the Population Special Reports. Washington, D.C.: U.S. Government Printing Office, 1971.

Vroman, Wayne. "Employment Gains of Black Workers" (mimeograph). Paper presented at 1974 Meetings of the Industrial Relations Research Association, San Francisco, California.

18

Health Services and
the Puerto Rican Elderly

Ruth E. Zambrana, Rolando Merino,
and Sarah Santana

The purpose of this chapter is to examine the use of health services among the Puerto Rican elderly in East Harlem and to examine the different modalities of delivery systems which can be used effectively with this particular ethnic group. Analyzing, evaluating, and proposing models of service delivery for any age group of Puerto Ricans, however, must be integrally related to an understanding of their community—in this case East Harlem—and of those sociocultural factors and patterns that have significant impact on the use of services by Puerto Ricans.

East Harlem as a Setting

East Harlem is a poor urban residential community of approximately 160,000 people. Traditionally it has been an area of tenement dwellings for the working and lower classes, and particularly for newly arrived immigrant groups. The bulk of the population still consists of migrants, mainly Black and Puerto Rican. East Harlem is a primary area of settlement for Puerto Ricans, and thus the community reflects Puerto Rican culture to a significant extent. Almost one-half of the population is of Latin origin, which is why East Harlem is called "El Barrio." Thirty-five percent of the community is Black and the remaining 17% is white (Johnson, 1974).

The majority of the East Harlem Puerto Rican population tends to be younger than that of the other ethnic groups, with almost two-thirds of its members under 45 years of age. In contrast, the white population has almost one-third of its members over 65. This age differential can be attributed to the fact that most Black and Puerto Rican residents in New York came to New York in the early 1950s, while the white residents are mainly part of the earlier pre-World War II migration.

No truly reliable sources of data exist on the Puerto Rican elderly population of the East Harlem area. Estimates determined by the use of the 1970 Census, data from Community Planning District 11, and projections by the Human Resources Administration, indicate that the number of persons over the age of 65 in the area varies between 11,000 and 14,000. Approximately 8,305 people over 65 receive Supplemental Security Income or public assistance.

Characteristics of the Puerto Rican Elderly

Demographic characteristics. Elderly Puerto Ricans represent the smallest percentage of elderly in East Harlem. Hispanic elderly, predominantly Puerto Ricans, constitute 13% of the over-60 population in New York City. However, the Puerto Rican elderly are not rigidly defined only by age. They must also be defined as those individuals who already have adult children and grandchildren and who perhaps have functional impairments and disabilities. Two major patterns emerge among the elderly population in East Harlem: the Hispanic elderly tend to live with a spouse and tend to be willing and functionally able to provide concrete assistance to their children especially in the area of child care. A significant dynamic of the Puerto Rican family structure is that many of these Hispanic elderly are helping their children and their spouses in the hope that they will earn enough money to return to their homeland to rejoin their own siblings. Consequently it is likely that the social problems among Puerto Rican elderly have not reached a critical point because there is a back-migration to Puerto Rico as soon as the elderly feel "very sick." It is commonly heard among older Puerto Ricans that they want to die *"en mi tierra"* ("on my land").

It is difficult to verify these speculations on the importance of migratory patterns of Puerto Rican elderly and their relation to health because there are few empirical data on the health status of the Puerto Rican elderly and/or on the outcome of treatment interventions on the health status of this group. In two studies by the New York City Office for the Aging, 8.3% of New York's inner city elderly (60 and over) were found to be severely impaired when compared to the national average (Cantor, 1974, 1976). The studies demonstrated that the East Harlem area contained the highest percentage of impaired elderly persons in the Borough of Manhattan. The Hispanics surveyed showed more than twice the rate of severe impairment than other groups. The number of seriously impaired elderly in East Harlem was estimated at 5,440. Another unpublished survey conducted by the Aguilar Senior Citizens Center in East Harlem identified 1,000 homebound elderly in only one-fourth of the public housing projects. Johnson's study in 1972 also found that Hispanics have poorer health status than other Black and white ethnic groups. These data and estimations of the 15 senior citizens centers and eight home health agencies in East Harlem indicate that there are approximately 4,000 to 4,500 homebound elderly in East Harlem, of whom approximately half are Black and Puerto Rican.

Language and cultural characteristics. A multitude of factors have affected the health care status of the Puerto Rican elderly in East Harlem. Language and cultural differences are major impediments to the adequate use of services. East Harlem has a wealth of health care resources—two medical schools, a community hospital, a municipal hospital, a group practice Health Insurance Plan (HIP) and over 20 *centros medicos*—most of which are dependent on Puerto Rican clientele. Health care organizations in the area, however, have not seriously addressed themselves to the linguistic and cultural reality of the urban ethnic Puerto Rican. In many instances the professional and paraprofessional staffing patterns of these health institutions merely represent a token gesture in their recognition of the cultural and linguistic barriers that Puerto Ricans must confront in their use of the health care system.

We find in the Puerto Rican culture what Shuval (1970) has called the "magic-science conflict." Puerto Ricans maintain a belief in the use of *espiritistas,* who are indigenous folk healers. There is a traditional belief in the powers of the supernatural, which is mediated through *espiritistas* and helps Puerto Ricans to identify the root of a problem and then suggest solutions to alleviate the causes of the problem (see Harwood, 1977). These beliefs are well-established among the elderly. It is interesting to note that *espiritistas* often provide herbal remedies, warm baths, and/or massage therapy, which are perceived as quite effective in alleviating a substantial number of presenting complaints. However, when the Puerto Rican elderly encounter the Western medical system, the cultural clash often results in the ridicule of their traditional belief system, with consequent alienation of the Puerto Rican elderly from the health system.

Factors in service usage. The lack of awareness of existing services within the community and how to use the services available skillfully is compounded by English language difficulties among East Harlem Puerto Ricans. This lack of knowledge usually results in misuse of services, fragmentation of care, costly duplication of health services, and increased rates of institutionalization of the Puerto Rican elderly.

Lastly, but of critical importance, is the lack of financial coverage available for the elderly with incomes barely above the poverty level. Medicare does not cover essential and common necessities that plague the elderly such as prescriptions, eyeglasses, hearing aids, and dental care (Hyman, 1973). The inaccessibility of health services to the poor Puerto Rican elderly is a result of the reimbursement mechanisms. Harris (1978) aptly describes the reasons:

> The fact that out of pocket expenses for the elderly have increased over 250% since 1966 and that the elderly now pay about 60% of their health care bill, with Medicare paying only about 40%, shows what a cruel hoax this insurance is for senior citizens [p. 3].

The fact that health care services are financially inaccessible to the poor Puerto Rican elderly presents serious problems for both the elderly and their immediate families. The lack of adequate financial coverage for the health expenditures of the Puerto Rican elderly militates against the maintenance of a strong family structure and the interdependence of generations.

In sum, an overwhelming number of East Harlem Puerto Rican elderly do not use the available services due to existing racial, class, linguistic, cultural, and financial barriers. There has certainly not been a comprehensive approach to the needs of the Puerto Rican elderly or to the delivery of services. The services that do exist are fragmented and inadequate, particularly in their lack of tertiary prevention such as rehabilitation services.

Since health services for Puerto Ricans are generally inadequate, the Puerto Rican elderly face special problems. Approaches to the care of the Puerto Rican elderly have generally taken two forms—traditional and alternative approaches. Traditional approaches are based on a medical model which is highly specialized, highly "technologized," and highly impersonal, and which is oriented toward diseases and emphasizes curative rather than preventive care and health maintenance. It is based on a doctor-patient relationship that responds to a specific problem and provides fragmented care. Alternative approaches are community-based and community-oriented with more focus on prevention and health maintenance. This alternative mode is also based on a team approach in order to respond to the varying needs of the individuals and provide continuity of care.

312Ethnicity and Aging

Traditional Health Approaches
for Puerto Rican Elderly

It is important to examine the acceptability of the traditional approaches to the Puerto Rican elderly prior to presenting a model that would be applicable in a community with a Puerto Rican population such as East Harlem. The traditional approaches most frequently identified for elderly care are institutional long-term care, day care, and home health care.

Institutional settings. In New York City, approximately 3% of the total elderly population resides in institutions such as nursing homes or public hospitals. In East Harlem this figure is much lower. There is only one nursing home in East Harlem, which recruits the majority of its patient population from areas outside East Harlem. The fact that this nursing home does not reflect the composition of its surrounding area raises questions both of accessibility and acceptability for potential patients. The greatest barrier of access is financial: the Puerto Rican elderly are unable to afford nursing home care but are often forced into public institutions such as psychiatric hospitals if familial support systems are not available. On the other hand, it is our contention that this type of approach is the least acceptable culturally to the majority of Puerto Rican elderly. It would alienate them from those social networks within the community such as family members and peers which are critical to their sense of life satisfaction, fulfillment, and ultimately maintenance of adequate or functional health status.

Day care. Adult day care is a relatively new modality in this country. It has been in use for several years in other countries, particularly England, where it is considered a viable alternative to long-term care. The major factors that work against the use of day care for Puerto Rican elderly are the reimbursement policies of Medicare and Medicaid, which do not reimburse for this type of ambulatory care service. Further, since it is a relatively new modality in the U.S. there is limited information on its effectiveness and efficiency. Evaluation in terms of its impact on the health status of elderly patients has been inadequate; and there is no assessment as yet of its cultural acceptance to the different ethnic groups. A study conducted by the National Center for Health Services in 1974 (Weissert, 1977), identified two areas that require further study: one is that day care encompasses a substantial number of submodalities, such as "hospital" day care, which have to be more carefully delineated, making it difficult to characterize this type of care; and second, day care costs were found to be higher than nursing home costs. (Comparison was made based on cost per day of both systems.) If the latter finding is proven accurate, it seems that this modality will not be an economically feasible alternative of care for the poor Puerto Rican elderly.

However, this type of modality should be explored as an alternative substitute structure for those Puerto Ricans who need institutional-based care. A "multipurpose" day care system would foster intergenerational linkages between the elderly and his/her immediate family because there would be daily contact. This modality would also enable the family to play a critical role in enabling the elderly patient to use services effectively and to comply with necessary treatments.

Home health care. Home health care includes a variety of health and social programs provided to the elderly in their homes. At present, great emphasis is being given to home health care as a viable alternative to long-term institutionalized care (Brickner et al., 1976). Many of the patients now residing in long-term facilities could optimally reside in their homes if health and social services were regularly provided in their homes or on an ambulatory basis. A recent study in New York City of a sample of skilled nursing homes found that 76% of patient-residents did not require skilled nursing home care but rather required health-related facility care, domiciliary, or noninstitutional (NYCHSA, 1977). Some evidence also indicates that the population using home health care in New York is comparable to the population receiving nursing home care. In a comparison of a sample of bedfast and fully ambulatory patients from each group, the only significant difference was found in the proportion of married patients: 50% of those receiving home health care were married, while only 12% of those in nursing homes had spouses. This finding suggests that this modality should be further explored as an alternative to care for Puerto Ricans since a substantial proportion are married.

The Chelsea-Village Program, administered by St. Vincent's Hospital in New York, provides care in the home to homebound, isolated, aged people; the program is economically advantageous as well as morally appropriate. Yearly nursing home costs for ambulatory, semi-ambulatory and bedbound patients were estimated at $8,266, $16,231 and $32,162, respectively. By contrast, the Chelsea-Village Program costs for these three categories of patients were $7,159, $8,606, and $12,697 yearly. In both samples, the patients suffered comparable ailments and required the same care (Scharer and Boehringer, 1976).

These data and the experiences at Chelsea-Village suggest that home health care programs are an important and viable alternative to long-term care, especially for those elderly Puerto Ricans who do not have accessibility to long-term or day care facilities.

For Puerto Ricans whose culture, language, family structure, and economic viability are not compatible with either a nursing home or

hospital environment, the traditional approaches to their old-age problems are cruel and ineffective. The overutilization of expensive professionals in settings such as nursing homes or hospitals inflate costs and
may indeed be not only unnecessary but detrimental to the patient.
Improvement in the provision of health and other services and the
development of community-based and culturally oriented health delivery models will provide the basis for an effective delivery of services to
the Puerto Rican elderly (East Harlem Tenants Council, 1977).

Alternative Approaches

From both an economic and humanistic point of view, alternatives to
the traditional system are necessary. We will discuss two: (1) a modified
traditional approach consisting of coordinated home/hospital/nursing
home care delivered by doctors, nurses, and social workers and (2) a
more unorthodox approach, also coordinating home/hospital/nursing
home care, but delivered mainly by nurse practitioners, elderly paraprofessional health workers, and those included in the social support
network of the patient (family, neighbors, mailman, grocer, etc.), under
the professional supervision of nurses, doctors, and social workers. This
latter approach we term *intracommunity* to reflect the high utilization,
whenever possible, of resources already in existence within the patient's immediate family system as well as his/her larger community or
neighborhood. The main objective of both approaches is to maintain
the patient living at home with a maximum of independence, thus
preventing institutionalization (see King, 1977; Blank, 1977; Rubin,
1977).

    Modified traditional approach. In this approach, a nurse, social
worker, and physician form the team assuming responsibility for the
health maintenance of the patient. These three professionals do an
initial evaluative home visit and decide on the treatment plan or course
to follow. Depending on the severity of the physical illness or degree
of impairment, follow-up visits are then conducted by both doctor and
nurse or by the nurse alone. The social worker may accompany them
or generate her/his own visiting schedule. She/he arranges for whatever social and income maintenance services are necessary (Medicare,
Medicaid, SSI, etc.), coordinates the use of homemakers and compan-
ions when needed, provides counseling, and helps the elderly make
contact with social centers in his/her community.

    The team is based at a community hospital, which becomes the
back-up and emergency service for elderly patients. Although the hos-

pital is not reimbursed for the home visits, the income generated by these patients' ambulatory visits and hospitalizations and the greater ease of caring for a patient who already trusts and has a relationship with hospital staff compensate for the expenditures. In other words, this type of approach is geared to foster continuity of care for the elderly patient.

Although the model is far superior to traditional approaches and provides good care for the patient, it is not cost-efficient due to the use of high-salaried professional personnel. The physician is the core of the team, and the traditional physician/nurse unit is used. Regardless of how attuned to the community the team may be, it always remains a group of professionals who invade the life of the patient, generally for the better, but who are usually distant and different in terms of age, social and economic class, place of residence, etc., even if they share the same ethnic background. For the team, the link with the community of the patient is the hospital, not the patient; they work *in* but are not part *of* the community.

This model has been implemented at St. Vincent's Hospital in New York City and appears to be successful in improving the cost-effectiveness and cost-efficiency of elderly care and is a great improvement to traditional care.

The intracommunity approach. This design is based on two premises: (1) that already existing resources in a community can and should be used to provide care for the elderly under professional supervision and (2) that the elderly are an integral resource of the community, the functionally healthy and willing of whom should be integrated into a team to help their peers. As we shall indicate, the intracommunity approach is cost-effective and cost-efficient. It provides the community an opportunity to act on its own behalf, and to employ currently idle capability, namely the elderly.

In keeping with the community approach, the team (which in this model consists of a geriatric nurse practitioner, a social worker, a community health worker, and a supervising consulting physician) is based at a community health center—a comprehensive, primary care, ambulatory facility. Back-up agreements and coordination are implemented with hospitals and nursing homes in geographic proximity to the community.

The Community Health Worker (CHW) becomes the core of the team. She/he is an active, healthy, literate senior citizen especially trained to monitor the health of the patient at home, render basic health services—measuring temperature, blood pressure, height, weight, pulse, respiration; perform vision and hearing screenings; collect samples (feces, urine, etc.); perform simple lab tests (dipstick); help patients understand and follow treatment, etc.—and serve as a bridge between the home-bound patient and the health/social services outside the home. She/he also acts as the patients' advocate and counselor, provides or arranges for transportation, meals, psychological support, and necessary social and income maintenance services.

A midlevel health professional, such as a nurse practitioner, provides technical supervision for a specified number of CHWs and their patients. In the same fashion, a social worker supervises the delivery of social services. The nurse practitioner and the social worker collaborate in a team approach to ensure comprehensive, coordinated services. In addition to supervision, the nurse practitioner makes professional house calls and serves as the patient's point of entry into the health care system. The social worker plays a similar role with regard to the patient's social and emotional needs.

An important function of the team is the reinforcement of the patient's existing social support network (Garrison and Howe, 1976). This network consists of the patient's family, neighbors, friends, and any significant others, such as bingo or domino partners or the janitor of their building. Because the CHW is a neighbor or nearby resident of the patient, the task of constructing or reinforcing a support system for the patient is simplified.

Since CHWs live in the community and would be assigned patients living very near them, it is assumed that travel expenses would be less costly than those based on ambulatory visits and institutional stays. However, a proper mechanism of funding must be identified, since available sources of third-party payments (insurance, Medicare, Medicaid) do not cover most of these services. There is a need to implement this model on an experimental basis to determine its actual cost-effectiveness.

For the Puerto Rican elderly, and more generally for any ethnic elderly population, this model integrates the elderly into their community, attempts to recreate, build upon, and expand the support and services rendered by an extended family, and does so within the context of familiar culture, language, community, and neighborhood.

Conclusion

The implementation of the intracommunity model for delivery of health care services has great implications for the health of the home-bound Puerto Rican elderly in East Harlem. At the community level it would improve the utilization of existing health resources, contain costs of services to the elderly, decrease duplication, and provide high-quality, humane, and culturally consonant care. It would also provide employment for a small number of functionally healthy elderly in the community. This program would provide them with the structure necessary to use knowledge and skills readily available not only for their own benefit, but also for that of their peers.

This program has several social implications for the poor Puerto Rican elderly and for a national health policy on the aging. Primarily the program would foster more effective use of the multiplicity of existing health and social resources in East Harlem by discouraging the duplication of services and encouraging the coordination of different community services to maximize the benefits to the patient. In other words, this approach would enhance the redistribution of community-based services and the development of more community-oriented services. The greatest need in many poor, urban ethnic communities is related to the lack of comprehensive services. Thus, there is a need to develop a continuum of comprehensive services that would better respond to the physical, social, cultural, and psychological needs of the elderly of different ethnic groups at different levels of functional health and impairment. It is important to develop a system that provides different levels of care (Abdellah, 1978). There is not just one type of care that would solve the entire spectrum of problems presented by the elderly population. A system of health care for the elderly population should integrate and properly use different services and levels of care: home health, ambulatory, and hospitalization/long-term institutionalization. For the Puerto Rican population, an intracommunity approach is the most viable in terms of cultural acceptability.

The development of a comprehensive system must be coupled with educational programs to inform all elderly groups, but particularly the poor Puerto Rican elderly, of the types of services available and how to utilize them. Unfortunately, the development of a community-based and comprehensive model cannot be implemented unless there is a restructuring of the reimbursement mechanisms and organization of health services for the poor and elderly. Changes are required in the reimbursement policies of Medicaid and Medicare in order to foster the use of ambulatory and home health care services and discourage the use of hospital-based services, which are monetarily beneficial to provider institutions but often detrimental to the well-being of the elderly.

The use of services by poor ethnic groups are not simply explained by financial constraints and attitudes of poor elderly. Serious structural barriers also impede Puerto Ricans' use of services. In her study, Dutton (1978) interprets her findings in the following way:

These findings suggest that neither improved financial access nor health education efforts alone will eliminate current income differentials in use, unless accompanied by structural improvements in existing delivery systems. Fundamental changes in the organization and distribution of care must occur, if equitable patterns of use are to be more than health policy rhetoric [p. 363].

The particular importance of our proposed intracommunity model is that it will take into consideration not only organizational issues of health care delivery but also factors such as culture, family support systems, and community resources. For the Puerto Rican group, the strength of this model rests with its ability to reinforce intergenerational dependency and to strengthen the fiber of the family. The incorporation of these factors is essential if a health and social services delivery model is to be an effective and efficient mechanism to provide care to the Puerto Rican elderly in a humane, culturally acceptable, and dignified manner.

References

Abdellah, F. G. The future of long-term term care. *Bulletin of the New York Academy of Medicine*, 1978, *54*, 261–270.

Blank, M. L. Meeting the needs of the aged: the social worker in the community health center. *Public Health Reports*, 1977, *92*, 39–42.

Brickner, P. W., Janeski, J. F., Rich, G., Duque, T., Starita, L., La Rocco, R., Flannery, T., and Werlin, S. Home maintenance for the home-bound aged. *The Gerontologist*, 1976, *16*, 25–29.

Cantor, M. *Functional ability estimates of the elderly for New York City Community Planning Districts*. New York: New York City Office for the aging, 1976.

Cantor, M. *Health of the inner city elderly*. New York: New York City Office for the Aging, October, 1974.

Dutton, Diana B. Explaining the low use of health services by the poor: costs, attitudes, or delivery systems? *American Sociological Review*, 1978, *43*, 348–368.

East Harlem Tenants Council. Neighborhood Health Center Proposal to DHEW, 1977.

Garrison, J. E., and Howe, J. A. Community intervention with the elderly. *Journal of the American Geriatrics Society*, 1976, *24*, 329–333.

Harris, J. (Ed.). *Economic Notes*. New York: Labor Research Association, 1978, *46*.

Harwood, A. *Rx: Spiritist as needed: a study of a Puerto Rican community mental health resource*. New York: John Wiley, 1977.

Hyman, H. (Ed.). *Policy recommendations for change.* Unpublished manuscript. Hunter College, Graduate Program of Urban Planning, New York, New York, 1973.

Johnson, L. *The people of East Harlem.* New York: The Mount Sinai School of Medicine, 1974.

King, S. Counseling the younger elderly: a responsive approach. Presented at the Annual Meeting of the National Conference of Jewish Communal Service, Washington, D.C., June 6, 1977.

New York City Health Systems Agency. *Home health care: its utilization, costs and reimbursement.* 1977.

Rubin, B. The role of the community center in meeting the health needs of the aged: an overview. Presented at the Annual Meeting of the National Conference of Jewish Communal Service, Washington, D.C., June 6, 1977.

Scharer, L. K., and Boehringer, J. R. *Home health care for the aged: the program of St. Vincent's Hospital, New York City. Philadelphia: Boehringer Associates, February 17, 1976.*

Shuval, J. *Social functions of medical practice.* San Francisco: Jossey-Bass, 1970.

Weissert, W. G. Adult day care programs in the United States: current research projects and a survey of ten centers. *Public Health Reports,* 1977, *92,* 49–56.

19

Neighborhood Capacity Building and the Ethnic Aged

David E. Biegel and Wendy R. Sherman

Considerable attention has recently been given to the mental health needs of the elderly, which are not being addressed by the current mental health delivery system. Federally funded community mental health centers see very few elderly clients. Recent legislation has set a goal for community mental health centers to have 10% of their clients 65 years of age and over, but centers do not know how to design and deliver services that are accessible, appropriate, coordinated with other human services needed by the elderly, and allow utilization without stigma or loss of pride.

Too often mental health services are seemingly "parachuted" into the community and operate with few, if any, linkages to the informal community support systems. In fact, mental health services often bypass those neighborhood-based organizational and cultural networks that have the capacity to support people. They fail to utilize fully the positive neighborhood identification of the urban elderly as a means of overcoming personal and institutional obstacles—administrative, fiscal, and legal—to seeking and receiving help.

The findings of the authors' Neighborhood and Family Services Project show that neighborhood attachment and neighborhood-based helping networks are of critical importance for the elderly, especially

This project is supported by a grant from the National Institute of Mental Health, #R01MH2653-01, Howard R. Davis, Ph.D., Project Officer. Principal Investigator of the Grant is Arthur J. Naparstek, Ph.D. Research in Milwaukee was conducted in cooperation with the South Community Organization, Inc.

the ethnic elderly, but that at the present time the elderly face a mental health system that is fragmented, dysfunctional, and not built upon this positive concept of neighborhood. We will review previous research findings that support the importance of neighborhood and neighborhood-based helping networks, discuss our own research findings, and then propose a neighborhood-based service model that can strengthen the positive attachment to the neighborhood by the ethnic elderly. This model enhances the capacity of the elderly to shape mental health services to meet needs they have identified. It creates a more cohesive helping system that integrates mental health services with other human service needs of the elderly.

Definition of Terms

Before previous research findings are reviewed, it will be helpful to define what is meant by the term *mental health.* There are a number of current definitions of mental health. In this analysis, we are using a community mental health framework that encompasses the concepts in the following two definitions. Staff of the Langley Porter Neuropsychiatric Institute in San Francisco have suggested that community mental health

> . . . is the broad multi-disciplined field concerned with the wide variety of forces and structures in a community which affect the emotional stability (positive growth, development, and functioning) of a significant group of its members. . . . The attention is directed at social institutions including those concerned with welfare, health, legislation, minority groups, employment, education, church, and their interactions which can in their functioning either enhance or hinder the emotional growth of a large segment of the population [Goldston, 1965, p. 195].

Lemkau, a psychiatrist with long and significant involvement in public health, argues that the concept of "community" in community mental health should be a central and not a peripheral part of community mental health. Lemkau states that

> . . . community mental health is a community-wide responsibility, that the program is to be under professional and lay auspices, and that mental health is promoted and fostered not solely through medical treatment but also through a variety of institutions and agencies with numerous disciplines joining in the effort. It is through this concept that the phrase "community mental health" becomes more than a pious wish, and is a living concept whereby concern with mental health becomes diffused throughout the matrix of the community itself. [Goldston, 1965, p. 197].

Using this framework, we see the mental health needs of the elderly being met by a variety of community and professional resources, including but not limited to community mental health centers. Community mental health services are thus provided by friends, neighbors, family, clergy, mental health clinics, physicians, welfare agencies, "natural helpers,"[1] health clinics, pharmacists, etc., as is evident in the review of the literature that follows.

Review of the Literature

People most often turn to relatives, neighbors, friends, and neighborhood institutions for support and emergency assistance. The importance of these neighborhood-based natural, cultural, and organizational networks has been noted by Breton (1964), Caplan (1974), Collins and Pancoast (1976), Glazer (1971), Litwak (1961), Slater (1970), and Warren (1977). These authors contend, in fact, that strengthening these neighborhood networks can provide a means of gaining a sense of control over one's life, reducing alienation from society, gaining a capacity to solve new problems, and maintaining the motivation to overcome handicaps and frustrations of modern society (President's Commission on Mental Health, 1978).

Berger and Neuhaus (1977) concur in their discussion of the importance of "mediating structures," such as the neighborhood, church, and family, that stand between the individual in his/her private life and the large institutions of public life. They state that the neighborhood should be seen as a key structure and argue that human service programs should be developed through these relevant mediating institutions. People working in small groups around concerns of the neighborhood strengthen their own internal networks and mediating institutions, making it possible to link with other systems for mutual problem solving (Berger and Neuhaus, 1977; Naparstek, Spiro, and Biegel, 1977). On a more psychological and individual level, there is strong evidence that the availability of social supports in the neighborhood acts as a buffer in times of crisis, making it easier for people to cope with and adapt to change (Caplan and Killilea, 1976; Warren, 1977).

Collins and Pancoast (1976) provide a review of the studies of informal care-givers and state that enough is already known about informal networks to indicate their tremendous potential as linkages to professional human services, since these networks do provide a vital

1. Natural helpers are community residents who provide helping services but are not professionally trained.

bridge between the individual and the environment. A number of recent studies of social networks report similar findings (Caplan and Killilea, 1976; Lee, 1969; Sarason et al., 1977; Snyder, 1971).

The importance of neighborhood and neighborhood-based networks for the general population have been shown to be extremely important for the elderly as well. Lawton and Byerts (1973) point out that the elderly meet most of their social and daily needs within a six-block radius of their home and various studies on relocation efforts note both the economic and psychosocial separation cost of moving for older persons (Birren, 1969; Fried, 1972).

The physical community, then, is an important concept for older persons. Regnier (1975) states that "good neighborhoods can provide a safe, convenient environment of social interaction as well as a location for basic life supportive goods and services." Cantor (1975) has underscored the importance of the neighborhood as a social center for older persons. Yet much of the gerontology literature emphasizes only physical planning and environmental modifications of neighborhoods.

Rosow (1967) further develops the concept of the neighborhood as a reference group for older persons offering potential mutuality and self-esteem through friends and neighbors. Cantor (1975), Lopata (1973), Lowenthal and Haven (1968), Rose (1965), Shanas et al. (1968), Townsend (1957), and others have shown that neighborhood networks of friends, family, community groups, and voluntary associations are of great importance to the well-being of the elderly. Cantor (1975) in her study of the social support system of inner city New York elderly noted the mutuality of assistance between neighbors exemplified by younger neighbors shopping for elderly persons while the elderly watched their children. Discussing the importance of voluntary associations for the elderly, Shore (1974) states that these organizations help sensitize the larger community to the needs of an often invisible elderly subculture. As regards voluntary organization membership, Hendricks and Hendricks (1977) state that after age 60 most participation occurs in church-related activities. The church has been found by many researchers to be a key resource that people use when they have problems (Gurin et al., 1960; Srole et al., 1960; Snyder, 1971). Others have discussed the important role that the church should play in the delivery of mental health services (Haugk, 1976; Rosen, 1974).

This review shows that neighborhood-based networks provide important mechanisms of support, assist in crisis, and provide the basis for linkages with professional human services. For the elderly particularly, the neighborhood is especially important. It serves as a locus for meeting daily needs as a social center and as the locus for support networks of family, friends, and community organizations.

Neighborhood and Family Services Project

Research Framework

Project description. The Neighborhood and Family Services Project is based upon the concepts just reviewed. The project, supported by a four-year grant from NIMH, is an action research and demonstration program designed to mobilize ethnic neighborhoods around mental health issues, to develop model programs to overcome identified obstacles to effective service delivery, and to develop policy initiatives on the national, state, and local levels to institutionalize project findings. The focus of our research is on personal problems people are experiencing, where people go for help when they have problems, how and when people make use of helping networks, what the obstacles are to seeking and/or receiving help, and how the factors of ethnicity and community attachment intervene in the process of defining problems and utilizing helping networks. Project sites are southeast Baltimore City, Maryland, and the south side of Milwaukee, Wisconsin. Since research findings from both cities were similar and space considerations prevent a full discussion of all the data, we have decided to present Milwaukee findings only.

Target area. The target area on Milwaukee's south side is composed of some 22 census tracts. In 1975 this area had a population of 66,074, down some 10% from the 1970 figure of 73,351. Of this population 5.8% is between the ages of 60 and 64 years and 12.4% is age 65 and over as compared to 4.6% and 11% respectively for the city of Milwaukee. Sixteen percent of the total population of the area is first- or second-generation Polish American, while 8% is German, and over 32% of the area's population is mixed foreign stock (i.e., foreign born, or at least one foreign-born parent). There are 18 Catholic churches and two Eastern Orthodox churches in the area. The 19 Protestant churches in the target area are mostly smaller in size than the Catholic parishes, and often the former draw parishioners from outside the area. The area, then, is heavily Catholic, Polish and working class, and is probably one of the most visible ethnic communities in the city. Not only are there many ethnics in the area, but their institutions and customs are readily discernible.

Research Methodology

The research methodologies utilized in this project consist of three principle data sources: helper and leader survey, community resident survey, and statistical data.

Helper and leader survey. We conducted 270 interviews of community helpers and leaders in Milwaukee—clergy, human service agency staff, natural helpers, neighborhood leaders,[2] pharmacists, physicians, and school personnel serving the target community. This survey, which utilized 100 open- and closed-ended pretested questions taking one hour to administer, was given to a 100% sample of leaders and helpers within selected neighborhoods of the target area. Refusal rates averaged below 25%.

The survey instrument asked community leaders and helpers what the major problems were for teenagers, families, separated and divorced, widowed, and the elderly. Interviewees were asked which individual, group, or organization in the neighborhood and which professional agency was most effective in dealing with particular problems. Other questions focused on obstacles to seeking and receiving help, neighborhood attachment, and help giving provided by the respondent.

Community resident survey.   A random sample of 197 community residents, age 18 years and older, was interviewed in Milwaukee. The respondents were chosen randomly using the Kish selection process and were interviewed face to face using a pretested instrument that took slightly over one hour to administer. Professional research organizations conducted the interviews through a subcontract, under the guidance of project research staff. The survey instrument focused on personal problems the interviewee had experienced, where they went for help, their attitudes toward seeking and receiving help, and their opinions of the problems of other community residents, as well as questions dealing with neighborhood attachment and ethnicity.

Statistical data.   Census data, utilization of mental health services, and social indicator data—crime rates, welfare, health, education statistics—were utilized as supportive data.

Description of Interviewees

Community helper and leader survey.   A total of 270 helpers and leaders were interviewed as follows: 25 (9.3%) clergy, 95 (35.2%) human service agency staff, 62 (30%) neighborhood leaders, 27 (10%) natural helpers, 33 (12.2%) school personnel, 12 (4.4%) physicians, and 15 (5.9%) pharmacists. Of the 270 interviewees, 19 (7%) were age 65 years or older. Neighborhood leaders included the highest percentage of interviewees age 65 and over (22.6%), with natural helpers, physicians, and pharmacists having no interviewees age 65 or over.

Community resident survey.   Of the 197 individuals interviewed in Milwaukee, 43 (21.8%) were 65 years or older, and 64 (32.5%) were

2. Neighborhood leaders are individuals who hold an office in a neighborhood association, ethnic club, social or fraternal organization or individuals perceived by others as leaders although occupying no formal organizational positions.

classified as Southern/Eastern European Ethnic. There were significant differences in ethnicity by age, with 69% of those 65 and over being ethnic as compared to 22.6% of those under 65 ($p < .001$).[3] Almost two-thirds (60.6%) of the interviewees stated that their country's background was important to them. For purposes of this analysis, ethnic includes those individuals who themselves or whose parents—one or both—were foreign-born, from one of these Central, Southern, or Eastern European countries: Germany, Austria, Switzerland, Italy, Greece, Poland, Latvia, Hungary, Yugoslavia, Czechoslavakia, and Russia (USSR). This definition of ethnicity is of course a conservative one, which does not include second- or third-generation ethnics.

Findings: Neighborhood Attachment and Use of Helping Networks

We will discuss research findings related to neighborhood attachment and use of helping networks from both our community helper and leader and our community resident surveys. Since the findings of our helper and leader survey have been reported previously (Naparstek, Spiro, and Biegel, 1977), we will not discuss them here in great detail. The community resident survey results are descriptions of initial findings. Further analyses will be conducted in the coming months.

Indicators of neighborhood attachment to be examined include satisfaction with neighborhood, perceptions of the size of the neighborhood, length of time living in the neighborhood, organizational affiliations, and activities done in the neighborhood. Indicators of utilization of helping networks to be examined include what elderly do when they have problems, knowledge of helping resources, factors affecting utilization of resources, and who interviewees talk with first when they have a problem.

Neighborhood Attachment

Length of time living in the neighborhood. More than half (53.3%) of the community resident interviewees have lived in the neighborhood for more than ten years. Of these individuals, 70% have lived in the neighborhood for more than 20 years. There are significant differences by age, with 88% of those over age 65 having lived in the neighborhood for more than ten years as compared to 44% of those

3. The Chi-square statistic was used throughout the analysis.

under age 65 ($p < .001$). This difference by age was found in both ethnic and non-ethnic populations, although the difference was much greater among ethnics. Among the ethnics, 97% of those age 65 years and older have lived in the neighborhood for more than ten years as compared with 41% of those under age 65 ($p < .05$). Ethnics have lived in the neighborhood for considerably longer than non-ethnics, with 73% of the ethnics having lived in the neighborhood for more than ten years as compared to 44% of the non-ethnics; however, this is a conditional relationship that holds true only for those age 65 and over when stratifying by age.

Of the leaders and helpers, all neighborhood leaders and natural helpers lived in the community, while a majority of the clergy, a number of agency staff, and no doctors or pharmacists lived in the community. Many neighborhood leaders and natural helpers lived in the community for 20 years or more.

Size of neighborhood. Residents view their neighborhoods as being small in size, with 82.9% of the interviewees viewing their neighborhood as less than ten blocks and 26.9% of the interviewees viewing their neighborhood as just one block. There were significant differences by age, with 44.7% of those age 65 years and older viewing their neighborhood as just one block as compared to 22.6% of those under age 65 ($p < .002$). This difference according to age was found to be conditional, holding true for ethnics but not for non-ethnics. Of ethnics age 65 years old and over, 53.8% view their neighborhood as just one block as compared with 22.6% of those ethnics under age 65 ($p < .03$).

Satisfaction with neighborhood. Over three-quarters (76.6%) of community resident interviewees expressed satisfaction with their neighborhood, with 35% being very satisfied. There were no significant differences by age or ethnicity. Over half of the interviewees (58.1%) stated that they saw their neighborhood as a place where they really belonged. There were no significant differences by age or ethnicity.

Natural helpers, neighborhood leaders, and clergy felt very positive about the neighborhood, with human service agency staff feeling considerably less positive. Attitudes toward the neighborhood were directly related to living in the neighborhood, with those helpers and leaders who lived in the neighborhood feeling much more positive than those helpers and leaders who did not live in the neighborhood.

Organization affiliation. Almost half of the community resident interviewees (48.2%) stated that they belonged to one or more organizations. Of those age 65 years and older, slightly over half (52.4%) stated that they belonged to one or more organization. Almost one-third (31%) of those age 65 years and older belonged to more than one organization as compared with 13.2 of those under age 65 ($p < .05$).

Activities done in the neighborhood.   Community resident interviewees were read a list of seven everyday types of activities (weekly
grocery shopping, making small purchases, going to church, movies,
doctor, work, and doing banking). For each of these activities they were
asked whether they do most of that within five blocks of their home, six
to ten blocks, or not at all. Only two activities were done by a majority
of the interviewees within ten blocks of their home: grocery shopping
(67%) and going to church (66.3%). A high percentage of respondents
did both of these activities within five blocks of their home: church
(50%) and grocery shopping (35%). The only significant differences by
age were due to the fact that many elderly do not work or go to movies.
There were no significant differences on any of the seven factors due
to ethnicity. Of interest is the very high percentages of elderly respondents who report going to church: 89% for ethnics and 82% for non-
ethnics.

Use of Helping Networks

What elderly do when they have problems.   Community resident
interviewees were asked what the elderly did when faced with a specific problem. Almost one-third (30.7%) see the elderly as seeking help,
24% as coping, and 20% as doing nothing; 13.3% did not know. There
were significant differences by age, with 60% of those interviewees age
65 years and older seeing the elderly as coping but only 15% of those
under age 65 seeing the elderly as coping. Similarly only 6.7% of the
elderly see the elderly as doing nothing, but 23.3% of those under age
65 see the elderly as doing nothing when they have a problem ($p < .01$).

Do individuals know where to go for help?   Community resident
interviewees were asked if they thought that individuals knew where
to go for help when they had a problem. Over half of the interviewees
stated that they felt that all or most individuals knew where to go for
help. There were no significant differences by ethnicity or age. However, when ethnicity was introduced as a test factor into the relationship between age and opinions, there were significant differences
among non-ethnics but not among ethnics, with those non-ethnics age
65 years and older feeling that people knew where to go for help. Of
those non-ethnics age 65 years and older, 69.2% felt that most or all
knew where to go for help, compared to 57.5% of those under age 65.
Nearly one-quarter (24%) of those under age 65 felt that almost no one
knew where to go for help, as compared to none of those age 65 years
and older ($p < .01$).

Factors affecting utilization of services.   Community resident interviewees were asked to imagine a situation in which they had a

problem for a number of months and had been very unhappy, with their work and personal life being affected. They were read a list of 17 factors and asked whether each particular factor made them more willing, less willing, or had no effect upon their decision to seek professional help for their problem. The factors ranged from location, hours, cost, auspices, referral source, and confidentiality, to sex and ethnicity of service provider. Five factors were cited by over 60% of the interviewees as making them more willing to use services:

• Doctor referral—81.3% more willing
• Family referral—74.6% more willing
• Clergy referral—67.2% more willing
• Service located in neighborhood—66.5% more willing
• Affordable fee—64.1% more willing

The auspices of the program mattered little, as did the question of whether they would be seen by someone of their own ethnic group. Slightly over one-third of the interviewees (36.6%) were concerned about privacy, saying they would be less willing to go for help if their friends or neighbors might find out. More than half of the respondents (59.4%) stated they would be more willing to go for help if the services were called a "family counseling center" rather than a "mental health center." The only significant difference by age for any of the 17 factors was the convenience of hours, with the elderly feeling that this was less important.

The community helper and leaders survey also examined factors affecting utilization of services. The following were the key findings:

1. While there is much seeking and receiving of help among the elderly in the south side of Milwaukee, the helping networks are fragmented; many helpers and leaders, both professional and community, are unaware of the major problems of the elderly and of the networks utilized for meeting those problems.

2. Pride and privacy are important obstacles that prevent persons from seeking help; lack of knowledge of available helping resources is also a problem.

3. Professional helpers are extremely unaware of the extent and operation of community-based resources for the elderly.

4. Community leaders and helpers are also unaware of the extensive resources that are being provided to the elderly in their neighborhood by community residents.

Who interviewees talk with first when they have a problem. Community resident interviewees were given a list of life events from the Holmes and Rahe Life Stress Scale (1967). They were asked which events had happened to them within the past 12 months. Interviewees were then asked who the first person was with whom they had discussed their problem. Over four-fifths (83.6%) of the interviewees stated that they discussed their problems first with a family member, over half with a spouse (52.5%) and 31% with another family member. More than seven out of ten (71.4%) elderly respondents discussed the problem with a family member first. There were no significant differences by age or ethnicity.

Summary of Findings

Data from the community helper and leader survey show present helping networks, community and professional, are internally fragmented. Although the survey shows that there are many neighborhood and professional helpers, this fragmentation prevents maximum utilization of community strengths. The fragmentation exists among particular groups of helpers as well as between professional and lay helpers and is a major obstacle to people seeking help, thus reinforcing the values of pride and privacy in a negative direction. We found, for example, that although many clergy provided supportive services to the elderly, individual clergy were not aware of other clergy only a block or two away who were providing similar supports for the elderly. In addition, clergy were also almost totally unaware of "natural helpers" who were also providing supports for the elderly. Finally, clergy had only limited knowledge of professional resources for the elderly. Similarly, professional staff at any given agency serving the elderly were aware of only some of the many agencies providing supportive services for the elderly. Professionals had little if any knowledge of community helpers serving the elderly.

The source of referral, cost of the service, and location of the service in the neighborhood were the most significant factors affecting whether or not one sought help for a problem. There were few differences by age or ethnicity on these factors. It is clear that for the community in general, a referral by a doctor, clergy, or family is a key in the decision to seek professional assistance. It is of significance that over half of the respondents stated that they would be more willing to seek help from a "family counseling" rather than a "mental health" center. The auspices of the service and the ethnic background of the service provider mattered little.

As already noted, the research in Milwaukee focused upon a community whose population is heavily Catholic, Polish and working class. While some of the findings may be peculiar to this community, the major thrust of the results should be generalizable to other cities with concentrated ethnic communities. This assertion is initially supported by the similarity of these findings to the Baltimore phase of the project.

Capacity Building Model

Model Approach

The results of the existing fragmented helping systems in Milwaukee are duplication, lack of coordination of services, to the evident detriment of the mental health of the elderly in the community. Neither neighborhood-based nor professional service providers were fully aware of the implications of positive neighborhood attachment of the elderly and of the importance of building services upon the strengths and resources of the community.

We have developed a model for addressing these issues through recognizing and utilizing the unique cultural and organizational differences among neighborhoods. The model also involves building and rebuilding neighborhood support systems and linking neighborhood with professional support systems. These latter two efforts are important in creating an effective helping network that minimizes obstacles to seeking and receiving help and maximizes neighborhood strengths.

The model consists of a community empowerment process that is community directed and agency linked. Through this process, the elderly become aware of their own strengths and resources and their own abilities to shape services to meet neighborhood needs. Central to this process model is the importance of neighborhood. As previously discussed, neighborhoods play a crucial role for people in their need for and use of mental health services. Neighborhoods contain the "locality relevant" institutions that form the basis for weaving the individual into the social fabric of the society—the church, schools, community and civic associations, pharmacists, doctors, and small businesses.

A systems approach is utilized in the model based upon the neighborhood as the locus for service and as the basis for preventative and rehabilitative programming. Our focus on the system rather than on the individual client is useful in understanding the interrelated administrative, fiscal, and legal obstacles that prevent effective functioning of community mental health services for the aging on the neighborhood level.

Assumptions

The capacity building model is based on the following assumptions that grew out of our experiences and are well supported in the literature.

1. We live in a pluralistic society. Different groups of people solve problems, face crisis, and seek help in various ways determined by age, class, race, ethnic, and geographic factors. Age, social class, and eth-

nicity, specifically, are very important variables affecting attitude toward and use of mental health services. There is a documented underutilization of professional mental health services in urban ethnic working class neighborhoods. Yet age, class, and ethnic differences are often ignored by the mental health service delivery system, which tends to be designed and operated on a monolithic framework model.

2. Neighborhood and neighborhood attachment are positive resources that can and should be used as a basis for community mental health services. People need to feel that daily life is being conducted at a manageable scale. In the urban setting this occurs largely within the neighborhood. Neighborhood has been used as a locus for service for some community mental health centers but as little more. There are many strengths and helping resources in communities (friends, neighbors, family, clergy, schools, etc.). Professional services should be designed to strengthen and augment these resources.

3. A sense of competency, self-esteem, and power is extremely important to the mental health of the community. Professional services should be designed to build competency and to build power for the community. This necessitates a radical change in the role of the community and the role of the mental health professional in the current mental health system.

4. The community, not agencies, needs to take primary responsibility for its own mental health. We need to rethink the role of professional services vis-à-vis the role of the local neighborhood in providing supports to community members.

5. The mental health service delivery system is not unique in its problems. As part of the overall human services system, it suffers from problems of accessibility, funding, duplication and fragmentation of services, lack of community involvement, and lack of coordination. These problems need to be addressed not solely through the mental health system but, of necessity, as part of an overall human services system approach to service delivery, in which mental health research, planning, service delivery, and evaluation will be coordinated with but not assimilated by the human service system.

Overview

The capacity building model uses a helping network framework with a neighborhood focus. The neighborhood is seen not only as a locus of service but also as

• a support system and a vehicle for the development and strengthening of networks, professional and lay;

• a basis for the development of mental health programming;

• a means of citizen/client involvement;

• a basis for citizen empowerment in mental health.

Such a view of neighborhood in the provision of mental health and community support serves to help overcome the obstacles of inaccessibility, fragmentation, and lack of coordination of services. It ensures that programs and services will be built upon the unique strengths and resources of particular communities.

In Figure 19-1 we have identified a lay and a professional helping network. The lay network includes those helpers who provide support services on a voluntary basis to individuals in the community. Lay helpers may have professional training but the helping services they provide are an adjunct and not a principle part of their professional training and practice. For example, physicians may provide informal counseling for their patients. The professional network consists of those paid to provide support services to individuals in the community These support services are provided in an agency or institutional context, usually by professionally trained persons.

As we can see from the diagram, there are actual and potential communication channels and linkages between and among the various helpers, both professional and lay, and to the macrosystem as well, which represents the larger forces that have impact on the relationship. This model represents an ideal. It is not a program model but a process model that needs to be developed over time through a series of developmental stages. We outline below the goals of the capacity building model and briefly describe issues that need to be addressed in achieving those goals based upon our work with the project to date.

Goals

1. Create community awareness by the elderly of neighborhood strengths and needs. Organizationally, one should work through a local community-based organization or develop such a group. This group should have a Task Force directing the project composed principally of the elderly. The sponsoring organization might be a neighborhood organization, a church or ministerial group, or ethnic club, etc., depending on the community. By placing the sponsorship and ownership of the process squarely with the community from the beginning, one automatically asserts that the elderly have the strength to define for themselves their own needs and resources. Estes (1973) offers support for this notion. Her prescription for overcoming the barriers to effective community planning for the elderly includes setting up an organizational structure that assures a meaningful role for the elderly and creating a role for professionals without subverting the role of the elderly.

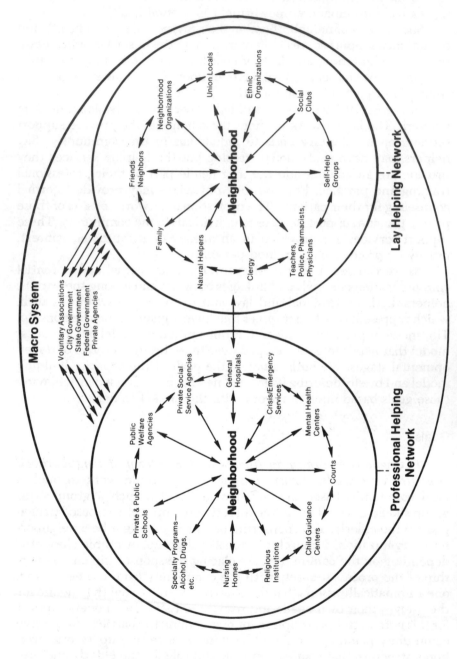

Figure 19–1. Community Mental Health Empowerment Model

Macro System

Voluntary Associations
City Government
State Government
Federal Government
Private Agencies

Lay Helping Network

Neighborhood

Union Locals
Ethnic Organizations
Social Clubs
Self-Help Groups
Teachers, Police, Pharmacists, Physicians
Clergy
Natural Helpers
Family
Friends Neighbors
Neighborhood Organizations

Professional Helping Network

Neighborhood

Public Welfare Agencies
Private Social Service Agencies
General Hospitals
Crisis/Emergency Services
Mental Health Centers
Courts
Child Guidance Centers
Religious Institutions
Nursing Homes
Specialty Programs— Alcohol, Drugs, etc.
Private & Public Schools

She suggests letting the elderly have their own consultants and define their own problems.

Self-assessment is an extremely important issue. If someone from the Mayor's Office says that the elderly in neighborhood A have emotional problems and are in need of services, then that neighborhood is immediately labeled a problem neighborhood and thereby stigmatized. If instead the people in the neighborhood talk with their leaders, doctors, pharmacists, school personnel, human service workers, and natural helpers and find out that loneliness and isolation is a problem, not only have they defined the problem but they have also begun to take responsibility for dealing with that problem, thus reinforcing the strengths of the community as well as attacking its problems. Using the clinical analogy, we know that to help someone we must begin with *his/her* presentation of the problem, not ours.

Methodologically, we have found action research to be an indispensable tool for self-assessment. Using action research, community residents, directed by a Task Force of elderly, gather data and information on giving and receiving help in the neighborhood through collection of "objective" statistical data and through "subjective" interviews with community leaders and helpers. In the course of gathering and analyzing data, issues are clarified and action plans develop for addressing them.

If a project is to be successful in developing linkages with the professional human service system, professionals from a wide variety of human service agencies need to be involved. A Professional Advisory Committee (PAC) should be formed with members holding decision-making positions in their agency so that they can help get agency resources committed to the project. This group would be advisory to the elderly Task Force and would meet on an as-needed basis. Individual members will be further involved as members of Task Force committees form to develop action plans to meet identified needs.

2. Strengthen neighborhood helping networks. This part of the process includes developing linkages among natural helpers in the community, among helpers and neighborhood leaders, and among neighborhood residents themselves. The planning process for developing programs in itself helps to strengthen neighborhood helping networks. Clergy, natural helpers, and neighborhood leaders will be brought together through workshops, symposia, and meetings as part of the action research process. They will then be further involved through working on committees of the Task Force. Also, one of the goals of any specific program, for example, a community-directed homemaker program, would be that it be organized in such a way as to strengthen neighborhood helping networks.

3. Strengthen the professional helping networks.   Professionals
will be advisors to a community-directed process led by the elderly, as
opposed to the more traditional model where citizens are advisors to
a professional process. The PAC process itself will help strengthen the
often fragmented and uncoordinated professional helping system by
bringing together professionals serving a common neighborhood who
were formerly not in regular contact with each other. By initially keeping the PAC and elderly Task Force separate from each other, the
elderly will have time to develop knowledge and expertise and the
professionals will be able to examine ways in which they can provide
increased support to the lay helping network.

*4. Form linkages between the lay and professional helping net-
works.*   As program committees are formed, Task Force members will
invite professionals to work with the committees, offering their particular expertise. By the time this occurs, the PAC meeting process will
sensitize most of the professionals to the ability of the community to
develop programs that would work. The two systems will then be able
to develop a partnership, aware of their differing roles and agendas.

In addition, programs will operationalize the concept of co-sponsorship to create broad-based appeal and legitimacy. For instance, a
publicity brochure for a telephone reassurance program could list all
the churches, agencies, and groups that were supporting the project. A
social center might be set up in a church and be run by the community
with professional consultation and assistance. Not only does such a system decrease the stigma of seeking help, it also links services for more
effective utilization, extends the resources of the community and agencies, and meets the needs for community control and agency support.

*5. Form linkages between the lay and professional helping net-
works and the macrosystem.*   Once the neighborhood process is well
on the way, the community needs to begin to look at the larger forces
that have impact on the process and that represent resources, obstacles,
and incentives to institutionalization of the community process. Task
Force and PAC members should put together a data base of information
regarding state and local mental health and human service plans,
United Way Funding patterns, agency program plans, major pending
legislation, etc. In addition, they should scout locally, making contact
with local foundations, industry, and other funding sources. This stage
of the process is critical if the accomplishments of the process are to be
long lasting.

Thus, the necessary linkages must take place at many levels so that
federal, state, and local programs do not create further obstacles and
disincentives to an effective mental health service system for the elderly.

Applications and Limitations

The capacity building model is a process, not a program model, and is thus difficult to replicate. We have developed this model through our work in urban, ethnic, working-class neighborhoods, but feel that it is applicable to other types of urban neighborhoods as well. Lay helping networks are present in varying degrees in all urban neighborhoods— white, black, or brown. Clearly the model is easier to replicate in stable neighborhoods than in transitional ones. Each neighborhood has its own peculiar set of factors that must be taken into account. Since our collective experience has been in urban and metropolitan areas, we will leave to others the question of the applicability of the model to rural areas.

Nevertheless there are a number of factors that may limit the ability of this model to be replicated. First, monies are needed by the elderly Task Force to hire staff to carry out the project objectives. This money might be difficult to obtain since most sources of funding for elderly services tend to be categorical. Second, professional agencies have to be willing and able to let the elderly themselves take the leadership role. Finally, the model takes several years to fully develop, and if a visible product is demanded too quickly, this process will fail.

Program and Policy Implications

If the capacity building process is to be successful, a number of policy issues affecting the elderly as regards mental health must be confronted. The answer to current mental health problems is not new programs, but a new policy framework. We must develop such a new mental health policy framework based upon the importance of neighborhood, upon the strengths of mediating institutions in the community, and upon the abilities of the elderly to identify their own needs and and to propose mechanisms to meet those needs.

Neighborhood groups must be given the financial resources to define their own needs and then to develop, in concert with professionals, intervention strategies to meet those needs. Such strategies must respect the values of each particular community and offer help in a way that can be accepted without loss of pride. We would recommend the following.

1. All federal and federally funded mental health programs for the delivery of services to the elderly should be mandated to incorporate plans that include impact of planned services upon, and planned linkages to, social support systems, neighborhood helping networks, and mutual aid groups.

2. The federal government should allocate personnel and service delivery demonstration monies that would mandate the training and retraining of mental health and human service workers on the nature

and function of elderly social support systems, neighborhood helping networks, and mutual aid groups.

3. Research and planning funds under the Community Mental Health Centers Act should be made available for studies of neighborhood helping networks serving the elderly. These should be aimed at studying how to re-focus the role of professionals into a consultative one vis-à-vis the community, and how to develop services for the elderly that build upon the strengths of neighborhoods and that link to and strengthen existing community helping networks.

4. A variety of funding mechanisms need to be explored that allow direct funding to the elderly for community-based mental health prevention, consultation, and education programs. Measures presently before Congress including ACTION's Urban Volunteer Corp and HUD's Neighborhood Self-Help Program are important steps in the direction of a National Self-Help Fund which would accomplish such direct funding.

To move from research findings to provision of services and formulation of supportive policy is a major step often neglected by social scientists and helping professionals. The model presented affords an opportunity to develop services in a manner that takes into account the general strengths as well as individual characteristics of neighborhoods.

In Milwaukee, the large number of white ethnic elderly were very attached to the ethnic neighborhood and had lived there a considerable length of time. The elderly tended to see their neighborhood as a limited area but were willing to and interested in expanding their boundaries of experience if services offered met certain requirements. Among such requirements was referral by clergy or a highly regarded professional. Such patterns of seeking and receiving help reflect, not only the ethnic value system of these elderly, but also the particular neighborhood institutions which develop out of that value system.

In other neighborhoods, characterized by different ethnic composition, coupled with different socioeconomic backgrounds of residents, responses will vary. The model proposed herein enables program development to take differences into account since the model incorporates members of the neighborhood helping networks as an integral part of the design team. Then not only does the mix of services to meet the supportive needs of ethnic elderly utilize all available resources, but it does so through meaningful linkage patterns that include the ethnic elderly themselves and the persons they turn to most often for help.

In this sense, the action research becomes an integral part of the planning process, exploring attitudes and needs of ethnic elderly and implementing the results. Finally, such neighborhood programming for

the ethnic elderly can be replicated in different neighborhoods if policies exist that allow for self-help development which, by definition,
acknowledges the importance of ethnicity.

References

Berger, P., and Neuhaus, R. *To empower people: the role of mediating institu-
    tions.* Washington, D.C.: American Enterprise Institute for Public Policy
    Research, 1977.
Birren, J. E. The aged in cities. *The Gerontologist,* 1969, *9*(3), 163–169.
Breton, R. Institutional completeness of ethnic communities and the personal
    relations of immigrants. *American Journal of Sociology,* 1964, *70*(2), 193–
    205.
Cantor, M. H. Life space and the social support system of the inner city elderly
    in New York. *The Gerontologist,* 1975, *15*(1), 23–27.
Caplan, G. *Support systems and community mental health.* New York: Behav-
    ioral Publications, 1974.
Caplan, G., and Killilea, M. (Eds.). *Support systems and mutual help.* New York:
    Grune and Stratton, 1976.
Collins, A., and Pancoast, D. *Natural helping networks: a strategy for preven-
    tion.* Washington, D.C.: National Association of Social Workers, Inc., 1976.
Estes, C. L. Barriers to effective community planning for the elderly. *The
    Gerontologist,* 1973, *13*(2), 178–183.
Fried, M. Grieving for a lost home. In R. Gutman (Ed.), *Peoples and buildings.*
    New York: Basic Books, 1972.
Glazer, N. The limits of social policy. *Commentary,* 1971, *52*(3), 51–58.
Goldston, S. E. Selected definitions. In S. E. Goldston (Ed.), *Concepts of commu-
    nity psychiatry: a framework for training.* Washington, D. C.: U.S. Govern-
    ment Printing Office, U.S. Public Health Service Publication No. 1319,
    1965.
Gurin, G., et al. *Americans view their mental health.* New York: Basic Books,
    1960.
Haugk, K. Unique contributions of churches and clergy to community mental
    health. *Community Mental Health Journal,* 1976, *12*(1), 20–28.
Hendricks, J., and Hendricks, C. D. *Aging in a mass society.* Cambridge, Mass.:
    Winthrop Publications, 1977.
Holmes, T., and Rahe, R. H. The social readjustment rating scale. *Journal of
    Psychosomatic Research,* 1967, *11*, 213–218.
Lawton, M. P., and Byerts, T. *Community planning for the elderly.* Washing-
    ton, D.C.: U.S. Department of Housing and Urban Development, 1973.
Lee, N. H. *The search for an abortionist.* Chicago: University of Chicago Press,
    1969.
Litwak, E. Voluntary associations and neighborhood cohesion. *American Socio-
    logical Review,* 1961, *26*(2), 258–271.

Lopata, H. Z. *Widowhood in an American City.* Cambridge, Mass.: Schenkman, 1973.

Lowenthal, M. F., and Haven, C. Interaction and adaptation: intimacy as a critical variable. In B. Neugarten (Ed.), *Middle age and aging.* Chicago: University of Chicago Press, 1968.

Naparstek, A., Spiro, H., and Biegel, D., et al. *Neighborhood and family services project, first year report,* 1977.

President's Commission on Mental Health. *Report to the President.* Washington, D.C.: U.S. Government Printing Office, 1978.

Regnier, V. Neighborhood planning for the urban elderly. In D. Woodruff and J. Birren (Eds.), *Aging.* New York: S. Van Nostrand, 1975.

Rose, A., and Peterson, W. A. (Eds.). *Older people and their social world.* Philadelphia: F. A. Davis, 1965.

Rosen, I. Some contributions of religion to mental and physical health. *Journal of Religion and Health,* 1974, *13*(4), 289–294.

Rosow, E. *Social integration of the aged.* New York: The Free Press, 1967.

Sarason, S., et al. *Human services and resource networks.* San Francisco: Jossey-Bass, 1977.

Shanas, E., et al. *Old people in three industrial societies.* New York: Atherton Press, 1968.

Shore, H. What's new about alternatives. *The Gerontologist,* 1974, *14*(1), 6–11.

Slater, Philip. *The pursuit of loneliness: American culture at the breaking point.* Boston: Beacon Press, 1970.

Snyder, John. The use of gatekeepers in crisis management. *Bulletin of Suicidology,* 1971, *8,* 39–44.

Srole, L., et al. *Mental health in the metropolis: the Midtown Manhattan study.* New York: McGraw-Hill, 1960.

Townsend, P. *The family life of old people.* London: Routeledge, Kegan and Paul, 1957.

Warren, Donald. Neighborhood in urban areas. In J. Turner (Ed.), *The encyclopedia of social work.* New York: National Association of Social Workers, 1977.

20

Ethnicity as a Factor in the Institutionalization of the Ethnic Elderly

Elizabeth W. Markson

In a speech to the Knights of Columbus in 1915, Theodore Roosevelt unequivocally espoused the melting pot premise that has characterized much of American ideology:

> There is no room in this country for hyphenated Americanism. . . . The one absolutely certain way of bringing this nation to ruin, of preventing all possibility of its continuing to be a nation at all, would be to permit it to become a tangle of squabbling nationalities.

For many years the notion that ethnicity, like the ideal state described by Marx, should wither away influenced both official policy and social research. However, it now seems dubious whether this postulate was ever valid in a consistently pluralistic society such as the United States. In fact, although immigration has indeed lessened and assimilation and acculturation have occurred, there is a resurgence of ethnicity as a salient social and political pattern in our social fabric. Ethnicity has come out of the closet. This is not surprising, for, as Michael Novak (1971) has commented, Americans have always been "ineffably ethnic

The research on old people in New York reported herein was supported in part by NIMH grant MH-16498. I am indebted to Elaine Cumming, Jennifer Hand, Ada Kwoh, Gary Levitz, and Suzanne Maurer for their ideas and inputs during that research project.

in their values and their actions." Novak has, incidentally, dubbed the 1970s the decade of the ethnics.

Ethnicity is particularly pertinent when we consider growing old in the United States. In 1970, for example, 15% of the elderly population were foreign born as compared to 5% of the general population. It is with the foreign-born ethnic that the majority of this chapter is concerned. Ethnicity has both objective and subjective dimensions. Both race and place of birth provide a very rough indicator of the former, including the extent to which a person is likely to be identified by others as a member of a distinct ethnic group. Subjective aspects of ethnicity are more difficult to tap, at least on a national dimension, for they encompass group consciousness and historical memory—both difficult to quantify.

The foreign-born elderly differ somewhat from the foreign born in the general population; they are more likely to reside in the northeastern United States and to have come from Eastern and Southern Europe than are their younger counterparts. Many foreign-born old people were pioneers of a sort who came to the United States in search of greater economic opportunity or political freedom. It is interesting to see how these new pioneers fared. A small segment of them ended up in old age being referred for mental hospitalization, often not because they were mentally ill but because there was simply no place else for them to go.

Double Minority Status: Being Old and Ethnic

If a minority group may be designated by its relatively subordinate position to the dominant social group, then the elderly qualify for this description. They experience many of the social and economic restrictions placed on ethnic and racial minorities. As Comfort (1976) has recently pointed out:

> ... old people need what people need: work to do, money to live on, a place to live in, and other people to care whether they live or die. At present they tend to be denied some or all of these by virtue of age [p. 6].

The economic and social pressures enforced by ageism often force the ghettoization of old people, an extreme form of which is institutionalization. (It is worth keeping in mind in this context that while one in every four elderly is poor, only one in nine among younger age groups is poor.)

Ethnicity, too, is a salient factor determining the kind and quality of life and concern that one will receive throughout the life span. As both Jacqueline Jackson (1973) and Hobart Jackson (1973) have reported, for the Black elderly, the problem is not to keep them out of institutions but to find appropriate institutional care when necessary. In general, there is an inverse relationship ($r = -.47$) between the proportion of elderly in the general population who are nonwhite and those in institutions (Caplow et al., 1978). Put differently, being nonwhite and poor are impediments to suitable institutionalization of the elderly (Kart and Beckham, 1976). For the white ethnic, it is suggested here that institutional patterns are somewhat different; poverty and low socioeconomic status coupled with being foreign born put one at a high risk of institutional care, including mental hospitalization.

Three points about American culture are relevant to the ethnic aged. First, personal worth in our society is largely determined by one's appearance of self-sufficiency and achievement, of which income and occupation are the most common indicators. Second, in an instrumental activist society such as the United States where work is valued as an end in itself and where belief in the value of productivity and the vice of unproductivity is strong, old age itself is an undesirable state. If social worth is measured by real or apparent productive capacity, the value of the American old person is low. Nor is their production needed. As Rosow noted in 1962:

> The aged are a problem precisely because we are such an affluent society.... We are too wealthy as a nation and economically too self sufficient as individuals to need the old person [p. 182].

To be over 65 is indeed to be at an awkward age: too old to work (despite recent legislative changes), too young to die.

Third, as various observers from de Tocqueville (1840/1947) to Philip Slater (1974) have commented, Americans stress conformity: similarity and agreement rather than uniqueness and originality are desirable attributes. Ethnic differences, like any other obvious divergence from the norm, are viewed by the majority society as undesirable deviations. This has decided implications for the ethnic elderly. Americans tend to classify each other both by socioeconomic position and by ethnic affiliation, so that one's social status depends upon both (see, for example, Wiley, 1967; Kahl, 1968). Milton Gordon has coined the term *ethclass* (1964) to refer to this subculture created by the conjunction of socioeconomic position and ethnicity. An ethclass thus is a "functioning unity that has an integrated impact on the participating individual"

(Gordon, 1964, p. 53), in which people share behavioral characteristics and a sense of identity. The combination of being old and ethnic also forms a distinct social category, albeit of heterogeneous individuals. They suffer from a double stigma, where they have perhaps been life-long victims of ethnic prejudice and now are victims of ageism. Pertinent here is the comment made by Alex Comfort (1976):

> One wonders what Archie Bunker would feel about immigrants if he knew that on his sixty-fifth birthday he would turn into a Puerto Rican. White racists don't turn black, Black racists don't become white, male chauvinists don't become women, anti-Semites don't wake up and find themselves Jewish—but we have a lifetime of indoctrination with the idea of the difference and inferiority of the old [p.4].

Ethnicity, Referral, and Hospitalization

What role does ethnicity, here narrowly defined as being foreign born, play in referral for mental hospitalization of the elderly? To determine this, the hospital records of 333 men and women, 65 years of age and older, were examined. This group encompassed 163 consecutive referrals to one state hospital during a seven-month period and 170 randomly selected patients referred to another state hospital during the same seven-month period.[1] Both hospitals served the New York City area. Not surprisingly, since women have a greater life expectancy, they outnumbered men; 62% of those referred were female as compared to 38% male. The median age of the elderly referred was close to 75 years of age, and the majority of patients were Roman Catholic (about 40%); almost as many were Jewish, and the minority were Protestant.

As Table 20-1 shows, the elderly referred for psychiatric hospitalization included a disproportionate number of foreign born; 59% of these were born outside the United States and its territories as compared to 43% of the general population 65 years of age and older in the standard metropolitan area of New York City. Most overrepresented in the sample referred for mental hospitalization are the elderly born in Eastern and Central Europe; Italians and those born in the British Isles (including Ireland) are also slightly overrepresented.

In general, the old people referred to the two mental hospitals reflect immigration patterns to the United States within the first 30 years of the 20th century. It seems unlikely, however, that a higher

1. A random sample of records was drawn from the second hospital because the number of referrals thereto far exceed the universe at the other hospital.

Table 20–1. Comparison of Place of Birth of the Metropolitan New York City Area
Population 65 Years of Age and Over and Patients of the Same Age
Referred to Two State Hospitals Serving the New York City Area

Country of Birth[a]	N.Y.C. Population (%)	State Hospitals (%)
Totals	100	100
	(N = 1,233,665)	(N = 333)
United States[b]	57	41
West Indies	2	3
Italy	9	12
Other Southern Europe	1	2
Eastern and Central Europe	17	27
Northern Europe (excluding Britain)	5	6
British Isles (including Ireland) and Canada	5	9
Other foreign born	4	—

[a]When foreign vs. native born are dichotomized, the underrepresentation of native born is outside the 3σ level, indicating that this difference would occur due to chance less than 99% of the time.
[b]Includes continental United States and territories.

incidence of mental illness in the last stage of the life cycle would be found among the foreign born than among native elderly, or that immigration at an earlier age has an impact on mental health in old age. It seems more probable that the high proportion of foreign born referred for hospitalization reflects career contingencies (Goffman, 1961), including level of education, occupation, and available community supports.

To test the hypothesis that level of education was indeed a factor relating to institutional referral, the educational histories of both foreign and native born were examined. About 51% of the ethnic elderly as compared to 31% of the native-born group had less than seven years of schooling; this included some people who were illiterate. Only slightly over one-third (34%) had completed elementary school as compared to 50% of the native-born sample.[2]

While all elderly referred for psychiatric hospitalization tended to be of relatively low education, the foreign-born group were more so. Their occupational status (using information on usual preretirement work) parallels their low educational status. Less than 2% had worked as professionals, administrators, or owners of even small businesses; 60% had been employed as unskilled or semiskilled laborers. The el-

2. Information on education was not recorded in the case records of 123 patients. No information on occupation was available for 97 patients. For women with no occupational history, the occupation of the husbands was used whenever this information was available. Thus, the above information is somewhat incomplete.

derly foreign born for whom information was available appear to be particularly disadvantaged, suffering from the traditional inequality associated with being an Irish or Eastern or Southern European immigrant to the Unites States. While a convenient and cheap source for labor—and, some employers hoped, an instrument for diluting the strength of trade union movements (Higham, 1968)—they were, as one immigrant summed it up, regarded as "dung" to fertilize the plant of rapid industrialization (Adamic, 1932, cited in Novak, 1971). They seem indeed social casualties in the race for mobility.

What is particularly interesting, however, is that many of these traditional "Nordic racist" barriers to mobility have disappeared for the majority of the foreign-born groups represented. In 1972, for example, the highest American family incomes were found among those of Russian, Polish, and Italian extraction; these were $13,929, $12,182, and $11,646 respectively (Thurow, 1976). The median family income for all Americans (regardless of country of birth or origin) was about $11,000 (Gans, 1974). As Blau and Duncan have shown in their analysis of occupational mobility in the United States, the difference in socioeconomic status due to ethnicity between native white men with foreign parents and native white men of native parentage is small. Even foreign-born whites, who have lower socioeconomic status in general than do either of the two native-born groups, have higher status on this dimension than do nonwhites. When occupation of father is held constant, socioeconomic status is most affected by level of education (Blau and Duncan, 1969). Put another way, while recent immigrants have tended to be at the bottom of the socioeconomic structure, at least in economic terms more than one ethnic group has not only risen to the economic position of the "average American" but has exceeded it. It seems clear that the elderly who were referred for mental hospitalization in this seven-month period in New York did less well than many of their counterparts and their own children.

They are victims of a mobility trap (Wiley, 1967) in which a few people in their own generation and many more in succeeding generations have begun to climb the tree of upward mobility while these elderly have remained at the base of the trunk. Their problems are not those of the ethnic who climbs up within his/her own ethnic group or moves into the dominant (nonethnic) socioeconomic structure; rather they are left behind, locked at the bottom of an ethclass, where, due to age, their productivity is no longer needed, and due to education and occupation, they have very few financial or political resources upon which to draw. In short, they have little power to manipulate or control their futures and change their fates.

Where are the Family Ties?

That the family has traditionally been *the* core institution for white ethnic families in the United States has been well documented. Greeley (1971) observed that ethnics spend most of their free time in the family. Ties are closer, parents and siblings are visited often, and one's best friends are also one's relatives. This closeness of the ethnic family differs from that noted for many WASP families, at least in urban areas. Among the foreign born and those of foreign-born identity, the idea of the extended family is more in evidence. If this is the case, why are the elderly ethnic who were referred to mental hospitals sent there rather than being cared for by the family? Two-thirds of them were, in fact, living with a family member prior to hospital referral. What happened to break family ties?

An examination of complaints made about patients prior to their admission indicates that the most frequent was that they were senile, that is, they were forgetful, confused, they wandered, left the gas on or the water running, etc. This described about four in ten people. The second most frequent complaint was major psychiatric symptoms, that is, severely depressed, suicidal, deluded or hallucinatory, or totally unpredictable. A small proportion were described as nervous, tearful, or anxious, and less than 1% were described as aggressive toward others. There were, incidentally, no significant differences in the types of complaints made about foreign-born versus native-born old people. Since about 45% had symptoms either of senility or nervousness, both of which might be managed at home within an extended or supportive family context, why were they sent to a mental hospital instead? The changing nature of the ethnic family seems especially relevant. While the first generation of an ethnic family may be very tightly knit, the second generation is expected both to succeed in the majority culture and to retain strong ties with their ethnic heritage. Choices must be made and, as Wrobel (1973) has pointed out, many ethnics in the second or third generation feel that the traditional ethnic family does not fit in with the desirable aspects of majority American culture. Often upward mobility can be won only at the price of rejection of parts of one's ethnicity. Care of a senile or neurotic elderly relative may be both an economic and a social drain on family resources.

In a series of interviews with elderly people hospitalized in a state mental hospital, I asked the questions: "How did you happen to come to the hospital?" and "If you could live anywhere you wanted, where would you live?" In response to the latter question, the answer was overwhelmingly "home," that is where she/he had lived just prior to hospitalization. Reasons for coming to the hospital varied, but often it appeared that there was just no other place to which to turn. The patients' families were not able to cope. As one elderly Polish-born Jewish woman summed it up:

> Before I got my stroke, I lived with my daughter. But then, you know, I got the stroke and I got depressed, afraid I was gonna die ... started driving her and her husband crazy. She's got a small apartment, 3 children, one in medical school . . . she goes out to business every day. So what does she need with me? I'm a poison, a bad poison, I make her unhappy. So, where should I go? Who wants me? I can't work, I can't cook, I don't walk good. They should spend the money on the children. My day is gone, I think I want to die—but you know I won't. I'm too strong.

In this case, family resources were taxed by this woman's stroke and depression. Never psychotic (her diagnosis was psychoneurotic depression), she wanted to live in her own apartment so as not to be in anyone's way; she had been in the mental hospital three years prior to interview. On this pathway to the mental hospital, shared by both foreign-born and native-born elderly, the younger generation was no longer able to cope with the older person, due to economic, social, or personal demands.

Another pathway to the mental hospital, confined almost entirely to the ethnic elderly, was death of a significant other. For example, Mrs. Raphael, age 92, was admitted to the mental hospital because she was allegedly depressed. She spoke no English, but through an interpreter she indicated that she had lived with her son and his wife until her son, at age 78, died of cancer. Her daughter-in-law was admitted to a nursing home shortly thereafter. Mrs. Raphael attempted living alone, but neighbors began to annoy her and, upon calling the police to complain about their behavior, she was admitted to hospital. Her dialect was heavy, she had no surviving relatives, and she was unused to living outside a family setting.

We observed a rather different pattern also, where sons or daughters may have spent the better part of their lives living at home. Upon the death of one or both parents, the child (by then over 65) became mentally disturbed, and no other community supports were offered. One Irish woman had spent her adult life taking care of relatives, including mother, father, and sister, all of whom she "buried." After the death of her father, she began to think that former President Eisenhower was contriving to take her small inheritance. Her brother and his wife referred her for commitment to a mental hospital.

The common denominator in these cases is the falling away of family ties, whether due to death of significant others with whom the person could communicate, or to the potential embarrassment and strain that the old person presents to siblings and children who have been more "successful" than she/he.

The ethnic elderly referred for psychiatric hospitalization in New York, like the immigrants and farm-born old people studied by Lopata (1975) in Chicago, were people without adequate systems, that is:

> a set of relations involving the giving and receiving of objects, services, social and emotional supports defined by the giver and the receiver as necessary or at least helpful in maintaining a style of life [p. 35].

That there may be no real role for old people without resources to exchange within the family structure or community is hardly a new finding. The elderly with little to give find that the only ones from whom they may expect support are those with a moral obligation to them (Hess, 1976), and this sense of obligation may wear thin in the face of competing obligations. Much of the plight of the elderly without resources has been laid at the door of the conjugal family. For years, social commentators have lamented the death of the multigenerational or extended family in the United States. What is often forgotten in this romanticized view of the "old" family is that, in the United States, as in other industrialized nations, this was never really a prevalent family form. The attraction of the multigenerational, agrarian Walton family on television is precisely its depiction of an idealized past, where each member of each generation played a vital role in maintenance of the family as the central social unit.

As Birgitte Berger (1971) pointed out, industrialization and urbanization over a period of centuries have shrunk the social and economic functions of families. The disintegration of feudalism, the rise of cities, political centralization rather than clan organization, economic differentiation, and the industrial revolution have all contrived to shift familial organization from an extended, multigenerational to a nuclear, conjugal pattern (Berger, 1971; Goode, 1963). Until relatively recently, the decline of the extended family presented little problem in care of the aged; there were simply not enough old people who survived. For example, the proportion of people in the United States who are 65 years or older has increased from 4.1% in 1900 to 9.5% in 1970; during the same time period, the number of old people has increased from slightly over 3 million to almost 20 million (Riley et al., 1971). The point here is that relatively few families were faced with the care of aged relatives. Those that were tended to be economically well off, for the life expectancy of the rich was, until relatively recently, considerably greater than that of the poor (Antonovsky, 1972). Since life was short for the majority of the population, those old people who did survive tended to be a biological and socioeconomic elite, possessing unusual social resources or physical health. Benjamin Franklin indeed lived to the age of 84 and was a productive elder statesman. But the average life expectancy for men in his generation was about 30 years (Antonovsky, 1972).

Many immigrants to the United States came from societies that had not industrialized at as rapid a rate and where the family was a relatively strong basis for social organization and source of stability (see, for example, Gambino, 1973; Hutchinson, 1956). While the traditional European peasant society had begun to break up prior to heavy waves of immigration to the United States, new arrivals to this country in the late 19th and early 20th centuries tended to seek, either as individuals or as families, people from their own village, region, or country and to use kinship and family relationships as a way of making contact with one another and to seek protection from and adjustment to American society (Greeley, 1971). As the children and grandchildren of these people became more assimilated in the socioeconomic structure, they developed social-class divisions that cut across ethnic-group lines. This in turn has tended to restructure their familial relationships, with less emphasis put on the family as a reference group and a source of support. The worth of the *individual* is asserted.

For white ethnics in the United States, too, aged relatives are a relatively new phenomenon, not only because of life expectancy patterns but also because of the nature of immigration itself. There are, for example, no visible grandparents in television's *Little House on the Prairie.* Although the Ingalls live in an ethnic community where family ties are heavily underscored, the thrust of effort is placed on present survival and future achievement. The grandparents apparently remained in the old country as they were unsuited to pioneering! Immigration, except in isolated cases, is more often a phenomenon among younger age groups.

Why Mental Hospitalization?

Comfort (1976) has proposed that "old people become crazy for three reasons: because they were crazy when young, because they have an illness, or because we drive them crazy" (p. 4). To this list I would like to add a fourth: they are labeled as crazy as a way of getting cheap, long-term, available care for them. The assumption behind this last statement is, of course, that mental hospitalization is cheap, home help or nursing home care expensive—an erroneous assumption, since the funds just come out of different pockets. The elderly who are sent to a public mental hospital are both old and poor, and in areas with large foreign-born populations, are likely to be white ethnics. When they experience social, emotional, or physical stress they are a group that is forced to live dependently: with relatives, friends, or in an institution.

Since the advent of Medicare and more especially Medicaid, use of the public mental hospital as a terminal-care facility has been considerably reduced; nursing home care is now available. Yet selective admission policies are used by many nursing homes and congregate care institutions; disabilities, national origin, race, and social class exist as barriers, either tacitly or explicitly. Admission procedures screen out the unworthy. A notable exception has traditionally been the mental hospital, which took all comers (Markson, 1971; Scheff, 1968). In recent years, with the advent of community mental health programs, nursing homes and Medicaid, and geriatric screening policies, it is more difficult to get into a mental hospital. I studied one state mental hospital that instituted geriatric screening specifically to exclude people whose prime reason for referral was physical illness, senility, or social problems such as lack of housing, low income, or paucity of family or community supports (Markson, 1974). I found that, surprisingly, the screening team behaved much as private practitioners and nursing homes have been accused of doing; that is, they *overchose* patients with traits like those of the clinicians, rejecting those with dissimilar traits: although the majority of old people referred were of low socioeconomic status (98% were blue collar), those people of the same sex and ethnicity as the examiners were most likely to be admitted; stated psychiatric criteria were unimportant. Presumably the examiners, who were proud of their hospital as an innovative treatment facility, felt that those most like them were also most likely to benefit from the program. Thus, the disadvantaged still lose.

Not all states have instituted a stringent geriatric screening program at state hospitals, however, and the poor, powerless, and ethnic elderly are likely to be represented in new admissions. In Massachusetts, for example, where there was considerable variation in local practice regarding admissions, those 65 years of age or over were slightly more likely to be admitted to a state hospital for the first time than were those in the 45–64 year age group; those catchment areas hospitalizing the highest rate of elderly also had large proportions of foreign born or Blacks. Their length of stay was greater as well; those age 65 or older who were admitted for the first time stayed in the hospital three times as long as those 21–54 years old and twice as long as those 55–64 years old. These data, while not conclusive, suggest that the state hospital may have been functioning as a nursing home substitute for the ethnic and Black old (Markson, 1975).

And Once in the Institution: What Then?

Ethnic ties and familial contact seem particularly significant for the institutionalized old person. They provide a reference point for self-definition, a way of relating "my kind" to "mankind"—the task of the last stage of personality development according to Erikson (1963). Such networks also aid and promote social interaction. Yet in most public facilities and in many private nursing homes, such contact is not feasible. The residents of the facility are heterogeneous and isolated from their families. A group home in New York City, in which elderly mental patients were placed after a period of hospitalization, served as the setting for determining some of the consequences of institutionalization. These findings are reviewed in this section.

As Goffman (1961) observed, institutions have documented side effects; the more pernicious ones include mortification of the self, loss of autonomy, and barriers to interchange with the outside world. The institution itself becomes one's social sphere. This is not always a happy process. As one elderly Russian-born Jewish woman described her contact with her son:

> My son, he comes up every Sunday. I bring him up in good shape. He's a businessman in Jersey. He has two stores, dresses, coats, like the Macy's. His wife, she's a big man, she takes $300 a week, a man. A half a day she works and a half a day she goes to business. She's a nice girl . . . she drives a car—everything. She's smart, like a shicksa, "Mama, don't worry, everything is ok. Mama, don't worry." She's good, like a diamond, a dress she brings me, a coat, everything. . . . I have no grandchildren. I told them, take 4 rooms, take a baby. They can't afford it! To take a baby they can't afford? They have plenty . . . two good stores. I don't have nobody. He can do what he wants. I told him, so you have something wrong with you, Mama go die, put me away in the hospital. Please do me a favor, I can die, I got nobody. He's got plenty; the truth, he's got plenty.

Her mortification and sense of isolation are evident.

Other residents complained of ways in which they had been stripped of their rights and possessions but felt powerless to do anything. For example, a 79-year-old Irish woman complainted:

> The only thing I want to know is about the paper I signed; if it is going to do me any harm. That's all I want to ask. . . . I want to ask the question and see if the paper that I signed will do me harm because I don't want to hurt my daughter-in-law and I know that I can't ask her for anything. So if I want a pair of shoes or I need something, I signed the paper that I don't need anything. Because on the paper it was stated I have clothes. Well, I

have enough, but if I need something, I can't get it. Because, you see, I signed the paper that I don't need nothing, and my daughter-in-law gives it to me. Well, I only meant on Christmas or Mother's Day, I didn't mean that they gave me everything. If you can't hear too well and you can't see too well, it's kinda hard. In fact, when I signed it, I couldn't hear all of it. But if I need a new pair of shoes—these are my marching shoes; they are very heavy and a high heel. I belong to the V. F. W. [Veterans of Foreign Wars] and when I march, I have to have shoes.

[You mean you couldn't ask your daughter-in-law to get you shoes?] I wouldn't do that because she's not my blood relative. My grandchildren are. And if I hurt her by asking her when she thinks I should wait until they are given to me, that she's smart enough to know. You see, they are very clever people, and I wouldn't hurt them for the world. And if I do hurt them, then I'm the one who is going to suffer. You see, I signed, so the Welfare and part, all of my Social Security and everything goes to the— this place. You see, I'm part paying and, they took the money from me. Twenty-five dollars you get for clothes, but I didn't get nothing; they [the managers of the group home] took it away.

This woman, who was receiving Social Security and Medicaid, had no spending money; the managers of the home apparently refused to give her the residue over and above the cost of her care. She had been afraid to ask anyone at the home and was hesitant to call any official agency because, as she said, "I don't go good on the telephone." Nor did she feel that she could turn to her daughter-in-law for help. (Finally, after her story became known, a social worker from the state hospital at which the woman had been a patient intervened, and was able to get her spending money and clothing.)

Social ties among residents tended to be slight; often people from different ethnic backgrounds came into open conflict. In the home, for example, weekly recreation programs were held where volunteer groups of musicians performed. The residents seldom seemed satisfied with the entertainment; one ethnic group or another felt left out. For example, on one occasion, musicians performed old popular songs, such as "The Sidewalks of New York," "Bicycle Built for Two," and "Daisy, Daisy." The performance was interrupted at frequent intervals by Jewish residents, who shouted *"Goyim,"* "Stop with the shicksa music," and other similar comments. On another day, when predominantly Yiddish songs were featured, Irish and Italian residents complained. One particularly vocal woman shouted, "Yei, Yei, Yei—makes no sense! Why don't they sing normal?"

Few personal relationships based on common ethnic background arose, perhaps because of personal feelings of alienation and despair, perhaps because no attempt was made to group people of common ethnicities together. Instead, room assignment appeared to be random. The results of this were often open confrontation between individuals of different national origins. As one Irish woman confronted her Jewish roommate:

> You can't call me a racist. I've known all kinds. But I don't see why I have to put up with somebody who don't speak English all the time and whose people crucified our Lord.

Nor were other people of different ethnicities much kinder.

It would be easy, of course, to say that much of the ethnic and familial isolation experienced by these people was the fault of the particular facility—it was just not well managed. But this obscures a major point about *many* facilities for the ethnic aged: because of a heterogeneous population, mixed staff, and limited resources, they become a simmering pot of discontent rather than a melting pot. It seems unrealistic to expect that, without planning, they would not.

Conclusion

This chapter has reviewed several factors relating to the institutionalization of the ethnic aged, including the role of ethnicity in referral for mental hospitalization, the breakdown of the traditional ethnic family as a support structure for the poor white ethnic elderly, and barriers and problems in their institutional care. Clearly, the problems described seem to be structural ones in American society. Where public facilities are concerned, little provision for the needs of the ethnic old person have been made. Instead, it is assumed that, because they are old and of low social status, their needs are similar—essentially custodial care.

Twenty years ago, Hollingshead and Redlich (1958) suggested that what was needed was a reevaluation of the kind of psychiatric care offered to lower-class patients—perhaps a good inexpensive psychotherapist. An evaluation of care offered the ethnic aged who have been labeled mentally ill suggests an elaboration on this point: what we need is more extensive, alternative facilities for care in old age. To institutionalize—and attempt to homogenize—the elderly of low social status may be cost-effective (although soaring costs of medical and institutional care open that assumption to question), but it is not effective or efficacious care for the elderly who receive it.

References

Adamic, L. *Laughing in the jungle.* New York: Harper, 1932. Cited in M. Novak. *The rise of the unmeltable ethnics.* New York: Macmillan, 1971.

Antonovsky, A. Social class, life expectancy and overall mortality. In E. G. Jaco (Ed.), *Patients, physicians and illness: a sourcebook in behavioral science and health.* New York: Free Press, 1972.

Berger, B. *Societies in change.* New York: Basic Books, 1971.

Blau, P., and Duncan, O. D. Occupational mobility in the United States. In C. Heller (Ed.), *Structured social inequality: a reader in comparative social stratification.* New York: Macmillan, 1969.

Caplow, T., et al. The elderly and old age institutions. Charlottesville, Va.: The Center for Program Effectiveness Studies, The University of Virginia. Cited in C. S. Kart, E. S. Metress, and J. F. Metress (Eds.), *Aging and health: biologic and social perspectives.* Menlo Park, Calif: Addison-Wesley, 1978.

Comfort, A. Age prejudice in America. *Social Policy,* 1976, *7*(3), 3–8.

de Tocqueville, A. *Democracy in America.* New York: Oxford University Press, 1947.

Erikson, E. *Childhood and society* (2nd ed.). New York: W. W. Norton, 1963.

Gambino, R. La famiglia: four generations of Italian Americans. In J. Ryan (Ed.), *White ethnics: their life in working class America.* New York: Prentice Hall, 1973.

Gans, H. More equality: income and taxes. *trans-action,* 1974 (Jan./Feb.), *11*(2), 62–6.

Goode, W. J. *World revolution and family patterns.* New York: Free Press, 1963.

Gordon, M. M. *Assimilation in American life.* New York: Oxford University Press, 1964.

Greeley, A. *Why can't they be like us?* New York: Institute of Human Relations Press, 1971.

Goffman, E. *Asylums.* New York: Anchor Books, 1961.

Hess, B. Self help among the aged. *Social Policy,* 1976, *7*(3), 55–62.

Higham, J. *Strangers in the land.* New York: Atheneum, 1968.

Hollingshead, A. B., and Redlich, F. C. *Social class and mental illness.* New York: John Wiley, 1958.

Hutchinson, E. P. *Immigrants and their children, 1850–1950.* New York: John Wiley, 1956.

Jackson, H. Planning for the specially disadvantaged. In E. Pfeiffer (Ed.), *Alternatives to institutional care for older Americans: practice and planning.* Durham, N.C.: Center for the Study of Aging and Human Development, 1973.

Jackson, J. Really, there are existing alternatives to institutionalization for aged blacks. In E. Pfeiffer (Ed.), *Alternatives to institutional care for older Americans: practice and planning.* Durham, N.C.: Center for the Study of Aging and Human Development, 1973.

Kahl, J. (Ed.). *Comparative perspectives on stratification.* Boston: Little, Brown, 1968.

Kart, C. S., and Beckham, B. Black-white differentials in the institutionalization of the elderly. *Social Forces,* 1976, *54,* 901–910.

Lopata, H. Z. Support systems of elderly urbanites: Chicago of the 1970s, *The Gerontologist.* 1975, *15*(1, part 1), 35–41.

Markson, E. A hiding place to die, *trans-action.* 1971, *9*(1–2), 48–54.

Markson, E. A touch of class? A case study of geriatric screening process. *International Journal of Aging and Human Development,* 1974, *5*(2), 187–196.

Markson, E. Geriatric first admissions to Massachusetts state hospitals during fiscal year 1974. Working paper prepared for the Massachusetts Department of Mental Health Task Force on Geriatric Services. Boston: Mass. Dept. of Mental Health, 1975.

Novak, M. *The unmeltable white ethnics.* New York: Macmillan, 1971.

Riley, M. W., Johnson, M. E., and Foner, A. *A sociology of age stratification.* New York: Russell Sage, 1971.

Rosow, I. Old age: one moral dilemma of an affluent society. *The Gerontologist,* 1962, *2*(4), 182–191.

Scheff, T. The societal reaction to deviance: ascriptive elements in the psychiatric screening of mental patients in a Midwestern state. In S. Spitzer and N. Denzin (Eds.), *The mental patient.* New York: McGraw-Hill, 1968.

Slater, P. *The pursuit of loneliness: American culture at the breaking point.* Boston: Beacon, 1974.

Thurow, L. C. Not making it in America: the economic progress of minority groups. *Social Policy,* 1976, *6*(5), 5–11.

Wiley. N. F. The ethnic mobility trap and stratification theory. *Social Problems,* 1967, *15* (Fall), 147–159.

Wrobel, P. Becoming a Polish American: a personal point of view. In J. Ryan (Ed.), *White ethnics: their life in working class America.* New York: Prentice-Hall, 1973.

Conclusion:
The Continuing Significance
of Ethnicity

Donald E. Gelfand and Alfred J. Kutzik

There is consensus among the contributors to this volume that ethnic factors must be taken into account in studying the aging process and providing services to the aged, but they differ regarding the relative importance of ethnicity. At the heart of their disagreement is the weight each author attributes to ethnicity and socioeconomic class as alternative explanations of social and psychological phenomena.

In our view, this is a false issue based on a mistaken understanding of ethnicity and its relationship to class. It results from considering ethnicity to be essentially cultural and existing separately from, even if closely intertwined with, social class. However, the ethnic groups that generate and maintain ethnic culture (norms, values, lifestyles, etc.) are social groups with social structure including a system of social stratification that interpenetrates the social stratification of American society. Rather than two independent variables, ethnicity and class can more validly be conceived of as a compound whose effect is unitary. From this perspective, not only is the priority of class or ethnicity a false issue, but questions can be raised as to the soundness of dealing with ethnicity in isolation from class and vice versa. Such a position led Milton Gordon (1964) to invent the term *ethclass* for heuristic purposes.

In addition to misdirecting research and analysis, viewing ethnicity as cultural rather than sociocultural leads to underestimating its significance. In the first place, with rare exceptions, social scientists have considered cultural phenomena secondary to if not derived from social phenomena. Ethnic culture in the United States is therefore considered tertiary since it is generally assumed to be largely derived from other cultures and to a small extent from certain ephemeral social conditions. The dominant scholarly as well as popular belief is that ethnicity is the transplanted "Old World cultural heritage" (Mindel and Habenstein, 1976) brought to this country by immigrants with some minor modifications required by immigrant life.

The fallacy of insisting that the vitality of American ethnic groups must be assessed according to the extent to which they retain their comparatively few and inevitably fading non-American and immigrant components results in downplaying the importance of these groups to their nonimmigrant members. While the misconception of ethnicity as being immigrant culture necessarily recognizes the importance of ethnicity for the first-generation and many second-generation immigrants, it negates the importance for later generations. In the field of aging, this translates into recognition of the importance of ethnicity for many of the present aged white population but a self-fulfilling prophecy as to its unimportance for the white aged population of the future. This, of course, also applies to the Chicano, Cuban, Puerto Rican, and similar groups irrespective of race. It even more strongly negates the significance of ethnicity for Blacks of any generation since they do not conform to the immigrant ethnic model.

Despite more or less sharing the erroneous approach, most contributors to this book and many others writing on ethnicity and aging have been able to do justice to the subject up to this point, since the aging population has been so largely first- and second-generation immigrants. As this population will soon predominantly consist of American-born offspring of American-born parents, it is urgently necessary that ideology be replaced by sociology in the orientation of those studying ethnicity and aging. This will not be an easy task since the position that ethnicity is immigrant culture functions as an ideological rationalization for assimilation in place of the now discredited "melting pot" approach. While it does not advocate assimilation to WASP norms on grounds of their superiority, it argues that such assimilation is inevitable on grounds of the transience of immigrant status.

What is required is more knowledge of the actual rather than presumed effects of ethnic group membership on those of different generations as well as different classes. We already have some information, as is evident in various chapters in this book. We need more studies focused on the lifestyles and attitudes toward aging and the service utilization of such ethnic subgroups as third-generation middle-class Italians. General information on Italians does not provide enough data on which to base sound policies, programs, and practice.

At the present state of knowledge, however, it seems safe to conclude that there are important sociocultural differences among ethnic
groups and that the salience of ethnicity in American life is not soon
going to disappear. This has long been evident in the case of minority
groups. A considerable amount of literature during the past decade
clearly indicates that such differences also exist and promise to persist
among white ethnic groups. This is also evident from recent social and
political developments. None of these is more striking than the land-
mark Bakke decision in which the Supreme Court ruled that "race" and
"nationality," i.e. ethnicity, can be taken into account in university
admissions. Significantly, the court used both Italians and Blacks as case
illustrations.

Irrespective of such unprecedented governmental recognition of
the legitimacy of ethnicity, an increasing number of researchers and
practitioners in various fields have recently become engaged in ex-
plicating the role of ethnicity in American society. They have now been
joined by gerontologists, as exemplified by our contributors.

Among the latter's major conclusions is that members of different
ethnic groups have varying role expectations of the aged. We suspect
that this differs by generation and class within given ethnic groups.
These differences, as well as the extent to which these attitudinal sets
are passed on from generation to generation within each group, are
areas for further research. Other related findings are the social and
psychological functions that the ethnic group performs for aged individuals when their circle of workmates, life-long friends, and family has
begun to shrink, and the dysfunctions of structuring interpersonal relations among ethnically disparate aged in institutional settings. This increased knowledge base challenges the assumed universal beneficence
of integrated, multi-ethnic programs and deserves further attention.

We suspect that well-focused studies will show that class and generation make a difference in both the nature and impact of intra- and
interethnic group relationships. Such information on the norms of not
only ethnic groups but ethnic subgroups is needed to provide the planner and practitioner with guidelines for the differential diagnoses and
treatment that the helping professions require. That this information
must be updated for each "ethclass" in each generation suggests the
demands on those studying and serving the American aged.

Hopefully, such knowledge will help mitigate the problematical
relationships that often exist between ethnically disparate providers
and consumers of service noted throughout this book. The complexity
of the problem is suggested by the frequently encountered preferences
by consumers for service providers of an ethnically *different* back-

ground from their own. Again, reliable research might well find a generational and/or class differential involved here. Other dimensions of this protean problem that need to be studied are those services for which the same individual (or cohort) requires intra-ethnic auspices or extra-ethnic auspices.

In line with a recent trend in the literature, several chapters deal with how neighborhoods can serve as a base of organizing and improving services for the elderly. While the authors justifiably advocate reinforcing the "informal support systems" and "natural helping networks" within neighborhood communities, a word of caution is in order. As demonstrated in this volume, formal, organized programs rather than informal help have historically been the mainstay of assistance for the needy, including the aged. In addition to sensitizing service providers to the preference of many aged individuals for neighborhood-based services, we believe it is equally important to support the preference of many aged individuals for services and activities outside of their immediate neighborhoods. While the neighborhood may have once bounded the lives of the immigrant aged, the American-born English-speaking aged of today are not so restricted. To afford aged individuals an actual choice of extra-neighborhood alternatives requires resources ranging from more adequate transportation to more adequate income maintenance, issues on which advocacy groups like the National Caucus on Black Aged and the National Council of Senior Citizens are already at work.

Another major problem is that many professionally staffed programs, whether or not neighborhood-based and under ethnic auspices, tend not to be successful at serving the elderly and other strongly ethnic clientele. Professional and bureaucratic norms of service providers often conflict with the social and cultural norms of the older generation of consumers. Failure to apply for service or continue treatment is often blamed by professionals on the resistance or ignorance of clients. However, such underutilization is often due to the professional's resistance or ignorance of the client's norms of acceptable service, which tend to vary among ethnic groups and ethnic (class and generational) subgroups.

With a new generation of almost entirely American-born aged about to replace the present heavily immigrant one, the field of aging is at a point of departure. The always questionable equation of ethnicity and immigrant culture will no longer be tenable, nor will the monolithic ethnic characterizations that once actually approximated the typically working-class immigrant communities. The Americanized, generally less impoverished new generation of elderly will probably require fewer services in areas like nutrition and housing but will certainly consume more physical and mental health care and sophisticated social services. Consequently, it will be more important than ever for service providers to have knowledge of the different ethnic and class norms governing the utilization of services and shaping the conceptions of aging among those they serve. We are convinced that in the future, understanding ethnicity will continue to be essential for providing adequate services to the aged—and that this can take place only in a health and welfare system in which older people have resource-buttressed choices of services under the auspices of their own ethnic or multi-ethnic ("nonsectarian" or integrated) groups.

References

Gordon, M. *Assimilation in American life.* New York: Oxford University Press, 1964.

Mindel, C., and Habenstein, R. (Eds.). *Ethnic families in America: Patterns and variations.* New York: Elsevier, 1976.

Index